ELVIS IN OZ
New Stories and Poems from the
Hollins Creative Writing Program

ELVIS IN OZ
New Stories and Poems
from the
Hollins Creative Writing Program

Edited by

MARY FLINN AND GEORGE GARRETT

UNIVERSITY PRESS OF VIRGINIA
Charlottesville and London

THE UNIVERSITY PRESS OF VIRGINIA
Copyright © 1992 by Hollins College

First published 1992

"The Dreams of Children" copyright © 1992 by Don Belton
Photos by George Butler copyright © by George Butler
"The Heart Operation" copyright © 1992 by Garrett Epps
"Hôtel du Roi, Nôtre Dame" copyright © 1992 by Richard McCann, from his forthcoming
novel to be published by Pantheon Books. Printed by permission of Brandt and Brandt
Literary Agents, Inc.
"Dance of the Dead Puppets" copyright © 1992 by Thomas McGonigle
Photos by Sally Mann copyright © by Sally Mann

Library of Congress Cataloging-in-Publication Data
Elvis in Oz : new stories and poems from the Hollins Creative Writing
Program / edited by Mary Flinn and George Garrett.
p.   cm.
ISBN 0-8139-1381-0 (cloth). — ISBN 0-8139-1382-9 (paper)
I. American literature—20th century.   I. Flinn, Mary.
II. Garrett, George P., 1929–
PS535.5.E45   1992
810.8'0054—dc20
91-31585
CIP

Printed in the United States of America

CONTENTS

Photos by George Butler and by Sally Mann follow page 278

FICTION

Preface

"What is the secret," I am on occasion asked, "of the Hollins College creative writing program? How does a program located at a small liberal arts woman's college produce so many successful writers, and writers of such diversity?" The faulty assumption behind those questions is that, since I have taught at Hollins since 1964 and have chaired the creative writing program since 1971, I actually know.

Usually I manage a somewhat inscrutable look and change the subject quickly, but reading through this collection of work by graduates of the program has given me at least a part of the answer.

Of course, I've always known that Hollins produces good writers because good writers come to Hollins to study. And I know that they come because of the vision of the program's founder, Louis D. Rubin, Jr., who had the courage and the energy to establish a graduate program in 1960 in a conventionally unlikely place and not to model it after programs that already existed elsewhere but to give it its own unique shape and feel. I also know that good writers come to Hollins to study with a writing faculty that has included such extraordinary writers and teachers as John Alexander Allen, Annie Dillard, George Garrett (who directed the program from 1968 to 1971), Marianne Gingher, Cathryn Hankla, Jeanne Larsen, M. Cronan Minton, Carole Oles, Greg Pape, James Andrew Purdy, Julia Randall, William Jay Smith, Leon Stokesbury, Katherine Soniat, Eric Trethewey, Allen Wier, and Dara Wier.

But seeing in this anthology the work of writers who lived and wrote at Hollins as undergraduates and graduate students over the last thirty-five years all gathered together in one volume (and comfortably, despite all the variety of manner and matter in their work) made me realize that the answer is actually a very simple one. It is that Hollins is a genuine community of writers, one that includes all these writers (and all the ones who are not here represented) without chronological or hierarchical distinction. We were all, students and teachers alike, writers together, and we remain writers together despite all the miles and years that separate us.

And that *is* the secret of the Hollins College creative writing program. If this is disappointing, I suspect it is because, like all great secrets, it is so obvious—or maybe it's that you had to be here. I'm sure glad I was and am, and I hope you'll be glad to be here with us as you read the stories and poems (and photographs) in this collection.

R.H.W.DILLARD

Introduction

Because of the prompt and astonishing number of manuscripts submitted in reply to the invitation to former Hollins students to submit poetry and fiction for this anthology celebrating the Sesquicentennial of Hollins College (the oldest chartered women's college in Virginia), we have had to pick and choose from among submissions of the highest quality. Many fine poems and stories (this book could easily have been twice its size) have been left out. And, at the same time, there were some distinguished writers who were unable to contribute. Tama Janowitz and Elizabeth Forsythe Hailey, for example, were in the midst of new work from which nothing could easily be excerpted.

We begin with that admission and acknowledgment because *all* the work, taken together, has created the context for our selections. Those pieces not included shadow those that are here.

Our choices were guided by the desire of being at once representative and diverse. From the beginning until now there has never been a Hollins "school" of writing, nothing, in fact, identifiable beyond excellence. The range of subjects, the rich variety of ways and means of dealing with them, both conventional and advanced, the diversity of person, place and thing, all bear witness to the energy of undiminished creativity.

A whole generation of writers, covering the more than thirty years' history of the creative writing program at Hollins, is represented here. There are some well-known names, and there are some new voices. There are three Pulitzer Prize winners present as well as at least one first publication. (In fact, of course, all the material in this anthology is published here for the first time anywhere.) What they share—it comes with the territory at Hollins—is a sense of adventure, a constant questioning of perceived literary conventions, and a cheerful willingness to take risks. The results for the reader are always interesting and usually exciting.

Another kind of shadow, influential without being inhibiting, falls across these pages—it's the shadow of teachers. In addition to the regular teaching staff, there were the full-time writers in residence who worked with students. Hollins was one of the first American colleges to bring in writers for a semester or a year as a matter of course. As might be expected, there are all kinds of writers who have come to Hollins. Among them are: Enid Starkie, John W. Aldridge, Jr., William Golding, Flannery O'Connor, Robert Penn Warren, Benedict Kiely, Colin Wilson, Malcolm Cowley, Shelby Foote, Louise Bogan, William Harrison, Mark McCloskey, Kay Boyle, Elizabeth Spencer, Diane Wakoski, William Goyen, Derek Walcott, Mark Smith, Alice McDermott, F. T. Prince, Richard Bausch, Stephen Becker, Alan Cheuse, Jean Gould, and Denise Giardina.

A word more about the wonderful photographs in this book. Two Hollins writers, George Butler and Sally Mann, have earned national reputations as distinguished photographers. They have generously contributed photographs, and we are sincerely grateful to them.

MARY FLINN
GEORGE GARRETT

A Beautiful Day
with a Red Parasol

When you cut an earthworm in half it becomes two worms. I've never seen this happen, but I place blind faith in the wisdom of my seventh-grade science teacher Mr. Welk. The seventh grade is now long behind me. I am what is commonly called an adult, but still I think about those worms, fat, pink, eternally divided.

This is what I wonder. You are digging. Maybe you are planting marigolds, maybe hollowing out a burial place for a dead rabbit, or heading down towards China. Anyway, you're digging. With a careless shovel you slice right through an earthworm, leaving two behind in its place. These two separate worms go their two separate ways, riding down different tunnels through the cool, brown earth. Their paths may never again intersect. But these two worms that once ate the same earth with the same mouth, do they see the same visions as they burrow through their blind tunnels? Would a worm that had been twained and twained and twained carry all the thoughts of all the worms it had been joined to? If this were true, this worm would be an invertebrate guru whose world enlarged only by severance and separation.

Sitting in the warm spring rain, I fill my mouth with loamy soil and think about Mary Louise and Julia, twained at birth. These two were severed by facts, the fact that they had two different mothers, the fact that they were born in two different hospital beds. It is a fact that Mary Louise was exactly one hour and six minutes older than Julia. This may be either important or completely irrelevant. Facts do have a way of slipping to one side or another, like the severed halves of earthworms.

We all know how vast the population of the earth has grown. There are 7,364,158 people in New Jersey alone. With these great numbers it might seem impossible that two people would ever meet. Julia and Mary Louise did meet. They met and became friends because their mothers met and became friends. They lived side by side in two nearly identical houses. Of course they met. It seemed obvious.

Mary Louise and Julia could not remember a time when they hadn't known each other. And, really, their first meeting could only have been uninspiring. In their infancy they had expended too much effort lifting their heavy heads and grasping at shiny objects to really notice each other. Let us just say that when Julia and Mary Louise began to speak, they were friends already. Maybe this was a good thing for neither of them, but so it was and will be forever-more, amen.

Their friendship lasted for twenty-one years, right up until the moment when Mary Louise pushed Julia off the Craven Creek footbridge. Such an incident must certainly sever a friendship for at least one of the parties involved, so you can see its importance. I promise to tell you all about the making of this day. I am Mary Louise, so you know that everything I say will be the unadulterated truth.

Since history is eternal repetition, I began as others have begun before me; I was born. I stepped from my mother's womb like some howling Lazarus just wakened from a dead sleep. The first thing in the world I remember is not my mother and not my father, it is Julia's face, red and wet like the inside of a melon, her eyes staring into my eyes.

I had a childhood; nearly everyone does. The best gift my parents ever gave me was a pair of eyes as green as new lettuce and the bottom tips of grass blades. I kept these eyes in two holes set right above my nose and wore them with pride for all to see. Julia had two eyes, green too, but a milky green like the color left in your white handkerchief when you blow your nose. It is a fact that Julia was very, very jealous of two lettuce-colored eyes.

When I was seven and Julia was younger, Elaine Thayer moved to our neighborhood. She had long blonde hair and a doll that cried real tears. She went to Bermuda for Christmas and came back brown. Elaine wanted a friend and chose Julia. They say that three is always too many, and so it was. If we played hide-and-seek, I was always It. I never could find either Julia or Elaine, because they were in Elaine's basement playing Jacks or "Barbie Goes to Shanghai." I had made up the last game. It was very elaborate and involved paper cocktail parasols and a carton of table salt. Ken was an English sailor. Barbie ran an opium den. When I heard they had played this game without me, I cried and cried. Julia looked right into my eyes and told me they were the color of vomit. "Vomit," she said. "Vomit. Vomit-eyes." Elaine said it with her. They said it and said it until I left.

My eyes. My eyes. They turned pink at the edges. I walked into the woods and sat by a tree. The creek flowed somewhere in front of me. Behind the creek, behind me, behind the woods, the suburbs rolled up towards the horizon. I stared down at my hands, wet from stray tears. My fingers tunneled into earth as sweet and dark as chocolate cake. I scooped up a handful and filled my mouth with it, letting it rest there until it grew wet and heavy. Like thick, gritty molasses it slid down my throat. Whenever my tooth hit a stone, it sent a tremor that traveled from my stomach down through my thighs. I stared up between the tree branches at the sun and looked it straight in its face until it turned blue. I shut my eyes tightly. Little pink and blue suns ran across my eyelids. I lay there, my mouth warm and muddy, feeling as voluptuous as a heavy-breasted odalisque. My body weighed as much as the whole world, so I floated far, far away.

I sit now in a gray room. All the people who pass me by have Julia's face. She gave it to them because she doesn't need it anymore. She took my face. All I have left is a smooth white globe. My mouth is a red wound, my eyes two bits of sharp, green glass pressed deep into my skin. Amanita-white, filled with spores, my heart swells ready to burst.

I promised you facts and forgot to give them. Here are facts. Elaine Thayer moved to Michigan. Perhaps you guessed that al-

ready. Julia was lonely. No one wanted her; she had buck teeth and
no chin. She sought Mary Louise. Mary Louise forgave her over and
over again. They spent most nights together sleeping in the same
bed, their ankles twined together. They talked through the long,
blue nights of boxes and the things they would fill up the boxes
with, of looping gray rivers, of a sky filled with endless white birds.
They talked and talked until they were no longer six, they were no
longer seven; they were thirteen or fourteen.

Then Mary Louise was embarrassed by her breasts. They were
new breasts, and she knocked them into everything when she
walked. Her mother bought her a special harness to hold them up.
Julia had no harness; she had no breasts. She spun naked through
Mary Louise's bedroom, singing, "I am a willow wand, a lithe green
bough." Each time she spun past Mary Louise, she smacked her
palms hard against Mary Louise's new breasts.

Once upon a time Mary Louise began to bleed from a secret
wound. Her mother gave her a white napkin to protect her from
harm. The napkin was the same as a white handkerchief spotted
with three drops of blood. It spoke with her mother's voice. Mary
Louise's mother showed her a photograph of herself at fifteen. The
faces and figures of mother and daughter were nearly identical.
"You see," said her mother. "You are beautiful."

When Julia turned sixteen she began to wear Mary Louise's
clothes. If she couldn't wear the clothes themselves, she would buy
clothes exactly like them. At first Mary Louise tried to combat it.
She would wear a red sweater, and if the next day Julia was wearing
a red sweater, then Mary Louise would buy a blue sweater. It was
no use. Julia usurped Mary Louise's tastes as soon as she developed
them. She ate her whole with greedy gulps.

Still they lay together, Julia's hands pressed close to those strange
new breasts. They talked on and on. Then when Mary Louise
listened to Julia speak, she heard her own voice. Julia spoke Mary
Louise's own thoughts, thoughts born on some blue night when
they lay twined, murmuring, watching the window-framed moon
where it hung as white-hot and sharp as the blade of a little knife. It
was no longer possible for Mary Louise to tell which person was her
real self. They spoke the same language, wore the same clothes, and
even walked with the same gait. "The Siamese Twins" was what

people called them. Julia's face was now a slick silver mirror, slowly erasing the face it reflected. Nights, Mary Louise caressed the lines and curves of Julia's face, burying her head against the neck below it to avoid a set of strange chalky green eyes. She would fall asleep with her nose full of the scent of skin and hair.

When a cat sits on your chest, it sucks the breath out of your body; you smother and die. I used to wake nights and feel cat's paws against me, its eyes glowing green above my breasts.

In this gray room there are no cats, but now I have no more breath. I stay inside all the time when it's not raining. The walls here are bone-hard, the floor soft as jelly.

Julia and I might have drifted on into old age, finally blending to become one whole person. We might have been happy, but into each paradise comes a snake, and we were allowed no fairy-tale ending. I say it is because we had climbed no glass mountains, plucked no magic fruits, guessed the name of no crippled dwarf. Our happiness dissolved into bitter, black mud.

This is how it was. When Julia was twenty-one and Mary Louise was older, Sebastian arrived from California. He had come to make his home in the New Jersey suburbs, no one knew why. He was a dental school graduate and planned to set up a practice. His teeth were white, white, white. Mary Louise said he applied his smooth golden hair with a paint brush every morning. And they loved him. He was so beautiful that they could see their own faces reflected over and over again on his shining hair. "We are infinity," said Mary Louise and Julia in bed that night. They scratched each other with their toenails and planned how to get him.

Getting Sebastian was no easy matter. Mary Louise and Julia were so much alike that he could barely tell them apart. It seemed for awhile that Mary Louise had gotten him. It must have been her eyes. Sebastian would stare for hours into those lettuce-colored eyes, his lips parted in a smile that showed his beautiful teeth.

But while Mary Louise opened her eyes and closed them, Julia was planning and planning. She caught Sebastian one day and told him lies, lies about Mary Louise. I never found out what she said, but Sebastian avoided Mary Louise after that. Did Julia whisper to him, vomit, vomit-eyes? I never found out, but once again Mary

Louise began to eat dirt. She ate this time in surreptitious pinches, her stomach no longer able to take larger amounts.

So, one day in the summer things happened. It was very hot. Mary Louise and Julia had just fallen in love with Impressionist paintings and were dressed all in white. They looked beautiful, like angels, but they sweated terribly in the heat. Julia carried a red paper umbrella to keep the sun off her face. It began to remind Mary Louise of fire engines, saint's blood, and the napkins they wave around in front of bulls.

They walked back and forth across Craven Creek footbridge, back and forth, up and down. You can guess what they were talking about. Sebastian, Sebastian, Sebastian. Mary Louise wanted him and Julia both. She said, "You can't have him; you are me." Julia said Mary Louise was ridiculous and a nuisance. She said certain white teeth were her territory and no trespassers would be tolerated. Mary Louise pressed her hands against her ears and began to say little things in a little voice.

The conversation went on and on like that. It twisted around itself and wound upwards in an angry spiral. Their heels banged back and forth across the wooden bridge like fists. Their voices grew loud, loud, until they were screaming. Then Mary Louise said that all she wanted, all she had ever wanted was to have her own face again. How Julia had taken her face and hidden it in the shade of a red umbrella and she wanted it back. And Julia began to laugh loud and fast and back away from Mary Louise. And Mary Louise held her hands over Julia's breasts to keep them there. Julia tried to leave and Mary Louise pressed harder and harder until there was no longer anything in front of her and all she heard was splashing and yelling. And Julia was underneath the bridge splashing about in the muddy water and shrieking that her arm was broken. And someone was yelling that they would tear the moon out of the sky and cut off the head that was their own. Then there was a long silence. Mary Louise looked down into Julia's eyes. Julia looked up into Mary Louise's eyes. Neither one had a face.

I sit, now in the rain, now in a gray room. I would like to say that Julia sends me flowers and chocolates wrapped up in paper bags and white twine, but I doubt that it's true. In this gray room I am happy for all eternity, my grin a constant gash below my sloped nose.

There is Julia. She was my face. We stared, pressed together, eye to eye, nose to nose, and lip to lip to lip to lip. I am a monster. We are an angel. And Mary Louise. Where is Mary Louise? Gone. Gone. Gone floating up to heaven on a bat's black wings. There is no Mary Louise. There is no Julia. Not now. Maybe not ever.

LEE ZACHARIAS

Weatherman Shot by MIA Mom

(from the novel *Infrared, a Wife's Story*)

> *Washington. March 9, 1982.* Former civil rights and antiwar activist Ted Neal was shot today after turning himself over to the FBI. Neal, who disappeared in 1971, was speaking to reporters outside the Hoover Building when the unidentified assailant opened fire.

It is the second death that is the cruelest, the child pulled from the lake only to perish in some other needless way. Reprieved once from the world of shadow, a young man should take care. His loved ones will not easily give up the miracle.

But she is not a widow, not even yet, though she has served for eleven years. That much Alex knows from the news, which she watches at lunchtime, at dinnertime, at bedtime, listening to the radio on the hour every hour between. Too late to meet her class, she hovers in the darkroom, waiting out the static and top tunes. A few of her students have refused the unexpected holiday and are printing; she sees Ross only when he passes so close she starts. "I thought you were sick," he says, and the eyes she turns on him are wide with alarm. "I've been meaning to ask you—a friend of mine is having some people for dinner Sunday, will you come?" She reaches a hand back to clutch at the counter. "I don't know," she blurts at last without knowing what he's asked or if she's answered, and flees to the room outside, where Kendrick is waiting to take her home.

"Come on," he says and lays an arm around her shoulder to guide her past the two students who gawk from behind the drier. He's left his station wagon in the loading zone. "Do you want to go to D.C.?"

he asks. "No," she whispers. She can't remember what they say on the way to his farmhouse. He fixes her a drink; in the freezer he finds two boil-in-bag dinners, and they eat without mentioning Ted Neal, though they sit on the sofa in front of Dan Rather. "Cognac," he offers, but the bottle stands with an unbroken seal on the coffee table all the four hours while they wait for the eleven o'clock news. "He won't die," she says once, so tonelessly not even she can tell if it is a lament or a prayer. "You don't have to do this," he answers, but they keep silent vigil until the update, and then there is no more news to wait for, no reason not to go to bed. Ted is at a hospital in critical condition.

"You should call," Kendrick suggests, but she doesn't answer, and still neither of them move for the stairs. Pity has melted over his features, and she can't bear to see their familiar landscape re-formed. "Would you like me to?"

Slowly, in an emptied-out voice, she says, "I thought I would learn something from my life. And when I met Ted I thought what I'd learned was that I hadn't been a very good person. I wanted to be better." She looks up. "So here I am." It is a joke of sorts, bitter.

"Don't," he says.

On the upstairs landing where he keeps his cluttered desk, a makeshift office between the large bedroom where he sleeps and the small one where she will sleep, they pause. She's reluctant to part with the day, for tomorrow will be the day after, and she will rise already stumbling into the shape of her sorrow. "I would tell you what I feel if I knew," she vows. "I don't want him to die." It's too simple. She can't imagine the rest of her life if he lives.

She wakes before dawn and watches the light come. Listens: a harbinger of birdsong; the abrupt blare of a clock radio; the muffled squeak and sibilance of Kendrick's rising. His socks whisper on the stairs, but what's the point of tiptoes, she won't go back to sleep. She meets him in the kitchen, where he pours coffee with a careful hand. He's not sure if her energy is a good or bad sign. "No news," he says gently. She cracks eggs into a frying pan. "I was going to call the hospital before you woke up."

"Too late now," she says, and his face folds. "I broke the yolks. You'll have to have scrambled." She pitches the shells into the garbage with a peevish lash of her hand. "And what were you planning to tell me if he died?" He shakes his head sadly, and at the table she repents. "They never give out information about patients over the phone."

The call comes after nine. "His mother," Kendrick mouths and motions her upstairs, where she sits with her head bowed at his desk, a sudden quease in her stomach, hand trembling toward the receiver. It releases Justine's sob like a gush of water. "Lexie," her mother-in-law whimpers, and Alex begins to shake so hard she has trouble holding the phone. "I'm sorry, I'm so sorry," Alex murmurs. "Justine, I'm sorry, I can't hear you, could you speak up?" She has to know if he's died. "Please, I can't hear you." It's monstrous, but she has to know what *critical* means.

Coma.

Dimly Alex hears the dishwasher throbbing downstairs. "I'm sorry," she whispers.

"He's on a respirator." Justine's voice chokes again. "How do they know, how can they tell—less than twenty-four hours later how can they say he'll never wake up?" When does the faithful wife know, waiting dinner, that her husband will never come home? Justine's message falls into the dead eye of a storm, the terrible calm of her heart. It is practiced at not beating. She takes the news as if she has always known it, there, in the comatose muscle where she used to think passion resides.

"There's brain damage."

"Is Jeannie with you?"

There is a long pause. "Jeannie's in Washington." Another pause, filled with the crackle of another conversation on the line. "The bottom line," someone keeps saying. "We haven't told her." Downstairs the dishwasher hesitates and thrums into a new cycle. "Jeannie's joined the Sikhs. They run a restaurant in Dupont Circle. I know what you're thinking, but it's not like the Moonies or those nuts in Guyana. Most of them are from very good homes."

For an instant Alex sees Justine: bare feet with bright red toenails tucked beneath her, black hair in a heavy bun, lips as thick with carmine as her nails. "Welcome to our family," Justine says, with a breezy wave from the terrace. It was the first time Ted brought her home. He hadn't warned her, and as she cleared the last step the spectacular charm of the scene struck her like knowledge. White petunias and red geraniums in bloom in the urns, a cascade of ivy over the brick wall, a perfume of roses from the garden, and overhead the elms, stirring a lace of shadows. It was so lovely it took her breath, and she knew then that to them she was already one of that legion of girls not good enough to marry rich sons. She had wanted them to like her. A year of wading through Marx, Marcuse, and Mills, watered down through the Port Huron Statement, and still she had wanted them to like her.

"It's a disciplined life. Maybe it will be good for her," Justine says. With a sharp twist of pain Alex comes back to the phone. Jeannie, they are talking about Ted's sister, Jeannie. "She's getting married again. A boy from the ashram; they've been given permission. They'll live in their separate—dorm rooms, I guess you'd call them—and meet once a month for intercourse."

"It sounds wonderful," Alex says weakly.

"Well, I don't know what she's thinking," Justine says. "If only Ted—he was always such a good one for giving advice, even when he was a little boy he was always a leader. Sometimes I think Jeannie would have, well, found herself if he hadn't disappeared."

A leader—the class president and good Eagle Scout, a son any mother could be proud of, and even when they didn't agree, his parents had to admire the courage of his convictions. She loved him, and all the years he was gone it never occurred to her to wonder anything but *where*. Alex shouldn't be so angry. She had loved him too.

Justine's voice fails again; there is only the faint sound of anguish melting into the long distance lines. *Welcome to our family.* Something tears loose inside Alex, she feels a rush of pain so dizzying that she flings an arm out, stripped of her moorings, standing again on a terrace stippled with shadow, as innocent of time as a tableau, all of them gathered before her mind's eye in the impossible grace of an irretrievable moment, such unwitting lambs in wait; and loss blinds her with a hot mist of tears.

". . . was it something I did? Lexie, he's been seeing other women."

Of course he would have seen other women, of course he would, of course. "Ted." The word falls from her mouth, stupid. Her breath comes in shudders and ragged gulps.

"*Dad,*" Justine says impatiently. "He wants a divorce. You wouldn't even put a dog out after forty years."

Please, Alex thinks, please, as she lays her head on a sheaf of pink papers and weeps.

"Are you there? I know it's not the time to tell you my troubles, but I wanted to prepare you. Are you there? What time is your flight?"

Alex stiffens and sits up. They mean for her to come. It is not an unreasonable expectation. The other conversation still echoes in the receiver. The bottom line, the bottom line, the bottom line. The phone feels clammy. "Justine," she says dully, "I can't."

"You mean you're not coming? *My god.*" Running her finger around the rim of the mouthpiece, Alex brings away a cold tear. "I can understand that you might feel bitter, but—oh Lexie—if you saw him, you'd have to forgive him."

If she saw him . . .

As in every day of her life? For how many years? When she thought any day might be the day, *hoped,* when all she had to do was close her eyes to see him. She was grateful when the image finally wore itself out, grateful to be without hope, because without hope it was done.

And then Cathy Wilkerson turned herself in.

A decade underground. Ten years since she and her Weatherpals blew up her father's house, and two young women stumbled from the rubble, leaving three dead behind. Justine had phoned, ecstatic with the news, which smote Alex like a stunning white light, and she understood that more than anything on earth she *feared* he would come back too. It's too late. She can't save him.

"No one blames you." Justine's voice is cold with reproach. "You've been lonely, you have another life now."

"I have no life," Alex says.

"Ted needs you, Lexie." But she can't—or does she mean won't? When they hang up, she splashes her face with cold water. Kendrick is waiting downstairs.

"Is it bad?"

Wordless, she nods.

"Dead?"

She shakes her head.

"I'm so sorry," he tells her.

She had forgotten the most staggering thing about grief—that the acts it inhabits are so ordinary. It will have to learn again how to live inside the routine of her needs, and she's boggled by the way the blind beast must try to fit itself to those meager gestures, to eat, sleep, turn on and off lights, go to the grocery, get gas, raging and twisting those deeds into sorrows until it can teach itself the limits of the life which contains it, until it shrivels, becomes a small thing you can hold in your hand. She makes herself meet classes, endures the calls from Justine, all those progress reports with no progress. "He'd be better off dead," Justine sobs. "I know it's wrong, but I wish they'd just pull the plug. Do you think I'm wrong? For God's sake, why can't you forgive him, why won't you come?" But still she refuses, as if to see him, to look upon his unthinking white face, might be to forgive him, to let him slip off, excused. And then he really would be dead.

The woman who shot him is in custody. Her son is an MIA. And once Alex thought it was just the little comings and goings of love that could break your heart. What did she know, a teenager reading romantic novels? What did he know, a teenager reading *Das Kapital?*

When Ross asks her to dinner again she accepts, because she feels helpless. Who is she to hand out excuses? As if her will could make a difference. "Don't answer the phone," Kendrick says, "I'll tell her you're out," but why bother to refuse phone calls when you can't refuse disaster? Kendrick makes her feel helpless: she needs him, and he's there. He's never failed her. Never mind how she left him, the day after Ted's disappearance he called. Came to see her, and later, when she showed him her photographs, almost shyly, her documentary of the Movement, he got her a show and then a publisher, and then it was school, encouraging her, practically ordering her to go, when she was still so lethargic she had trouble leaving the warm, numb place she had worn in her bed. Maybe he already knew he would offer her a job when she finished. He's let her play the faithful widow, though she knows how strongly he's disapproved, just as now he disapproves of the cranky apathy she passes for mourning. For her sake, he's with them: she should see Ted, howl it out, and be done. "So I've wasted the best years of my life," she snaps. "What else is new?" She can't seem to thank him; he's so necessary he makes her cross. If she is the faithful wife, what does that make him? At least she has a husband. Where is his wife or lover?

When she tells him she is going out, he brightens. "Have a good time," he says heartily. He is happy to see her trying. Or maybe he's just happy to be off the hook for a night. It's only a student dinner, she tells him, but he says it again: "Have a good time."

Ross's directions take her across the Lee Bridge to a horseshoe drive in what used to be country but is now the scraggly hem of the city's south side. The loop of red and white cabins in need of new paint has the configuration of a wagon train under attack, though it more nearly resembles a tourist court. Toys are scattered over the common grass lot. Though she's lived in far more dilapidated places, she feels a tug of pity. In the gloomy dusk, the settlement has the forlorn look of occupants who have found themselves stranded.

"I'm glad you came," Ross says as he opens the door. The guests are already assembled in the cramped living room. One she recognizes from the Art Building, Lorraine. "This is Alex," he announces, but Alex will have to pick up the conversation to guess the names of the others, a boy in a Kafka T-shirt and the girl on the long, sagging brown sofa beside a couple who have the insular look of serious students married too young. The wine she hands Ross is meant as a gift, but he leads her to the refrigerator and hands her a glass decorated with pink cartoon figures. From the end of the sofa she can see bunk beds in the bedroom, with two giggling children dressed in pajamas crawling in and out. Their mother, Marjean, is Ross's friend. Her clear, buoyant voice rises and falls from the bedroom in the cadence of a story, and Alex feels something catch in her throat, something that has to do with the small, serviceable rooms, with the domesticity in which they have gathered, that transports her to the house where she lived with Kendrick in Limestone all those ages ago, before her history had begun. A lost sentiment, a road not taken. Since the shooting she has been, constantly, on the verge of excrescent emotion.

When Marjean turns out the bedroom light and joins them, she sits on the arm of Ross's chair, brushing her short brown hair back from her forehead with a careless sweep of her hand. She is not pretty—short, nearly dumpy in her jersey and jeans, with wire-framed glasses that are too colorless for her pale face, but there is something appealing about her, an unaffected grace and good humor. Alex would have expected a girlfriend more like Lorraine, an *artiste* in gauzy cottons, jangly bracelets, and gigantic hoop earrings, or perhaps a petite blonde sorority sweetheart. But Marjean is impressive, chatting easily with her handsome boyfriend's sour friends (or is it Alex's mood? perhaps they are just reticent and solemn) and serving a poorly made dinner off mismatched china, which they hold on their knees, poking at the ground beef, canned corn, and noodles bound in a Campbell's soup sauce. The room reeks of air freshener. Marjean takes in kids for a living (where does she put them?), can have little in common with Lorraine, and yet Marjean draws her out until the girl's hands flutter in the air as she describes the geometry of light that links all her paintings. Alex feels herself close to tears again; Marjean's talent recollects Ted's. When Alex looks for Ross's eye (for what? to signal her ardent approval?), he is watching her with a concentration so searing she drops her fork to her plate with a clatter that pops the children from their room. Marjean rises to shoo them, but nothing will do until Ross bears the girl, Karen, adorably blond and curly, about the room for kisses. She is two, and her warm cheek is as silky as water. Her brother Billy makes the rounds himself. "Gimme five," he says, but when he reaches Alex his hand locks and he turns to his mother. "Who is *she?*" he asks, and Marjean laughs. "She's Ross's teacher. Isn't she pretty?" And the evening is ruined.

On Saturday her picture was in the *Times-Dispatch*. A local reporter picking up a local angle—it's a bigger story than was first expected, WEATHERMAN SHOT BY MIA MOM. On the day Ted stood in front of the FBI Building, he was just another of those underground creatures hatching like locusts. Now he's an editorial, and Alex is obliged to correct headlines: Ted was never in Weather; his heart would go out to the woman who shot him. *Her* heart goes out, it makes her sick, why do they have to hype it as if all history rides on the balance?

"Do you still believe in the Revolution?" the reporter had asked her, pulling at his tie. She used to meet his type all the time: strangers who seemed to feel they owed her a personal apology for never having joined the Movement; they were embarrassed to have missed the big party. (What was it Tulip, the girl who worked just as hard as they did but never had her face on Huntley and Brinkley, what was it she had said so spitefully at one of those all-night

sessions where they started out to plot a more perfect world and
ended up taking potshots at one another? "They make Revolution
look like a commercial—buy this and you too can be gorgeous." But
she meant Alex. Ted was above her reproach; it was not only for his
face that she festered in secret; nor was it for her face, pinched,
mousy, that he wouldn't have her. Or had he?)

"Goodnight, puddings," Marjean says firmly. When Alex makes
her excuses, Ross leaps to walk her out.

"You forgot your wine," he says as soon as they step off the slab
stoop, ready to drag her back to retrieve it.

"That's okay, keep it." Once again she is fighting back tears,
almost considers confessing, but what can she say? I'm sorry I'm
such a wet blanket; you see, my husband's been shot and he's in a
coma. Apparently he does not read the paper. She pulls her jacket
close against the chill of the early March evening, more penetrating
for the stuffy warmth of the house.

He takes her keys and opens the door of her Toyota. "Thanks for
coming."

"Thanks for inviting me."

"Marjean's not a very good cook."

"No, but it's unkind of you to say so." They are still standing
beside the car, their awkwardness lit up for each other by the small
lamp on the ceiling. "Well," she says. The sweet scent of tobacco
from the storage shed chokes the air. On the highway a truck grinds
gears.

"I don't live here."

He wants her to know that the children aren't his and Marjean is
a part-time lover. She's embarrassed for him. For herself. She
knows now why she chose him: his height, the steady cast of his
eyes, his somber bearing. Marjean's manner, Ross's looks: it is her
eyes that are clouded over with Ted's image. She should have
noticed before tonight that the foolish attraction was returned. She
slides into the car, refusing to take his meaning. "It's a funny place,
all these little cabins. All it needs is a lake."

"She's had a rough time—Billy's got a hole in his heart, and her
husband skipped out on the child support. She's a good person."

"I can tell."

His hand still rests on the door. "I wasn't apologizing for her."

"I'm sorry." She puts her face down on the steering wheel. What she means is that she doesn't want to know anything about his life. "I have to go home now."

And so how does it happen that after Tuesday, when he slips in and out of her class so inconspicuously he seems, conspicuously, to be avoiding (fine—she would like to avoid him too; maybe he'll drop and that will be the end of an infatuation she sincerely recants)— how can it happen that on Wednesday, checking the darkroom, she should find him printing and walk to his cubicle to stand behind him until the air sharpens with her intent and he turns around, without a word packing up his negatives and paper? He's a good student, precise, careful to seal the foil inner pocket. He knows what she means, all right, but he's not sure it's worth forty bucks of paper. Already half of her regrets, but half and half make a whole, and that's what she wants, to be wholly occupied in whatever fractions, nothing leftover to think about Ted Neal.

But on the sidewalk of West Avenue, she loses purpose. It's a pretty street, tucked like a secret into the Fan, three quiet blocks whose house numbers skip without apology from eleven to fifteen hundred. She was lucky to get into one of the last rentals in this row of town houses painted with pretty pastels or sandblasted down to the red brick and gentrified. It's so well tended and charming that at first she felt as if she only sublet while rich owners trotted the globe. Now, as she sidesteps a tricycle on the walk, even her own footsteps feel like someone else's. She hasn't been home for more than a week, and the woman who drove off to the Y that morning seems a stranger, as impossibly innocent as the girl who stood a little dazed on a brick terrace beside a boy who wore the world's sorrows like honor on his high cheekbones. She doesn't have enough resolve to get through this without parlance. "How late did your guests stay?"

"Not late. Marjean has to get up with the kids."

"I liked your friends," she says, although they are already blanks.

He grabs her wrist and turns it, almost as if he's inspecting for razor stripes or holding her against permission. "You didn't tell me you were married."

So he knows. That's how he understands her. It happens all the time, people in pain and shock cruising for the fuck that will shake the broken hearts right out of their bodies.

"I go to school on Monday, everyone's buzzing. I felt like a fool."

"Maybe you should read the newspaper," she says and the hollow place where her breath should be lurches. She can't get rid of it, this ache that is like the wind knocked out, a collapsing void inside her lungs. She should stop, cancel out. Is she supposed to explain that she doesn't wear her wedding ring because she doesn't want to explain? He doesn't know what it's like to find out that your husband's left you from UPI.

He lets go. "Why did you come and just sit there?"

"Why didn't I stay home and just sit there?" she says bitterly. "It's been a long time since I've seen him. There's not a whole lot I can do."

"I'm sorry." He means it. "If you want to talk . . ." She shakes her head. His brow is troubled with sympathy, or maybe he's just not sure that fucking the bereaved is polite. She doesn't know him well enough to predict. (Is it polite for the bereaved to fuck strangers when they can't summon the interest to give the occasion a social side?)

Her apartment smells of disuse, like a motel room that needs the air-conditioning turned on, where a thousand occupants have left no trace but the brown cigarette scar on the tub. Her plants need water; while she attends them, he busies himself checking out what he can read of her from her possessions. White walls with good prints; lots of greenery; note the Turkish rugs, hardwood floors sanded and gleaming with polyurethane. All the flea market finds, and any artist or academic could live here. He could have imagined it if he tried.

"This your work?" He's looking at the walls. "I liked your book on the sixties. I didn't know you'd done anything else."

"Time marches on." She feels nasty.

For a moment they stand, caught in the arch between living and dining rooms, out of conversation. It's the same awkwardness that kept them beside her Toyota on Sunday night, an ineptitude at the inevitable, or perhaps it's only the predictable. Whatever, they're dignifying it beyond its deserts with their hesitations. She sets the watering can on the dining room table. "The bedroom's this way," she says and takes his hand to lead him, but for the strange warmth of his palm against hers, a realtor showing a floorplan. She turns down the quilt, and when she turns her depression back to him, he is already undressed, his lean chest polished with the late afternoon light. He springs with the merciless art of a cat, a thin coil of muscle pressing through her flesh to her bones, and though she bends into the embrace she feels assaulted, afraid their ribs will give way and their organs mix themselves up together; when they finish she will have to sort out their lungs, hearts, and stomachs like a jumble of clothes. But the pressure is really just her own resistance, less a struggle of flesh than an unyielding of her spirit. His mouth explores hers with a sensual tremor—plain-Jane Marjean has got herself some lover, who lifts Alex like a dancer, locking their eyes for the look of it; this is a performance, and he means to bring her house down. Lowers her to the sheet in the same fluid ballet, strips off her shirt and jeans, touching all over her body. She should close her eyes to him and give in, but she's fascinated to watch him work all the frail, curled tendrils of her nerves, his fingers stroking like questions (this? here?). She has to see the quake in her thighs to know she is coming, but her body opens to him in a way she regrets even as she is thinking why not? Eleven years. How many wives would have been so faithful? She can't find the rhythm. Her body knows the notes, but it's the beat that distinguishes the thing. When he shudders into the moist nest of her arms, they hold him, relieved, though her skin still shivers and trills. "You're quite the athlete," she says flatly, but he's no novice and knows better than to try sealing his bargains with words. B+ (Ted would have laughed at the tart compliment). But she should be nicer; she supposes she's sorry only that now it will be awkward in classes—for all his skill he embarrasses himself with his shyness and lack of humor. It's a mean thing to do, but while he's in the shower she dresses and sneaks out.

He does not show on Thursday, and she scans the class with a small sting of conscience—she hasn't been thinking about him. She won't think about Ted, and so she has been studiously thinking of nothing. (Who would guess what a demanding, full-time job that is?) The class's attention seems soiled. Ross has warned her—the mongers are out. Up and down the hall they whisper.

He turns up at the farmhouse that night. Drooped on the sofa in the robe Kendrick fetched with her things from West Avenue, she's sure it is Ross even before she rises, and she cinches the wide satin sash tighter, bunching the neckline between her fingers at the cleavage. Kendrick has a class. She opens the door, looking beyond him to the streaky sunset, and sighs. For something to do she brings him a beer, but he holds it unopened, leather jacket slouching from his shoulders in an easy fit that is too sexy to be unstudied. Neither of them sit down. "You weren't in class today."

"You weren't home when I got out of the shower." He's angry. "Whose apartment was it, anyway? You didn't tell me you live with the head honcho."

"I don't," she says. "I didn't tell you this, I didn't tell you that. What is this? I skipped a couple of lines on my application?"

"Whoa," he says. "You're pissed."

"What do you expect?" But if he reminded her of Ted and is only himself, is it his fault? And if she is pissed, is it with him? Bad train of thought—she needs to get off before it arrives at its destination, for it isn't entirely Ted or even herself, and she doesn't want to discover what she's really mad at is just *things*. "We're friends. Very old friends. I've been staying here since . . ." Her eyes fill as she moves to the sofa and picks up her tea. "I can't talk about this. I'm not angry with you, I just don't want to have to go through all that information."

"You want sex with no questions." It's not quite a statement or a question.

"That was a mistake," she says. He opens the beer, still watching her with a wary, skeptical expression. "I'm sorry. Look, can you accept that I am just possibly not in my right mind? It's nothing you did. I just don't want to get involved."

"You've got a funny way of not getting involved." He sips. The fingers wrapped around the can are slender, like his elegant long nose. He has the slightly punk look of a European aristocrat. He lacks Ted's breadth, the sturdy weight of his shoulders.

"It was a cowardly thing to sneak out. I apologize."

"I don't want you to be sorry." When she doesn't answer he examines her photographs framed along the wall that opens into the staircase, and she cuts past him to sit on the steps, as if to block him as he glances upward, at the prints ascending to the second floor. "You all must use a lot of Windex." Underneath his jacket he wears a thick cotton shirt and baggy pants with complicated pockets. "I found Steve Kendrick's book in the library. *Memen-toes.*" He is watching her face; there is more to this story than she's told.

She stares at the floor, hugging her knees. "That was a long time ago. I guess, for both of us, our material just kind of dried up." But that's unfair to Kendrick, whose vision has always focused inward, on the texture of his own imagination, even in the days when he was photographing her. For him the whole fascination is form. "At least it did for me."

"The sixties?"

"I don't know. Maybe it was only my attitude." Her eye had looked outward, but she hasn't worked well for almost two years. "He taught me how to use the camera and the darkroom—that's where I learned. I was sitting for him, so he did me a favor." She looks up. "I was fifteen years old, with a crush on my teacher."

He flushes. "I'm not fifteen."

"Twenty? Twenty-one?"

"Twenty-three—I was in Europe a couple of years."

"Dropped out of school to paint." He nods. "And now you feel old because you're a twenty-three-year-old senior with Paris. But I'm thirty-six, and twenty-three seems very young to me." Numbers. Ted was only twenty when he bound her forever with his grave voice; she was nineteen. But she has grown older while he's never changed, twenty-seven when he vanished, twenty-seven all these long years. And when Kendrick was twenty-seven, she was fifteen. What counsel can she give this boy? Except that he will grow older too. If he's careful. In a year he'll bemoan twenty-five as a looming watershed and mark it in a morose funk. In ten years he'll wonder how he ever could have been as young as twenty-five. "Besides, I don't think teachers should sleep with their students."

"You think I screwed you for a grade?" Resentment splotches his face. "If you're so fucking moral what are you doing here with your old boyfriend while your husband . . ." But he wants to keep her and cannot go on.

"Do you know who he is? Was? Don't you *understand?* You're too young, you don't remember! He was a *hero*."

"So you left him."

His words hang in the air. Outside there is a faint stirring toward summer, a sound of crickets, things hatching, that cannot quite yet be heard. Her voice hollows. "He left me. He was wanted for questioning in connection with a bombing." She looks up. He's listening. "Questioning, that's all. He *hated* that the Movement turned violent, and if he even knew anything it was against his will. Maybe he did; he heard things. You see the pictures—*Hey-hey-LBJ-*

how-many-kids-did-you-kill-today—you think we were together. It wasn't just methods; we couldn't even agree on the issues."

For a second her ears ring with the discord of all the old debates that played from shabby living room to shabby living room that first summer on Crow Hill. Stokely had stolen the blacks and left them the poor, the whole disorganized mass of it. Welfare mothers, the homeless, the substandardly housed, students, sharecroppers, migrant workers, the Third World, the laborers of the first world who didn't dare vote themselves unions. That was the year when they could strike up a conversation on the corner and come home with a new cause, a neighborhood center, free lunch, better garbage collection. And while their rhetoric rattled against the paper-thin walls, outside, in a landscape of tarpaper shacks, cars on blocks, rusted wringers, the lowly citizens of a crueler kingdom lifted wordless voices in song, the sweet harmony of tree frogs, crickets, cicadas. When they left the poor for the war, they had yet to decide who their constituents were.

"So he disappeared. Like the rest of them the year before, oh you wouldn't believe how excited they were when they planned it, Underground, Weatherman in Babylon. But I couldn't believe it, it wasn't him. I used to think they'd killed him."

"The government?" He's incapable of shock. His generation grew up expecting its government to be corrupt.

She shakes her head. "Oh at first, sure. The FBI—we used to call them the Shoes—the CIA. We were paranoid, we thought they were out to get us—and actually they were. Roseann Guston—you never heard of her. Wellspring? It was the commune where they trained the SLA—of Patti Hearst fame? Tribal Thumb, May 19th Coalition, The Family. When you open this can of worms, the connections just don't quit coming. Or are you one of those people that believe Charlie Manson was a common criminal and our dear departed peaceniks saints? Bernardine Dohrn: 'Dig it, first they killed those pigs, then they ate dinner in the same room with them.' *They couldn't tell Manson from Che.* She—Roseann Guston—tried to leave, and they shot her in the head, *murdered* her—"her voice breaks—"just like the Mississippi rednecks murdered Schwerner and Goodman, for betraying their white cause. I saw it happen to others, people I revered for their courage. They had ideals. Peace, justice—and maybe that's vague, but do you hear your president promising something more specific? It was the hippies who added love and reduced it to silly slogans.

"And the government didn't want peace and wouldn't have justice. So you start with ideals, you want to save the people, that makes you a prophet, pretty soon you've got an ego instead of a conscience—by God if the country doesn't want saving, you're going to cram it down their throats. You break one law, you march where they told you not to—is that a crime?—and then another, you occupy an office, you burn your draft card, and another and another, and just like the war it escalates, and still the government won't listen. So why shouldn't you bomb buildings, why shouldn't you kill anyone who threatens your noble ideals, except somewhere along the line they got stained of course, and you're not prophets or even political agitators anymore, you're just thugs. They got drunk on their power, and it's all a bad joke because after that the only power they had was to self-destruct. *We were too young.*" She raises her eyes to meet his. "But not Ted."

"Only now you know better."

She turns her face away. "They should have killed him and left him a hero."

He sits beside her, but she's not ready to give it over to tokens of comfort yet. "He always did have a genius for timing. When it was time for civil rights, he made his parents think about the discrimination they had always taken for granted. When it was time to put a stop to Vietnam, he made them think about a war that was good for business. He pulled out of civil rights *before* black power, because he saw it coming and knew that it should come. Maybe that was the flaw—he never had a cause that was his own." She sighs. "Now here he is again, with a truly contemporary dilemma: to pull or not to pull the plug. And among all the other things—the grief and anger and exhaustion—I resent it. I loved him better than that, and I resent having to wish he were dead."

"You think they should pull the plug."

She turns her face back. "I have wished he was dead, but it's not the same thing. Now that he's alive I can't wish him to die."

"But if he's suffering . . ." He livens to the argument, a freshman warming to the thesis statement of a paper he's been assigned. Why I believe capital punishment should/should not be abolished. Five reasons to ratify the E.R.A. One syllogism in favor of euthanasia.

"*Suffering?* How the hell would he know?"

She straightens, shrugging his arm off. "You wanted to know what I'm doing here. Steve Kendrick's been everything to me but my husband, and I was going to marry him once, but then I met Ted, and for a while Kendrick was married to someone else too, and then, after Ted disappeared, something about us just crippled us for anyone else. I should be talking to him, I don't know why I can't." But they never have talked about Ted, about Kendrick's marriage. They were closer than that; they had learned loneliness and respected private sorrows. "I love him. He's my best friend. I don't know why I have to be so bitchy to him."

"I don't think you're bitchy." He smiles. "You were pretty nice to me yesterday, until you snuck out."

That. Her mouth tics in annoyance: he still thinks this has to do with him. "Look. Ross." She takes his hand, streaked with umber across one knuckle. "It's very nice of you to listen, I mean it." But before she can tell him again that anything he might have considered between them is finished, gravel sprays in the driveway, she drops his hand but reacts too late and stands only at the clap of Kendrick's boots on the steps.

"Hi. How was your class?" She is bright and a little bit breathless as, much too late, Ross scrambles to his feet beside her. "This is one of my students, Ross Walker."

"How are you doing?" Kendrick sets a slide tray on a table and crosses the room to hold out his hand. She's never noticed before how the light creases beneath his eyes. He looks tired.

And Ross looks so guilty someone should laugh. A quick mumble, shake, and he's gone—can't wait to get out. His hand might as well have come away from hers marked.

"Nervous young man," Kendrick remarks.

"He's shy." She is embarrassed to catch herself bunching the vulgar neckline of her robe again. "He's one of my students."

"So you said." Kendrick sinks to the sofa. "Another poor moony-eyed pupil. You do attract them, my dear." He is going through the mail on the coffee table. "Have you eaten? Want to get a pizza?"

"You don't?"

"Nope. Must be losing my touch. Haven't had a nibble in years." He tosses the mail aside. "So, did he come to confess or just ask about the assignment?" He jingles the keys in his sportcoat pocket.

He's the only man she knows who still wears blue work shirts with Harris tweed jackets.

"I don't feel like getting dressed. It's easier to make clam sauce and pasta."

"Sure?" He follows her into the kitchen, linoleum counters the right height for midgets, the original glass-paned doors still on cupboards sloppy with paint, drawers warped beyond closing, the door to his darkroom sealed with black rubber strips. He's always going to renovate, but then a pipe bursts or another ceiling falls, and he spends all his time just patching the place back together. "Well, I imagine he appreciated the outfit. That robe's a pretty sexy number. To a kid . . ."

"He's twenty-three," Alex says sharply.

"Sorry. I didn't know you were enchanted. He *is* pretty. I overheard some girls in the elevator—he's got his admirers, and you've got some female students who don't mince words. I was blushing by the time we hit first. Whoop." He backs off from the knife as she turns from the board where she's mincing garlic, though it was only her look that she meant to warn him. She's afraid they will quarrel, and like a slap in the face she'll snap, "I slept with him." Which would be stupid—if she expects Ross to be discreet, *hopes,* she'd best start by keeping her own secrets. At another time Kendrick might have been happy to hear it, or at least to hear that she was sleeping with someone, but hardly a student, and certainly not now, when he would know how seriously she's failing—it's not exactly a sign that she's getting on with her life, and if she can't talk to him it's for that: he knows her too well for her to think she can test words on him as she stutters her way back to whatever the truth of her heart is. The best audience is always a stranger.

Do you know anything about a person, she wonders, until you've known him twenty-one years? Kendrick's fine blond hair is raddled with silver now, thinner, his face has a little more bulk, the line of his body has slackened, changes so subtle she can't say when they happened. It's not that he looks old, only that for the first time she sees how malleable the flesh is to life's seasons. One knows this, and still has to learn it: the slow tick of time is really so fast.

When the water boils, he breaks in the linguini. Years ago she used to wonder what made him so loyal. He is loyal because it is his nature to be.

Twenty-one years. And what will she know after forty? For it doesn't end with this milestone that's almost a joke—their friendship has reached its majority—even at this moment, in this stasis, it is evolving, and though she cannot imagine how, she cannot imagine that she will ever be without him. If *he* should die? The thought softens her face into a semblance of sorrow.

"Any word about Ted?"

She shakes her head. "Actually it was you I was thinking about."

"Ah."

"You should take better care of yourself. You don't eat right. Pizza—do you know how much fat there is in pepperoni?" She stabs the third clove of garlic and turns back to him, nattering fury. "You're forty-eight. People your age have heart attacks, they get cancer." The words fly from her mouth like small fists. "You need fruits and vegetables. Fiber. You should exercise, watch your cholesterol, get checkups . . ." In a second he is beside her, taking the knife from her hand as the hot wave of tears breaks.

"It's okay, it's okay; Alex, it's okay," a lullaby jarred by a noise that she hears far away in the warm, damp cradle of his shoulder, only the noodles boiling so furiously they rattle the burner.

But it's not done yet, and in the morning nothing is changed. The bread is moldy; they're out of eggs. At McDonald's they drink bitter coffee, and she gazes out over the styrofoam litter with dull, beaten eyes. "You should go," he advises.

"Whose side are you on? I've got enough problems." Her voice is too exhausted to flare. "I'd prefer not to take on Brad and Justine's divorce. Every time she calls, she asks me, and I have to tell her I always thought they were very happily married. I've told her so many times I don't remember what I did think."

"You don't have to see them."

"Why? I don't hate them. Anyway, I think Justine's holding vigil at the bedside. She's got to sit long enough not to look callous when she goes to court to get the life-support shut off."

He's set his empty cup aside to fold arms on the table, leaning forward with a judge's irritating impartiality. "If you don't want her to, get a lawyer. You're his wife."

"What's the difference?" she says.

"Get his lawyer. The guy probably knows a lot. Where he's been, what he's been doing. You're an experienced gumshoe—this is a lead, right?"

She shrugs.

"You want to know."

She shrugs.

He sits back. "Are you afraid of what you might find out?"

"It doesn't matter."

"Bullshit." She plays with the plastic salt and pepper shakers, not to meet his eyes. "Cut it out. Spilling salt's bad luck." So? her lifted eyebrow says. She's being a bitch and should quit it but can't.

"Dammit." He yanks the shaker from her hand and slams it out of reach. "You don't want to know because you're angry. You hate his guts, you don't give a shit where he's been or what he's done—fine, admit it, it's nothing to be ashamed of. But quit wallowing. Get professional help if you need it. And don't roll those eyes at me."

She straightens, ashamed. "I'm sorry," she says in a dead voice. "You've been very good to me, and I know I should thank you, but I can't." She bows her head. "I don't hate him."

"It's a noble thing to save the world, but he didn't quite finish the job, and he put you through hell. You don't have to hate him, but it's also a decent thing to stay home and love your wife. He wasn't an MIA, Alex."

For a stunned second nothing happens. Then she flinches, and a whimper escapes the hand cupped to her mouth.

"What do I have to do to shock you? When are you going to react? Your mother all but abandons you, your father kills himself, and you'd rather lock it in a suitcase and drag it around for the rest of your life than get mad. There are some subjects on which you can't have no opinion. It's called repression, Alex, and it is every bit as bad for you as pepperoni."

She takes her hand away from her mouth. She hates words like *repression,* she hates the "professional help" that use them. Man and his therapist instead of man and his conscience. She hates the way they talk about feelings, as if they are growths to be poked at and prodded like tumors. She doesn't need a licensed Ph.D. to tell her she's malignant. She doesn't need him, daring her to get angry, waiting to win the Nobel Prize for discovering the miracle cure: take a little tantrum and call me in the morning.

But he's not smug. For that matter, he's even right, but she's right too: it doesn't make any difference. She is what she is, and a long time ago she learned what horror can come of trying to change that.

Kendrick sighs. "The point is he had a choice. You have too."

"Love him or leave him?" She snatches her hand from the table before he can grab it, but he's not going to let her off light.

His eyes are steady. "Something like that."

"There weren't even any charges. There wasn't a warrant, he could have just as easily gone home."

"It was a grandstand act."

"I never renounced him. I never renounced the Movement." But she had withdrawn. The Underground denounced her, and she never knew if that was why she couldn't find him or if Ted himself had put the word out. "The government was *wrong*."

But so had the government of the Movement gone awry. It is hardly a coincidence that, in the fallout, the country had turned so conservative. She's not even sure it's ironic. In 1964 some radicals had hoped Goldwater would win. No regime lasts, and every action is a reaction. What is so hard, what is *unendurable* for her, is not his loss—she lost him a long time ago—but to imagine him all along, waiting. What did he see, nights, in the silver stretch of her body? An eternity of moonlight or the commemoration of shadow? Or did he just reach in the dark, eyes shining on the vanward masses? History is a dark story of enlightenment. Mankind as the great amoeba. Sometimes she does hate him, for being so dumb.

But in the end, for all their misplaced righteousness and rigid party lines, their politics were no more calculated than a dare. In dreaming a future for mankind, they discovered their own present. It turned out that revolution was fun. What they protested was as much the fact of government as its crimes. Authority. Parents no less than presidents. She had shared their anger, but not their archetypal fury.

"The government *is* wrong," Kendrick says. He is thinking of El Salvador, where the death squads patrol at this very moment with its blessing. "Do you still believe in the Revolution?" the reporter had asked her. *My god.* "I'm a photographer," she answered. "By definition an observer." Which wasn't the truth, because the eye is never neutral and every picture comments on the heart of the picturemaker.

"Is wrong," she agrees. Not that it matters. "Winston Churchill: 'If you're twenty and not a liberal, you have no heart. If you're forty and not a conservative, you have no brain.' " Let the platitude sum her, even though something inside her wants to argue that justice is a matter for both. What she has learned from her life is that people rarely speak of freedom without coming to mean power. The angel of destruction plucks at the sleeve of the prophet's rag coat. She will never again trust herself to know the hairsbreadth of grace between God's pointed finger and the angel's mad claw.

"Go see him, Alex. You owe it to yourself."

She sighs. "It was all such a long time ago. I wanted to forget it."

"That's why. See him. Let it go."

But she won't, and in the afternoon she changes her mind and goes looking for Ross.

Circle Track—1958

(from the novel *Aqua Velva Man*)

"How can a man with good sense risk his neck to go running in a circle like some harebrained dog that can't find a scent?"

Tom froze, bending over to get the garbage out for his mother as if he was waiting for Zack to kick him.

"He's just reading the paper," Zack whispered in his ear.

"Dumbest thing I've ever heard of," Hershal went on. "A grown man driving a car as fast as he can go in a circle so small he can't help but run into everybody else's cars. That's not what a car's meant for. What's the point of it?"

"I'm sure I don't know, Hershal," Gladys replied from behind a pile of envelopes that she was stuffing for Summit Savings and Loan. "Some men like to do things for the sport of it, I suppose. I have never seen why there'd be any sport in going out and shooting a gun, just to be killing, myself."

"Hum. Says here the fellow who took first place up at Greenmont Speedway got two hundred eighty-six dollars. Little Joe Weatherly. I've heard Marvin Simmons make mention of him. Cousin or something." He paused, then repeated: "Two hundred eighty-six dollars. Must be a lot of people paying to see it."

Tom winked at Zack before he went out the back door.

At first Tom and Zack went to the Yellow County Speedway on Friday nights to watch from the bleachers. Buck and Lanky met

Tom after work; Zack rode his bike down to Parsons when he finished his chores, telling their mother he was going to the show in Summit. As the cars started to hot lap, the boys rushed into the empty seats in the turns where flying mud balls pelted them. When they undressed for bed after the races, clods fell out of their clothes. They swept them up—Tom called them track turds—to flush down the commode before their mother saw them.

After Tom graduated from Summit High in 1958, he went to work full time at Parsons as a mechanic, giving his mother ten dollars a week out of his fifty-four take-home pay. "We can hire a colored boy for half that to do farmwork," she told Hershal after Tom took the job. The forty-four dollars he had left went for his cars: either the Chevy or the '34 Ford race car at Parsons that had been sitting in the weeds since Clyde Henry ran out of money two summers before.

Zeb Parsons took Tom aside: "Old man Henry is over the hill, if you know what I mean. Don't say I told you, but I believe that car's yours for the asking. See if you can talk him into building you a motor. That he can still do."

Hershal and Gladys didn't know about the race car. Hershal thought a boy's interest in cars was something he would outgrow as fast as a pair of shoes; that when the novelty wore off it was just transportation. He never bought a car himself because the trunk wouldn't hold three bushel baskets, never mind the cab had to hold five people. Tom worked nights on it; every day after school, fourteen-year-old Zack got off the bus at Parsons instead of at home.

During their evening conversations in bed, Tom allowed he no longer planned to be a genius. Zack had shown him a copy of **CAR CRAFT** that pictured men racing a thing called a go-cart that resembled Tom's Speed Seat stored in their workshop, but Tom was no longer interested. Also Tom read in a car magazine that being champion of the world in one of those open-wheel cars like Carmichael had in his garage was pretty much for rich foreigners. The boys had seen a movie: *The Crash Helmet* about racing in Europe. Everytime they saw it, Tom disliked the heroine a little more, who no sooner than she got the race driver to marry her, started whining for him to quit racing. After the fourth time they saw it, Tom decided he wouldn't give up one trip around a race track in that car for ten women like her.

"I'm going to be a stock car driver," he told Zack. This time his choice of vocation moved a little closer to reality.

Soho, the palmist, lived in a rusty house trailer that sat in the middle of a pig lot near Summit. As Tom and Zack approached, she threw a pan of slops to the pigs so they snorted away from the doorway towards their food. When they got inside, Zack, who was known to be tight as a drum with his money from the day he got his first new dollar bill from Uncle Vernon at Christmas, wouldn't pay a nickel to see his future. They didn't tell Soho, but Tom had put down his dollar to find out if he was really going to be a stock-car driver.

Soho read great things ahead for Tom in his hands, the standard fortune-teller fare: adventure, fame, beautiful women, he was going on a long journey, far away from Summit, with a dark and beautiful woman who was very rich and loved him dearly. Every time Soho mentioned a new fact, Tom rabbit-punched Zack's arm and laughed. So far she hadn't mentioned cars.

"Night owl," she said. Tom was astonished; Night Owl was the name of his old car club. "Night owl eats the crow at night," she went on, "but the crow eats the owl by day. The common crow tricks the owl into turning its head until it wrings its own neck." Then suddenly Soho frowned, her ugly brown face like a peach seed with eyes. She pointed into his hand with her yellow hook of a fingernail.

"What? What?" Tom asked. "Hurry up."

She had found a blank spot. A nothing. A big hole in his life that extended to his death. "The lifeline stops. There is a hole."

"A hole? When does the hole come?" Tom asked weakly.

"Soon. With the start of the new year. Very bad. Very bad," she said sincerely.

Tom didn't punch Zack again. On the way home, Zack tried to make him feel better: "She was just trying to get you to come back and give her a dollar again."

But Tom worried over that blank spot until he went back to see her, after Christmas when he was eighteen, the time when the hole was to come into his life. He borrowed all the money Zack had on him—fifty-three cents—to put gas in his car.

On the way over, Zack attempted to entertain with his latest **Tales from the Crypt:** "Mr. Bigsby, who was a rich man, thought this medium was a fake so he decided to trick her. He went to a séance and told the medium he wanted to talk to his dead wife. See, his wife wasn't really dead because he just left her at home. Then when the medium talked to her, he said, 'See, she's a phony,' and when he got home, guess what?"

Tom wasn't in the mood for games. "Dead as a doornail, right?"

"You musta read it."

"That wasn't too tough, Zack. What did being rich have to do with anything?"

Zack thought a minute. He didn't remember any souls for sale in that one.

"I don't think the Crypt Keeper likes rich people."

"That makes two of us," Tom answered.

Soho's trailer was being slept in by three colored men. Her Palmist sign was leaning against the outside, the fingers pointing at the ground. Zack stood behind his brother while he talked to a man, tipping his head to read the writing on the upside-down hand: *Job XXXVII, 7: He sealeth up the hand of every man, that all man may know his worth.*

"Where is Soho?"

"Pigs eat her," the man mumbled.

Zack shivered. "Why?" Tom asked.

"'Cause she dead."

This time Tom was quiet when they were driving home, while Zack chattered: "Listen to this, Tom. There's this fortune-teller and she makes a fortune reading palms, always telling everybody how rich they're going to be. She's making so much money that she just keeps buying hogs and fattening them up and eating a pig a week. Ham everyday and not just Sunday. Then one day when she goes out the door to carry all her money to the bank, she falls down and breaks her leg, right in the hog lot. And every day those pigs keep getting hungrier and hungrier. And they keep oinking for her to go get their food and she keeps beating on their snouts and saying leave me alone, you rotten old hogs, I've got a broken leg. Guess what happened?"

Tom had it all figured out. "It wasn't my dark hole she was looking into last time I talked to her, Zack. The reason Soho saw my life go into a dark hole was that was where she was going."

"I like my story better. I think it's even better than the one about a man who got accidentally locked in a masoleum and was forced to eat the body of his embalmed girlfriend and pickled himself."

Tom laughed and hit the steering wheel with his fist and said something Zack spent the rest of the ride home trying to figure out: "I don't have anything to be afraid of, here or in hell. I won a race against the devil, Zack. Everybody else is just second best."

One afternoon at Parsons when Tom was pulling the bottom end of the engine apart for Clyde, and Zack was sitting in the floor with a pan of solvent between his legs, scrubbing parts with a wire brush; a figure appeared at the door to the shop. Clyde Henry and Zeb Parsons leaned against the workbench, watching the boys work. Clyde had been telling about the time he won the feature at Statesville in 1947; it was the second time that week they had heard it. His voice stopped in his throat as though someone had hit a switch. The figure who had appeared at the door wasn't the silent type.

"Tom Pate, I have been waiting for you to pick me up for an hour."

Tom jumped to his feet. "Holly Lee. I forgot. You get off early today, huh?"

"I get off early every Tuesday, if it is any concern of yours, which it doesn't seem to be. If it hadn't been for Buck Herndon giving me a ride over here, I'd be standing there till the cows come . . . Tom Pate, that is the ugliest old junk pile I've ever seen," she exclaimed.

Tom stopped what he was doing and stepped backwards, squinting at the car as though his eyes had lost their focus. Clyde and Zeb were struck dumb.

"Don't you tell me," she went on, "that this is the reason we don't ever go to the show anymore? This is a race car?"

Holly Lee stepped inside the shop and walked over to the car, her hands on her hips. Zack had never seen her move without her skates; her movements looked jerky and it took her a long time to get to the car. She tipped her head sideways, staring at Tom as if he was a crazy man. Tom grabbed for the words in his throat because he had to stop her from saying anything else in front of Clyde and Zeb:

"It's a different kind of racing, Holly Lee," he stammered finally. "It's not like drag racing where people don't ever run into each other. You get hit a lot so you get a bunch of dents. No need to waste your time beating them out . . ."

"Get hit! You mean you wreck?" She crossed her arms and stepped back, a pink bubble rising out of her mouth, popping and getting sucked back inside as she wheezed: "This thing looks like it's done got wrecked one time too many already."

"That's just the body," Tom defended. "Inside this engine, it will be perfect. That's where the money goes, in the motor."

"All your money in that greasy old pile of nuts and bolts? How about me? I want to see *Seven Brides for Seven Brothers* this Saturday. You told me we could see it."

Clyde Henry could take no more. "Get that woman out of here. Can't have no woman hanging around a race car. Bad luck."

"She doesn't mean any harm, Clyde," Tom put in quickly. "You know how women are. She just doesn't know any better."

"What do you mean I don't know any better? I have two eyes same as a man, don't I? I've been to the movies. I know what a race car looks like. And I betcha I know a lot better than a bunch of men I see when I'm looking at something the cat wouldn't drag in."

"Heard of a man got killed up at Hickory." Clyde insisted. "Some woman hanging around his car let one of them bobba pins fall outa her hair. Right into his carburetor. Stuck it wide open." Clyde's mouth stayed wide open when he finished talking, tobacco juice running out one corner and stopping in the stubble on his chin.

"I think you better go, Holly Lee," Tom added.

"Woman got no business around a car," Clyde went on. "Man don't keep his mind on his work when a woman hangs around. He's the one who pays for it."

"I don't even use bobby pins," she snapped. "Bobby pins are for tacky hicks."

"Woman was eating peanuts down at Cowpens. Shells got sucked right in a fellow's engine. Ruint it."

"Tom Pate's the one who eats peanuts with shells," she retorted. "Not me. I don't even like 'em, except the salted in the can."

"Joe Weatherly and Curtis Turner love their doll babies much as the next man," Clyde went on as though Holly Lee didn't exist except as a pair of ears, "but they'd be the first to tell you, they got their place. And it ain't around a race car. They keep a count, those two. Hundreds of them."

"That's what you got in mind, Tom Pate? A hundred women?"

Zack looked at Tom. His brother couldn't find any words except:

"I don't even know a hundred women, Holly Lee. Don't know a dozen pretty ones."

She put her hands back on her hips and wheezed again. Tom froze like a man trying to fend off a striking snake.

"I know how to handle another pretty woman," Holly Lee said flatly, and spun around to leave as if her feet had sprouted their own wheels.

"Clyde is an engine man," Tom explained to Zack. "His car isn't pretty, but that doesn't bother him one bit."

To hear the engine they were working on rev up in the back of Parson's Garage or to make a few hot runs down 43, ducking back behind the building before the state man came to check it out was one thing; or even dragging his Chevy over in the Solomon Mill parking lot. But the first time Clyde's flathead started up at Yellow County Speedway, with the sound bouncing back down off the bleachers, was like the first time Tom heard Elvis sing. Nothing else was ever going to compare, except maybe going to Darlington to the big one.

Tom let the engine warm up slowly the way Clyde had told him to. Clyde kept the carburetor in the refrigerator. He wouldn't tell anybody why, but they believed he knew what he was doing even if they didn't know why. The old driver had promised to give Tom a lesson before he let him run the car, but he arrived at the track hunched over with aching kidneys. Zeb and Tom had to help him through the window. After he took the Ford around for a few laps, they pulled him back out. Clyde stood in a seated position:

"If a car don't bust up your top half, it'll get you on the bottom end," he moaned. "Remember I told you that when your hotshot days are done. My guts are ruint." That was the last time Clyde sat in the driver's seat. Tom grabbed the doorposts and swung through the window like a gymnast. He waited for Clyde's instructions, but the old driver ambled away towards the outhouse.

"Take her out," Zeb offered. "Get the feel of it."

Tom headed for the track before the words were out of Zeb's mouth. On his first lap around, he drove in the center of the road. Then he tried giving the engine more throttle, feeling the car slide sideways. The Ford bounced across the ruts left from the last race, and yanked the steering wheel from his grip.

Since the track hadn't been wet down yet, the dry clods off his wheels hit the board fence like bullets. Each lap he came around, he caught up to his own dust. The cloud thickened until he was driving half blind. But each lap he went faster.

"Your brother is going to be a talent to be reckoned with," Zeb Parsons told Zack. "He's got a feel for it that you just have to get born with. And don't tell your daddy I said that. He'll tack my hide to the smokehouse wall. Lord knows why, but his kid's a natural."

Each time Tom revved the engine higher, cleaning it out, looking for traction as he threw the Ford into the turns; a feeling went through him, making him want to run faster. His speed increased until the pedal was on the floor. Suddenly he felt the car lean into the wall, and heard a scraping sound on his right side. Tom had slid up too high and rattled down the outside fence, adding another body crease.

"He'll really get going as soon as he finds some decent equipment," Zeb added with a whisper after Clyde walked out of the outhouse. "He ain't scared to hang it out a little already."

Tom drove until the engine sputtered, low on fuel. As he pulled down into the infield, he saw Clyde and Zeb coming to meet him. He was smiling as Zeb pounded on the roof.

"Whatcha think, Leadfoot," Zeb asked.

"Fill 'er up," he answered. "And check the oil and water. How did I look? Did I look fast?"

Zack ran for the gas can.

"Hold your horses, boy," Clyde added. "There's some pretty impatient fellows wanting to get across that track that figure they get to race too. Leadfoot has to stay off the track for a while." The infield started to fill up with cars as the other racers streamed across the track into the pit area. The water truck went out to prepare the surface.

Zack caught a sad look in Clyde's eyes as Tom pulled himself through the window and dropped to the ground. Then Clyde straightened his body and took Tom's shoulders in both hands: "Hot damn, we got us a racer."

The Night Owls out at Soloman's Mill were left to fight among themselves with Buck Herndon and Jigger Carmichael sharing the rewards. Holly Lee gave up waiting for Tom to pick her up at work, while Buck seemed to always be there when she needed a ride. Tom still kept his Chevy clean and running smoothly. If Zack's clothes were greasy, Tom made him sit on a towel, sweeping the dirt from his feet off the floor mat with a little broom.

But the race car was treated differently. When Clyde hosed the Ford down after every trip to the speedway, the dirt dropped from under it like cow piles. Tom added more dents that he quit trying to pound out. Number 7 looked as if it had been painted with a broom dipped in white paint. Yet inside that engine went every extra cent Tom earned and every dollar he won when he placed.

By the time Clyde allowed Tom to write his name over the door in the summer of 1958—he carefully lettered the name: *Casey Searles*—Tom knew a race car fit him like a new skin on a seven-year bug that left his old shell stuck on a tree. In fact he knew from the first lap he took around the Yellow County Speedway that if life was in colors, then racing was red and everything else was a pale shade of pink.

Every Saturday night for two months, Tom ran the car without his parents' knowledge until one Sunday, Marvin Simmons said to Hershal at church.

"That boy of yours is getting to be a real hotshoe."

"How's that?" he asked, not understanding what Marvin meant.

"Down at Yellow County. He'll win a race before summer's over, you can count on it."

"Is that so?" Hershal answered, never admitting he knew nothing about it.

Zack ran out to tell Tom, who was washing his car. "Tom! Daddy knows. Marvin Simmons blew the whistle on us at church."

For a moment, Tom stood motionless, then he began to twist his chamois between his hands. "What'd Daddy say?"

"Nothing. He acted like he already knew."

Tom swept the chamois across the hood of the Chevy, shaking his head. "If he didn't say anything, he didn't even know what Marvin was talking about."

The boys waited all week for their daddy to confront them, but he never did. On Friday as soon as they finished up their chores, they planned to leave for Parsons to help Clyde load the car on the trailer. Tom had the motor running in the Chevy when Zack started to go out the back door. His mother stopped him in the kitchen.

"Where are you headed off to so fast, young man?"

"I'm done. I've got to go help Tom with something over at Parsons."

"I don't think it's a good idea for you to spend all your weekends hanging around a filling station with grown men."

"I'm not hanging around the station."

"Oh, you aren't. Well, where are you hanging around?"

"Uh," he stammered, "Zeb wants Tom and I to take this car out for somebody."

"Out to where?"

"Out to Yellow County Speedway," he blurted.

"The race track! Zachary, those fast cars are too dangerous for you to be around."

"I've been around them already with Tom and lived to tell about it, Mama." While he began to dance around, the horn blasted on the Chevy.

"Tom's getting mad at me for holding him up, Mama."

"Those cars might blow up or run you down. You just haven't heard all the awful things that have happened at that terrible place. The Perkins family lost their oldest son when a car turned over and mashed his head and . . ."

"Mama, that was five years ago."

Zack was afraid she was going to tell him about the guy who got scalded when a radiator broke and the one who got his arm ripped off. He didn't know his mother read that part of the *Summit News.* The horn blew again. Gladys wound her hands in her apron and no more horror stories came out. Instead: "Well, just so long as you and Tom don't even *think* of driving one of them," her voice like a child who had just asked for the moon for Christmas and was smart enough to know it wasn't going to be in her stocking.

They got to the track later than they had hoped, because Zeb made Tom change the points and plugs on Unis Treckler's Rambler before he took off work. Tom had planned to get in some practice before the track got too crowded, but when they arrived, they were stuck on the outside until hot lapping was over. Tom got out and paced back and forth like a cat in a cage before they were allowed to drive over the sticky mud of the track into the infield.

By this time, Zack wore glasses all the time, so when his family walked across the bleachers and sat down, he knew who they were, even before he saw his mother holding onto Annie's shirttail to keep her from running across the seats after the man selling boiled peanuts.

Annie had put on her favorite yellow shirt with the front and the rear of a rabbit on her front and rear; her shirttail hung out where her mother kept grabbing at her. Rachel hadn't changed since she got home from work at Simon's Department. Gladys had recombed her hair that would be frizzy by this time of the day because it was as smoothly rolled into a bun as it was in the morning. She had on the blue dress she wore to go shopping in town and a sweater over her shoulders, latched by the pearl strand with a clip on each end that Rachel bought her at Simons.

When Gladys realized she was dressed too nice, she called the crowd "rough" to Rachel and tried to keep Annie close. She trembled when she saw first Zack facing them, then Tom's back as he bent over a car.

Annie jumped up on the seat. Zack could see her face, her eyes little dots under her bangs, and though her buttonhole mouth was too small to see clearly, he knew she was smiling when she found him by the way she started bouncing up and down on the bleacher bench. He waved.

Gladys grabbed Annie's shirttail again, this time because the little girl wanted to come down where they were and didn't understand why she couldn't. First Gladys told her it was because she was a child, then Annie saw a little boy in the pits, holding his father's hand. Then Gladys told her it was because she was a little girl. Annie had to believe her then because she couldn't find a single girl, little or big, among the cars.

"Look at that clodhopper up there," Tom remarked to Zack without turning his head.

"You mean Daddy?"

"You know who the hell I mean."

"Yeah, I didn't know he was a racing fan."

"Why didn't he stay the hell home? Marvin Simmons oughta learn how to keep his big mouth shut. Daddy didn't even bother to show up when I graduated from high school. So he comes to see me race looking like he just slopped through the hog lot."

Hershal wore his bibs. The cloth from the knees down was red with mud, the way his pants always were except on Sunday. Once when the hogs got out on Sunday morning and he had to run them down in his suit pants, he went to church that way.

"You think he's going to come down and say you can't race?"

"Let him try."

When the boys got caught up in the action of the night, getting the car ready, Tom didn't mention the family again. Zack didn't look again either after the stand filled with people, their family melting into the crowd.

Something was wrong with the car. Clyde started the engine. It ran rough at first which wasn't unusual, but the way he listened, stopped, and turned screws, indicated that the carburetor that had come out of the icebox with frost on its sides wasn't right. Tom took the car out for a practice lap and drove back off the track without passing the pits. The engine made small explosion noises out of the short pipes underneath when he came towards them. Clyde mumbled a cuss word before walking back to his tool box.

When Clyde lifted the hood, Tom shook his head. He began banging his fist on the steering wheel.

"Stop that, will you?" Clyde growled. "I can't think."

The speeds picked up with engines snarling around them as the cars went sideways into the turns, fighting for traction. The evening was hot so the track dried out fast. The thud of mud balls on the fence died down as the air filled with dust and exhaust. Before they could get Tom back on the track, the cars lumbered back into the pit area to line up for qualifying.

"Damn it, Clyde," Tom finally blurted, "if you don't get this thing going soon, we might as well go home."

The complaint made matters worse because Clyde stopped working, using it for a breather. With his face flushed and his hair stuck to his forehead with sweat, he looked too old to ever have been a driver.

"If you think you can do it better, get your lazy ass out here and try. You sit in there like you're too high and mighty to get your hands dirty anymore."

Zack had never heard Clyde, or anyone except their daddy, talk to Tom like that. Tom slid down in the seat, took a pack of cigarettes from his sleeve and lit one up.

"Go draw a qualifying number," Tom ordered Zack. When Zack returned, he showed Clyde the number thirteen, earning him a disgusted look.

The cars shut down their engines. When a preacher started talking on the loudspeaker, all the men took off their caps except Clyde who kept working. Tom didn't bow his head. Zack half bowed so he could keep watching. A scratchy recording of "The Star-Spangled Banner" made it halfway through before the needle skipped over to the end. People in the stands looked around and sat down slowly, not sure if the song was finished or if they were going to try again. Nobody had remembered to put up the flag. When a few men started yelling and clapping, the crowd dropped to the bleachers to wait for qualifying to begin.

The first car went out. Thirteen was reached and passed as Tom lost his place in line. Clyde, Zack, and Zeb Parsons pushed the car aside. Tom climbed out and went to watch beside the track. Drivers were setting times that he had beaten before easily.

After Tom walked away, Clyde asked Zack to get in the car in his place and turn the engine over. It wouldn't fire at all, the battery worn down. Zack could smell gas. He had sat in the car before and pretended to be a driver, turning the wheel and making engine sounds. His imagination wouldn't work. He felt sad, like the game was over.

Soon Clyde stepped back and crossed his arms. He didn't tell Zack to get out. Other mechanics began to gather around the car, pointing, making suggestions. Zeb drove his wrecker over and hooked jumper cables to the battery.

"Hey, how do you tell who's the groom at a colored wedding?" someone joked. "He's the one with the new jumper cables."

Zack couldn't hear what Clyde said, but he watched him shake his head. Then Zeb reached behind the wrecker seat and pulled out a spray can. For the first time, Clyde looked interested. After he lifted his eyebrows and nodded, Zeb bent over. When everyone jumped back from the engine, for a moment Zack felt panicky, wondering if there was some reason that he should dive out the window and roll away from the car before it blew up. Then Clyde relieved his fears.

"Try her again, Zack."

He cranked the motor over and to everyone's surprise, it started. Clyde disappeared beneath the hood and Zack felt the gas pedal under his foot moving on its own.

"Hop out," Clyde told him. No sooner than he did, Tom climbed in, the engine sound calling him back to the car like his mother's supper bell. A strange smell hung in the air, not just exhaust, or the smell of raw gas from the flooded engine. It smelled like somewhere else, a hospital or the vet's office. Zack felt a little dizzy.

"Ether," Zeb replied, answering his question.

Tom rushed to the staging line. Clyde ran behind him and began to check the tire pressures, hooking up a bicycle pump and pumping frantically. He tossed Zack the gauge and waved him to the other side. When Tom's turn came, he took off, the pump ripping from Clyde's hand.

"Hold your horses, goddamn it."

A man at the exit held up his hand, while Clyde stumbled over to unscrew the pump from the tire. Tom took off again before he could screw on the cap.

"Asshole," Clyde mumbled. "Your brother is a asshole," he told Zack, but watched intently as Tom took his warmup lap. "Don't sound right yet. Goddamn it. The best motor I ever built and some chicken shit little thing is messed up. . . . You got the watch?"

Zack had forgotten it. He turned to get it, but Clyde said, "Never mind," and walked over to Marvin Simmons who was already clocking Tom.

Tom qualified tenth that night, the worst of the summer. He felt too surly to talk to anyone before the race started, walking away or backing up everytime anyone came up to him. He never liked to talk much before a race, but tonight he was unapproachable, trying to put his anger through his hands and feet, to make him drive faster. Clyde worked over the engine until time to roll the car to the grid.

When the green flag waved, Tom was already on the gas, passing two cars before they crossed the starting line. The starter didn't flag him out for jumping the start. Ahead a car went sideways in the second turn, sliding towards the wall. By the time Tom got there, the car had moved back down into the groove, so he passed under him, so low that people jumped back from the corner. The track was so rough down low, Tom's teeth jarred.

Clyde cheered when he passed. Tom had made it safely through the traffic, popping out at the end of the first lap, already in fifth place. By that time, everyone was watching one car, Tom Pate's. Zack thought that maybe this day, the worst beginning for a race they had ever had, was going to be the day that Tom won for the first time.

Then the roar began to subside. The cars slowed for a crash. A man stood beside the track, holding a yellow flag to keep the cars from passing each other until the wrecked cars were cleared off the track. Tom's number 7 went past, it's white paint peppered with mud dots. Zack and Clyde waved at him, but he wasn't looking. Zeb took his wrecker out and headed for the backside, riding down on the apron against the traffic that ran slowly now, single file, bouncing along the rutted track.

"That sonavabitch thinks Tom passed him after the accident," Clyde said.

"I b'lieve he did, Clyde," Marvin Simmons replied.

"I'll be goddamned. He was clear of him before those assholes even thought of crashing."

"You can't even see the backside from here, Clyde."

"You don't have the slightest notion of what I can see," Clyde snapped.

Marvin laughed and turned to another man who laughed with him.

"Naw, Clyde, I guess not." Clyde, determined to have the last word, let his words turn to mumbles about not letting that sonavabitch get around. A mechanic from another team went up to the flagman and started talking, pointing angrily at Tom each time he came by. The flagman began pointing the flag stick at Tom, before hiding it behind his back, trying to communicate to Tom to let the driver around. Clyde went over, talking into the flagman's other ear. He started shaking his head, his mind made up. He wasn't going to restart until Tom got back into fifth position. Zeb brought the wrecker back into the pits, dragging the wrecked car that zigzagged in, resting on rear wheels that weren't turning.

Tom watched the flag stick. With each pass the starter got angrier at him for holding up the restart. He knew he was long around that car before the crash, but the starter wasn't going to back down.

When Tom dropped back, Clyde stamped his foot.

"Forget it, Clyde," Zeb said. "Either he falls back or we stand here all night."

"Put that sonavabitch in the fence," Clyde shouted.

When the green waved, Clyde's anger was instantly replaced by excitement. Tom easily repassed the car on the first lap and began to press on third place. But as he let up for the first turn, Zack noticed a little puff of blue smoke. "Clyde, the engine's smoking," he said.

Clyde looked at Zack with such a mean look that he wished he'd kept his mouth shut. "I didn't see nothing. Just loaded up from running all them slow laps. Clean your glasses, boy." On the next pass, the rear view of the car was lost in traffic, but Zack kept watching for the smoke.

"How many more laps?" Clyde asked him.

"I don't know. I forgot to count."

"You're useless as tits on a boar, boy."

Clyde walked over to ask Marvin and Zeb, getting two sets of answers: anywhere from five to ten more laps.

"Now you can count them, boy," he said to Zack. "Let me know when there's . . . Oh my god!"

Tom's car was wrapped in blue smoke, pouring from around the wheels. As he came off the last turn before the pit entrance, there was an explosion under his feet. The steering wheel ripped from his hands. Before he could grip it again, the car snapped around. He saw the front of two cars coming at him. Then they vanished and he saw the fence. He was spinning. Fence boards filled his vision before the impact.

Zack and Clyde watched the field split to go around Tom as he bounced back off the wall into their path. The field didn't split soon enough. The first hit was hard and in the passenger side, tipping Tom's car up on two wheels then shoving it sideways into the wall again. When he came down on all fours and was struck the second time from the rear, the Ford shot forward like a bumper car at the carnival.

Tom felt each blow harder than the last as he groped for something to grab. The car was hit again and again, spinning, one way then the other, out of control. When he grabbed for the steering wheel, trying to brace his arms against it to stop the lashing movement of his upper body, his shoulder hit the door. The car steered itself as the wheel ripped out of his hands again. His chest struck as one of his arms buckled and was slung out the window like a rag-doll arm.

People ran from the edge of the track as the rest of the pack dropped down to miss the crashed cars. Clyde shoved Zack backwards and he sat down hard, then scrambled to his feet. He was sure he saw Tom's arm fly out of the window. It was as if his brother was a magnet drawing every car there, all the cars he had passed, hitting him now. By the time Zack got to his feet, the track was blocked; the terrible movement stopped. One car trickled around the pileup. The flagman threw down his yellow flag and grabbed a red one, waving it frantically even though no one was passing the start-finish line. The last running cars coasted into the pits and shut down their motors.

Men went running to the pileup, tugging drivers out of the windows. One driver crawled across a hood—he wore an old air-force helmet with a star with wings. Tom didn't wear a helmet. Zack ran to the wreckage. People were pushing and shoving, all trying to get to their drivers. A wide ooze of oil was coming down the track; two men slipped and fell on their hands and knees in the black stream. When the siren blasted on the Summit volunteer fire department pickup, everyone ran away from the track. Zack smelled the gasoline then. Instead of running back, he ran towards the cars, climbing up on the fenders, across the hoods and tops, trying to get to Tom's car. He snagged his jeans on something that cut through to the skin. Finally he saw the hood of number 7; it was shorter, stuffed like ham in a biscuit. He crawled on top and hung off the roof, looking inside. The seat was empty.

"Zack, get your ass out of there!"

He turned around. It was Tom. He was standing beside the track. How could he have been in the accident if he was standing over there? Zack scrambled back over the cars, even faster than he went in. When his feet hit the sticky track, Tom grabbed his arm and pulled him away, back from the pile of twisted cars that had people moving around it now like a beehive, the fire truck shooting water on the steaming cars, diluting the gasoline that splattered on the clay. As Tom kept pulling him, Zack felt as though they were running away, trying to escape from the scene of the crime before someone grabbed them and blamed them. Instead Tom led Zack to a spigot.

"Here, wash your knee off before Mama sees it."

Zack pulled up the leg of his jeans. His kneecap was brown with blood and oil. The cut stung when Tom washed it out with an oil rag. After Tom pulled the pant leg back down, blood trickled inside Zack's jeans, soaking into his sock. Tom rubbed his wrists and stared at the pile of cars. His shoulders were hunched forward, making him seem shorter.

The wreckage never caught fire. Zeb Parsons cautiously approached the outside car in the pileup, like a cat sticking out his paw and tapping a mouse he had killed. When he decided it was safe, he hooked up the cable off his wrecker to the outside car, a '36 Plymouth, and began yanking it away from the others. Five cars were finished for the night. A man on a tractor came out and began dragging a harrow over the ruts. The wrecks were dragged outside the speedway into the parking lot, Tom's car the most damaged.

"Your engine let go," Tom began to explain to Clyde as the car passed through the gate, swinging on the wrecker hook with its rear wheels buckled. "I didn't do anything wrong. It just spun around on its own. I was going to win that damn race. I know I was. Nobody in the world could've beat me tonight. Fireball Roberts couldn't have beat me tonight."

Clyde didn't respond for awhile, just kept packing up his tools. Then he looked up at Tom. "Go tell Zeb to set it down on the trailer. It sure ain't gonna roll up the ramps."

Tom and Zack went to the parking lot. Zeb had already deposited the car on the trailer. Listening to the cheers and roar as the engines restarted inside the speedway, Tom felt a flash of anger. What right did they have to go on without them? Zack stared at the car; it sat sideways, hanging over the edge of the trailer. When he looked inside, he saw the seat he had padded with cotton he brought from home was shoved up against the door.

"Tom, don't you think you ought to get one of those helmets?"

Both boys turned around in surprise. Until they heard their mother's voice, the boys had forgotten the family was there. She stood in the muddy lot, her black Sunday shoes stuck with clay, but her blue dress as crisp as when she went shopping. Rachel and

Annie weren't with her, but Hershal walked over to look at the car on the trailer.

"What did you say, Mother?" Tom asked, as if he was talking to a stranger.

"I said, you should get one of those helmets. A lot of the boys have them on." Her eyes were shiny in the weak light.

Tom shook his head, so she stepped back and brought her purse around and pressed it to her stomach, her fingertips making dents in the patent leather.

"Why don't you give me one for Christmas?" Tom replied. Zack had tried to get him to wear an old football helmet that Coach Beal gave him at school, but he refused because it looked chicken.

"Hello, Clyde," Gladys said, undaunted by Tom.

"Howdy, Mrs. Pate. Surprised to see you here," he said dumbly.

"Yes, me too," Gladys answered.

Hershal was walking around the car, studying it. In his muddy bibs, he looked like the one who was properly dressed. Gladys was out of place, her heels sinking in the mud. Zack tugged on her arm.

"Mama, you're messing up your shoes."

She looked down at them and back at him with no surprise on her face. "Yes, I know." She hesitated, then took Zack's arm. "I told the girls to go on home with Mrs. Spencer's son," she added. "They needed to get their dresses ironed for Sunday school." Zack led her where there was a patch of grass. She slipped a little walking there, tightening her grip on his arm. "Your britches are going to need a patch," she said to him, not noticing the cut. Zack glanced down and saw that the blood had blackened like oil in the faded blue of his jeans. She frowned at the car on the trailer. Oil dropped out and splattered on the trailer bed. "Imagine how I felt when I saw you get in that car, Zachary."

"Me?"

"Yes, when Tom got out. Before it all started."

"Oh, then. Well, I wasn't planning on driving it. Not yet, anyway."

"Oh, Zachary," she said and looked up at the dark sky. "What did I do wrong?"

"You didn't have anything to do with it, Mama. The engine blew up."

Tom watched his father's moves as if he were a thief. Hershal walked around the wreck as though it was a cow he wanted to buy.

Clyde was the first person to speak to Hershal: "We had us a good one going there, Hershal, until the damn engine let go. Excuse me, Mrs. Pate," he added.

Gladys didn't flinch. She wasn't responsible for Clyde's language.

"Spun in my own oil," Tom put in, relieved that Clyde had understood what had happened. Zack remembered the ominous blue whiff out the pipe that Clyde didn't want to see.

Finally Hershal walked away from the car towards his wife. He still hadn't spoken. He took her by the arm where she waited to be led like a dance partner in any direction he chose to go, even if it was back into the mud. When it looked as though he was going to leave without saying a word, Tom moved quickly, jumping in front of them. Hershal stopped suddenly, pulling his wife to a stop beside him. Face-to-face, Hershal was still bigger than Tom, even with his hat in his hand.

Tom stood there like a child who had gotten everyone's attention, but had forgotten what he wanted to say. He started to speak, weakly:

"Well, what did you think?"

His daddy stared at him. Zack moved where he could see his father's face. Hershal looked puzzled, as if he was trying to figure out how to make something work without reading the instructions. He started to walk again, but Tom stood his ground, moving into his path again. Tom's eyes flitted around nervously.

When it was certain to Hershal that his wife wasn't going to answer the question for him, he regarded the car again, slowly. For a few seconds Zack felt sorry for his daddy, the way he did for a dumb kid in school who got called on, but couldn't answer the teacher's question. The race car groaned instead, settling into place on its oil blackened trailer that Zack had painted red. Hershal turned back to look at Tom, squarely in the eyes.

"I guess you ain't gonna to get killed today," he said and smiled the kind of smile you know won't get returned. Then he led his wife away.

TOM WHALEN

Notes from the Tower

I am, at the moment, in my tower atop the mountain from which I can see all that has been and all that will be and where I've just been, namely to the laundromat down the street in which I deposited my laundry, two weeks worth, into the hands of the laundromat person, who took it gladly and smiled upon me and blessed me with, "Thank you, monsieur, I love you, monsieur, I have always loved you, monsieur, I hope someday you rot in hell for not returning my love in like manner, monsieur."

Either the world is dissolving or it's getting dark or I'm going blind. I turn on the light in the tower that illuminates whatever I want it to illuminate. Door one darkens at approach, but when opened reveals the kneeling woman with her hair down to her knees and music of Penderecki buzzing like insects from the insectlike earphones of her Walkman. Door two opens upon the writing woman at her desk writing writing writing, while above her head parakeets swirl in a delirium of parakeet screeches. And what is the writing woman writing? Door three is made of glass and behind it sits the glass woman before her mirror. Door four I open with a silver key because behind it is the silver woman who must forever polish herself so she will not tarnish. Door five creaks on its hinges—the old woman in her cage trilling her song of age all night long. Door six—but I am tired of opening these same doors; why can't door six contain the lass with golden hair I saw out my window rolling a hoop up the road? Why can't, say, door six hold a different woman each time instead of the forgetful woman and her dead starlings? Door seven, should I open it (but I shan't), would swing wide upon a landscape where the sad woman lies surrounded by four thousand television sets all tuned to the same channel, an underwater show whose light casts an underwater glow upon the mountains and valleys that are the landscape of the sad woman. It would make me cry if I weren't the one who bought her the TVs.

Rumors of war, rumors of peace. The gods and devils are convening again in Roanoke, and I'm in charge of their meals. Who wants the little children? Who wants the rabbit? Who wants the raw roast beef with blue cheese? Apple pie? I wheel my cart down the aisles and listen to their discourse, if discourse it can be called, more a gaggle of contradictions and well-wishes and vituperations followed by professions of the most sincere and deepest and deadliest and dullest and damnedest love. Ah, these devils and gods. What fun they have when they mate. And what a mess is left for me and my nimble tower servants to clean. Like trying to start the alphabet with, say, *O* or *T*. Each letter with its own smell, each letter with its own taste. I've had enough. The sky lowers. The bombers begin their runs. I am folding up my tent. The landscape darkens with blood. Locusts eat their way out of the enemy's throats and eyes.

The writing woman writes: Why is it that you still persist, gaptooth, why is it that you persist longer than other gaptoothed fools? When everyone had long since given up on the study of tides as a means to understand the relationship to the other (that's Sartre's other, *not* Rimbaud's), you were still on the beach with your compass and ruler and Blue Horse notebook calculating the recession of the waves while sand crabs scuttled about your feet. Of course I am writing to you from a faraway land. You've banished me here, haven't you? The months are circular, children must learn to fend for themselves at far too early an age (seven months). Baths are taken with a mixture of oil and sand. Heavy weaponry rolls past beneath my window. A flight out? Someone whispers to me that this is possible. I'll never write to you again.

In my anteroom I hear a humming noise, so I follow it out the door and down the hall and into the kitchen and out of the kitchen and into the garage and out of the garage, and back into the garage, and into the closet of the garage that leads into the cellar. And in the cellar it's louder, and I follow the humming noise to the back of the cellar, where it changes directions and I run back up the stairs and into the servants' quarters, but there the humming noise is very faint, so I follow it out of the servants' quarters and into the library where the humming noise is very loud, so loud that I can't locate it anywhere, it's everywhere and nowhere, therefore un-locatable, so I move into specific areas of the library, for example, where the dead queen lies on her velour sofa dreaming the dream of oblivion which dream she has been dreaming for god knows how long, but what am I to do, I inherited her, I did not marry her. But the humming noise does not come from the dead queen or her dream, so I retreat back into my antechamber where I first detected the humming noise and follow the thread of sound again, this time into my mistress's chamber where my mistress lies dreaming the dream of I-Will-Murder-You-If-You-Do-Not-Appear-At-Once-At-My-Bedside, a terrifying dream, it plays nightly on the TVs of all the kingdom's subjects. But the humming noise is not here either, it moves, the humming noise, it takes me out the door of the castle into the landscape, out of the situation into the nonspecific, out of here into elsewhere. And I follow the river of elsewhere along which the humming noise sails, and know that at the river's end, in a clearing, a bower, a glade, you will be there, humming and naked and waiting only for me.

So I visit The Premises where works the bartender, or *bar-tendresse* whom I think I love, but she refuses to serve me, though I am her only customer and have laid a substantial amount of money (you see, I am monied, I can take care of you for as long as the two of us think it wise) on the mahogany counter. Her eyes are gray, her upper lip brushed lightly with hair. Her jeans sag off her ass in a way that causes my heart to stumble up the stairs. So I visit the bar where she works, but she's not there. Where is she? She's not here.

It's a circular bar. I walk around and around it. No *bartendresse,* only three bartenders who pay me no heed.

Thank god I write these notes to myself. Who else would forgive me for writing them?

The old woman sings her song of the old woman again and again, but I can remember only a snatch of the tune, a fragment of the lyrics—something about birds on frosted glasses, patternless cloth, incomprehensible bells. Her hair is skygray, it covers her face, the floor. When I open the door where the old woman abides, her hair rumples like waves.

Lately, a breather has been calling me just before I go to sleep. He breathes for a bit, then says, "I want you," in a whisper. Only last night have I got him to talk to me, though admittedly he doesn't say much. "I want you," he says. "I think you're attractive," he says. I ask him if he knows me. He breathes for a bit, then says, "Yes, I know you. I know your name. I want you." I ask him his name, but of course he refuses to give it to me. I tell him, then, that I understand his need for sexual companionship, that I find it one of the very best kinds of companionship that companionship has to offer, but that, you know, if you want to have an affair with someone, the best approach is not anonymous phone calls in the middle of the night. He breathes for a bit, then whispers, "You're very interesting. I want you, I want you, I want you."

The writing woman writes: A woman in a black cape carrying bread in a basket passes in front of me. Beyond my range of hearing, brown forms appear, come closer. They are schoolchildren carrying their drawings of the moon that they will bring home to their mothers. When do we have enough of being and wish not to start all over again? When do we long for the poison or the leap from the window? Should I ask the woman for some bread, some milk? How did I come to be here? Did you banish me here? The woman looks dumbfounded. She raises her finger, points to an inn, then turns away. I let myself be led in the direction she has pointed. I am given the same meal you used to give me—salad and beer. Beneath the bar a dog with only one eye growls. Women are not allowed to stay the night in this castle, someone whispers. Are these more of your rules? The little room I'm in fills with the ceremonies of rats. Two hats lie crushed on the bureau. A painting shows a demon (the resemblance to you is uncanny) sitting on a stool, cleaning his nails. An angel (the resemblance to me, etc.) bows before him. Wind rattles the milk can where I have placed my umbrella. Outside my window a father and daughter, the latter in a yellow wedding dress, bounce up and down on a trampoline.

Through the crack in the door to the forgetful woman's chamber, I hear her chanting, "Whose room is this, whose bed? Whose hands are these? Are they mine? Did I forget my name? Whose tongue speaks these words? Are these my hands? Have I left the last words in the rain long enough now for me to have forgotten the river's name from which they were dredged? Whose hands are these? Are these my hands? And the birds, how did they come to be on my bed? And why do they remind me of something that I no longer can remember? Is this always? Am I of this or this? Am I? Which? Who left me in this room? Did I once love? Did I answer that? Have I forgotten something here? Are these my walls? Were those scars made by me? Is that my shadow? Are those starlings or sparrows? Have I a name? Did I forget something? Are these my words? My bed? My hands?"

During lulls in the war, the city, too, dreams, which is why I must be careful on its streets. A bicycler might roll up like a tongue, and the street itself might be a door I have mistakenly opened. A family of four invited me to join them at their table. The father spread his fat hands, and meat appeared for our delectation. The children, a boy and a girl, both bald, were especially ravenous. Of the mother, I can only say I fell in love with her on first sight. But was it because of her eyes, into which like a rock I tumbled, or her nose, or her smile which said nothing to me? Her wings were moulting, and throughout the meal she kept them tucked close to her sides. I wanted to wrap my arms around her trembling body, but her husband smelled of ash and the children whispered over their plates in a language I could not understand.

I open the door to the room of the silver woman where she is busy polishing her smooth surfaces. Then I open the door to the room of the glass woman where she sits in her glass chair before her mirror. First I open the door of the silver woman, then I open the door of the glass woman. I open one, then I open the other. I open the door of the silver woman and then the door of the glass woman. Glass woman. Silver woman. I open their doors again and again and again. Silver, glass, silver, glass, silver, glass, silver glass silver glass silver silver glass glass glass glass silver silver glass silver silver glass glass silver . . . open close open close again and again and again . . . until between the one and the other I can no longer see any difference.

*   *   *

Overheard the following yesterday between the dead queen and my mistress:

Mistress: Found a gray hair right on my young or youngish head.

Dead queen: Either he choked me or I hung myself, I can't remember which.

Mistress: Gray hairs! At my age! I can't stand it!

Dead queen: Could use a little more air in here, don't you think, awful stuffy, and why does it always smell like a manger?

Mistress: Manger?

Dead queen: Barn, then.

Mistress: He wanders the corridors at night thinking up conspiracies when in fact there are no conspiracies or everything is a conspiracy, there's no middle ground, so there's no reason to worry about it.

Dead queen: I know what you mean.

Mistress: And not a gray hair on his head, that's what dogs my ass, not a gray hair on any part of his skinny frame. And on top of that, he seems to be growing younger, not older!

Dead queen: (snores)

Mistress: (is consumed in the flames of her distress)

Embarrassed, I withdraw.

*   *   *

I ask the kneeling woman if she would, you know, mind turning down her Walkman, I can hear it even with the door shut, like mindless, meaningless insect chatter, but she disobliges me.

Now the writing woman writes about entering the tropical birdhouse for the first time: First there's the music and the John Gould

prints and tribal bird artifacts (masks and such like), and then the
doors that have bird handles and then it's the birdhouse proper. I am
writing this to you because I abhor the way you are acting, you must
stop acting the way you are acting this minute, otherwise you will
never be a better person, and god knows that above all you need to be
a better person. Then you enter the birdhouse proper, as I just said,
a bit small it is, surely, but still OK, and there you see palaver
peacock pheasants, wrinkled hornbills, green jays, buffalo weavers,
red-billed hornbills, fairy bluebirds, bay owls, red-crested cardi-
nals, saffron toucanets, yellow-naped amazons, red-billed magpies,
gray touracos, plate-billed mountain toucans, all of a very definite
oddity and beauty, and beechey jays who are crow-sized and have
solid black bodies and solid blue wings, and handfuls of free wandering birds including whistling ducks, and if you would stop doing
whatever it is you're doing, you might have a shot at entering this
space with yours truly and there we could listen together to the
cacophony, and I would stroke your ears, assuming you have stopped
doing whatever it is you're doing, and whatever it is you are doing
you should stop this instant, moment, minute, second, now, presto,
because it's a bad thing you are doing, even if it's nothing you are
doing, it's a bad thing you are doing, because whatever you are
thinking you should not be thinking, which assumption I can make
based on past experience with your thoughts, donkey face, fig tree,
old apple head, I will not love you ever again, and yet you imagine I
will, harebrained rascal, honestly, honestly, you should be dragged
out by your elongated ears for doing what you did with me and in a
foreign clime to boot! As soon as I'm out of this prison, you'll know
about it.

"Then what method," the breather asked me, "is most efficacious
in bringing people together in a manner that will eventually lead to
their sexual conjunction?"
Shoulder massages, I told him.

More static than usual tonight. It's raining. On this channel, my
dead father. On that channel, my dead mother. I twiddle the knobs
until I hear the voice of my professor.
"The self is not the counterpole of the world, my boy; it is the
point of reflection, the golden egg, the irrational third in the music

scale. If you crack open a word, what do you suppose you will find—
a purer form of water, white light? Once you fall into this, there is
no assurance you will ever get out. Language assumes some riddle
that only language itself can solve, but not during this eternity.
The will does not interest me. After a few moments, its little
escapade ends, the world is reconstituted as the world only, a
limited implacable whole you can't pull your finger out of. I, too,
was once in love. My heart, too, seemed to bound into my mouth.
The visual field has no limits. How curious, I said to her, that your
feelings in no way match mine, that this remarkable missile assumes . . ."

Static. Static.

The rain has turned to sleet.

The war continues, the war always continues. I am broadcasting
this to you atop my tower. The frequency is low, but sustained.
Possibilities of peace exist. I believe in little, but in possibilities I
believe. I wander the corridors at night picking up strange noises.
Somewhere out there someone is making love to someone I, too,
made love to, and I grant them this indulgence. The laundromat
person waits for me to pick up my laundry. Does she await with a
shiv or a kiss? The breather does not call. Do I mind? Is this a new
song I am singing or an old one? Which door do you suggest I open
now?

ANITA THOMPSON

The Garden

Last summer, I wanted a garden. I wanted to see flowers pretty from the window. They would be quiet, hushed in the winter. As I laughed in the grass, they'd whisper secrets in my ear. Tickle the inside of my elbow as if to take my blood. Under the tree by our bedroom window, I looked for roots. I took a seed from the cup of my nail, planted it three times until it was perfect.

Inside, I leaned over a sink, cleaned my hands until white. The drain fell further, deeper down to black. When I went to shut the back door, I saw caterpillars in cracks. They crawled inside, wanted to make nests in the corners of my house. I didn't want to find cocoons in the folds of my sheets. Butterflies would land on my eyes, make me blind. They'd bleed if I cried.

I told him I was pregnant five days after I heard. I had been busy with the garden, stacking stones I found in the soil. He told me he loved us, put an iris in my hair. That night, he took me to the opera and kissed me the rest of the night. In the morning, he said he wanted to crawl under my skin and watch it grow.

When I was young, my dad used the edge of his thumb to count the inches I stood in the doorway of my bedroom. You're growing up fast, he said. The brush of his breath closed my eyes. As he pulled the sheets straight across my chest, he didn't want me to move. He tucked me in tight every night, kiss behind the ear. With my shoulders pinned, I cried until the covers came wet.

In the mirror, I got bigger each day. The baby pulled my skin tighter. When he kissed me, I couldn't feel his lips. He touched only my stomach, never a crease at the bottom of my back or the hollow of my neck. If he walked in while I bathed, he wanted to wash my stomach, pat it dry. Don't stay in too long, it's not good for the baby. It might drown, he said as he looked into the mirror, staring at my reflection. The walls sweated from the steam. I watched water vein from the ceiling to the floor.

I pressed the tips of my fingers down into soil, pulled apart roots. The tree hunched over to touch my ankles. As I vined against the trunk of the tree, I looked up to the sky. Quiet, I whispered over and over. Leaves fell in circles around my head and covered my eyes. I wondered if the baby's head folded upside-down. If its fingers tied in knots.

Late at night, he traced pictures with his finger on my stomach. I lay on my back with my head falling, looking at the ceiling. I watched rainwater split straight down a window. Birds hid under eaves, their eyes black as they stared at us. My shoulders almost cracked, snapped in pieces. They bent around me as I folded inside myself. When I curled round, the skin of my back stretched tight, wrapped me and the baby. He pulled me under his arm like the sun pulls a moon into night. Let the baby fall asleep to the sound of the rain, he whispered close in my ear. The garden flooded that night.

One day I left water running in a sink after I splashed my face and neck. I watched his eyes follow a drop streaming between the halves of my back. You haven't been getting enough sun, he told me. Sit here in the light so God can watch you, keep the baby warm. I told him it was hot and I wanted to sleep. Sleep in the sun, he said. He put his hands over my eyes and took me to the back patio, sat me in a wooden chair. He said it was good for the legs. I wondered if he meant mine or the baby's.

The neighbors brought me feathers. Stuff a pillow for the baby's head, they said. As they stood hot in the kitchen, their faces swelled. They wrote down songs I should sing to the baby. It will look like his father, they said. I thought of my father's scar down his right cheek. They asked me if I will breast-feed, if I will cut my hair, if we will have another. On the window, a beetle was dragging another. As I walked closer, stuck my eye to the glass, I noticed one was dead. After I watched the neighbors leave down the sidewalk, I checked to see if they had taken anything from the back of the cabinets.

I started knitting again this winter. He got me needles and colored yarn. Bought me thick cushions to sit on, vitamins to swallow, and herbs to boil. Sometimes in bed he rubbed lotion on my stomach in perfect circles. When I pushed in to feel the baby, he squeezed my hands, told me I would poke its eyes back. Then he joked and tried to see it through a pinhole in my navel. During the winter, I couldn't sleep at night. When it got too cold, he wrapped me in soft blankets. Keep the baby warm, but don't smother it, he said as he tucked me in. I watched moonlight cut shadows into his face. In the distance behind his head, a wooden cross hung on a wall. Under the touch of his hands, my back arched high. I thought I was dying.

I called the man at the drugstore. When he answered, he was out of breath. I heard two women laughing in the background. They sounded like the two women who sat behind me in church one Sunday. I told him I was pregnant and needed more vitamins. He said he knew my husband and would give them to him. The man asked when it was due. It's good to have a baby in the spring, he said, they say it will live longer.

He woke me one morning. I told you not to sleep on your side, he said. You'll press the baby flat, stop it from growing. He asked me if I loved it. He began to rub my breasts in circles, said we had to get the milk ready. I told him to kiss me, and he kissed my forehead, then set his ear next to the baby's. It's almost time for its birth, and you should stay in bed. I'm going to keep you here until it takes its first breath. He put a pill on my tongue, told me to swallow. I stretched my arms to the ends of the bed, my legs straight, center to the bed.

This morning my water broke into puddles on the floor. He grabbed towels, told me I was killing it. I closed my eyes and hummed a lullaby. Hush little baby. In the car, I rubbed its round-ness with my hands. It swelled, and I felt it turn over and over. When we got to the hospital, everything seemed quiet—the second hand behind the watch glass, no bigger than my eye, the bird perched under a roof, eye not blinking, its head not moving. It was past noon.

When they sliced me, it felt like ice melting, sliding down, forming into oceans. He looked at my stomach, to my eyes, then to my stomach again. The light above hung from the ceiling on a thin wire. He turned and walked out. I wait to hear its first breath.

Under the tree today, I see cracks in the ground left from the winter. I pull up the dead roots of the garden.

Washer Woman

Hey, how are you doing? The place is pretty empty to-night, huh? I usually don't find anyone here this time of morning. What is it, two A.M. maybe? Do you have insomnia too? I was trying to find something to do, so I decided to sort my laundry. Then I thought, hell, why don't I just go on over there and do it. You like coffee? Here, I got an extra cup. It's Sanka. I drink it so I won't stay up. A lot of good it does me. That's a nice sweater, you should use a little Woolite on it to keep the color fresh.

Where do you live? I live on the corner of Madison and Broad. Want to hear something interesting? In the past ten years, I have been in twenty-six different laundromats in ten different cities. I have spent over five thousand dollars washing and drying: seven white shirts, twelve pairs of underwear, two pairs of boxer shorts (leftovers from my marriage), five pairs of jeans and fourteen T-shirts. Isn't that something? I figured it out the last time I was in here. Wait a minute, I forgot to put this shirt in the second load . . .

Once in Chicago, I counted the number of days I had been alive and the number of men I had slept with. Thank God, the days outnumbered the beds. That was a little place called "The Lost Sock." Where do all the lost socks go to anyway? There must be a place in Heaven where, when you die, you get back everything you ever lost. It must be full of car keys, odd-matched socks, cigarette lighters, and dry-cleaning claim checks.

I'm bilingual, you know. Yeah, I speak English and Southern. Don't laugh, it's a very useful language. Why, in Macon, Georgia, I met a woman in an all-night diner who told me how to get rid of wine stains. "Awal tempa chair," she said. Now if I didn't speak Southern, I wouldn't have understood a damn word she'd said. By the way, club soda works better than Cheer. She was wearing this black, strapless number. I think she had just been crowned Queen of the Pork Festival. Jim, my ex-husband, and I had stopped there to go to the bathroom. We were on our way to Florida to visit his cousin, Mae. A big fat woman with little pig eyes. Eight kids, she had! A regular breeder.

Want a magazine? It's *Ms.* I got it from a lady in Pittsburgh. She needed a quarter for the dryer and she gave it to me when she left. I got a big kick out of reading a feminist magazine while folding my husband's undershorts. I put a little too much starch in them that day. Maybe that's why he left?

I know all the Beatles' songs by heart. I sing them to myself when no one's in here with me. The "Spend A Dime, Wash Some Grime" in Cambridge has the best acoustics. I wrote my thesis there. Uh huh, I bet you didn't think I went to college did you? My thesis was a novel dealing with mushrooms. The protagonist was in love with a morel; but it gets killed in the end when his mother makes a salad. I got an *F* on my thesis. I guess the committee just wasn't interested in human/fungi relationships. Is that my buzzer? I'll be right back. I have to put my clothes in the dryer.

I have seven new white sheets. You can see them over there in the dryer. I bought them at K-Mart. A television reporter in Utah told me that people who buy white sheets were sexually repressed. He also said that chewing gum can give you cancer. Want a stick? No? I stopped watching TV right after that broadcast.

How many kids do you have? I saw you had a box of Ivory Snow. Jim and I never had any children. It's just as well, Ivory Snow is too expensive these days, anyway. A dollar eighty-four at the Safeway. When the first one died, I washed those sheets I know at least a hundred times. Just couldn't get the blood out. I bleached them so much it ate a hole right through. Jim didn't have a clean shirt for weeks. I spent all my time trying to get those sheets clean. He left me after the third one died. He pinned a note to the top of the laundry basket and left. He said, in the note, that I was deformed because I couldn't have kids. It wasn't my fault. I just couldn't hold them in. They kept——. Is that my buzzer again? The sheets must be dry.

Do you like movies? My favorite is *Saturday Night Fever.* I just loved the dancing in that movie. My mother thought I could have been a dancer, you know. She taught me ballet, tap, and even square dancing. Southern women make their children dance a lot. I think it's to keep them from thinking about sex.

Gee, it's four A.M. Well, once again I have clean underwear. I finished this article on PMS. The *Enquirer* says it could save my marriage. I'll leave it here for you. I got a few quarters left, want them? I'm going to Boston to see my sister. She has her own washer and dryer, so I won't be needing them. Take care, now; and don't use dryer number twelve. I think the lint trap needs to be cleaned.

Valentine

The great-uncle is as heavy as dark bread. Emphysema punctuates the weighty words that form near-perfect English phrases so careful that they announce his German past. He is as English as the Londoners will let him be. He imagines himself more so.

"Ambition," he wheezes. "You went to a very fine school for which your parents paid a great deal of money, and now you must do something to warrant this gift. You are very lucky, but you must now choose a career and embark upon it with all your time and energy."

I am nodding with shame. I am saying to myself, I know, I know, I know.

"When Tom, my son, was younger and wanted to go into film, he went to Italy to work with a director there. He had no money but he taught English to many fine Italian girls of good families, and he made a living for himself. This you could always do. When you were in Rome, what use did you make of your time? Did you study?"

I could lie. I am thinking fast, the story coming together before I can distinguish truth from fabricaton. He is looking straight at me, leaning forward in his armchair, breathing heavily. Up go his eyebrows as he waits for me to justify myself. Nothing moves. The light is turning to evening, receding dreamily from the rim of the teacup on the table before me. Everything in this room seems covered with a fine layer of dust.

"Yes," I answer. "Yes, I studied Italian with a young man who roomed with my friend."

He is pleased. I have in my answer given him both hope and a bone to gnaw on.

"Oh, yes?" He inhales what sounds like a breath of crumbs. "You studied?"

"Mmmm. Not for long, but I learned enough to get by." I am groping for images that would to my great-uncle represent a satisfactory version of getting by. "I could order food and make myself understood in the train stations."

This is true. The implied connection between studying and being able to communicate, however, is false. I acquired these skills otherwise, mostly by copying those around me. I did study, for a week, perhaps, declining verbs on a legal pad and scribbling vocabulary words in the margins, but such exercises ended when my tutor's Italian half got the better of his British restraint. This led to a depressing lovers' weekend in Venice, which, by this time, had been abandoned by the tourists due to the cold, constant drizzle. Vincenzo took photographs of everything, with me in the foreground. He taught me how to use his camera, and I took photographs in which I was careful not to include him. Our room at the hotel was a box with a low ceiling and a cold linoleum-squared floor, much like the classrooms that mushroomed overnight from the side of my elementary school. The sex was pedestrian, instructive. I slept with him for the sake of it, because I had never had sex with anyone but my first boyfriend, who was waiting in New York for me to return.

I am thinking of Vincenzo's earnest orgasms when Uncle Kurt revives the conversation.

"And now what will you do?"

Never have sex again, I think. Have indiscriminate sex with every attractive person I meet. Move to Greece.

"Go back to the States," I say in my most sensible voice. "Find a good job."

"And where will you live?"

"New York, probably. I have friends there, and an apartment I can live in."

He stops listening after New York.

"Your family is in Denver. You should return to Denver and let your father find you a good job there, so you can be close to them. I don't understand why you want always to live so far away from your parents."

"I don't want to live far away from my parents," I say slowly. "It's just that there is nothing for me to do in Denver. I mean, nothing I want to do. I'd like to find a job in publishing."

He bends forward over his knees, peering at me in puzzlement.

"Ja?" he asks. I nod and say, "Ja." He bobs his head as if to say this is all very well, but, and I prepare myself for the lecture I know I am about to receive. Publishing is Uncle Kurt's life. In his grimy Spartan flat there are precious first-edition books signed by the authors. The gray walls boast original etchings by famous German illustrators, colorful child-like line drawings from the twenties and thirties. The great men were my great-uncle's friends. Like him, they were great in a country that disowned them, but even stateless, they managed to leave some impression on the world.

Before Kurt can lecture me, Friedl shuffles in. She is my great-uncle's live-in companion, and has been for forty years. He still refers to her as "my girlfriend."

"Kurt," she yells. "Kurt, it is time for the television." Panic has pushed her eyes open wide. Her eyebrows strain to meet the wispy white hair above them. She stops next to Kurt's chair and waits for him to tell her what to do next.

"Don't yell at me," he says, looking at the low table in front of him. "I hear you perfectly fine." He turns to me and asks earnestly, "Have you seen this television program called *Dinasty*? It's American. Trash, really." He dismisses it with a wave of his hand. "But some fine actors."

Friedl is making her way across the carpet to the large television set.

"*Dynasty*?" I ask, pronouncing it the American way.

"Na, ja." He grins, ducking his head. "You know?"

"Yes," I say. "My English friends like it so much that they videotape the episodes."

"Really?" He is surprised. He thinks about this. Over the noise of the television, which Friedl has adjusted to full volume, he shouts, "And in America? Do they watch?"

"Yes." I nod vigorously, not sure that he can hear me over the TV. "Many do."

"Your parents?"

I shake my head scornfully and say "Nooo" in the long drawn-out way my father uses to tell people, mostly strangers, that they have asked a stupid question.

"But," I shout, "it takes place in Denver."

Uncle Kurt nods wisely.

"Ja?" screeches Friedl. "In Denver?"

Kurt raises his head to look at her. "Eh?" he grunts in annoyance.

"In Denver," she screams. "The program is in Denver."

"The program?"

"Ja. *This* one." She peers desperately into Kurt's eyes and flaps her arm at the screen.

"We know," he says.

Friedl clucks in disgust and turns her head toward the television. Uncle Kurt shrugs and looks at me. I pretend to watch the show.

A distinguished-looking white-haired man with a square jaw is saying curt, unpleasant things to a woman in an emerald ball gown. The woman's fuschia lips part in outrage. Friedl, now sitting in the armchair to my right, watches, transfixed. To my left, Uncle Kurt also stares at the screen. He breathes heavily. I can't hear him, but I see his shoulders rise and fall with the effort.

The show lasts for an hour. More people in tuxedos and ball gowns fight, embrace, talk on the telephone, change clothes. The room grows darker. When the credits roll, I stretch my legs, and Kurt twists his head to see what I am doing. I shout over the triumphant theme music that I must go soon.

"Hmm?" he says.

"I have to go soon," I say, pointing first to myself and then out the window.

"Oh," he says. He looks at Friedl, who is still staring at the TV screen. "Friedl," he shouts. She jerks and cries, "Wass?" Kurt points to the television set.

"You want off?" she asks. He nods. "But the next program," she says. "We watch."

Kurt leans forward for emphasis, glaring at Friedl but pointing at me. "She must *go*," he says.

Friedl turns the corners of her mouth down and pushes herself up out of the armchair. Her slippered feet propel her small body across the carpet with measured strokes. When she finally reaches the television set, she gazes longingly at its screen for a moment before shutting it off.

The silence stuns me. I wonder if Kurt and Friedl are less aware of it just as they are less aware of loud noises. By the light of a streetlamp outside, Friedl shuffles over to a standing lamp and pulls its chain. The room seems to shrink.

Kurt puts his hands on his knees. "Well," he says, "where do you go now?"

"To work," I say.

"To the club."

"Yes," I say, "to the club."

Friedl makes a strangled noise in her throat to indicate disapproval. I tell myself that she is old, that I should humor her.

"This I really do not like," Kurt says. "To what time do you work?"

I know that this is not a question but a prelude. I have been working at the club for four months. Every visit I have made to Kurt and Friedl since starting at the club has ended in a lecture on the dangers of nightlife. At first I told them stories about the interesting people I met at the club, about the exciting, creative, productive lives those people were leading, in the hope that at least Kurt, if not Friedl, would understand that the nightclub was not a sleazy dead end. But the names of the famous pop stars and movie actors to whom I serve overpriced drinks mean nothing to either Kurt or Friedl, and so I have given up.

"Till three," I say. Friedl sucks in a loud breath. Kurt shakes his head.

"There is now a movie," he says, "the advertisements for which you have perhaps seen in the newspapers, which is about a young woman who works in a club. It's true. The story is true. I have here some clippings about the woman on whom the movie is based, and I think you should take them and read them and think about what you are doing with yourself."

He leans forward slowly and takes from the table two articles, one from the *Sunday Observer* magazine, the other from some chatty magazine I don't recognize. Both articles are about Ruth Ellis, the subject of a recent movie called *Dance with a Stranger*. I've heard about this woman: a curvaceous bottle-blonde, she ran a London nightclub in the fifties. It was at the club that she fell for an upper-class ne'er-do-well whose cheating ways drove her to such distraction that she eventually shot him and killed him. She was then executed.

I don't know what to say. I study the articles with what I hope is a serious expression. When I can no longer maintain this expression, I look up.

"Thank you, Uncle Kurt. I appreciate these."

What I mean is this: Thank you for finding a place in your brain, which is far more cluttered with memories than mine, in which to keep a mental map dotted with pins to mark my path. I know that I am an anomaly for you. You want me to be ambitious, and to succeed, as you have done, but I am a girl, and your instincts tell you that I should be protected by my parents, or perhaps even a husband. You are as confused about me as I am. Kurt looks at me. By this look I understand that whatever he is about to tell me is the last piece of advice for today's visit. I also sense that it is something I am supposed to take with me and apply to my life.

"You know," Kurt says, "sometimes on the weekend when I am going past the park I see people sitting on the grass, talking and so on. They sit there and enjoy themselves, and many years later when they get arthritis, they don't think that maybe the grass was wet and so they should not have been sitting there."

At first I think he is joking. I realize when he looks at me that he is not. I nod gravely in response.

Uncle Kurt stands to see me out. I notice that his suit is not as wrinkled as I would have expected it to be. Each time I visit, he is wearing a dark suit and tie. His office, as he calls it, is the third floor of this three-story house. Every day, a secretary comes to type his correspondence and organize his papers, a Frau somebody-or-other who is probably only a few years younger than Uncle Kurt. I wonder what the third floor looks like. I am willing to bet that Friedl wonders, too.

Friedl, Kurt, and I walk to the door. "Is that your coat?" Friedl asks, examining the Burberry raincoat as I slide my arms into its sleeves.

"Yes," I say.

"But iss so big!" she cries.

"It's Opa's," I say. "He gave it to me."

My grandfather didn't really give me the coat. He sits in a wheelchair in a spotless, sunny room in Zurich, surrounded by other old people who thank God that they are not as bad off as he. He no longer recognizes his wife, or his son. When I visited him, he took my fingers in his elegant, spotted hand and, with his other hand, stroked my cheek, but as the doctors explained afterward, "He likes young girls." One of the nurses told us to take some of his things. "He has too many," she said in stiff English. "He does not need them." I picked the Burberry as mine, and a fine cotton nightshirt, while Opa sat slumped in his wheelchair across the room. I felt then that he was already dead.

My Oma, Uncle Kurt's sister, still walks every day on the arm of a starched Swiss nurse along the carpeted corridors of the home to check on her husband. She finds him the same each time, and no longer expects to find him otherwise. The doctor suggested once that for her sake, as well as for Opa's, she not see him so often, and for about a week after that she stayed in her one room "apartment" on the other side of the building, surrounded by chocolates and photographs. Then she resumed her daily visits as though she'd never heard the doctor's advice. She walks into her husband's room in the infirmary and sits across from him at the square table, he in his wheelchair, she with her cane. For the next half hour she watches him, first talking to him as though he were a baby, and then saying with sorry disgust, "Ach, he does not speak. He is not there. Look, he doesn't even know what he does." After a few minutes of silence, she begins again, like a bird pecking at a wall. Opa just sits, looking at the television set behind her. A nurse has placed a brown felt fedora on his head at a jaunty angle. The television set is always on.

Uncle Kurt calls my Oma every week. I have been present at both ends. When she speaks to him, she brightens. Kurt, on the other hand, maintains his businesslike manner, asking her practical questions about her health and her finances, and nodding while she answers. "And the hip?" he says. He listens, the receiver pressed tight to his ear. "Aah," he says seriously. "Aah, ja."

Oma doesn't like Friedl much. Opa didn't either. I'm glad now, standing half out of Kurt and Friedl's doorway, that Friedl thinks Opa's coat looks silly, because Opa thought Friedl was silly. Opa would probably have thought that the Burberry looked ridiculous on me, but it was his and now it is mine, and I can pretend. I can imagine him doing a Friedl imitation and a wicked little dance, and the two of us laughing and laughing.

"Good-bye," Friedl says uncertainly. I kiss her on the cheek. This seems to startle her. I kiss Uncle Kurt on the cheek and hug him. He hugs me back and smiles.

"I'll see you soon," I say. "Perhaps in a couple of weeks."

"Yes," he says. "Good. Let us know of your plans." I walk down the dark staircase, waving at them. Uncle Kurt waves back as though the gesture were foreign to him, the way someone in an expensive suit would eat a melting ice-cream cone. I want to make plans so I can call him up and tell them to him.

Just before Uncle Kurt dies, I get a letter from him. I had written him from New York to tell him that I had found work as a free-lance writer. I explained in my letter that Europe had made me appreciate New York, and that I felt better equipped to find my way now that I had a sense of my parents' pasts. "I knew nothing about the family," I wrote. "Talking with you and Oma and the other relatives helped me place myself. This in itself was an education."

He writes back, a typed letter on his business stationery, dated February 14th. I can hear him dictating the letter to Frau some-body-or-other.

"That you already have a job writing for a magazine is a wonderful start," he writes. "It is not so important which magazine as long as you write good articles which you can send to a more important magazine and so, little by little, carve out a career for yourself. If you are talented and if you get good reviews and people like what you write then you can become a good writer and have no longer got to do odd jobs.

"We carry on with life as usual and I still do my work every day in the office on the floor above the flat. Every day I spend approx. 6 hours there and at the moment I pass my time with reading the newspapers and books and also a little TV. One of the lowest standard programs on TV is *Dynasty* and yet I watch it, because it is surprisingly well acted.

"I was indeed very pleased that you wrote to me and I would like to keep in touch.

"I do hope that one day you will achieve what you would like to achieve and you will by then also know what is important in life and the things which are less important. As you know I saw both your parents on their last trip to Europe and I had to notice again what wonderful people they both are—you can be proud to have such nice people as your parents. My best regards, from Friedl as well, Love, Kurt."

Scrawled in blue ink beneath his signature is a sentence I should not be able to read, because it is illegible, yet I know immediately what it says. "Send me some articles you have written!"

Two days later I call my Aunt Hilde in Queens. She is Uncle Kurt's youngest sister, the baby. She was a kindergarten teacher for many years, and now, at eighty-six, still talks to everyone in the voice she used with her five-year-olds. After forty years in the States, she has picked up many American expressions, but her accent is thicker than that of her siblings in Europe. She refers to Oma and Opa as "Grainma und Grainpa." She is tiny, energetic, and in perfect health.

"Did you know that your Onkel Kurt iss in hospital?" she asks.

"What?" He is so far away, I think. What if something happens. What if I can't talk to him again. Why didn't I send the articles sooner?

"Iss not serious," Hilde says in her singsong voice. "Tom sess that he reads every day and does also his business from hospital. Iss not serious. Not to vorry."

As soon as we hang up, I call my father to ask him what's going on. He says that he had no idea Kurt was in hospital, that he had spoken earlier with Oma and she hadn't mentioned it. Therefore, he figures, Hilde is probably right. It probably isn't serious.

For the next week, I think about sending Kurt the articles. Maybe I should send them to the hospital, I think. I wonder about postage. Will they get there quickly enough to reach him before he leaves the hospital? Will it cost more than I can afford to send them by plane rather than by boat?

And then my father calls to tell me that Kurt is dead. I am glad I am home, because I don't know what my father would have told my answering machine.

"Oh," I say. "Oh."

STEPHEN STARK

The Customary Sin

He had expected tears, at least something more concrete
than the silence that had billowed out through the late afternoon
and into the early evening like excessively calm weather. But there
had been no tears, no acknowledgment. It appeared now that the
thing had never existed, that nothing had happened, and that nothing would continue to happen. It was like half of the day had not
existed, and the other half was still waiting to begin.

They had gone to Sherrills for pastries late in the afternoon. It
was decided, though now he wasn't sure exactly how, that she
needed something sweet to help replenish the blood she had lost.
The pastry she had ordered, a fat croissant filled with chocolate,
had lain on her plate for most of an hour before the waitress had
taken it. He had eaten his immediately, and as soon as he had, felt
mildly guilty for having had an appetite. But he had needed something to concentrate on, some practical matter that would occupy
his hands and eyes.

The restaurant was busy; it was at the corner of Pennsylvania
Avenue and Third Street on Capitol Hill, and the dinner crowd
had come while she stared at the pastry. He could tell that the
waitress—an older, impatient woman with heavy legs who called
both of them "dear" when they ordered—was anxious for them to
leave. The restaurant was small, and they took up valuable space.

"Do you want to go or anything?" he said. "Are you okay?"
Though it was at least the tenth time he'd asked, he could think of

little else to say. He felt outside, strange. He should have been more emotional about the morning and afternoon, more involved, yet he could feel nothing at all, only a kind of inertia.

"I'm okay," she said.

"All right." His hand went to his chest, touched the package of cigarettes in his shirt pocket. "All right."

"I'm fine. Really." It was dark out now—through the arch of windows over the doorway at the front of the restaurant, he could see the glare of headlights and streetlamps. He wasn't sure what time it was, or that any time had elapsed at all since waking too early that morning. That was all he could think of now, naked in bed, the raw half-born taste in his mouth, waiting out the silence of the house and dawn.

"What do you—" he started, but she didn't hear him, and cut him off.

"I'm okay," she said, smiling. "You can stop worrying. It's nothing. Millions of women do this. Really." She stopped, frowned. "Millions of people, millions of people do this every day."

He looked at her and frowned himself. It didn't make sense. He took his cigarettes from his pocket and offered her one. She shook her head.

"You're not quitting on me?" he said.

"No," she said. Her lips were even, tight, as fine as if they had been pencilled on blank skin by an architect.

"Don't go getting wholesome on me."

"I wouldn't think of it," she said. "I plan on spending the rest of my days as a profligate." Then, after a moment, "With you." She smiled, but the humor faded quickly. "I just don't feel like a cigarette now."

He took one from the pack and fingered it, but then, looking at the ashtray—the waitress had not emptied it for some time— thought the better of it and put it back into the pack. "Maybe *I'll* get wholesome," he said, "Maybe I'll sell the Citroen, go back to law school, and become one of those boring law firm types—hate my job but revel in the money—"

"Please."

"You know, all smoky and important-looking in blue and charcoal pinstripes."

"Stop it. You don't have to do this."

"I'm sorry," he said, and again there was silence, this one not as long and obdurate as the ones that had preceded it, but with a fragile sort of calm, like a water surface, waiting for wind or thrown stones. He knew, now, that it was his fault. He could not have done what he had just said. It was impossible.

He remembered one of the first times he had gone out with her. He had had little money, and after they had left the first club owing money on their tab, they had gone to another, this one with no cover. She had hustled drinks, then brought them back to share with him. Right now it was difficult for him to reconcile the woman that night with the woman sitting across the table from him. In learning about her, in knowing her, there was something that had been left out—the key to the reconciliation of those things. But what it was escaped him.

He said: "Did you ever see a movie with Katharine Hepburn and Spencer Tracy?"

"They made a lot of movies together. They were lovers for a long time."

"Well in this one, there was a scene where the two of them were sitting together at a piano—like, romancing, seducing each other with the piano. It was fabulous."

She raised her eyebrows and gave a little cluck.

"I saw it one afternoon on television when I was out sick from work. I wish I could remember the title. Their conversation was almost like fencing—cautious, oblivious, in*tell*igent. I remember thinking, that's how I wish love were. But it's not, you know. It's not. It's never that intelligent."

She looked at him and waited. "What's the point?" she said. No pain or anger in her voice.

"I don't know," he said. "No point, I guess." It bothered him that he couldn't feel anything right now except guilt. It bothered him that he couldn't remember feeling anything.

"Do you feel like walking a bit?" she said.

He nodded. He was glad to leave the restaurant. "You feel up to it?"

"I'm fine. But if you wouldn't mind, I'd like to stop at the liquor store and get some beer."

"Okay," he said, his excess of sympathy matching her excess of politeness. "I think I'd like a walk."

They had not eaten dinner, and neither, it occurred to him as they left the restaurant, had they eaten lunch. Beyond the simple mechanism with the croissant, he had not thought to eat, and it surprised him vaguely to think that he was not hungry.

They headed north on Pennsylvania. Ahead, the Capitol dome was bleached in the darkness with hot white light. The liquor store was next to the bagel bakery, and he followed her in. He had no idea if beer was a good idea at the moment, but he wasn't prepared to stop her.

The liquor store was bright inside, and cluttered with steep walls of bottles. She browsed the wines for a moment, idly, silently. He followed behind, staring at the labels. Poilly Fuisse. Zinfandel. Petit Sarah. Trockenbeerenauslese.

She turned away from the wines and shuffled along the dusty floor, past the imported beers, and picked up a six-pack of Pabst in bottles. He watched her pay for them, and listened to the worried buzz of the overhead lamps. He bought more cigarettes and followed her out again into the dark of the avenue.

She walked inside of him, dangling the bag heavily from her fingers. He thought he should carry it, but made no offer. At the corner of Pennsylvania, where the street turned into Independence, there was a man lying on the sidewalk on the other side of the street. He seemed to be dead. A policeman and policewoman were prodding him with their feet. The man did not move.

It was cool out, the temperature like late summer, even though it was July. The days were warm, but the nights were easy and comfortable. Not like Washington at all.

All day she had worn the same pale green dress with a sash at the waist. It seemed to him like a peasant dress. She wore darker green sandals with thin straps that bound above her ankles. She was an unexceptional-looking woman, though in this light, depending on the way the shadows fell, she looked very pretty, or very old.

They walked for some time—down Independence, across Union Square between the Mall and the Capitol. The front of the Capitol was dark with scaffolding.

They went up the hill at Constitution, then turned at First and headed toward home.

"Do you want a beer?" she said. "Do you want to drink a beer?"

"I don't know," he said. "I don't know. I don't really feel like a beer this second."

She stopped and turned to him. "Listen," she said, shifting the bag between hands a moment, looking at him nervously, then looking away, tucking the bag beneath an arm, "I think I want to quit. I think I want to quit all of this." She bit the inside of her cheek and looked at him, then turned and started walking again as abruptly as she had stopped.

He had not expected it, but it did not surprise him. He thought he should be horrified, but he didn't feel anything, and then he wondered if she had really said what he had heard.

He caught up with her, and, watching the trees, the hard, blue sidewalk, sidled up to her. Now she held the beer to her breast, her right forearm crooked beneath the dampening bag. He did not look at her. Suddenly he wished that he had not refused the beer—and wished that he could say something, do something that would make the day seem small in comparison. The taste of regret came into his mouth, but it was not only that.

When they got home, they sat on the stoop in silence. If she really wanted to quit, there was a lot to figure out.

She took the six-pack out of the bag, then crumpled the brown paper and tossed it toward the garbage cans. It bounced off one of the cans and over the short fence, then rolled toward the sidewalk.

He said, "You'd better practice up before the playoffs."

He didn't look at her, but thought of the thick tangle of scaffolding surrounding the Capitol. The world tearing itself down and rebuilding every minute. He took the beer she offered him. It was warmish, and the bottle was damp. The taste of it made him feel vaguely ill.

"Do you want to go for a drive?" he offered.

"Where?" she said.

"I don't know. We could get into the Citroen and drive out to the country. There's a little shop out at Occoquan that sells miniatures. It's fascinating." He didn't look at her, and there was silence. He hated the silence. "Once they had a tiny Mozart piano," he said, "a pianoforte, I think they call it. With the black keys." He breathed heavily. "This one wasn't much bigger than a box of kitchen matches." He was nervous and weary, but everything felt light, almost weightless. "They have tiny beds, tiny chairs, tiny fixtures. We could go press our noses against the windows."

She smiled. "And seduce one another over the miniature piano?"

He laughed tentatively, testing new ground. She peeled the label off of her bottle and rolled the paper between her fingers. "I hadn't thought of that," he said, "exactly."

"We could take the Concorde to Paris."

"I think the miniature shop is more within our means," he said. Again, once he had said it, he regretted it.

"Any people?" she said.

"What?"

"Do they have any miniature people?"

He shook his head. "Not that I know of."

"Did you wonder about that? Ever I mean? How a miniature house could be so wonderfully furnished, but then have no people to go into it?"

"Never spent a great deal of time worrying about dollhouses."

"I always did. I mean wonder. I know the thing you were supposed to do was extrapolate, imagine yourself living in this marvelous little house. Sitting on the miniature chairs, taking the miniature pup out for miniature walks on miniature streets. Same theory, I guess, that keeps miniature trains and race cars moving. It was never quite satisfying."

It was the longest string of words she had managed since the morning. Thoughtfully, quietly, he said, "I always wanted things on a much larger scale." He could feel the bitter beer warming through him, filling his ribs with a strange, almost giddy lightness. Finishing the first one, he took a second. "Funny how age can change your desires."

"You're such an old man." She took another beer too.

"I don't know," he said, feeling as though he were floating away from her involuntarily, "The way I figure it, everyone is old as soon as time starts becoming like something you feel." He coughed, put his beer bottle down on the step and lit a cigarette. "Should we go for that drive?"

When she turned to him, it was a sudden, jerking movement. "What did you want?" she said.

He felt nauseated. "What?" He looked at her, then away. He

made as though there were tobacco on his lip, and spat air. "I don't know," he said. He drank long and deep from the beer.

She sighed. "Maybe it was the lights," she said. "Maybe it was the lights. I've always hated fluorescent lights. They make everything seem unreal. I kept looking up, because that was the only place to look. I stared at the lights, and they didn't even hurt my eyes. I thought there was something wrong with my eyes."

Again, he expected tears. She was bent forward, one arm circling her knees, the other dangling by the neck her almost-empty beer bottle. Again, there were no tears. Her hair was pushed behind her ears. She stared over her knees at the dark street. Perhaps there had been tears—of a kind—and he had missed them.

"Awful, huh?" he said, his throat dry.

"Not awful," she said, hesitating. "Like anything. Not awful, no."

He thought for a moment of buying her a miniature house. But it would have been a cruel consolation prize.

"Last call," she said, putting her empty bottle into the paper carton and getting herself one of the two remaining bottles. He accepted the last when she offered it.

"That poor waitress," she said. He couldn't listen. "She must've thought . . . ," she said, but let the thought trail away. And in her breath: "We must have cost her twenty dollars."

He bit his lip and looked at her. "Shall we go for that drive?" He didn't want to push it. The thing that kept her on the porch with him seemed fragile, like moth wings.

"As long as I can bring my little pal here," she said, lifting the bottle.

They stood up. He took her hand. It was damp, noncommittal. They waited at the edge of the street, between parked cars, as a panel truck hissed past, then walked into the vacuum left in its wake, and headed for the Citroen.

LEE SMITH

Down by
Grassy Branch

(from the novel *Shall We Gather at the River*)

R.C. BAILEY

When Mama run off with the medicine show, I was working days at that lumber camp out from Holly Grove, old man Beady Nolan's outfit, and fiddling someplace nearabout ever night. I could fiddle all night and work all day in them days, and never think a thing of it. I was wild as any young buck, but I never let on to it when I'd go back over there on Grassy Branch and see the folks. Why I'd go right along to meeting with the rest of em, and sit in a row on them old hard benches, and sing them old high hymn songs. *What Daddy and Mama don't know, don't hurt em,* I figgered then, for Daddy didn't hold with fiddle music nor with dancing, and I didn't have no intention of running up agin him iffen I didn't have to.

Nor Mama neither, for I helt Mama up in my mind as a flat-out angel in them days, her always so nice and sweet and pretty and all, not a thing like them other old women around here. Why you could of knocked me over with a feather when she run off.

Durwood was the one told me. He come over to the camp a-purpose to do so, and then me and him got good and drunk, and I laid out of work the next day while Durwood went on back home. Somehow I couldn't go over there just yet, I couldn't look Daddy in the face, and I had to play for a dance in town that night anyhow.

I reckon I had been drinking some when I got there. I was bad to drink back then. Well they was this purty little redheaded gal that caught my eye. She was dancing up a storm. And I could tell that she was cottoning up to me, making eyes and such, so when me and the boys took a break, I says to her, *Let's you and me take us a little walk, honey,* and we done so.

We walked off from the hall a little ways, and we was just commencing to get acquainted good when I felt of somebody a-grabbing me around the neck, liked to choke me. *What the hell air ye a-doing?* I heerd him say, and hit turned out to be this great big old boy that was that little redheaded gal's regular fellow. Right then I knowed I wasn't going to fight him, for he would of made two of me.

Now Lonnie, now Lonnie, she was a-crying. Her name was Shirley Hash. *He didn't know no better,* she said to Lonnie, and I'll give her credit for it, so then he let go of me and grabbed *her,* twisting her pore little arm up behind her back.

I was not too drunk to say I thought he ought to turn loose of her.

I reckon you do, he said, *and just who the hell might you be, anyhow, over here a-rubbing on my girl?*

So I said who I was, and then Lord if he didn't start up laughing. *Oh so you are that Melungeon feller,* he said. *I reckon I know about you.*

What the hell are you talking about? I axed him, and then he liked to bust a gut laughing. They was some several fellers gathered up about us by now, a-listening to all of this.

Shirley, this here is a woods-colt that don't even know it, he says, and at least he lets go of her arm. *My grandma was Mrs. Rice that used to run the boardinghouse in Cana, the one that stood where the lumberyard is now,* he goes on to say, *and she tole it for a fact that yer momma done tuck up with a Melungeon man that was staying up there in her boardinghouse, and yore momma tried to run off with him too, but he wouldn't have her, and then she had his baby. Hell, it weren't no big secret at the time. Everybody around there knowed it.*

Liar, I hollered, and I lit into him, and he liked to change my looks afore they pulled him offen me.

Well it seemed like I couldn't work no more after that, or do nothing afore I got to the bottom of it. We had got paid two days prior to this dance I am telling you about, so what I done, I just tuck my pay and tuck off from there, and the firstest one I went to see was Tom Kincaid that taught me to play the fiddle, and knowed me since I was a boy. He was some kind of a cousin of Daddy's. He run the dry goods store in Cana.

I reckon I looked pretty rough when I come in there, for Tom jest laid down this roll of oilcloth he was a-measuring, and said, *R. C.,* *let's me and you go in the back here and eat us some lunch,* and he tuck my elbow and tuck me back there, where he doctored up my face some and give me some hoop cheese and crackers to eat and got us some sweet milk to drink, and said, *Son, it's a mighty hard thing, I'll grant ye,* for he thought I was all in a swivet over Mama running off with the show.

Then I told Tom what all that old boy had said about Mama and the Melungeon, and his thin face got kind of a cagey look.

Well, is it true or not? I axed him pint-blank, but he jest shook his head. He tuck off his glasses and polished em and then he put em back on. He had these little bitty gold glasses.

I heerd something oncet to that effect, he allowed finely. *But if you live long enough, you are likely to hear anything oncet.*

I reckon I could jest ax Daddy, I said, but Tom said he didn't believe I ought to do that, that Daddy had moren plenty to bear and there wasn't no reason for me to ax him nothing about that Melungeon. Tom says this real forceful.

So you are telling me hit's the truth, I said, for even if I was a fool, I wasn't a tee-total fool.

I am not telling you nothing, Tom Kincaid said. *I am not telling you but what's the God's truth, you had best fergit this whole business, and get on back home and help yer pa,* he said.

I can't do that, Tom, I said. *I am bound to go around here axing some more folks, I reckon, iffen you won't tell me.*

You will do nothing of the kind, Tom said. He was getting all riled up. *Listen here boy. Hit is best to leave well enough alone. Hit is best to keep yer goddam mouth shut, if you foller me.*

Well I don't foller you, I said. I stood up, I was fixing to go.

Tom kept pacing back and forth on his little office there, with the door shut. *All right,* he said. *All right, goddammit. I tell you what. If you are bound and determined to ax somebody, go up there on Cherokee mountain and ax old Willie. Tell him I sent you up thar to ax him.*

I will, I said, and I done so, fer I was bound to get the straight of it oncet and fer all. I got up there about dark the next day.

I found Old Man Willie Malone a-setting out on his porch all wrapped up in a quilt, and hit August. But old folks gets cold real easy. He was so little and dried up, he put me in mind of a grasshopper a-setting there.

Howdy, I said, and said who I was, fer I knowed he couldn't see nothing there in the dark.

Zeke's boy? he said, and I said Well that's what I had come up thar to ax him about, and I allowed as how Tom had sent me up thar. I knowed him and Tom used to be running mates, and my daddy with em afore he got religion so bad, for many's the story Tom had told me about them and what all they used to get into. I had knowed *Daddy* weren't no saint, but I had never knowed no such of a thing about Mama.

So then Uncle Willie Malone told me what folks said about Mama and the Melungeon, and by then it had growed so dark that it was like I wasn't talking to a man atall, jest a old voice coming from noplace, from the night and the mountain hitself. *And now, if I was you, I'd fergit the whole thing,* Uncle Willie said when he had got done telling it. *For yer daddy raised you as hisn, and used to trot you on his knee and walk you of a night and play with you by the hour,* Uncle Willie said. *They is not many men that had a daddy to set so much store by a baby as yourn done you,* he said.

But I was young and hotheaded then, and three or four days drunk on top of it. I had heerd what I'd come to hear all right, and I splunged off down that mountain hollering in the middle of the night, I didn't give a damn. I went over to the camp and got my stuff and then I went over to Grassy Branch and gathered up what I had left there, and told em I was leaving for a while.

They said that that strawberry-face ugly old sister of Mama's had come over here wanting to stay and help out, and Daddy had run her off in a New York minute. I reckon I was still drunk, for when Durwood told me this, I says to Daddy, *Daddy, if I was you, I would of let her stay on here. I would of just put a bag over her head,* I said, *For hit's all the same in the dark. I bet she wouldn't of felt no different from Mama,* I said.

Well Daddy whupped me good then, and after he whupped me, he gone to praying over me, and I raised up long enough to say, *Quit that praying over me, for there aint nothing to it. Hit aint nothing to Heaven, nor nothing to Hell. Hit aint nothing, period,* I tole Daddy, fer it seemed to me like that was the bare-bone facts of it all. Then I past out finely and slept all that next day through, and woke up to see Lizzie thar by the bed crying. *What are you looking at?* I said.

Then I left. I didn't never mean to darken that door again. I went over around Bluefield, then up in West Virginia, doing first one thing and then another, fiddling here and there and drinking steady. Best I can recall, my thinking run kindly along these lines. *Mama is a whore, and I am a bastard,* and so by God I set out to prove it. It seemed like a great storm was raging in me. I figgered I might as well get out there and fuck my brains out or do whatever the hell else I could think of, for it wasn't no pleasure in this life nor nothing beyond it, nothing, nothing, nothing.

I didn't want nothing but pussy. I'd tell a girl anything just to get in her pants, and you'd be surprised how easy that is, iffen you go projecting around with nothing but that on your mind. *They're all whores,* I says to myself, and I proved it pretty good too.

I stayed gone for some several years, drunk moren not, beat up frequent, in jail a couple of times too. Then come a pretty spring morning when I woke up in a woman's bed in Huntington, West Virginia, and didn't have no memory at all of who she was, or how I had got there, or where we was. Hit looked to be a room in a cheap hotel, or may be a boardinghouse. I could hear somebody walking overhead, and then I couldn't hardly hear nothing, fer the sound of this little old baby that started up crying to beat the band. It was in a dresser drawer over there in the corner, I reckon it didn't have no crib. And Lord it could holler! It just cried and cried.

I rolled over and looked at the woman that was laying there in the bed with me. She didn't look too good. Matter of fact, I couldn't tell if she was breathing or not, she had dried vomit all over her face. She was laying on her back with her mouth open. She was a curlyheaded blond woman, vomit in her hair too. She looked awful. I felt of her arm, which was warm, but I swear I couldn't see her breathing. I don't know to this day if she was dead or not. I don't know if she was a whore or not. I don't know how I got there. I couldn't remember nothing about the baby. I couldn't remember nothing about the whole week prior, in fact. I got up and pulled on my pants, I was shaking so bad all over I couldn't hardly buckle my belt. The baby had set into a hard thin wail, like it was hopeless or something. The room was a wreck, liquor bottles and drinking glasses and cigarette butts and clothes throwed all over the place. They was a gun on the floor by the bed that was not my gun, it did not look much like a lady's gun neither. The woman on the bed was not moving. She was a big woman. I reached down and got something to cover her with, or part of her anyway. Then I got out of there. I remember standing on the street in the blazing sunshine and looking back up at that window. I could still hear the baby wailing, but it sounded real far away, like a baby in another world.

Then I heerd my mama speaking to me, plain as that blazing sun. *Go on home now, Son,* she told me, and so I did.

I got back to find that Daddy had had a stroke and couldn't say a thing, nor move his left leg. He could walk after while, he got some better, but he dragged his left foot the rest of his life. Durwood and Lizzie and me figgered out later that Daddy had had the stroke just right about the time that I had heerd Mama speaking to me up in West Virginia. Somehow it didn't surprise me none to learn this.

I am home fer good, I told them, and even though Daddy couldn't talk none, he could understand me. Tears came up in his old blue eyes. I hugged him as hard as I could. *You took good care of usuns,* I told him, *and now I aim to take good care of you.*

A True Story

—for my mother

Mr. Warner was a big man who lived with his big wife and two big daughters in a cement house by the Newton Hook Rod and Gun Club. The daughters rode the bus to school, and afternoons they trained to be clowns. Their big mother sewed their costumes, the ruffled white collars, the orange and blue balloon pants. The girls painted sad faces on each other for fun, drew stars around each other's eyes, tied each other's floppy cotton shoelaces. They gallumphed around the house trying to make each other laugh but of course neither ever did, because good clowns don't laugh. Their mother never laughed either; what did she have to laugh about, living side by side with two clowns and a big grumpy side of beef of a husband? Next door at the Newton Hook Rod and Gun Club the guns went off, the arrows flew. "Now don't you girls go out in the yard," the father would say. Someone should have laughed at that, because the girls were such wide targets: when they walked the road past the Allens' farm to the bus stop the farmer chuckled, thinking they might better belong on the pasture side. Mr. Warner didn't know it but he was proud of his big family. All that flesh under one roof, all his flesh: he ate and ate and swelled with pride.

Then one day Mrs. Warner drove the station wagon out of the dirt yard and didn't come back. A month later she called and asked to speak to the girls. The older daughter took the phone from her father and shooed him out of the kitchen.

"I'm living the fast life," the mother said.

"Is it true you're a blonde now?" the older daughter asked. The younger daughter, on the phone in the bedroom, looked over at her father sinking like a punctured dirigible onto the bed.

"Where's the fast life?" she asked, ignoring her father's hissing sigh.

"In the next town," the mother said. "Whenever you're ready, come and join me."

Clowning lost its lustre in the weeks to come. One day in the middle of their best routine, just as the little red wagon's bottom drops out and dumps the younger daughter in the dirt, while the older daughter strolls on unaware, one or the other girl suddenly giggled, in a burp, and then the other's choking giggle followed, and the two sisters found themselves rolling on the ground in inexhaustible laughter.

"You-look-so-funny," the older daughter gasped.

"Look-at-you!" the younger daughter howled.

Using their father's unpracticed cooking as an excuse, they stopped eating for good. One night they packed their two nightgowns in a paper bag and snuck out of the cement house. They hitchhiked to the next town, and eventually the next one, and the next. Finally they arrived in New York City, where the older daughter met and married an heir to the Beatrice Food Company, a very nice young man who has made a hobby of finding dates for the younger daughter, though he and his wife are beginning to suspect she's too picky to ever make a match.

Mr. Warner folded up the girls' abandoned clown costumes and put them in a drawer. I see him sometimes, early in the morning, and late at night, walking by my house; and we often pass each other on the way to and from the post office. His hands, slender now, are always empty. Sometimes I don't mind these silent meetings, but there are days when the sight of him—a tall, narrow man, swinging his hollow arms, one white greasepaint tear fixed to his drooped cheek—scares me, and I cross the road. I regret this, when it happens, but I can't help myself, perhaps because as a child I always cried at the circus.

KATHERINE REED

Daylight

The woman on the other side of the desk wears a high-necked blouse and seems to unfold words onto her chin. Beth watches each one fall from the woman's lips and onto the sheaf of forms under her clasped hands. Beth wishes the words would arrange themselves into new sentences so she will not have to make any more to say or to put in the blank spaces of the forms people keep handing her.

This is the day after.

She leans hard toward the desk, wrestling her stare away from a diamond ring on the woman's hand. What is her name? Beth tries to remember, searches the desk for a clue. A nameplate says, "Margaret Handler" in fancy lettering. She tries to look into Margaret's eyes, but she gets only as far as her lips, which curve. This is what a smile looks like, Beth remembers.

"We will try to contact you first, before the police, but sometimes it doesn't work out that way," Margaret says, and hands Beth a pamphlet.

It is glossy red with black lettering, but the words don't make any sense. Beth puts the pamphlet in her purse with the other papers.

"Read it over when you have a chance. It may help you understand some of what you are experiencing." Margaret breathes out through her nose, making her eyes soft as Beth stares into them. "I never know what else to say except that I hope you'll call me if you need help. Do you have any questions right now?"

Beth looks away, out the window of the office. It is a spring
morning. There is light coming through the leaves of a tree. She
wonders when the night turned to day, how she missed it. Was she
at the hospital? Maybe she was in the room where she was questioned. She remembers the men, wonders why there were so many.
Will it take that many to find him?

She looks at the woman whose name she keeps forgetting: Margaret. Beth notices how patiently Margaret is sitting, without fidgeting. She must be very good at this job, Beth thinks, then swallows
in preparation for speaking. "Do you have a card or something? In
case I forget your name?"

Margaret nods, almost fiercely. "Of course," she says, and hands
Beth a card.

Beth stands up slowly, reading it. "Margaret Handler," it says in
gold lettering and underneath, "Victim's Advocate/Fourth Judicial
District." She feels strange in the clothes she is wearing, the ones
they gave her to wear home. She asks, "When will I get my clothes
back?"

Margaret shakes her head, slowly. "It's hard to say. Sometimes it
takes a long time."

Beth nods. As she turns to leave, she has one clear thought that
surprises her: There is a name for everything that has happened in
the last twenty-four hours. It is part of someone's routine.

She steps out into the hallway where a police officer is waiting for
her, smoking a cigarette. The officer stubs out the cigarette and
directs Beth out of the building and into the parking lot, where a
patrol car is parked.

Beth touches the handle of the passenger's side door.

"Excuse me, Mrs. Casey," the officer, a young blonde woman,
says. "You'll have to ride in back. It's just—the rules. I'm sorry."

Beth nods and waits for the back door to be opened for her. She
looks through a partition of wire mesh at the back of the officer's
head as the car moves into the street. Then she leans back and
tries to relax the muscles in her back. Suddenly she sees herself
from behind the car, a woman in a cheap, coral-colored polyester
blouse—not her own—being taken somewhere in a patrol car. It
occurs to her that someone might wonder what she has done
wrong, but there is no hard grip in her stomach—no shame. It is

just a thought, barely formed, and it is gone before she has time to feel it.

Her house surprises her by looking the same, at least from the outside. As she walks past her sister-in-law, who is standing in the doorway, crying, with Danny in her arms, she expects something to be different. Somehow she expects pictures to have fallen off the walls, pipes to have broken, windows shattered. She walks through each room, except the kitchen. The stuffed animals on Danny's bed stare at each other, tongues lolling. There are Matchbox cars on the floor.

Beth's bedroom seems darker than usual. Someone has pulled down the shades, which have never been used—at least not that she can remember.

Back downstairs, in the living room, Danny is sitting on the floor playing with a Sesame Street puzzle and talking a mile a minute to his aunt Carol. He looks up when Beth comes in.

"Hey, sport," Beth says. Her voice will not smooth itself. "Come and give me a hug."

The boy gets up and drags his feet as he comes over to her. She stoops to pick him up and hug him. Carol cannot seem to stop crying.

Beth looks at her sister-in-law's smeared eye makeup and flattened hair. Carol glances up, shoulders hunched, and pulls a tissue out of the front pocket of her tight jeans. "I know, I'm a wreck," she says. "I just couldn't sleep last night . . . in this house. I'm sorry." Carol's voice rises to a squeak as she says, "Nothing like this has ever happened to me."

Beth puts Danny down and tells him to go play. When he's gone, she realizes she has nothing to say to Carol. They stand in the middle of the room, for a minute. Then Beth feels herself sway with exhaustion.

"Oh, God," Carol says, grabbing her by the arm. "Sit down. Here."

Beth lets herself be lowered into Jim's old La-Z-Boy. Carol adjusts it, yanks up the footrest then steps back quickly, chewing on a cuticle. Her nervousness is like a strong scent in the room—too much perfume or something, Beth thinks, foggy headed. She wants

Carol to go away. After a moment, Beth takes a deep breath and gets out of the chair. Her feet feel strange, like balls, but she aims herself at the front door and concentrates on each step.

Carol follows. "Beth, I can stay."

"No, I'm all right now," Beth says. She unlocks the door, which someone has triple-locked. Even the old hook has been fastened inside the screen door.

Beth notices how Carol won't look at her. She keeps fidgeting, touching her hair, tugging at her blouse. Beth says, "Go on, go to work." Words tumble out. "Get your hair done. Get a manicure." A smile cracks Beth's face. She touches her teeth, amazed at how just anything will come out of her mouth. She can't stop talking. "You'll feel better if you just do what you usually do. Stick to the routine."

Carol takes her finger out of her mouth and says, "Are you sure you're all right?

Beth looks out onto the street at Carol's car, which is badly parked at the curb. She can't recall its arrival at that spot. She wants it gone. "Go, Carol," she says, hearing the strange hardness in her own voice. "I mean, I appreciate everything you did, but I am really okay now." She feels that she might be about to laugh, so she coughs to stop herself. "I—I'll call you later."

Carol takes her handbag from a table near the door and leaves, looking back only once as she scurries down the sidewalk. Beth thinks the look is full of fear, but she can't put together what it is Carol is so afraid of.

Sleep is what she thinks she wants, all through the phone calls, which she handles briskly and efficiently, and all through a neighborly visit from nervous Mrs. Harmon, who brings a casserole of dried beef, hard-boiled eggs, and cream of mushroom soup. It is so salty, Danny and Beth drain three Cokes, washing it down. Danny asks why they are eating on a blanket in the living room and Beth tells him they are having a picnic. She chews food and stares at the living room drapes, pulled tightly together.

She puts Danny to bed with his usual three stories and endless made-up songs. But tonight when they do the song about the soap bubble that grows and grows until it has to leave the house and is finally popped with a pin, Danny changes the words, not seeming to realize that he has done it. He sings, "Good-bye, bubble. Good-bye, bubble. Good-bye, bubble. I pop you with a knife."

In the hallway, outside his room after tucking him in, she mutters, "All I need is sleep." She whispers it over and over to herself to block out her thoughts as she takes a scalding bath, puts on a flannel nightgown, and crawls in between the sheets. She imagines how sleep will feel as she finds a comfortable position and rearranges the pillows. Then she closes her eyes.

The little flecks of light and halos that usually move around in harmless, meaningless patterns form lines and make a shape, two shapes, emerging like a photograph dipped in developer: eyes. Beth's fly open in the dark. She closes them again. The flecks march like ants in lines: eyes. They become clearer: his eyes. Beth sits up in bed, breathing quickly. This is impossible, she thinks. She stares into the corners of her room. There is something there that she did not see before. She turns on the light on the night table.

Nothing. She sits, listening for a while. She can hear breathing—her own and another's, lagging just behind. She holds her breath to listen. Finally, she recognizes the tiny whistle of Danny's sleeping breath and exhales. She turns out the light and stares at the ceiling in the dark, hoping sleep will shut her eyes, before the vision has time to slide into place.

Somewhere between awake and a dream, she sees light spilling into the room as she opens the front door and says "Yes?" to the man on the other side.

He is young, about twenty, dark haired. He smiles, seems shy, as he says, "I'm sorry to bother you so early in the morning." He glances over his shoulder at a black Ford Mustang parked at the curb. "My car quit on me. I just need to use a phone."

She notices his belt buckle; it says "Copenhagen" on it, like those in the booths at the county fair. She tries to look into his eyes, but he peers over her shoulder, into the house.

"I'm still in my robe," she says. "I will be happy to call someone for you."

He starts to move around on the stoop. She feels bad that she can't quite overcome her city-bred suspicions, even now that she lives in a small town where nothing ever happens. She congratulates herself when she remembers to leave her car doors unlocked in the parking lot at work and is pleased when she and Danny take a walk around the neighborhood without first locking up the house. It is a real effort, unlearning old habits.

The young man decides to give her a number to call. In the kitchen, she writes it down on a piece of paper and dials. She can't remember anything from one minute to the next. Jim used to call her forgetfulness, "Mommy lapses." He'd say, "You just have too much to do, Beth, between Danny and working. Don't be so hard on yourself."

There is no answer at the number the young man gives her. She goes back to the front door and tells him. He doesn't seem to care. "Well, okay. Thanks," he says, and walks down the sidewalk to his car, stepping lightly in a pair of steel-toed cowboy boots.

She goes to find Danny, to tell him to get dressed for school. He is in the kitchen, digging all of the Cheerios out of the box to find the sticker inside. She is chasing him playfully past the front door and upstairs when she sees the man standing there again.

Before she can think, he says, "I'm sorry to bother you again, but I think if I just had a screwdriver or something I could get this car cranked."

Jim used to stick a screwdriver in the carburetor of her old Dodge Charger when it wouldn't start. So she nods. "Okay. I have to remember where it is." She knows there is a box of tools in the gardening shed next to the garage. She looks at herself in her pajamas, long, blue terrycloth robe and moccasins. "I guess I'm okay to step outside for a second."

She smiles at him and he smiles back as she steps out onto the stoop. But she is falling, reaching, and it isn't there—it disappears as she falls more deeply asleep. Then there is something in her hand—she hopes it is the railing. She unfolds her hand and sees a pair of garden shears, cutting deeply into her palm, and forces herself to wake up.

The next morning, Danny won't let her talk on the phone. "Mom," he keeps saying while Beth argues with her doctor's answering service. She knows she is being unreasonable, but can't stop herself. She says, "I don't see why you can't have him call me at home. *Now.*"

Something is said about rounds at the hospital, babies needing to be born. The woman on the other end of the phone is trying to be patient, Beth knows. She asks for Beth's name and phone number. Beth has to think before answering, glancing at the little card on the bedroom telephone.

Danny tugs at her nightgown. "Mommy, *now.*"

She tries to pretend she is not in the kitchen as she pours cereal and milk into a bowl, finds a spoon and puts Danny in his booster seat at the table. She leaves the room without drawing a breath and sits down on the living room couch. She wants the phone to ring. Her lips move as she rehearses what she will say: "Doctor, I was wrong about not needing any medication to sleep." Waiting on the couch, she listens to Danny hum to himself as he eats.

When Jim comes to take Danny to nursery school, she is dressed. She looks in the mirror before going to the door, but she can't quite see herself clearly. Her blouse is tucked in, her belt through all of the loops. But she is not sure about her face. It won't stay still to be examined. Something keeps moving in the way of her seeing it.

She looks out the living room window to be sure it is Jim at the door, then opens it. "Hi," she says. "Will you pick up a prescription for me if I call you at work?"

He comes slowly into the house and stands in the entryway.

Her chin is suddenly shaking.

"Beth?" He looks down at her.

She can feel his eyes on the top of her head, remembers her hair. "Oh, shoot," she says. "Is my hair all screwed up?" She tries to smooth it down.

He grabs her hand. "Beth?" He tries to look into her face. "Is everything all right?"

Danny comes down the stairs. He has dressed himself, blue jeans over footy pajamas, carrying a toy gun. "Hi, Daddy," he says, smiling. "When the bad man comes back, I will be ready."

Before bed, Beth takes one pill then waits with the light on. Danny is sleeping peacefully already. Listening to him breathe, she feels envy. How can it be possible to sleep so easily, she thinks. She tries to remember falling asleep, before. She tries to remember what the difference between night and day used to be, before a day became an endless succession of slow-moving minutes with slight variations in color, before the thing that happened in broad daylight.

She pulls the covers over her head and hopes the lack of air will help her fall asleep. She is glad that Jim did not insist on taking Danny home with him, to his apartment for "a week or so however long you need." It is nice of him not to make her beg, she thinks, beginning to feel drowsy.

It begins again, from the beginning, with the door opening, the face, Danny going up the stairs. The images move so quickly through her mind, she can't stop them. She is too tired to stop them. Her hand is on the door handle of the gardening shed.

"Just a second," she says to him, as she reaches into the air over her head, looking for the dangling bulb. She can't find it right away, keeps bumping into it. She feels him behind her in the doorway— there isn't room enough for two people inside. She tries not to be nervous. There is no reason to be afraid.

"There," she says, when the light is on. She comes down from tiptoes into a hard embrace. Something presses into her throat—a forearm. "No," she starts to say, this is wrong, you didn't mean to do this.

But he tells her not to scream, tells her what he will do if she does.

She says, "No, no, no" but her voice is not hers, what is wrong, why do I sound like a child?

She wakes up to the sound of Danny screaming.

"He is having nightmares," she tells Margaret Handler. "Last night he woke up screaming."

Beth talks into the telephone for a long time after Danny leaves for school. Margaret says the nightmares are normal. Then she asks Beth if she is having nightmares.

Beth hesitates. "Just the one."

Margaret asks her to get a pen and a piece of paper so she can write down the name and number of an excellent therapist. Beth says hold on and goes to look for a piece of paper, wandering into the kitchen without realizing she is there, alone. She sees the shining edge of the kitchen table, the telephone, the drawer. She sees herself walking stiffly into the kitchen, him behind her, pressing the garden shears into her side.

She slides to the floor. The only way to get out is to crawl. She keeps crawling until she is in the bedroom again with the telephone in her hand.

"Beth? Beth?" Margaret sounds worried on the other end.

It is some time before Beth can answer. Finally, she says, "I'm here. I'm here now."

When the phone rings, Beth is sitting on the living room couch, watching television. As she passes the bedroom clock on the way to the phone, she notices it is 1:30. She has been watching television since 9 A.M. She is thirsty and her bladder is full.

"Hello?" She can hear someone breathing on the other end. She remembers what he said, that if she called the police he would get her. She is sure that he wanted to kill her, that the only thing that stopped him was Danny. Her heartbeat is so fast, she cannot breathe normally. "Hello?"

"Mommy?"

"Danny." She breathes.

"Mommy. I had pizza for lunch."

Before she can say anything, another voice is on the line. "Hi, Beth," Jim says. "Danny fell asleep on the way to school so I figured he'd be better off coming to my place for the day."

"Don't you have to work?"

"It's okay. Don't worry about it. Listen, I'll bring him home in a couple of hours. Then Carol's going to watch him tonight."

"Why?"

"I'm taking you out," he says. "Dinner and a movie. It's time you got out of the house."

She catches a glimpse of disheveled hair in the bedroom mirror and whispers into the phone, "It is?"

Getting ready takes so much time, for some reason. Each motion is deliberate—blow-drying hair, applying makeup, choosing clothing and getting it on right. She looks at herself in the mirror. Her eyes are red, but there are no drops in the house. She looks more closely into the bathroom mirror, at her eyes, and a transparency glides over them: a face, a mouth, then words begin, "Tell me how much you . . ."

She falls back against the towel rack. The pain between her shoulder blades ends his sentence.

There is not enough time to prepare for getting out of Jim's car at the restaurant. She sits and drums her fingers on the seat. Jim lights a cigarette and blows smoke out the window.

"May I have one of those please?"

He looks at her. "You quit."

"Please." The word makes her shudder. She lights up and looks out the window.

"You know," he says, "Danny's going to think we're getting back together."

She can't think of any way to respond. They sit and smoke for a while. Finally, she puts out the cigarette and fumbles for the handle of the car door. Jim has to help her get out.

In the restaurant, everyone stares. Beth sees two familiar faces and remembers work, knows that she will have to go back soon. One of the other news clerks is there and a photographer, who has been teaching her how to shoot pictures. Neither of them comes over. John, the photographer, seems to avoid passing Beth and Jim's table as he leaves the restaurant.

She asks Jim to order her another drink. He blinks at her and chews. "Why don't you eat something? It's your favorite."

She stares down at her plate of Greek chicken and potatoes. Her stomach feels full. "I'm not hungry," she says. "I'm thirsty." Then she reaches across the table for Jim's cigarettes.

They go to the theater and stare up at the titles on the marquee: There is a movie about a woman being terrorized by a psychopath, the sixth sequel to a horror film and a romantic comedy.

"I guess that one would be all right," she says, pointing at the third title.

Inside, Jim strides toward the first row of the theater, as usual. Beth feels people behind her in the dark and turns around.

Jim whispers "You don't want to sit here?"

She shakes her head and he sighs. "Okay."

When they are seated in the back row, she realizes he is angry. He never wears his glasses, so he can't see. She sits uneasily, trying to look only at the screen. But she is sure someone is watching her. To her right, at the end of the row, a man is sitting. He seems to be looking at her. She looks away, then back at the man. His head seems to move slightly in the dark. Her heartbeat is out of control again, so she tries to concentrate on her breathing.

Jim touches her arm. "Are you okay?"

She shakes her head and gets up.

As they are leaving, Jim tells the girl in the ticket booth his wife is sick and gets two movie passes.

She is dreaming about the flowers—the daffodils and the tulips in the beds behind the house, the wild violets in the grass and the one that isn't up yet, the popcorn plant along the wall of the shed. She goes from flower to wall to the cool darkness of the tiny shed, where someone is speaking. She moves closer to listen; she has never heard a voice so full of rage. He tells her to walk up the driveway and into the house, through the side door into the kitchen. She notices a Tom's Snack Foods van and a souped-up Volkswagen beetle going by on the road in front of the house. How odd, she thinks, that mind and body still work.

She opens the kitchen door and goes in. He presses the shears more deeply into her side and tells her to take off her robe.

She fumbles with the belt, thinking about Danny. Stay in your room, stay up there, take forever to get dressed, she thinks. Her hands are shaking. This is impossible, she thinks, not happening. It isn't going to happen.

He tears off her pajama top, pulls down the flannel pants, then yanks open a drawer near the stove. He is holding her by the throat with the other hand. He fumbles around, looking over his shoulder into the drawer, and pulls out a steak knife. The shears are dropped to the floor and kicked out of the way as he pushes her toward the kitchen table.

I am not dreaming, I am awake, she thinks, falling back on the table. She puts a word to every thrust: "Not. Here. Not. Here. I'm. Not. Here." She is staring through yellow, ruffled curtains at nothing, doesn't realize she is crying until her shoulder slides into something wet.

"Mommy?"

The weight and piercing are gone. She struggles to sit up. "Danny. Go. Go to your room."

His face darkens. He is a bad boy, so he leaves. A hand on her throat again, a hiss in her ear: "If you call the police, I will kill you. I will kill him."

Danny is back. She is struggling to get up, why can't she get up? She has to tell him again, to leave, but she can't. He is beside her, saying, "Mommy? Mommy? Wake up. Wake up."

It takes forever to wake up, to find herself not on the table.

The phone wakes her up in the morning. Danny is asleep beside her. She reaches over his tiny shape to stop the ringing.

"Yes?" Her voice is rough.

"Mrs. Casey?"

It is a man's voice.

"Yes."

"This is Lieutenant George from the sheriff's department. I don't know if you remember me."

She thinks of uniforms, suits and ties, cowboy boots, a cigar. "No," she says. "Not exactly."

"Well, that's understandable, of course." He pauses to clear his throat, loudly, like a longtime smoker. "Anyway, I sure have a piece of good news for you."

She tries to open her eyes. "What is it?"

"We got him," he says. "Of course you deserve most of the credit for writing down that phone number. All we had to do was wait for him to go home to his mama's house from wherever he was. Sort of stupid of him to give you his own phone number. Guess it was the first thing to pop into his head. Then of course I guess he didn't figure you'd write it down."

"I have a bad memory," she says, wishing it were always true. "So he's in jail."

"Yep," he says.

She waits, thinking. This could be anyone. She doesn't know the voice. Maybe she is supposed to let her guard down now. She sits up in bed. "Tell me your name again."

"Lieutenant George. Lieutenant Luther George."

She nods. "Okay, Lieutenant. Do me a big favor. Have one of

your officers come over here and tell me this in person. If it's not too much trouble."

There is a hesitation, then he says, apparently pleased with himself, "I understand, Mrs. Casey. It's perfectly understandable."

At 10 A.M., Lieutenant George arrives in person. He is, as it turns out, the cigar smoker, so Beth asks him to come outside with her while she does some gardening.

The lieutenant is a wall of a man, in a light blue and white pin-striped suit, a crisp white shirt, and a yellow tie with navy stripes. His haircut makes him look like a retired Marine, about fifty. He lets Danny see his badge and pats the boy on the head as Danny runs around in the backyard, pushing a toy wheelbarrow. Beth kneels in front of the flower beds while he tells her about rapists, how stupid they are. Every time he says "rape" or "rapists" he drops his voice to a whisper and looks around to see that the boy is not within earshot.

"There was this one fella, raped a woman in Gaffney, drank a bottle of her liquor and fell asleep on the living room couch. Which is where we found him," he says, then laughs to himself.

Beth is picking daffodils, pulling them out by hand.

"You're gonna have a nice bouquet," the lieutenant says, relighting his cigar. He blows out a huge cloud of smoke, which Beth watches float up over the garage and into the clean, blue air.

Danny looks at his mother and begins, tentatively, to pick the wild violets, pulling their purple heads off the frail stems. He lays them next to her and goes back for more. She notices that he is going blonde again, then she goes back to pulling out the daffodils. She lays them stem against stem in the grass.

"Maybe you ought to get you some shears," the lieutenant says.

Beth stands up and picks grass out of the creases in her knees. "I'm done," she says.

He nods. "Well, anyway, all that's left to do is put the boy in the penitentiary for a long, long time. I know you'll be good on the stand. Now, it'll be kind of rough, but I bet you're not the kind to fall apart under pressure."

The lieutenant keeps talking about evidence and testifying. Beth sees two faces: hers and the jailed man's. She realizes she will have to see him again. And then again and again and again. It is complete. She sees it before her, every night, every day. She wonders if there is a way to stop it that she has yet to learn.

The lieutenant is edging toward his car, so she scoops up the flowers and follows with Danny behind her. She stuffs the flowers into a garbage can next to the garage. The lieutenant is still talking as he removes his jacket, puts it on a hanger, and slides heavily into the front seat.

He squints into the sun as he looks up at her and says, "The important thing, of course, is that it's over." He smiles. "It's over."

CONSTANCE J. POTEN

Heading Home

On the last Saturday in November the Arctic blizzard blew in, howling down the east wall of the Rockies. Ninety-mile-an-hour winds derailed an eastbound train, and snowdrifts the size of small mountain ranges blocked the roads. Food would have to be air-dropped to the plywood Indian community of Heart Butte; five people would die of exposure. Ruby Red Willow's house sighed and collapsed at three o'clock that afternoon.

Ruby was feeding the chickens, bunched against the cold between straw bales, their bald eyes staring up at her, bright and appalled. First came the sagging, then the great final *whoosh*. The crashing house exploded noise around them like a bomb dropped from inside the storm. A tornado of slashing feathers whirled up, screeching and clawing around her head. Gusts yanked at the wall planks like a crazy man, slamming the boards against the barbwire fence from the pile that had been her house.

Ruby stood with hands over her ears, eyes clenched. She pictured flying shrapnel in war movies. She heard her husband saying the hits were indiscriminate, the ground shook so constantly that he thought the earth itself conspired with the Vietcong. Some feared an uglier hell was in store for them; it was wrong to survive the fabulous bombs. A few went deaf, they watched the tracers and sizzling impacts like children at a carnival.

When the noise diminished, she peered around the barn door. The house was flat, the gray tin roof thrown over her furniture and kitchen appliances like a stiff new blanket. If the place had to fall apart, Ruby figured, it was dumb luck she was out, already out wearing gloves and her husband's parka. The first thing she thought of was the picture of her son Wolf, and the second was her electric coffee maker. The oil furnace was on, and Ruby thought that it might blow up so she decided to go to Uncle Willie's. The old house, nailed up when her great-grandmother was a young girl, had stood its limit of winter blows.

Ruby pulled a two-by-six from the sprung doorframe and used it for a walking stick. She set out in the direction of Willie Wolf Eyes' house three miles away around the hill. When a roaring built up behind her in the mountains she could no longer see, Ruby plunged the board into the nearest snowdrift and wrapped her arms around it behind her. She planted her feet downwind because the weight anchored her better that way.

Ruby Red Willow could have been out fixing fence in a summer squall. Some people thought her tendency to ride out trouble rather than buck it just asked for a beating, but after random calamities, like what took her husband and son, she quit worrying about herself. Now, except for occasional bartending in Atlas for grocery money, she hardly saw anyone. What was the use? No one had a magic wand to make things right again. She couldn't stand the heaviness, the unspoken accusations, she felt from her family. Because she didn't come for help, the family gradually narrowed its eyes, as if she were white, living solitary like that, and stayed away.

There was the wedding picture of Frank holding her hand at the Baptist church, and Frank's rodeo poster, the picture on the dresser of her mother, a young solemn girl, at the boarding school. She knew there must be more important things, but what were they? It was funny how snapshots, not even pawnable, were suddenly more important than real things, her bed and clothes, the television. Silly pieces of colored paper. The wind screaming off Elk Calf Mountain bent Ruby forward and buffeted her. She held onto her post like the maidenhead of a ship's prow, snow roiling around her soft brown face.

Ruby opened her eyes after a while. She'd been picturing herself riding the wind like a redtail, letting it carry her across miles of prairie, skating with it over dry coulees, banking with the runnels of terrain. Then the wind swept on past her and she was back on earth, holding her post. Uncle Willie was surely drinking coffee at his kitchen table by the window, his horses lined up in the lee of the house. They were good insulation, he said. She began the march forward.

Thirty miles south, the snow had come in before the wind. It goosed the blood of hunters fanning west in their pickups to scan the foothill drainages. It was the second to last day of hunting season and legions of them hoisted guns and walked up coulees, hopes pinned on the silence of their movements and the confusion a sudden storm brings on wild animals.

Bryan Dooley tried to glide uphill through the pines but he couldn't keep his eyes off his Uncle Calvin, ten yards away, which caused him to trip over fallen branches and make enough noise to flush a fool's hen. He knew the safety was off Cal's .308 Winchester, which is why he kept looking at him, to make sure Uncle Cal knew where he was. Then Bryan would fumble on a snag under the snow, Cal would swing his rifle at him and Bryan would throw his hands up in the air. "Goddamn," Calvin would hiss. "Get off the ground, boy."

When they topped the hill, Calvin motioned Bryan to his side. Calvin's orange camouflage suit bulked out like a blimp. The extra-large beaked cap made him look like Woody Woodpecker. It was hard to concentrate on the hunt when your partner looked like a large plucked bird, a goofy mascot for the football team, and also had the safety off his gun. Bryan wanted to giggle. But close up, the pale blue eyes behind Calvin's glasses pulsated, Uncle Cal looked like a mountain man, single-minded, wild around the edges, the kind of guy Bryan wanted to be.

"This, son, is where we'll get him," Calvin panted, jerking his hat bill toward a beaver pond meadow down the slope in front of them. "It will be the most important moment of your life," he breathed, "banging your first elk."

Calvin's heavy whisper stirred a tingle in Bryan's loin. He was about to kill, to become a man. A rush of wind rolled uphill, spraying snow in their faces. "Excellent," said Calvin. "We're downwind from the bastards."

If the sky had been clear and a hawk was to take the southerly thermals down the eastern reefs of the Rockies, its shadow would

have drifted over Ruby inching along the smooth side of a small
volcanic cone, a few miles southwest of a dark rectangle with horses
bunched up against it. The shadow would have bumped over the
crescent of forest covering two spots of orange, a pair of hunters,
Bryan Dooley and his uncle Calvin Fowler, beneath the branches.
Sailing south, tracing a crooked line over the rocky outcrops of
Antelope Butte, the hawk would have circled for rotting flesh, its
shadow growing larger as it dipped down over the prairie archi-
pelago of the Surfening Ranch. It would have passed near a wolf
threading through boulders down a coulee wash. The hawk would
have taken a closer look at two dogs scurrying in the junipers near
the county road, the kind of activity that might scare up some prey.

Moosejaw, the spaniel, and Frenchy, the black labrador, were
bustling over the snow from thicket to thicket, pushing their noses
under rocks and logs, snorting at gopher burrows and mouse holes.
Frances Bowl followed them, letting them run before the weather
closed in. The atmosphere was a busy quiet at the base of the
mountains, as though molecules were lining up to face the oncoming hordes.

Frances and the dogs were looking for a cabin to rent, which is
why they were out in a blizzard 200 miles from home on a Saturday
afternoon. Jed had suggested it, a vacation house, and wanted
Frances to find some places for him to choose from. She'd fully
expected to settle on a house at Flathead Lake, where they could be
near their friends who all had houses at the lake. But on a wild hair
she'd headed from Missoula to the desolate east side of the mountains, just to take a look. An excuse for another weekend trip. Jed
gave her two hundred dollars and told her to be careful.

The storm front had blanked out the northern horizon. It was
eerie to Frances the way air could gather in such force that the
8,000-foot rock wall dominating the western horizon appeared di-
minutive and naked by comparison. There was power in motion.
For instance, here she was traveling, in flight actually, and already
she felt stronger and younger.

For a moment, the headwall, rising from a dark-green flame
stitching of pine forest, reminded her of Jed. Proud Doctor Jed.
He'd never entertained a deviation from the family profession. It

was unorthodox enough to choose sports medicine, and his mother had to soothe the southern patriarchy by saying it was just a modern name for orthopedics. Mawdn naym fuh awthuh*pee*ducs, Frances could hear the silvery voice ringing all the way from Savannah's historic district. Jed had chafed under the reins of parental approval but he couldn't throw them off. Frances hadn't paid attention. She was busy writing poetry about the impermanence of cows in pastures.

She'd found his sense of destiny under that langorous voice and thin, blond hair exquisitely manly. He was silky rock. After six years of marriage, though, she was still trying to find a soft crevice. Whom would she ever tell that Jed fell asleep most nights in the bathtub reading war stories? He was safe in that secret. When he did come to bed on the rare occasion, afterwards he'd laugh, "Women turn to mush after sex. See? You'd do anything for me now." Or he'd be mute, resentful.

This trip away simply enlarged his boundaries around her, and she was allowing it. Here she was mulling over him. She expected that was the price of holy matrimony but sometimes it felt like a terrible loss. Before they'd moved west, he liked to hear her travel stories, reported from short trips with her friend Caley. He would marvel at how she had slipped past the muggers of the French Quarter, or evaded the bandits of Mexican beaches, dangers that lurked in the unexplored regions of his imagination. I can't allow you to go without me again, he'd say. (He always had a reason not to go, but it was routine he couldn't leave.) Then he'd kiss her gently, hold her as if she was a messenger from Marco Polo, and for a moment she could watch pass like a train, she thought they were happy.

Without fail, that little ritual opened up a deep sad pit in Frances. She'd wait it out, and the pit would slowly be subsumed again. She couldn't figure out why the unbearable emptiness came over her with her own husband. Their marriage was forever, he'd insist.

Jed had coerced Frances west from her lush southern coast, saying how wild and rugged Montana was, implying that he would become wild and rugged too. It turned out that she was the one who went native. He'd sought out all the things that were eastern and controlled, and preferably indoors. His time went to the clinic, the spa, the golf club. The bathtub. He tried to embrace an independent air, but when something came up, even going into the woods to cut firewood, he'd mock himself, saying his style didn't run to logger wear. Then, feet up in front of the Sunday game, he'd pull out his harmonica and play a plaintive Civil War tune. "This old soldier," he'd smile at her, "just hopes his woman'll stick by him 'til the war's won." It was one of those passing moments.

Jed charmed people with his warm, bourbon-flavored disdain. The phone rang for him often. Yesterday she'd heard, "So you're not Tom Watson. You're just another Yankee carpetbagger. Come in Monday and I'll remove that knee." Ha, ha, ha. Out here, sports medicine brought him glory.

Their Kentucky Derby party was an event on the small city's social calendar. Jed set up the big screen and elaborate betting chalkboard on the front porch. Frances draped Spanish moss, sent out by Jed's mother, on the birch tree, and the dogs would take running leaps at the salty sweet hair. The dogs Jed could do without. He played bookie with his Deep South auctioneer's voice and bartenders from the school's basketball team served mint juleps at tables on the lawn. They were aristocracy again, Jed would murmur to her, bringing civilization to the rubes. His pleasures could be horrific if you thought about it.

What Jed really liked about the west were the visits home to Savannah. He'd tell his old friends about bird hunting on grass prairies (he went once) and trips into the mountains, neglecting to say they were by car. He made himself into a Prince Maximilian, gathering exotica for display to the statuary of his past. "And Frances," he'd boast, "She's out there digging up the flora, hauling home rocks. You can't find the debutante in those canvas get-ups anymore." That raised the collective brow, and made her smile.

One time she had stopped at a roadside bar and cafe after a hike with Frenchy and Moosejaw. A drunk logger saw the rocks piled in the back of the Jeep. (Jed had always wanted a Jeep Cherokee but he never drove it.)

"Rockhound, eh?" the logger said, leering. "You know about people who save rocks. Yeah, people who collect rocks are insecure." He made himself at home draped over the back fender. "They say people who keep rocks had bad childhoods. Old rocks, you think about it, lady, old rocks ain't gonna fill the hole."

After her surgery, Jed wouldn't consider adoption because he didn't want a little gene problem running around the house. Maybe it was the end of possibilities that pushed her out here. The wind had picked up. Snow lifted in curling waves and whirlwinds like frothy Japanese seascapes.

The dogs led Frances over hummocks through sage bushes rising out of the snow. They entered denlike shelters, walled by magnolia-green firs and junipers, and chokecherry thickets. Frances and the dogs sniffed around in these hollows. The faint smell of salt, the isolate extravagance of vegetation reminded her of lagoons left by retreating tides, teeming with strange fish and mollusks, the occasional shark. In a large hollow she sat on a boulder, fingering the chartreuse and orange lichen splashed on the limestone and felt her legs pumping the mushy sand under loblolly pines to the V of endless metallic water, then breaking wide open onto the beach, arms high. Frances headed out to a shallow cutbank, a dry creek bed lined with shaggy cottonwoods. She strode through the trees as if she were retracing an old, familiar path.

Fifty yards away, Frances spotted a rangey animal loping across a swale of prairie. It looked like a coyote with a thick peppery coat, but it seemed bigger, taller, The animal stopped and stared sideways at her. The clear concentration in its dark eyes penetrated right through her, like a drum. She stopped breathing, trapped by the power in those eyes. The animal turned then, and moved on, steady-paced, dropping out of sight.

Frances stayed in one spot, straining to see it again. Something in that animal was correct and grand. She'd seen wild animals on her hikes, and they'd seen her, even a grizzly bear once. But none ever made so startling a connection—a *recognition*. The animal lifted her out. Walking on, flushed and racey, she panted, found herself trying for the keen, liquid grace of that animal.

Then the snow came in blankets, all she could see of Moosejaw and Frenchy were the orange sweatshirts cut to fit for hunting season. When she called them to head for the Jeep, Frances became aware that she was home. This was, of course, where she would find her cabin. She would think about it later, the odd idea of being comfortable in a wildly tenuous, in-between region, where the plains smacked into mountains and weather rode rocks and sediments to the plains, where no people ever settled.

Giddy, she pictured the cabin. It would be by a stream at the edge of cover. She looked west, up the canyon where dark pines stood out now against the low gray sky like arrowheads. Off the front porch would be absolute space. It wouldn't have to have running water, she could rig that up, but it would have electricity. And be where grizzlies still find quarter. Oh yes, the grizzly requirement was basic as a canary in a mine. If the grizzly was pushed out, it would no longer be safe haven for her either. She could hear her sister, "Honey, that's *pre*-rustic. Don't you want visitors?" Frances remembered folds of dark shining green—looking up when she was tiny. It was the brief, taffeta rustle of her mother's lap before she swept off to a dance.

Frances walked a mile down the road to her Jeep. The storm wheeled low on fast gray clouds but she grew drowsy, her vision shut down by the thick, white bombardment of snow. She stopped and opened the back gate of the Jeep. Something soft bumped her head. Frances turned and froze. She found herself under the nose of a mule, dozens more mules and horses moving up behind. The dogs jumped into the back, daunted by the crowd. They had moved in, quiet and quick as a swarm of fish except that they were big, snow-blanketed, hungry animals backing her against the Jeep, nudging her, trying to chew the bumper, the rearview mirror.

Mushing through the darkening snow, Ruby remembered when her sister-in-law converted to a Seventh Day Adventist. Winona got intolerant and yelled at Uncle Willie for scaring her children with his animal hobgoblins. Willie smiled gently and explained that they were wolf guardians watching over the children playing in the river; so many kids had drowned by slipping under logs. The children hadn't been scared, but Winona demanded that Willie keep his "evil spirits" away from her family. Her words stung Willie, but he agreed to send them away.

Then, no one knew why exactly, but six-year-old Ellis had been kicked by a mule in the head and hemorrhaged. A few days later, driving to see him in the hospital Winona slid off the icy road and rolled her car over the embankment. Little Stevie broke his collarbone in the accident. They were trapped for six hours in the borrow pit before another car happened along. Accidents happened like that on the reservation, as if an invisible army was attacking.

Willie Wolf Eyes was a Blackfeet medicine man whose wife had died three years ago. He was tall and walked with a limber, straight back, despite his eighty-six years. Willie kept a garden and spoke French when he planted. He blessed his house with a twig of burning sagebrush each morning and evening from a bundle he kept in a basket beside the kitchen door. Controversy embattled his brother, the tribal chairman, but Willie was a demilitarized zone, a last spiritual ember of the tribe. His gentle presence stilled even the angry young people.

Willie never said I told you so. He told Ruby that his wolf guide taught him to raise his children and let them learn on their own; the clever ones would make it, and the tribe would be stronger. His wolf spirit told him that his people depended on his own straight heart. Ruby had never seen a wolf, they'd been gone from Heart Butte since her great-grandfather's time, but she knew from stories that they had been skillful teachers. The Wolf Clan was still the biggest clan of the tribe. Still, Ruby told Willie, she didn't see how non-existent wolves could help someone trying to get a BIA loan. Times were hard enough, without wasting hope on the power of animals the whites erased in their spare time.

Willie told Ruby this wasn't so. He believed the talk of ghost wolves on the plains; some people claimed to have seen them. They were white, they ran past cars at night and scouted from the buttes. Willie told Ruby that wolves never abandoned their own. They had long-distance cunning and were all around, watching with patient eyes. It was part of a game, he said, a game too big for him and Ruby to see.

Neither Ruby nor Willie knew wolves were moving outward from their new mountain foothold on the Canadian border, retracing ancestral trails. Everyone knew about the wolves slipping into Glacier Park from Canada because it was a miracle, with so many guns pointing at them along the border. They were called the Magic Pack. But almost no one suspected they had in mind to leave their mountain safety and head east across the Continental Divide to open space. Glacier was simply a camp along the way. Wolves belonged on the plains, they were carrying back their instincts, cargo that once shimmered on the prairie and enlivened the grasses. They were heading home.

Ruby had named her son Wolf, partly after Willie, but also partly to give him the stamina and talents of his animal namesake. Wolf had been a good boy, too, but he hadn't lived long enough to grow into his name.

Five years ago, in the middle of the summer on a hot afternoon, the lazy kind where you'd think nothing could go bad, he fell off a hayrake. The ground snapped the breath out of him with no coming back, only seven years old. Ruby's life imploded at that moment, it felt as if her heart had collapsed. For months, she had to remember to breathe. It was worse for Frank. He paced the house and finally left in the fall, turning up on the streets of Great Falls.

It was a long drunk that lasted into winter, froze him out. Or maybe somebody killed him. Ruby didn't know. The body was recovered from the Missouri River in the spring, sixteen years after they stood on the steps of the Baptist church. It was so decomposed that the coroner wrote the incident up as accidental drowning. Why anybody would accidently drown in the cold of winter, Ruby couldn't guess, but it was out of her hands.

The gusts had dropped to a steady brace with darkness. Ruby concentrated on gripping the post with her fist. She couldn't see anything, and she was moving slower, her feet were numb.

When Frances went into the Antler Bar and Cafe, the snow in Atlas was a foot deep and blowing high as the town's three street-lights. Inside, the heat, noise, and pulsating bar signs hit her all at once, and she waited to adjust to the careening room. Men's faces were turned toward her. She moved out of the doorway to the quieter, darker side of the bar and found a stool. On the wall a thick pelt, huge and luxuriant, in striations of white, silver and black trapped her eye. She wanted to lie down in that fur. It was surrounded by a facing of blue felt, like an ocean boundary on a topographic wall map of some large, rich continent, some nourishing place that drew her in.

The bartender was smiling when her gaze dropped to him, and she ordered a draft beer. When he brought it, she asked him what the fur was. "Wolf," he said. "Some guy brought that down from Alaska last week. The genuine article. Nice, huh?"

The man on the next barstool turned and stared at her. "If I saw a wolf, I'd kill it. I'd kill every damn wolf I could," he declared.

Frances looked at him. He looked like he boiled skulls for a hobby. His teeth, glasses, and the whites of his eyes gleamed in the half-light. He was dry and bald. She found this conversation starter so outlandish it had to be a joke. She smiled rather gaily. "Oh?" she said, "why's that?"

"I don't need wolves going after my elk," he said, accusingly. "Management has replaced the wolf. *Hunters* are the wolves now." Western men, her mother had observed on her only visit, do not appreciate women.

"The wolf," he was saying through his teeth, "is vermin." He glared at her so, Frances shrugged innocence. The situation was absurd. She was a debutante from Savannah and she didn't give a rat's ass about him, his tirade, he didn't even know her. But he was waiting for a response. She finally said, "Isn't there room for both of you?"

"No. No room at all." He was primed. "It's hard enough to get an elk without any damn wolves. There's no use for them around here."

"Maybe you should become a better shot." She smiled lightly, joking, backing off.

The man squared his shoulders sharply. "I *teach* hunting."

"Really? That's interesting," said Frances, looking around for escape. But the bartender had receded to the brighter end of the bar. The hunter kept staring at her so she asked distractedly, "Where do you teach, at the Vo-Tech?"

"No!" he snapped. "I teach my sons, and Bryan here, he's almost a son."

Frances looked past the hunter at a boy about eighteen who bobbled his head in confirmation over a glass of beer. He was round and soft as his uncle was crisp.

When the hot gaze of Uncle Cal fell on him Bryan said, "He's right, yeah. Fish and Game manages the elk fine here. Wolves would mess it up. Wolves would be bad." He said this with the diffused enthusiasm of a cult addict. The boy was disarming, with gold fuzz for a beard, still unformed.

"Did you get your elk this year?" Frances asked him. Bryan and his uncle exchanged looks. After a moment, Bryan said, "Nah, weather came in too hard."

"That's what it is," said his uncle. "Hard work. That's what I mean about no need for wolves." He nattered on about wolves tearing apart cattle alive. No, he wasn't a rancher, but he'd heard the stories. It was not for nothing bounty hunters were paid to exterminate wolves, vicious thieving killers. His face seemed to get flatter as he talked. His long white hands moved as if he were loading a gun.

Bryan took a gulp from his glass. His uncle sounded like he was afraid he couldn't compete with a wolf. And this woman with the southern accent acted as if elk hunting was impressive as catching a chicken or kicking a mule. Bryan had been brought up to believe hunting was the only real way left to prove yourself. Prove what, though? Something he'd depended on and never questioned seemed to be collapsing right in front of him.

At her voice, Bryan glanced up and saw the woman smiling painfully at Calvin, excusing herself. Cal didn't seem to hear, although he was still speaking directly to her. Bryan watched her stand, pick up her hat and gloves, and head for the bathroom. She looked at him once, and smiled. Calvin turned forward, directing his oration at the bottles on the back bar.

"People like that," he said finally, "are going to cause our extinction, son. They don't even know what survival is." Cal looked at Bryan frankly. His anger was gone and he appeared sad, almost scared. Bryan nodded and looked away, embarrassed.

Out of sight of her recent barstool companions, Frances sat at a table near the jukebox, eating greasy fried chicken. The preening positions of a group of young men hoisting beer and talking in loud voices at the bar caused her to glance around for females. In fact, there were four young women playing pool. Their hair was all the same in different shades, the rural shoulder-length frizz that looked undecided, as though any time now style would descend and give purpose to their heads. Frances settled in to watch courtship display in Atlas as she churned over what it would be like to have it as her closest town, and the Antler Bar the center of social life. She was trying to see it as adventurous.

A lean man in jeans, plaid shirt, and red down vest was walking through the bar in her general direction. He was wearing a Con-Agra baseball cap and had the lined, ruddy face of someone who worked outdoors year round. He walked with an easy disinterest that set him apart from the once-a-year outdoorsmen crowding the bar in camouflage hunting gear.

He stopped in front of Frances, leaned his hands on the table and said, "Excuse me." She looked up. "I heard you're here to re-introduce the wolf."

Frances glanced around, perhaps he was trying to talk to someone at a table behind her. "You see," he said, looking right into her eyes, "I'm a rancher here and I have a stake in it."

Frances shook her head. "No, no. I have nothing to do with wolves." She swept a flat palm across the table. "Nothing." Then it occurred to her she was lying.

"You mind?" The rancher grabbed a wooden chair from the next table and sat down. He was younger than he'd appeared from a distance, probably late thirties, and he was plainly concerned. A ribbon of anger fluttered through Frances; some justice had been invaded. "Really," she said, wiping her mouth with a wad of paper napkin. "All I did was ask about that wolf skin on the wall."

He sat, waiting. "How'd you hear that, anyway," she asked.

The rancher smiled a little and pushed his cap back on his head. "I was in the bathroom. You know," he said. "This guy comes in all hot under the collar. He says to me. 'That goddamn, ah, woman out there is bringing back the wolf. We haven't had wolves around here for a hundred years and now she wants to ruin this whole country.'"

"Jesus," said Frances. Her face flamed. The Antler Bar took on a new life, as though all eyes and ears pointed at her. She was a participant and she didn't even know it. She looked around at the faces of the men standing and drinking, talking and gesturing. They were watching her, from corners of eyes. They were calculating the exchange between her and the rancher. A feeling of being powerful quarry crept over her. An unknown woman alone in the Antler Bar in Atlas was probably as odd and menacing as winter lightning.

She saw the wolf moving across the roll of land, an animal that belonged, like she did, in this country. The wolf held her with its eloquent eyes, telegraphing secret intelligence. Its face was clean and strong as a diamond, streaked white and black. Everything else dropped away. Frances felt again the cold, serene air against her face like a soothing hand. So, the character at the bar had known her connection with the wolf even before she did, had sniffed it out in that creepy way obsessive people sense things.

Frances started to laugh. Her back eased and the brittleness broke out of her. She had to close her eyes to stop laughing. The rancher smiled a little. She leaned forward. "What would you think," she asked, "If the wolf did come back?"

He raised his eyebrows and looked around. Then he hunched in and said, "I asked myself that when that guy told me you were bringing them in." He looked at his hands on the edge of the table as though they were ghost crabs. "You know, they'd lynch me in here," he said slowly, "but I thought it would be kind of nice to see wolves back in this country."

Frances smiled broadly. She looked around at the men watching her, and let herself settle on the rancher. His head was tilted wryly at his own disclosure. Frances studied him, the gentle frankness in his black-specked, olive eyes, watching her. They held her with a dark, steady flare of collaboration. She looked down at her plate of glistening chicken bones. "You know of a place to stay around here?" she asked. "I've got a couple of dogs."

Ruby's bones were cold, she could feel it in her wrists and arms, but she was sleepy. She thought about lying down and letting the snow build up a little shelter over her, like an elk would do, and wait for morning. It didn't seem so important to keep moving anymore, her sense of direction was totally dependent on the wind now, and she wasn't sure it hadn't shifted on her. Her wool hat and mittens had soaked and frozen stiff and her back felt like cold water.

She'd heard about people dying fifty feet from their own front doors in blizzards, and wondered if she would see her son and her husband if she died tonight. Or if her soul would just rise up, hover a bit, and disperse into separate atoms with no identity attached to them, no piece of her left. Then her body would lie there like ashes after a fire. Momentarily, she thought she saw something white drift past her, almost like her ghost already leaving.

The image gave her new resolve. She wouldn't let Winona say nasty things about her like she said about Frank after he was found in the river. This pain was her own pain. The numbness that had been inside her for a long time was burning away. She was afraid, but mingled with the fear was a tingling sensation, as though she were coming out of a long hibernation. Ruby clumped on, holding her post as if it were again the door to her house.

When she finally stopped and let the post drop, Ruby decided it was okay, better than a car accident. Breathing fast and shallow now, dizzy, she let herself sink on her knees. Anyway, lights might become visible if she stayed still. After a long silence, something tangible moved, passing very close to her. A shock of fear coursed through her numb body. It was an animal and it almost touched her. She stood and grabbed the post with both hands. The animal glided back and forth in front of her like a shark angling through black water.

Ruby decided to keep walking. It occurred to her that the animal might attack if it sensed she wasn't strong enough to keep moving. She held the post up like a bat. She couldn't smell or hear it, but the low silvery movement with the flickering, thick tail was the only thing she could see. Ruby wanted to keep it in front of her.

The wind let up some, and Ruby followed the animal as it methodically stitched a seam toward the small house where Willie Wolf Eyes rested in his big chair beside the woodstove, eyes closed.

What a Man Eats

(from the novel *Life and Letters*)

His brother's wedding was over, and more than anything else, Michael Zatulofsky wanted a cheeseburger. For all his hard-won refinement—he was not, as Sally was, to the manner born and made no bones about it—there were things he would not eat. His father called him a snob, a phony, but it was mostly real, Michael's refinement. His love for literature, for theater, for music, was deep and sustaining. His attention to matters of courtesy and kindness and form, his respect for tradition (nonfamilial) was, if somewhat belated, strong.

He was not quite the genuine article. He was purblind to the visual arts—painting, sculpture, photography—and got wobbly in museums. He had little patience with ballet—Sally, who danced, went regularly, polemically, by herself—hadn't a clue about the opera, and found Ingmar Bergman tedious and laughable. Several years ago he and Sally and some friends from the college drove to St. Paul to see Bergman's *Magic Flute*. Michael was well-rested, sociable, good-sporting, nearly keen, and dead asleep before the overture was done. He awoke once, near the end of the film, read the subtitle: "Let us hurl our bodies into the void," and went quickly back to sleep. Michael retained a proletarian fervor for pickup basketball and played intensely, often with pain, three times a week at noon. He could not bring himself to wear suits in any season; but most damningly, there were broad categories of stuff he omitted without exception from his daily diet.

Two of the seven basic food groups, for instance, he neglected. Shunned brussels sprouts. Broccoli. Eggplant. Spinach. Green leafy vegetables, raw or cooked. He would not eat these; had never, in fact, tasted them. Cauliflower. Okra. Avocado. Squash. Green and black olives, green and red pepper. Pickled cukes or capers. He rejected out of hand whole rubrics of food. No fish at all, fresh or salt water. No lobsters, no crabs, no crayfish. Nothing that slithered or pinched. Nothing phlegmy. Nothing with antennae. He hated shellfish on sight. Like eating large, oceangoing insects, he thought. He was fussy at table. Skittish, careful, resolutely unadventuresome. In unfamiliar restaurants, especially in those on either coast, Michael did not order chicken salad for fear of getting crab. Without regret he skipped whole pages of the most elegant menus, and reflexively declined, whoever the chef, his specials. Three rooms off he could not stomach the smell of asparagus cooking on the stove. Beyond salt, he had no truck with spice, pedestrian or exotic. No basil, dill, cumin, tarragon, nutmeg, garlic, paprika, arrowroot, chive, coriander. He passed on condiments and garnishes, ate his hot dog without mustard, without relish, without kraut. He preferred his food unadorned and put his sprig in the nearest ashtray. He had no food-related interests or hobbies. He did not especially like to eat, and he did not garden or fish or cook or go to farmers' markets. He would not join a co-op and could not imagine eating soya meal or bulgur in any form. Michael was very nearly isolationist. He would not eat food from, or prepared in the manner of Mexico, India, Thailand, Norway, Louisiana, Vietnam. In Japanese restaurants, he had steak. In Chinese restaurants he ordered batter-dipped fried chicken and refused to share. No measure of national guilt could stir him to sample Hmong cuisine.

As a result of his heterodoxy he had spent childhood, adolescence, most of his adult life smiling in the face of evangelical table talk. His mother wheedled. "Take a bite. I'll put a little on your plate; you don't have to eat it. A bite. What's the matter? A taste. It's good. Close your eyes. See?" Sally, less concerned, was more genteel—"Would you like to try some of mine?"—and Jacob, whose tastes were catholic, was forthright: "Eat this mussel, Dad." Michael had perfected his demurral. "That's okay. Thanks. I'm sure it's delicious. You go ahead. I'm fine." He was grateful, polite, unyielding. Sally, who loved to cook, and who cooked imaginatively and well, found his range stultifying. He was, he knew, a vexing dinner guest, a nuisance, and fretted about it. Often he'd trail his hostess into her kitchen, where he'd apologize. Once, confronted with a tureen of shrimp creole preceded by a cream soup's worth of lobster bisque, he wept. Michael hated to offend, but there were things he would not eat.

Dietary law had, in his case, nothing to do with it. He didn't know trayf from truffle, and his parents mixed milk and flesh scandalously. His mother ate buckets of steamers and collected lobster bibs up and down the south shore of Long Island. As a boy he'd eaten rashers of bacon, tins of spam. He had trouble with dishes traditional and festive. He did not eat knaidlach, kreplach, kishke, gefilte fish, grebenes, or borscht. Bitter herbs all. Chopped liver made him jittery. He wanted his meat served up in recognizable, geometric forms. He wanted it circular or rectangular, and out in the open. He did not trust it to come pureed, pasted, bernaised. He liked meat—beef and veal and pork and poultry and lamb—and he liked it grilled. In its own juice, with some butter and sweet corn on the cob, and a well-cooked baked potato, and a lettuce and tomato salad—the lettuce and the tomato wedged—with an oil and vinegar dressing he could blend himself. He stopped gratefully at restaurants with *Angus* or *Steer* in their names, and was happiest, easiest in Minnesota roadhouses: small wood-framed places on flat county roads just outside of town, near grain elevators, salvage yards, and sod farms, with a short bar and a jukebox and a raised parquet dance floor nobody used; where the patrons wore baseball caps, there were plenty of high chairs and booster seats for the kids; the waitresses were the wives of farmers, had quick feet, strong hands, and knew their trade; and where they had hashbrowns and fruit cocktail and Sara Lee cheesecake, and nine kinds and cuts and sizes of steak—8 oz., 12 oz., 16 oz., New York strip, porterhouse, rib eye, T-bone, sirloin, top sirloin, London broil, filet mignon, and on Saturday night, prime ribs of beef au jus.

Michael liked Italian food, northern and Neapolitan, German food, most desserts, barbecue—pork and beef and baby back ribs—some nouvelle cuisine, and several things to confute those who'd chalk him up as pill. Beaten biscuits, for instance. He could eat, at one sitting and straight from the carton, a pint of sour cream. When he could get it, he drank Dr. Brown's Cel-Ray, and he loved tongue.

At Sally's request, and for the sake of the boys (Jacob was om-
niverous, lean and always hungry, and needed no example), he had
cautiously extended his repertoire. He ate grits ("If they could see
me now . . ." Michael thought) and had recently worked up a taste
for snow peas and fresh green beans. Although he liked stew, with
cubed meat and carrots and new potatoes, he did not eat soup: not
chowder or gumbo, not minestrone, not leek or lentil, not cream of
anything, not gazpacho, not even chicken noodle. He saw no point
to consommé. Michael, alone in the English department, paid no
coffee mess, and he had never in his life had whiskey or a beer. He
was, in the broadest sense of the word, abstemious. His tastes in
food and drink were not inherited, one deficiency for which he
could not blame his forebears. Nor were his tastes eclectic. They
were crotchety, stunted, pathologically narrow. And except for
a somewhat dubious physiological clue—a doctor in Nashville,
checking Michael's throat for yeast, gasped: "Dad-gummit. Look at
that tongue. Those are the biggest taste buds I've ever seen. Hyper-
trophied. It's a wonder, son, you can eat anything."—there was no
accounting for them.

It was nine o'clock, Saturday night on the Pacific. The wedding
had been over for two hours. From where he stood on the West
Coast, at his windows on the sixth floor of the Hotel Durant,
Michael could see and hear the crowds and the cars on Durant and
Telegraph. He could see the Pacific Film Archive, where tonight
they were screening a Russian documentary about a woman basketball player, and, behind it, the university's pale bell tower. In
another direction, bayward, he could see the tail of lights on the Bay
Bridge, and across the dark water—the night was clear—the lights
on the hills of San Francisco. Michael dismissed all the sourdough,
north-to-Alaska, Frisco flap. It was a city for children. A theme
park of a city, a magic kingdom (the venereal epidemic harrowing its
homosexuals was a slaughter of the innocents), and he wondered
how any serious work got done there. But it was invigorating and
fantastic—he preferred it hands down to Berkeley or, for that
matter, Boston, both weltering in undergraduates—and was determined, when the cable cars were running again, to bring the boys
out.

It was eleven o'clock in Minnesota. The house was empty, deep-
frozen, the pipes, he feared, fit to burst. It was midnight on the

Atlantic, balmy and breezy in Delray Beach where, he hoped, Sally
and the boys would be asleep. It was too late to call again. He missed
them, and he was concerned about Peter.

As soon as the wedding had ended, Michael came back to his
room to call Sally.

"I can't talk to you now," she said. It was ten o'clock, eastern
standard time. "I'm sorry. How was the wedding?"

"Fine," he said. "You were missed. What's wrong? Is there
anything wrong? The kids alright?"

"Peter's got croup. It's a mess here."

"What's croup?" Michael asked.

"He can't breathe," Sally said. "He can't get enough air."

"Is it serious?" he asked. "Is it dangerous?"

"Sure," Sally said.

"Where is he?"

"Right here. In my arms."

"Have you seen a doctor?"

"What doctor?" she said. "It's Saturday night."

"What about the emergency room?"

"I can handle it," Sally said. "Let me go."

"Gosh," Michael said. With "Golly," it was a locution he'd picked
up from Sally's father, the Very Reverend Walter Lines, who, as did
Michael, used it calculatedly, to express concern or wonder. In the
way Ruggles and Ives used folk song: to disclose a childlike sen-
sitivity and freshness of vision beneath a manifest wealth of sophistication.

"Will he be okay?" Michael asked. "Can I say something to him?
Will that help?"

"I don't think so," Sally said. "He needs to go to sleep. We all do.
We'll see you tomorrow. He'll be okay. Good-night."

After the call Michael felt disoriented. He was sad, cut off,
useless. He knew, and was consoled by the knowledge, that even
had he been there, across the continent, in the thick of croup with
Sally and Jacob and Peter, he would have been useless. Wherever
he was, it would be Sally handling things, in charge, delivering
primary care.

In time of illness and injury, emotional crisis or collapse, in tight
spots, Sally's wisdom and grace and sanity prevailed; and he was, at
best, subaltern. When things got dire or dicey, Sally was gentle and

compassionate, tough, capable. Michael tried to be, and to a degree succeeded at being, all these things, and, unlike Sally, he was funny and could occasionally defuse the tension. He was not a crier or a swooner. He had watched both his sons born. He'd caught Jacob on the way out; with Peter, the midwife asked him to cut the cord. Michael declined, as if he'd been offered eel—"That's okay. I'm fine," he said. "Why don't you do it?"—but he did not buckle. He could be hard and decisive; word among students was that Michael was growly. But about the boys and their well-being, he was squeamish, tentative; in situations requiring prompt and right action, he did Hamlet. Lord Jim. The lobster quadrille. He loved Jacob and Peter so much he was afraid of botching the job. Sally loved them more, he supposed, and she moved surely and stayed compellingly cool. Michael supported her, coveted the intimacy she had with the kids, kept out of her way. When Jacob, learning to eat spaghetti, sucked a strand down the wrong tube, Sally reached in and fished it out before he'd missed a breath. She bathed and bandaged wounds, tended smashed fingers and toes. She administered eyedrops with touch and precision. She swabbed ears, aspirated noses. She applied salve to desiccate umbilical knots and to the tips, tender and purple, of circumcised penises. She held the boys' heads, stroked their hair, while they vomited; Michael stood at the bathroom door and asked, "Is everything okay? Shall I make tea?" She toweled up their piss when they shot wide of the bowl. She caught in her lap, in bedclothes, sportswear, evening dress, every conceivable bodily fluid; and through all the bleeding and breaking and oozing and sneezing and puking and coughing, Sally was loving and calm. Michael did the dishes, paid the bills, went for medicine. If, an emergency seen to, Sally was peevish, Michael let her take it out on him.

Sally was no simple shepherdess. No suffering servant. In her, Michael had married no Grisilde, nut-brown and patient, no Tess, no unlettered, uncomplicated, intuitive tender of hearth, no submissive, grateful bed warmer. She was not by nature, or by breeding, an angel of the house. Certainly not the angel of a blockish, drafty, ill-convenienced, whitewashed house in a small southern-Minnesota town. When he met her—she was in Princeton for a fall weekend, staying at the Graduate College with a friend from Nashville—Sally was twenty-two and just finished Sweet Briar. Captain

of the field-hockey team. Phi Beta Kappa. A philosophy major with
distinction; she wrote a senior thesis, one hundred pages long, on
Tillich's *Systematic Theology*. She played violin and piano—for a
wedding gift the Lynes gave them a Steinway parlor grand, in the
family for a century, that had once been played by Rachmaninoff
after cocktails on a southern swing. She'd lived in Oxford, Paris,
New Haven, and breakfasted with the archbishop of Canterbury.
She spoke fluent French and was, upon reaching majority, independently wealthy. She'd ridden steeplechase and the hunt. She'd
refused to come out. She'd dropped acid. She was a competent
draftsman and, when he met her that fall weekend in Princeton,
she was on fire and way out of his league. Had she not agreed, for
whatever reason (he still couldn't tell you why), some two years
later to marry Michael Zatulofsky—that lucky, upwardly mobile,
duck—she might have danced professionally. She might have done
anything; she was too good to be true, and he often felt guilty having
married her.

Sally's subsequent swerve to domesticity, her decision to dedicate
heart and mind to family affairs, was unpredictable, radically un-
fashionable, and, in retrospect, inspired. It was an act of free
will—although he benefited from it, was, in fact, redeemed by it,
Michael had nothing to do with her choice, had long since quit
trying to influence her. Before Jacob was born, Sally was anxious
about the prospect of rearing boys. She'd grown up with three
sisters, all of them belles, with cut flowers, Cartier pearls, crème
caramel, Chippendale sideboards and secretaries. She said she
knew, or cared, nothing about men pre their pubescence.

"What do they do?" she asked him. "I mean how do they pass the
time?" He told her what he could remember of his own boyhood,
which, in the telling, took on a decidedly Dickensian cast. When he
got out of line, he told Sally, or when she was cranky, his mother
threw ashtrays at him—big brown ceramic bowls with stubby
handles, which, as he slipped them, splintered on the walls. Out of
ammo, she chased him with a broom.

"What do they talk about?" Sally asked. "What will I say to them
at dinner?"

She bought books on the subject, but found them programmatic
and trivial.

"Do I give them pulling chores?" she asked. "Do I hang salt licks on trees? Must they scratch themselves in public? Will they pick up the seat? Do I thump them if they sass me? What on earth do they wear?"

By the time she was carrying Peter, Jacob was four, distinctively hers, and she prayed for another boy. She told Michael she found the little girls Jacob played with prissy and timid and too self-conscious. "My God," she said. "Was I like that?" She admired Jacob for his spine, for the hardness of his body, for the way he kept falling out of trees. She was glad he wouldn't, and couldn't, color within the lines. She loved him because he never backed down. She was delighted to have produced a thing so markedly unfeminine and, at the same time, so unaffectedly sensitive and soft. Jacob worshipped her—as did every other kid on the street; between three and five on school days the house and the yard were filled with children—and he was ferocious in her defense, when she and Michael argued. Michael taught the boys to play ball—by the time he was six Jacob could hit right- and left-handed, run a down-and-out, dribble behind his back—and gave them nicknames. He taught them to swagger, to tease, to whistle (Jacob could whistle all of "Sweet Georgia Brown"), to walk with their hands in their pockets. That they were fine boys, Jacob and Peter, exceptionally fine in body and mind, mien and spirit, there was no mistaking. Michael was a good father and he was proud, but he knew they were principally Sally's doing. With her around they'd assuredly survive croup, and they'd very likely survive whatever it was that ran riot and foul in their Zatulofsky blood. Michael watched Sally with her boys—teaching them to cook, to dance, giving them manners, bearing, soul. He watched her giving them their lives— she was, for them, a mediatrix of grace—and he envied his sons their mother.

The wedding had been over for two hours. It was nine o'clock in California, where there was no time to speak of, and Neal and his new bride, Maia, were driving north in Neal's old Datsun for a week on the Russian River. Michael's father was paying for the trip.

" 'Pick an island' I said to Neal and the girl," Michael's father told him as they left the reception. "I said to Neal, 'Don't be a schmuck, go to Aruba. It's warm there. They've got trees that grow on one side only.' " Michael's parents had been, the previous spring, on a cruise to the Netherland Antilles. "What do they want with

Russian River?" his father said. He smiled. He would tell a joke. "I
say to them, 'island,' and you know what they think? Out here?
They think Tahiti. They're upside down. Pogo Pogo. 'You like
Hawaii?' I said to them. 'Go to Hawaii.'"

For a wedding present Michael and Sally gave them just what
they'd asked for: a painting by a Japanese artist, a friend of Neal's in
Berkeley. Michael had no special feeling for the piece—it was
abstract, which to his mind meant merely ornamental, and murky.
He liked it no more, though no less, after Neal told him the artist
had done it by covering herself with paint and pressing up against
the canvas.

Michael wished them Godspeed, and in his hotel room he thought
about marriage. Their marriage, his own, his parents', marriage
more generally. Like his own death, it was not a subject he could
look at long without blinking. The birth of a baby with all its
equipment, whatever it looked like—Jacob and Peter looked like
pattypan squash—was cause for rejoicing, with all the stops out.
But a wedding was not a thing he took gaily. Each summer he was
invited to four or five, former students partnering up in Fargo,
Rapid City, Cedar Rapids, Racine, Duluth, all over the Great
Plains. These invitations were largely matters of form, and he'd go
only as far as Minneapolis to attend. He sent the rest of them woks.
A wedding, for Michael, especially involving one or more persons he
cared about, was occasion for serious reflection; although serious
and protracted reflection had brought him no new insight. He
wished Neal and Maia luck. He was no philosopher. Had Neal
asked his advice, Michael, irrespective of the bride in question,
might have counseled delay, indefinite postponement. The burden
of proof, he might have posited, lay heavy on the connubial side.
When in doubt, balk, leave waiting at the altar, hop on the bus,
Gus, annul. Under the best of circumstances—trust funds, good
health (Michael's father said, "Before you marry the girl, look at the
teeth. Then at the mother."), gratifying work, fresh and imaginative
sex—they'd need luck and more. Watching Neal's and Maia's wedding Michael was relieved to be married to Sally. She had, as it were,
perfect teeth, and he had enjoyed the best of circumstances. Yet it
had been, being married, even to Sally, woefully, searingly hard.
Those people who cried at weddings had the right idea. No matter

how you structured it, how you opened it up or held it close, marriage was, too much of the time, lower bolgia stuff. Paolo and Francesca. You drink my blood, I eat your skin, til death do us part. All this the world knows well, Michael thought. In every way Sally was more than he deserved; and even Sally, in twelve years of contiguity and routine, had frequently become insufferable. They had knocked it down, dragged it out, over every sort of problem— short-lived and chronic, trivial and grave. There were times, in a good year three or four, when neither he nor Sally wanted to continue. Tonight, in the pacific afterglow of Neal's wedding, Michael was glad, for his own sake, for the children's sake, they'd gone on, but he wasn't sure how, or why, they had. He loved Sally— not the way he loved the boys, of course; it was love more contingent, more complex. She apparently loved him; but he knew that for Sally there had been moments in their marriage, black holes, when no earthly reason could have kept her at it. He could not imagine how other people stayed married. What arrangements did they make? How baroque? How dear? And how had his parents, of all people, survived forty years of hip to haunch?

Michael hadn't a clue. About any of it. He would have, by way of advice worth hearing, nothing to give. Except, maybe, this (Sally was the metaphysician; Michael's vade mecum, like Polonius's, was rooted in the small): Avoid terms of endearment, pet names, unless they are ironic. Never straight-facedly say "Honey" or "Sweetie" to anyone you live with. Go to the early show and eat dinner afterward. Don't have too many children. Cultivate physical modesty. Smash the TV. Don't collaborate on household budgets. Use neutral tones and fabric with some body to it; stay away from venetian blinds. Don't dress alike. Don't share a sink. Go to bed when you're tired. And, above all, be no seeker of truth in marriage; leave all stones unturned; steer clear of family therapists. Especially those practitioners who see the truth as instrumental in sustaining or saving a marriage. Those who, for a fee, elicit a "Just this or that in you disgusts me" kind of candor from man and wife. Certain mechanisms—carburetors, doorknobs, cribs, bridles, marriages— once lay out all the parts for inspection, can never—not all the king's horses—be brought together again. What God has joined. Certain things, say them once—viva voce, *mano a mano,* in the service of truth or vengeance, impulsively or measured, in public and recorded on audio cassette or legal pad—can never be gainsaid. Or forgotten. Or forgiven.

This Michael knew to be true. He had watched the marriages of too many friends disintegrate, the works come unsprung, in the well-meaning, truth-trading hands of the family counselor. Like all marriages, these were delicate, but, so far as Michael could see, they were good or, at the very least, serviceable marriages, until the lamp affixed its beam and all the confessional chitchat began. Looked at head-on, the light could be blinding. There were things—her physical imperfections; unappealing patterns in her behavior, gesture, speech; his dreams, delusions, nasty habits— Michael would not talk about with Sally. Or with anyone else. To think them was one thing; to let them loose, giving them voice, substance—"The hair underneath your chin is appalling."—was another. He was sure there were things Sally did not tell him (though, admittedly, he sat less easy with this). A good marriage, their marriage anyway, depended, in the face of disappointment, disillusion, or vexation, on some holding back, some keeping mum. There were simply certain truths you could not tell and hope to continue. It was less a matter of a mute and stoic willingness to endure, far more a matter of courtesy and taste. These couples would have fared better, he thought, if instead of going for their weekly dose of slash and burn—"How does it make you feel, Marge, when John says he hates your thumbs?"—they had read late-James, together, aloud. A good marriage depended on a sufficient spread of uncommon ground, on areas of thought and feeling and experience not shared, on privacy and a private life. Michael did not advocate or practice downright deceit, baldface lying; he just withheld evidence, was less than forthcoming—the distinction was nice but crucial—in cases that might have caused Sally needless, peripheral pain. Infidelity was another business altogether. There was no withholding it—he, at least, had not been able to contain it. It was shattering, scarring, better not messed with.

Still, he admired women—girlish, tight-legged, small-breasted, long-fingered, fresh, sure women—and he reserved, jealously guarded, some solitary space and time in which to think on them. He did not tell Sally about the women—strictly speaking, about the parts of women: mouths, hair, hands—he fell in love with almost daily and everywhere he went. When he got to Florida he would not tell Sally about the blonde in the blue dress at Neal's wedding. Or how, between 7:15 and 9:00 that night, after calling Florida—there was nothing more he could do for Peter—he'd left the Hotel Durant, and, as he'd thought about doing for hours, walked up and down Telegraph Avenue trying for another look at her. He tailed several women who, from behind, might have been her. He followed one of them into the netherworld of a lesbian coffee shop. He ran into, and quickly dispatched, a timid blonde who, some time ago, had been his student and was now a librarian in Berkeley. Given his behavior in similar situations, it was unlikely, had he found *the* blonde, that Michael would have spoken to her. Nor would he have kicked himself for refusing the jump. He was only vaguely interested in, and virtually incapable of, maneuvering her to bed, and even less interested in deepening their acquaintance. What he wanted was to see her again, to get a clearer, more extended, less complicated look at her. He wanted to confirm or, if need be, to revise his initial impression. He wanted to watch her move when she was herself, at ease, composed. He wanted to see enough of her so that he could hold her in his mind. So that he might think about her later, on some severe February night in Minnesota, say, when Sally and the boys had gone to sleep and he sat downstairs, a book, half read, in his lap. Not to draw invidious comparisons. Sally was beautiful, and his imagination big enough for all the beautiful women in it. He would think of her the way you might curl your hands around a mug of hot tea and press it to your cheek. A beautiful woman recollected in tranquillity. For him the most estimable form of visual art.

He did not see her and didn't really expect to. His walk, fraught with that off chance, was none the less inspiriting. The night was clear and cool. The bay breeze was soft. Michael was pleasantly hungry; he felt trim and vital. He liked being out at night on the streets of a city. Even Berkeley. Blonde or no blonde, in spite of some disturbing thoughts—Peter's croup, for instance—the walk was delightful. Because in Berkeley—he wouldn't have lived there for anything—except for the cataloguing mouse who knew him, he was anonymous. And exotic. On his person, for instance, he had nothing inflatable, nothing waterproof or organically grown. He had with him no toxic or controlled substance. He had no decorative scars or tattoos, no rivets in his ears or nose. He was not wired for sound. He carried no backpack, no tote bag, and except for pen, wallet, spare change, and hotel key, no paraphernalia of any kind. He had nothing to sell or toss or kick. He proceeded on foot, in a relatively straight line, without moving his lips. He wore no jewelry, no bandana, no artificial hair, no rope. He did not watch himself in store windows. None of what he wore had come in the mail. Nothing he had on sparkled, jangled, whistled, or bounced. He wore what he wore most of the time: chinos ("Get another pair of pants, Dad," said Jacob.), button-down pinpoint Oxford, knit tie, leather belt, black socks, rubber-soled brogues with leather uppers. He was, in Berkeley, outlandish. He imagined young women on Telegraph Avenue, particularly those who'd lived nowhere else, thinking as he passed. "Check it out. This guy must be from Switzerland."

In California it was nine o'clock. Neal and Maia, newly wed, were heading north, and Michael was in his room at the Durant, back from his walk. It had been an escapade, and he was hungry. His father was right. The food at the reception—though colorful, undoubtedly healthy, and not birdseed exactly—was insubstantial. He'd walked briskly, expectantly, for nearly two hours, and now he was starving. He had a lot on his mind. Peter. The blonde. But more than anything else, he wanted french fries and a cheeseburger. He lived, in this instance, under no delusion. What a man eats when he is on the road, away from family and friends, disassociated and possessed of virtually free choice, when there is no reason to eat anything but precisely what he wants to eat, what he answers, asked "What'll you have?" defines him. He wanted his french fries crisp and his cheeseburger medium rare. California style. Run through the garden. No pickle.

My Southern Gothic Story Called "The Honeymooners"

"You sure took your sweet time coming to fetch me," complained Carla Sue. She had been kidnapped from the Greyhound bus station some fifty miles earlier by Tyson and his mother, and she was still letting Tyson know that, in *her* estimation, two weeks was too long of a time to let a wife be estranged. Carla Sue sat in the bucket seat beside Tyson, the little puppy in her lap giving off a dreamy whimper now and then, which she hushed with quick rubs of her hands. Carla Sue wore a gold chain necklace to accentuate her freckles; and her hair had just been permed; and she was eating a Snickers bar washed down with gulps of Dr. Tichner's that the old woman—now in the back seat—had abandoned. Tyson's mother had her own Dr. Tichner's, but was mad at being made to sit back there alone. She complained every other mile that there was too much wind on her and that the puppy stank and agitated her allergies. Tyson suspected his mother was angry too that she had lost control of the kidnapping. Tyson considered his mother more than a little crazy, but he saw himself as rather enlightened; and proof of his enlightenment was his ability to tolerate his mother's abnormal psychology. Many times, when he tried to envision the world the old woman held between her eyes, he envisioned a primitive state of mind where superstition and scientific fact co-existed hand in hand like a string of paper dolls. His wife wanted the finer things in life for them both, and was very practical, and did not ponder too deeply beneath the surface of things. Tyson had married her three months earlier for love and for what she would make of him. He saw himself as something to be shaped, to be handled, to be handed instructions which he would then dutifully carry out. Even the kidnapping was his mother's—not Tyson's—idea, dreamed up one Arkansas afternoon over chicken with white gravy. His mother had been drinking her Dr. Tichner's and belittling Tyson for Carla Sue's estrangement. The old woman rattled a magazine article in front of Tyson's nose for him to read. She smelled of baby powder and alcohol and Kent cigarettes. She wore a tennis visor Tyson had given her as a joke but which the old woman liked and wore so much that it seemed to have become a part of her head.

"See here, Tyson." She jabbed at the print with a stubby finger caked with gravy. She breathed over Tyson's shoulder as he read. "See here. We'll do it like that father-son pair in Wyoming, except with us it will be mother-son, and it'll work." Then she had thrust at her son Carla Sue's good-bye note: ARKANSAS IS A SUCK ASS STATE AND YOU ARE A LOUSY PROVIDER AND LOVER. Tyson regretted ever having shown his mother the note. In a fit of extreme melancholy, he had sold his and Carla Sue's double-wide trailer, quit his job as a convenience-store clerk, and showed up at his mother's doorstep with the note in hand. Tyson opinioned, though he made no outright accusations, that his mother was very much to blame for his wife's leaving. Ever since his father had died, his mother had found new and inventive ways to make Tyson's life miserable. Just a week after the newlyweds had returned from their West Memphis honeymoon, the old woman had left her perfectly liveable but somewhat broken-down house to move in with the freshly married couple.

"It's either that old bag or me," his bride had threatened one night in bed after they had made love. It was their second month of marriage.

"You two hold it down in there!" the old woman had yelled from the adjoining bedroom.

Tyson had struck what seemed an amiable compromise; he worked evenings for a solid month repairing his mother's abandoned house. He did such a fine job that Carla Sue suggested the old woman keep the trailer that they might move into the more roomy house. The old woman held the lease and would hear none of it.

Carla Sue moved the puppy to the floorboard, hiked her legs apart so that the air blowing through the vent would cool her thighs. The window was rolled fully down, and when the wind in gusts mussed her hair she smoothed curly strands with quick little pats of her hands. She still smelled of the beauty shop's mystery. She had gotten a rush appointment just that morning, when Tyson's mother had called with a not-so-successfully-disguised voice to congratulate Carla Sue for winning the Disney Land Trip Sweepstakes. The old woman stipulated that Carla Sue must show up at the Hickory, North Carolina, Greyhound terminal by noon or forfeit the tickets. Carla Sue had a weakness for sweepstakes; she would even crumple each of her multiple entries so they would have a feel different from the thousands of others in the drawing barrel.

"What if she hasn't entered any sweepstakes?" Tyson had protested.

"You can bet your ass she's entered about a hundred since she estranged herself to her people in North Carolina." His mother was right. What neither Tyson nor his mother had expected was that Carla Sue had been *counting* on them to come get her. She had shown up at the station with her bag packed and a smart, new hairdo. In her other hand she carried her traveling bonnet and a sack. Inside were a jar of pickled tomatoes and the smelly, just weaned puppy. Carla Sue's aunt took great pride in her pickling abilities; a visitor never left her house without a jar of pickled something. Tyson's mother was very partial to such briny delicacies, and she fell quickly to eating them, stopping between bites to complain about the puppy. The first real argument had started over the animal.

"I ain't riding to Arkansas with that thing," Tyson's mother had said. Then she suggested just leaving it or at least putting it in the trunk. Carla Sue threatened she wouldn't let them kidnap her if they so much as touched the puppy. The old woman said she would bind and gag Carla Sue if she had a mind to; after all, she was being *kidnapped.* Tyson saw the moment as one wherein he should take control, and he did so by rocketing from the bus station with a peel of his tires. For nearly fifty miles the road had been treacherous and uphill and winding. They were rising over the Smokey Mountains. And for most of the fifty miles, Carla Sue had been explaining what an awful time she had had being estranged.

"They had me sleeping in the same bed with three little towheads. The house smelled like vinegar. The TV didn't have the cable channels, and they let the kids run wild, half-naked and beating on the doors with pots and pans. You would think they would treat company—especially kin with serious marital problems—special." She said they had made her cook, too, and the old woman observed it was a wonder there were any survivors. Tyson reminded his mother that Carla Sue had won a blue ribbon once for her biscuits. The old woman chimed up from the back seat that the judges had mixed things up, that they had been drunk and thought they were giving her a livestock ribbon. Carla Sue promised to pour out all of the old woman's Dr. Tichner's. The old woman reached up to get the front-seat bottle. Carla Sue mistook her actions; she thought Tyson's mother was trying to get at the dog and give it a fling. They grappled and Tyson yelled for them both to shut up, but they ignored him and so he pulled the car over. They were sitting at a scenic roadside stopping place, high on a mountain ridge that overlooked, in the distance, a waterfall and a valley. The air tasted thinner, and the sight below them of farms with neat wood fences was one to be imprinted on postcards. Tyson felt dizzy from the altitude and the arguing. He honked his horn for their attention.

"I'll drive right over the mountainside if you two don't shut up." Carla Sue squealed girlishly while the old woman dared him.

"Would you just look at that view!" said Carla Sue. Tyson's mother complained she couldn't see well from where she sat.

His mother read aloud a billboard that said VISIT VIRGINIA, LAND OF THE PRESIDENTS! She said she had never been there and confessed a weakness for seeing Ole Virginny. Tyson knew something was up. Carla Sue said that part of hers and Tyson's problems was that they had never been properly honeymooned. Tyson reminded her they had stayed in West Memphis, and Carla Sue started crying, saying that the Ramada Inn thirty miles from home was not her idea of a honeymoon. She cried in short, sharp bursts that sounded like hiccups. She said it was a crime to be on the road and to not go anywhere. The old woman leaned forward and began jabbing Tyson on the shoulder. She let Tyson know that, in her time, people had had proper honeymoons, and that his own father, God Rest His Soul, had properly honeymooned his wife at the eloquent Peabody Hotel in fashionable downtown Memphis. She claimed the mezzanine was made of Italian marble and that every morning at six sharp WHOOSH! opened the elevator doors and out came a procession of mallards not of a group but Indian fashion. A tiny, red carpet ran from the elevator doors to the duck fountain. The ducks were followed by a bellhop in a monkey suit who chirped duck instructions while the self-playing piano played a rousing march. The old woman said Tyson's dear, dead father had been so taken by his bride gazing at the ducks that he had offered to buy a brace right there on the spot. She told the story as a testimony of their love and her now-gone beauty; had not her husband been so bedazzled by his bride and his feelings at that moment that he wanted to purchase for her a rare token of his adoration? Tyson hated it when his mother talked like this, and as far as the ducks went, he thought it said more about his dead father's taste for game fowl than anything else.

"You forgot to tell Carla Sue how he wanted to cook the ducks up in sweet sauce."

"That made it all the more special." The old woman pretended Tyson hadn't made a mockery of her memory. She said it was a shame the Peabody was not the crown jewel of Memphis any more, but that with the world the way it was, what could you expect? The president couldn't handle the country any more than Tyson could manage a wife, and besides, with crippling arthritis which caused her to need her medicine, and at seventy, she had gotten used to a world without Justice and one wherein two people couldn't keep a simple thing like love working.

"If you really loved me," said Carla Sue, touchy that she had never stayed in the Peabody Hotel, "you wouldn't just kidnap me, you'd take me someplace special."

"In *my* time," said the old woman, "a honeymoon was a serious occasion, and marriage was not taken so lightly." She was leaning in the space between the bucket seats, her tennis visor's bill pulled low and her sunshades clipped to her glasses, looking like a criminal. She said *her* husband would have never let his wife become estranged. Carla Sue corrected the old woman; she had estranged herself, and it just went to show you how weak the old woman was to have never even once left her husband. The old woman said to leave Tyson's father out of it; he had been a kind and good man every day of his life and had even fought in the Pacific theater of World War II. Carla Sue said Tyson would have fought too had there been a war in his times. The old woman said Tyson's and Carla Sue's real

problem were that he had never been tested on the battlefield and
she had never known the dread of waiting for the evening mail each
lonely afternoon. She said they had both never been caught up in
the conflicts of the time. A tear came from behind the old woman's
sunshades and worked its way down the powdered little hairs on her
cheeks. She took a pull of Dr. Tichner's for solace and pointed out
that in earlier times men fought for such things as peace and a
woman's honor. She claimed much of the world's sorriness boiled
down to people like Carla Sue and Tyson not establishing a solid
foundation. She made it very clear she considered them both children attempting to play at life's seriousness.

"Moments like my husband wanting to buy them ducks and cook
them up are bygone notions."

Carla Sue remarked she had no use for ducks or the Peabody
Hotel or Memphis for that matter.

The old woman pointed out that everyone knew the Delta was
the heart of Dixie and that it started at the doors of the Peabody and
ran to the Mississippi's mouth. Carla Sue said Dixie, Smixie; she
would *have* a proper honeymoon and it would be a sojourn in
Virginia. The old woman agreed because she wanted another adventure. She quoted a bumper sticker she had once seen that read:
VIRGINIA IS FOR LOVERS. Then the two women joined forces and
chorused Tyson was being selfish. The old woman claimed Virginny
the Mother of the South and said it was an ungrateful son who
would not pay homage. She would expect such irreverence from a
tenderfoot who had never fought for his country. She lied that
Tyson's father had promised to take her to Virginia, but he had died
before he could keep his promise. She suspected he was groaning
and gnashing in his grave, for it was a son's duty to keep his father's
pledges. Tyson said he felt no obligation whatsoever. His mother
said that proved her point—such ideas as beauty and responsibility
to your own blood kin were bygone notions. Carla Sue reached over
and nibbled at his ear and asked could they rent a bridal suite? She
gave his thigh a jostle and sprinkled his cheeks with little kisses.

He pulled back onto the highway and followed directions while
the two women bickered. The old woman scoured the map and
rerouted their journey. Tyson's mother wanted to visit the old places
while Carla Sue preferred spots like Busch Gardens or the Amazing
Rock City. They descended down a gap in the mountains. They

passed a barn with sides on which slogans had been lettered. VISIT
NATURAL BRIDGE, ONE OF THE SEVEN WONDERS OF THE WORLD was
alongside JESUS SAVES and AMERICA, PREPARE TO MEET THEY GOD!
The barn was on a hill in a meadow whose far fringes gave way to an
immeasurable, ancient forest. The air smelled of things in mysterious bloom, heavy with summer. The forest seemed at odds with
and winning against the patches of green cultivated land. Tyson
could not see very far into the forest, and its darkness scared him.
Tyson suspected the trees had been there since long before he was
born, that they would outlast him; and this thought gave him a
heaviness he could neither name nor contain. It occurred to Tyson
that many other travelers, some of them even honeymooners, had
worked their way North or South through this same mountain gap.
In the backseat the old woman worked a crossword puzzle whose
theme she announced as American History. Now and then she
chirped out a clue and an answer. She licked at the pencil's lead in
between thoughtful intervals. Carla Sue sat scribbling something
on the candy wrapper. She pushed it at Tyson.

THAT OLD BAG IS GETTING ON MY NERVES.

"What's that address of Lincoln's about the house divided?"

"Second Inaugural Address." Carla Sue had been president of
the high school history club.

"Too many letters."

"Then just try Lincoln's address or second address."

"Tyson, honey," said Carla Sue. "Let's pull in up yonder for some
coffee."

The old woman complained that coffee was bad for her blood
pressure. "Besides, it's a shame to stop when we're making such
damned good time."

"It's *my* honeymoon and I want some coffee."

"Don't get so uppity," the old woman warned. "You're being
kidnapped and you got no say-so in the matter. Besides, real honeymooners have just gotten married and their car is all decked out."
The old woman made a haughty noise through her nose.

"If it were a real honeymoon, we wouldn't be carting your flea-
bitten carcass around," was Carla Sue's reply.

"Don't let this kidnap stuff go to your head," warned Carla Sue.
She inserted another dollar's worth of quarters into the vibra bed's

slot. "You better get a few things straight. Number one—I'm not going back to that tin can trailer. Number two—we're going to find someplace better for you to do besides convenience-store clerking. And number three—you *did not* kidnap me; I came because I was fed up with being estranged." When she was not explaining things to Tyson, or complaining, or dropping quarters into the vibra bed slot, she was bothering the TV's remote control. The constant flashes of channels combined with the bed's motorized motion to make Tyson queasy. They were lodging at the Famous Rock City Motor Lodge and Continental Restaurant. Rock City was a haven of minerals and geological formations, and everything that could be so fashioned was made of cemented stone. The bedroom's bathroom was tiled with chunks of obsidian. They had just made love rather successfully in Tyson's opinion, and while he had pulled his pants on again, Carla Sue was still naked and reclining. She looked like something rare and beautiful cast up by the ocean.

"It would suit you and that old bag just fine to keep me under lock and key like some family heirloom, but it won't happen."

Tyson told her he had quit his job clerking.

"Great. Just what I need—an unemployed husband."

Tyson lied and said he was thinking about night school.

"Uncle Hersh makes a good living at taxidermy, and he learned it correspondence." She said you could get any number of good degrees by mail. "Then there's Raymond, my old beau from my summers in North Carolina, and I heard tell while I was back that *he* makes baskets of money selling satellite dishes to folks stuck out in the country with poor reception." She eyed Tyson and pushed back her new perm. Never had he known a woman so particular about her hair, even in bed. Carla Sue said it was a marvel of modern technology, putting those little satellite things up in outer space like little stars. Tyson said he thought real-estate night school was a more solid bet, but Carla Sue scoffed at the idea. "I sure would admire a man who sold little pieces of stars. It gets me right here," and she touched at the fleshy crease between her breasts.

His mother in the adjoining room knocked on the door and said she was hungry. Carla Sue yelled back they were talking serious honeymoon business, for her to drink some Dr. Tichner's and call up room service. The idea of being served must have pleased the old woman, for the knocking stopped.

"Would you just look at that!" Carla Sue had found the Playboy channel. Two women were entangled with a man. They seemed to all be wrestling. The perky Muzak was punctuated with quick gasps and drawn-out moans. Carla Sue observed it was probably as fake as wrestling, but Tyson wondered how three people could get so close and entangled without it being real. Carla Sue was lost in the channel a while; what had happened to the innocent girl he had married? He thought for a minute that he might have made a mistake getting her back, but then, no, he started remembering her as the girl in high school who had won *both* Sweetest Disposition and Most Practical. The first time he had kissed her she had blushed and gasped. On their wedding night he had imagined her as an angel, something not of this world which he should strive toward and admire. That first week she had covered her mouth whenever she laughed. Once, the day before she had estranged herself, he had asked her what inside her was changing. He explained to her that he didn't know if he liked the way she was becoming.

"You should've married a kewpie doll or a poster if that's what you wanted."

"But I married you, honey," was his reply.

"I aim to shake things up a little. I don't plan to spend my afternoons making pillowcases." She said she had bided her time for some eighteen years, and if they pooled their resources, the sky was the limit.

"Two women and one man," Carla Sue complained. "I could think up a better fantasy."

Tyson left the bed and sat at the pressed-wood dresser-desk. Someone had stolen the Bible or else the Gideons had neglected to put it on there. Carla Sue had insisted on the bridal suite, and their room had CONGRATULATIONS! on a faded banner across the wall. The wallpaper was of cupids that looked like fat babies with clipped wings and toy bows and arrows. The bed had a canopy with a few shreds of old crepe paper left over from a former celebration. The desk clerk had even sent over to the Magic Mart for a bottle of pink champagne. It was cooling now in a styrofoam bucket of ice.

"We're honeymooners fresh from Arkansas!" Carla Sue had announced upon checking in. The old woman had stated flatly that if they were real honeymooners she was the man in the moon. She had drunk two bottles of Dr. Tichner's and walked in a tipped-forward fashion. When she tried to stand still she swayed as if a strong breeze was pushing against her. Carla Sue rolled her eyes at the desk clerk and touched her forehead to indicate the old woman's insanity. "Dementia praecox," she had said; she had read of it in a mystery book somewhere. Tyson, worried that his mother might fall, helped her into a chair.

"Isn't it a shame when they get like that?" Carla Sue had whispered. The clerk nodded his head.

"She has no one on earth but us, and we just *couldn't* leave her behind. Why just last week, she tried to kindle a fire in a gas oven!"

The clerk had bleary eyes that seemed to have seen most everything. "Ma'am, we all seem to lose a little on the road of life."

This struck Carla Sue as particularly witty. She repeated what he had said. She exclaimed he was right, right as rain.

The clerk confessed that his own momma had thought she could fly before the swine flu epidemic got her. He said his wife died two years ago—a slow and painful death of cancer. He said when it came his time he wanted it fast, like his daddy. His daddy had been killed like that—he snapped his fingers—by a bolt of lightning while plowing a field just before a thunderstorm. That he had sold the farm and bought this piece of property in Rock City because he liked the idea of giving safe lodging to travelers and of living in a city made of solid stone. That it did a motel owner's heart good to see a couple such as them starting out on life's winding road. "And you all taking your mother along—that's what's special."

The old woman was banging on the adjoining door now, demanding to be let inside. Carla Sue got up and let her in. The old woman went straight for the champagne, but had trouble uncorking the bottle. She kept saying, "What's this, now. What's this, chicken wire?" Carla Sue walked over and unfastened the wire catch and unstoppered the bottle. It made a festive pop, and then she poured Tyson's mother a full glass. The old woman didn't seem to notice or care that Carla Sue was standing before her naked. She drank the glass quickly and stared at the TV while Carla Sue poured her another. She watched the naked bodies on the screen curiously, like an old family album peopled with faces she could remember but not yet place. She sat in the chair and finished her champagne. Her head dropped and she began snoring. She was lost in a country of dreams where beauty did not fade and well-dressed gentlemen paid her the continual respect of a bridegroom on a honeymoon. She dreamed of a garden noisy with fountains where they were all three splashing, but as children. She giggled girlishly, for in her dreams the three of them as children playing seemed to contain everything that ever would and would not happen. She felt herself on the threshold of an unfathomable mystery, about to be carried inside. She had the sensation of falling before hearing the voices which would pull her toward consciousness.

"Poor Momma," said Tyson to Carla Sue. "She looks as innocent as a babe when she sleeps like that."

"Poor momma my foot," said Carla Sue. "She's as mean as a snake and as bossy as a preacher's wife to boot."

The old woman eased open her eyes like someone returned from the dead. She took in Carla Sue with a face that appraised. She gave a high-pitched cackle. "*You,*" she said to Carla Sue. "You're buck-naked." She told Tyson he should pity himself, not her. She carried the bottle of champagne by its neck as she picked her way toward the door.

"You think you're so damned special. I got news for you both, you ain't."

Tyson paid their admission fee at a little cabin that had once been a slave quarters but was now renovated into a tourist information center. Carla Sue chewed some Dentyne behind him while the old woman snuck to the ladies room for fortification. A short, fat woman with quick hands passed him his change through a moon cut in the protective glass. While the bus that would take them up the hill to Monticello idled and awaited more passengers, a slender woman in a suit much like a stewardess's but without the cap welcomed them and asked that they refrain from smoking. She said once inside the mansion they could ask all the questions they wanted but to please refrain from touching the Jeffersonian arti- facts. Carla Sue and Tyson sat near the front of the bus. Carla Sue began chattering to a group of old people about how important it was to recapture your heritage. She told them she and Tyson were newlyweds taking a breather before beginning life's journey. She quoted the desk clerk's line about losing bits and pieces along the way. The group she talked to nodded in agreement to most anything she said. Two of the women wore what were noticeably wigs; the men had bald patches not on the tops of their heads but on the sides. Tyson estimated they were either chemotherapy patients or mental patients. They had the coherence of a group led out on an expedition. One man kept looking at his watch and feeling at his pocket for either a cigarette or pen that just wasn't there. Tyson's mother got on the bus and ignored her son and daughter-in-law. She worked her way to the rear so that she could sneak her Dr. Tichner's into a cup when she needed. She had been adamant that they visit Jefferson's homeplace, and as it was on the way to Busch Gardens, Carla Sue had conceded. The whole of the journey to Charlottesville the old woman had recounted what she knew of the Declaration of Independence and the causes of the American Revolution. She said wasn't it a wonder that the founding father's dream had so blossomed and prospered. Carla Sue had interrupted now and then to point out likely spots for satellite dishes. She said that as soon as they got back to Arkansas, Tyson could look into what it would take to get the satellite-dish ball rolling.

"Tyson and I aim to make a few changes. That trailer for instance. I reason it's just the right size for a widowed old lady."

"Over my dead body."

"The way you go at those Kents and that Dr. Tichner's, it won't be too long."

"Besides, your husband's done sold the trailer."

Tyson prepared himself for Carla Sue's wrath. Instead, she had commended him.

"It's the smartest thing you ever did. You'll need the capital to start your satellite dish business." She turned to the old woman. "I hear tell old age homes ain't so bad."

Carla Sue was talking now of how humble a place like Monticello made you feel. Most everyone on the bus was smiling blandly and listening. "It gives you a sense of. . . ." and she said she just didn't know the word.

"A sense of living on the backside of a nickel," Tyson's mother remarked from her backseat perch.

It occurred to Carla Sue that, as they had gotten on the bus separately, no one knew they were together except the silent woman behind the glass that took their money.

"I wonder who *she's* with?" Carla Sue confided to the sick-looking group across the aisle. "I bet she's escaped."

One woman leaned over and whispered something to another who said something to a third in the seat above her. The first woman gave a quick glance to the back of the bus.

"Do you think she's *dangerous?*" the woman asked. "Do you think we should report her to the *authorities?*"

"More likely she just aims to be a nuisance," said Carla Sue. "Old people get so jealous. And senile. Why, I wouldn't be a bit surprised if she claimed she knew us. When you get her age, you're liable to get most anything confused."

The old woman was talking to herself about staying in the Peabody. She was quite drunk and soon was babbling that it was a sorry world where the elderly were not respected. She said her own son had abandoned her for some hussy who wanted her locked away. Tyson burned with guilt but would not turn around. She said that as far as she was concerned, she didn't have a son and she never did.

"By the way," said Carla Sue. "We are Roberta and Humphry Mullberry."

Greetings were exchanged all around.

"Those two are phonies," hissed the old woman. The bus came to a stop at the top of the hill. Everyone arose and filed formally out the open doors. The tour guide said it was permissible to take outside photos of the mansion. One woman snapped a picture of Monticello while several others oohed and aahed over the commanding view of the countryside. Someone remarked that the spectacular view seemed patent-made for the mansion. Another lady said it was the house she had imagined all her life in her dreams.

"You dopes have it bass-ackwards," said Tyson's mother. Everyone pretended she did not exist. "The view was here first and *then* they stuck the fancy house on top of it." It seemed to her in her drunkenness that this was what history was all about—a dreamy house tacked onto a hillside that tried to make sense of something as jolting as a range of worn mountains. Again she had a revelation that they were all children, playing at things. She saw the mountains as covered mounds which hid the bones of the innocently slaughtered. It was as if the earth had opened up and showed her the skeleton of a terrible secret. She felt an urge to prophesy doom and destruction like a prophet of old. A man in a monkey suit nudged her. He asked was she all right, and had she bought a ticket?

"Jefferson was no saint," she said. "He kept slaves."

"It was a convention of the time," the attendant assured her. Then he urged she catch up with the group on the portico about to be ushered inside.

When Tyson and Carla Sue returned from viewing the mansion, a crowd stood gathered around Tyson's mother. Someone had propped her against an old oak. A little tag on the tree assured visitors that Jefferson had planted the oak himself. A stranger was fanning the old woman with his handkerchief. Someone else had gone in search of a spigot for water. The group of cancer patients moved as a unit to see what was the matter. Tyson stood with Carla Sue on the sweeping steps of Monticello, wondering if his mother was dead, and if so, what to do about it.

"Shit," said Carla Sue. "This is embarrassing. Leave it to your momma to pass out at Monticello."

"What if she's had a heart attack?"

"She's had two bottles of Dr. Tichner's this morning—that's what's the matter. And us on our honeymoon."

Tyson wondered if Carla Sue had said it so much that even she was beginning to believe it.

Someone said, "Make-way, make-way," and a cup of water was poured on the old woman. She sat up sputtering. She looked around her at the concerned faces as if not sure who she was or where she was. Someone asked the old woman her name and she didn't reply. "Think hard," said a man, but the old woman stared at him confusedly. One voice kept insisting the old woman looked like someone's mother or grandmother.

"You go get the car and leave this to me," said Carla Sue. Tyson started off at a run down the winding path to the parking lot. He stopped to catch his breath and looked back. The crowd had dispersed, and Carla Sue was standing over his mother. He could tell by the old woman's jerking arms and Carla Sue's working hands that the two were arguing. They were silhouetted by the house, and it seemed to Tyson, as he turned and began running, that they were arguing over what it might cost, or what it might be turned into. He got in his car and drove back up the hill as fast as he dared.

"You either see it my way, or we leave you," Carla Sue was saying. The old woman seemed still in a daze. She kept asking where her son was; had anyone seen him, and could they just please go home. A guard came up and asked was everything all right; they had called him on his walkie-talkie to say there was an incident at the gates. Carla Sue assured him it was nothing, that this poor woman here had a fainting spell and that, as a nurse, Carla Sue had everything under control. The guard got another call on his walkie-talkie saying some kids were smoking dope and necking in the woods. He told them all to stay put; he would be right back to handle everything.

"Get her in the car quick," Carla Sue said. The old woman said she would go nowhere with the two of them. Carla Sue said for her to suit herself, that it didn't matter to *her* what the old woman did.

"It would serve you right if we left you here. *Then* how would you get back to Arkansas, huh? You could just stay up here and rot on this hill, for all we care. Then they might pickle you and put you on display like all the other old notions they got behind glass around here. Would you *like* that? Would you like to be stuffed like some dummy so's they could charge four bucks for people to come gawk at you? They'd sew your mouth shut so's you couldn't talk, and that would be pure hell—you with your mouth sewn shut so's you couldn't make wisecracks and so's you couldn't drink no more Dr. Tichner's."

"NOooo," said the old woman. She was still more than a little drunk; and she had suffered a heart attack; and it all seemed like something from a dream to her. She was not so sure this woman couldn't sell her to the Thomas Jefferson people; he had kept slaves, hadn't he, and had not the very earth opened up just a short while ago and whispered to her that the mountains were made not of stones but of the dead?

"I don't want to die," she moaned. "I don't want to end up no museum piece."

"Then get in the car and lay down in the back and shut up." The old woman acquiesced. "Here," and Carla Sue gave Tyson's mother what was left of the front-seat Dr. Tichner's. Tyson began their descent down Mr. Jefferson's mountain. When they got to the highway, Carla Sue turned and spoke to the old woman.

"I don't want you to ever forget we could have left you back there. Or that, any time we want, we can have you put away." She waited a while before speaking again so that the message would sink in.

"Now," she said, smiling, "about that house you got back in Arkansas."

They kept the old woman tied loosely on the way back to Arkansas. Carla Sue was mad that the old woman was dying on them and that they had had to miss luscious Busch Gardens. The puppy roamed freely through the bucket seats' gap into the front and back. Tyson's mother sneezed a lot and once took a swipe at the dog. That was when Carla Sue decided to tie the old woman's hands. The dog used the old woman like a jungle gym set and teethed on her legs. The old woman complained that they were kidnapping her, holding her hostage for her house. Carla Sue said she would untie the old woman when she was good and ready, that turnabout was fair play, and besides, it served the old woman right because kidnapping was against federal law. The old woman was in a stupor and did not recognize her son. She asked for him as if he were not driving the car. Carla Sue said playing stupid would get the old woman nowhere with her. Since the attack back at Monticello, the old woman had been genuinely confused. Her chest ached, and her heart beat against her ribs like a caged bird.

Around Bakersville, Carla Sue decided the old woman wasn't a threat anymore and untied her hands. She gave her a pack of Nabs to eat. She said wasn't it a wonder how the land changed the further west you went? She wondered what it looked like, say, in Arizona? The old woman claimed to have visited Arizona once, and she said it looked a lot like the moon. Carla Sue shut her up by humming a few bars of "This Land Was Made for You and Me." Then Carla Sue started daydreaming out loud about how easy it would be making barrels of money selling satellite dishes to people in New Mexico. She said they could sell the house and start out fresh like pioneers. The old woman asked could she come along, said that she had forgotten at the moment who she was, or where she was headed, but that they both seemed like a fine couple, and she would be very glad to do chores in exchange for a warm bed and adequate doses of her medicine. Carla Sue remarked that the old woman had lost a piece of her mind back there at Monticello. She said that Tyson's mother was not long for this world; they had better hurry back to Arkansas so she could die proper. The old woman claimed to be seeing a well-furnished room with an open door and someone calling her. That, and a garden with fountains and children playing.

Carla Sue observed that being on the road like this, footloose and fancy-free, made her feel special inside, like when you went to the photographer and stood for your picture. She said she was very sorry for hurting the old woman's feelings back there at Monticello. She suggested they all just forget what had happened back there— wasn't life too short to hold grudges? The old woman said nothing because she was dead and past caring. She was beyond the realm of satellite dishes.

Tyson remarked how everything turned out for the best. He gave his bride a playful squeeze. He stated that he had been somewhat disappointed with Monticello. From the way it looked on the back of a nickel, he had thought it would have been much more imposing and impressive. He praised Carla Sue on her insight that everything turned out for the best. He claimed he felt like a new man now. He said the more you thought about it, the better selling little pieces of stars sounded. He reflected that a man could want little more than riding westward with his two girls (at this Carla Sue giggled) safely in tow. He confessed to loving them both greatly. He felt as if he had captured the essence of a dream.

"Hot *damn!* I feel so. . . ." but he didn't know the words to frame his feelings. Up ahead, some men were gathered around a harvester broken down midfield. Tyson began honking loudly. As they rocketed by the men and the machine, he yelled that he had just gotten married. He yelled it as if they might actually understand what he said or remember his car's noisy passage. His eyes teared with the emotion of the moment, with the sweet prospect of a full life that the land seemed not only to yield up but also to promise. It would be a few miles before they realized they were traveling with a corpse.

~~~~~~

The Happiness of Angels

(from the novel *In the Open*)

Elizabeth Taylor is on three different covers. She would be warm against him, and he trembles in this ugly buzzing fluorescence, his wrist a knot, a swelling, white watchband of skin. Tanya Tucker hugs a baby.

"Mister, this ain't the Mission," the 7-Eleven guy says. This guy's already given up on the big dreams, Earl can tell, if he ever had any, with his black, mannequin toupee, and his regulation red smock zipped clear to his Adam's apple. Christ. The guy eyes Earl with both hands planted on the counter. "The snow's stopping anyhow." Earl pushes his good hand through his hair, his full head of hair, and flicks the water off his fingers to the floor.

"Hey . . ."

"What's your problem?" Earl says. "I got money." He holds out the wadded bills, spits right in front of the counter, and says, "Doesn't that qualify me, big shot? Or are you some neo-Nazi survivalist cretin likes to hate all life-forms?" Earl raises his hands above his head, and the guy is coming around the counter. "Go ahead, big shot. Do it. Assault me, asshole, and I call the cops. Do it!"

That stops the guy, panting, his beer gut moving under the smock, and he sure as hell isn't pregnant. Earl laughs and says, "I like you."

"I told you, Mister—"

"I like you, because you're working for me. You've got what I want, one new carton of Pall Malls. Simple." Earl lowers his arms, and the wrist throbs. "You need to see my ID?" The guy stays put. "Do you? Come on, don't be a spoiler."

Headlights jump in out front. The guy says, "Sometime . . ."

Earl should buy something for the wrist, the cold, but what? Robutusin? Hell, he could buy half a dozen. This is complicated, and he has forgotten complicated. Two older guys in Rainbow Bread shirts jangle through the door and cut down an aisle.

The hairless 7-Eleven asshole tries to hold back the change, so Earl says, very quietly, "I'm not above busting out your front windows I don't get the eight bucks I have coming." The guy shows his teeth but delivers, and Earl buys a *Parent* magazine, which he rolls up and sticks down his right sleeve. The bread men laugh at the counter.

Under the overhang out front, Earl tears a pack out of the carton, which he tucks in with the magazine. Sure he's quivering, his teeth nuts, but he can light up out there, and the snow has stopped, the last snow of the year, of the century if this greenhouse thing is real, of all time, a drizzle now, a fuzz in the air, snow patched on the ground, asphalt shiny. Smoke. Loosens him. Rises from his head.

He sees what Earl the Pearl has done. His sister Marcia had her only baby die in its sleep. No gore. No negligence. No blame. And she landed, didn't crash, at AA, while old Ed, her hubbie dear, shacked up with a reconditioned ski bunny in Park City. She landed, yeah—needed AA more than she ever needed booze—but her spunk was gone. Okay, she's some big department-store buyer back east now, but that's just money. What's money? Spunk, goddamn it. Through the thick through the thin, the fundamental denominator. "You ain't got it, you ain't," their cleaning lady scolded him when he hung around the house as a kid.

Marcia never wrote. She never came to the hospital.

Holding white cups with lids, the bread guys climb into a snowy Caravan.

Earl takes a last hot hit and flips the butt into the drizzle and pushes back through the doors. "Got to piss," he says.

"Out of order," old hairless says.

"Unless you goose-step, that it? You know, I like pissin' on sidewalks." Earl starts to turn.

"Five minutes is all," the 7-Eleven guy says. "You hear me? Or I call the cops."

The worst of it is that he is sober, sober in a goddamned ice storm. The mist hardened over everything. What's control now? His butt-smooth, clumsy-ass army boots shoot out from under him anyway—and he feels it, slamming down on his side, the squirt gun snapping in his pocket, his elbow on the same goddamn arm, his funny bone exploding, one big nerve peeled raw, pain pinning him on his back, his head over the curb. Christ, the cold saves him, numbing his arm, but it is a big cold, a heavy cold, squeezing down on his lungs, his heart, the works. He drops his feet over the curb, counts to three—"One, two, three"—and rises. "You bet," he says.

The next worst part is being awake, and seeing that he will most likely not sleep till dark tomorrow, which is now today with all this pain. The sun won't be worth a damn today with all this haze, with all this slippery goddamn ice. Ruined arm or not, he keeps smoking, smoking, smoking, keeps his feet moving in their short sliding steps. And he gets there, Holy Cross Hospital, and half the windows glow, but still he wants a drink, needs one to fight the cold, to celebrate. Sure.

4:23.

A lard-assed bearded guy in blue coveralls and moon boots tosses rock salt from a bucket down the sidewalk. The white specks crunch under Earl's boots, but the man doesn't turn. The darkness roars over Earl, and a helicopter whirling with lights throbs onto the roof. Dies in a silence of tires squealing far away, the salt crystals showering the sidewalk, like breathing, the match rasping over the matchbook into flame under his shaking cigarette. Dies. A nun looks from the front window, a nun who loves him, right? a nun who would turn him out, he knows from nights trying to doze in the lobby, who would call the brain-dead goddamn security bums. "You may sleep in the chapel," she'd say, but who can sleep in a chapel with everywhere Christ nailed up like that, whoever He was? Who can sleep?

His fingers burn with frostbite, for God's sake, pressure under the nails like blood blisters. And his wrist, and his elbow—and his ribs so tight he can hardly breathe. He has to smoke to breathe. The trees are slick with, glazed with, trapped in ice. Ice. "Her water broke," the ambulance woman said. Warm, warm water. A siren now.

An ambulance howls onto Tenth Street behind him. The man sowing salt does not break stride. This ambulance—orange, more like a hearse, its exhaust sweet—fishtails into the Emergency alley, and its siren fades into this ringing like a phone in the center of Earl's head.

Dripping outside the bright, new Emergency entrance, the orange ambulance is open, empty. Earl considers climbing in, lying down under the white blankets, but the building's automatic doors slide for him, meet him with heat. He smells heat. There is no blood anywhere. No one stops him. No one should, not now, with this chill right inside his bones, and his arm, Christ, his arm . . .

Earl drops into a soft brown chair across from a TV, beside a youngish guy holding a woman's purse in his lap, a guy with a small girl asleep in the next chair over. The TV is on without sound, a fuzzy black and white with Jane in her dumb jungle tree house. Cheetah the chimp sits on her table. They are hot. Where is Tarzan?

The Coke machine in the corner kicks on. A lady with ratted hair and dark glasses is here, too. Her hand is wrapped with a towel. The guy with the purse and the girl checks his watch, sighs, scopes Earl he can feel, smells Earl most likely, the cigarettes, the Thunderbird: thinks, I don't know if I can stand this on top of everything else, this wasted nobody parked right here with all these other empty chairs. Earl wants to say, "Hey, who the hell do you think you are? It's tough for everybody, even me." But his teeth are chattering, and the warmth ignites his wrist, his elbow, his hands, his feet. He shivers as he burns. Jesus.

Earl should be dead. He was the firstborn, forty-two minutes before Eli, and Eli never writes, never calls. You'd think Earl would die. Your average American dies so easily, he thinks. A steering wheel jumps two inches too far. A chunk of sirloin in the throat, a fall on stairs. Flu. Salmonella. Clogged arteries. Hypothermia. A bee sting. Earl's father died of a heart attack at sixty—ten years older than Earl is now. His mother is eighty-three and she will never die and she believes he should be dead.

Nobody on the street dies. Well, almost nobody. That big lady from Hawaii died, but Christ look at the change of climate. And every winter a couple of liquored-up guys kick. A couple get knifed. Nobody he knows. He'll see the same goddamn emaciated no-bodies—at the Mission, the shelter, in the parks, under the via-duct—forever. God is using them, Earl knows, to spoil the Mormon empire, to show the lie for what it is.

Still, you'd think *he'd* die, should have, should have frozen back there with the Indian, but no, he's strong enough to kill, that's the truth of it, unlucky enough to twitch out of a goddamn stupor and kill a baby. He cares. That's his bad luck. Twenty-some odd bucks in his pocket now, he could be soused till Tuesday noon, but he's here, he's no drunk. He could go to the hospital coffee shop, but hell, they'd give him the boot. Send him to the chapel. Tarzan rides an elephant.

An Italian looking lady with a name badge touches his shoulder. "Please register at the desk," she says, and he wants to tear off his frozen clothes. Christ, he made it this far. Can't they leave him be? God, and now the wailing way off somewhere. It is not an elephant. It is a baby, come to life, going to death. He had two, two boys, bright, spunky boys. They knew what it meant to be alive. Good boys. Would they know him? If they came in right now, would they see their father in this wreck of a degenerate failure? Would he know his boys? Four years easy since he's had a word. The family stage is over for him, like some damn documentary. Mantises. Salmon. Tarzan yells in the jungle. Jane abides. Abide, abide, o. Earl's in the cold stream where he was born, drifting. You'd think he'd die.

"A rest room," he whispers. The lady nods with her lips turned in, and helps him up.

He runs hot water over his fingers. He smells cherry cough syrup. Cough syrup could save him. He holds his head under the blowing, hot hand drier on the wall, the clean wall in this new bathroom. He is stiff. No one has written in the stall. The toilet is spotless. He inhales one last cigarette. He can breathe, and the pain is where it can be stopped now. They will fix his arm. To hell with forms, the permanent address/social security bullshit. His elbow is swollen, he can tell, but bends. He can wiggle his fingers some, so his wrist can't be busted. Painkillers. He needs painkillers. He can breathe.

The cap's still on his felt-tip pen! He takes time with each letter: "The Pearl is everywhere!" above the four bars, the last a feather.

The Italian lady's gone. Just security to watch for—and nuns. And apparitions, his brother or his father mostly. Not ghosts. Materializations. Making sure he doesn't crack. That's what they do.

His boots squeak in the empty corridor. Any faster he might slip. Any faster his arm would bounce. He stops at the directory just long enough to find the floor, the first, up one, right over him, that close. Christ. He squeezes through the heavy door of the stairwell. He shivers as he climbs, but he 's hot, too, his face, his throat, breathing so loudly the whole state must hear him. Shadows slither from the railing, red shadows, orange shadows. His mother's crying seeps in. It stops on the landing when, by God, Earl lights another smoke, and the singing starts. The voice of his oldest friend, his only lifelong friend, for that matter, Vic, Victor Sorrell, is faint:

> *Whistle while you work,*
> *Stevenson's a jerk,*
> *Eisenhower's full of power,*
> *Whistle while you work.*

Earl remembers the words from junior high. He sings, too, a round, starting when Vic gets to the end of the first line again, but, shit, this commotion will get him tossed and he tells Vic to shut the fuck up, only Vic isn't dead yet and neither is Earl's mother, and this must be his father singing but he's too old to know that song. Eli? Earl crushes his cigarette. He can breathe. Who cares who sang? He knows what matters.

This is it, right here: "Maternal/Infant Units—Nursery." The dim yellow lights hum. Across from a side room with a miniature plastic table and chairs, a regulation Mary and baby Jesus hangs between dark windows. The waiting room is narrow, the nurses' station empty. One with a clipboard crosses from right to left in the first corridor. Behind the window to the nursery, two in white sweaters talk at a counter. If he moves, they'll spot him. He must move to know. He would not kill a baby. Not its mother with the spikes. She looked at him, she loved him.

He would kill somebody who tried to kill him. He would have to if he had a weapon. Some rules you have to recognize. He would not kill a baby. Babies are blameless.

DANIEL MUELLER

Ice Breaking

Sy Johnson trudged onto the frozen lake toting the dismembered body of his lover on a red plastic sled. He walked perhaps two hundred feet, then turned around to look at the gold Mustang he had driven north from Isabella and parked on the public landing. Its grill was rusted and caked with brown snow. Its left headlight was busted and dangling from the wires. It was a sad piece of machinery. To his Auntie Barto, when she came looking for him, the car would be a prelude to terror—like a torn scrap of shirt on the trail to a scene of bloodshed. Already she had seen that her fifty pounds of birdseed wasn't in the spot where she'd told him to deliver it, behind the porch swing between the cedar planters. Perhaps at this moment she was shaking the shoulders of her neighbor, old Heck Miller, and swiveling his hairless, arthritic legs off of the bed. To Wallace Triangle, whose fine white body lay in four parts in a gunnysack on the sled, whose own fingers had tied the piece of rope which supported the Mustang's muffler and pipes, the car had always been a source of joy. But then, Wallace Triangle took joy in sad things.

On the southern horizon, light poured from the slit of moon onto the snow and ice. Soon it would be daybreak. Across the frozen bay rested the island he and Wallace named Baskatong Hump because its high cliffs were shaped like tongs and in the summer, when the northerns and walleyes slowed in the afternoon, they had basked on the exposed rock above the lake and their beached canoe. Now the island blended with the strip of shoreline and with the sky. Yet Sy had walked with Wallace across the ice to the tiny fishing shack so many winter nights, he could have felt his way using only the ice pick. From time to time, the red plastic sled caught on the snow, and Sy yanked the cord until Wallace, the styrofoam bucket of minnows, and the four Fish-N-Flags skimmed smoothly again at his side.

"Wallace Triangle," he said, "you remember once telling me that anyone could be made to buy any product, provided he had the liquid assets to make the purchase?"

He'd met Wallace in Finland, Minnesota, at the Baptism River Bar in 1983. At the same bar in the same booth one year later, Wallace had told him about his scheme to unload five thousand inflatable decoy geese. The gunnysack rolled a little on the sled as if to say, *my mind's grown feeble, Sy, you've got to help me now to remember.* "We were drinking stingers, Wallace, your drink. You said, so long as the need is made known."

"That's what I said, Sy, and for a number of years now, we've lived a tidy life."

Sy nodded. They'd unloaded all but three hundred of the semi-durable vinyl geese, each with its own twenty-five ounce steel sinker, in less than two weeks. Those that remained, Sy had peddled to members of his immediate family, which spanned the region from Lax Lake to Cass Lake north to Kabetogama. With the profits, they'd repossessed the fishing shack which had once belonged to his brother, Dean, and had even used it as an office for a time, until, unloading an assortment of plastic lawn ornaments, they'd had the capital to buy up a small warehouse in Isabella. This they had filled with birdseed of the highest quality, in sacks ranging from five pounds to fifty, and had even made a name for themselves, Johnson-Triangle Birdseed Outlet.

"But what you don't understand, what I lacked the heart to tell you, Wallace, is that the only need we ever made known was our own. Our customers were every last one of them family. My family, Wallace. Johnson blood. That's what kept us afloat, and it's a fact I feel ashamed. I do and I know it."

The gunnysack rode easily on the sled, Wallace's legs, torso, and head having settled finally into the jerk and glide of Sy's pace over the frozen lake. The fact was he could not visit a single relative's home for supper without confronting a half dozen of the smiling green and yellow turtles, the frogs with tongues in full extension, the elfin toadstools and grazing deer, all of them cast out of a shiny synthetic that would outlast the people who owned them by thousands of years. Worse was finding his stock still on the racks of small retail outlets. Family, themselves the struggling owners of bait shops and groceries, laundromats and hardware stores, had, in kindness and love, taken on merchandise that hadn't moved in years and wouldn't till they took it home themselves.

"No, Sy," came Wallace's voice from the silhouette of pine tops and across the ice in an eerie gust, "we beautified."

"That may be easy for you to say."

"You're forgetting, Sy, about the sunflower seeds and suet, our stock for the past eighteen months."

"Good acts don't cancel bad ones. You should know that."

"But the good ones count for something. Think of the white-throated sparrow, the yellow-billed cuckoo, the black-throated blue warbler. Think of your grandmother Fern."

"You've never seen a brown-headed cowbird perched on one of our fourteen-foot plastic windmills."

"There's beauty in that."

"That's not a sight you'll have to live with. And if you think I'm going to, Wallace—"

"*Both* of us will, Sy. That's the beauty."

In a lagoon of the island he and Wallace had planted the four cinder blocks on which the tiny four-hole fishing shack rested over the ice. The sun had not yet risen, but its legs streaked upward into starry space like the blood splashes of a creature pulverized in a single blow of god Kawishiwi's stone mallet. Four hundred feet from the shore sat the shack, a toolshed really, the scarred remains of a house that had been. Its walls of asbestos and ceiling of tin had withstood the flames of arson as well as any chimney—the winter night Dean took himself, Sara, and their two boys out of the world. Sy pulled the sled up to the rickety plywood door. Behind the shack, he opened the valve on the tank of propane, then he picked up the gunnysack and carried Wallace inside.

"You cold?" Sy asked.

"Cold?" the gunnysack replied. In the cupboard above the sink,

Sy found the box of matches where he and Wallace had left it less than a week before, nestled in among kitchen utensils, old invoices, tools, and miscellaneous scraps of tackle. The stove lit, he took the crowbar from the cupboard, removed the entangled confusion of bobbers and fishing line from its neck, and applied its head to a plank in the floor. As he pushed down on the forked end, the board reared up, making an opening fanged like a snake's mouth. He gripped the board between four rust-encrusted nails and pried it loose from the crossbeam at the far end, exposing an eight foot long strip of yellowed snow and ice. As the stove warmed the air inside the shack, Sy moved methodically from board to board until he had made a rectangle to the ice the size of a coffin. Then he took the ice pick from where he'd propped it outside the door, and began chopping around the perimeter of the oblong opening.

"Talk to me," Sy said.

"No, Sy, you talk to me." In the light of day, which streamed in through the double panes of plexiglass, Sy saw the strange lumps in the coarse-weaved jute, angles made by Wallace's elbows and knees. Blood seeped from the burlap across the boards of the floor and stained the snow in the hole. Wallace's head, arms, and a portion of sternum had been the first segment he'd discovered under the moon's albino glow. As a consequence, it rested at the bottom of the sack. The center bulged with Wallace's torso. Clipped at the thighs and chest, it had drained like a water main open at both ends when he'd picked it up. A hundred feet from the tracks in a clump of dead milkweed, Sy had found the legs; as if under such awesome weight, they'd snapped like matchsticks and been hurled straight, or almost straight, into the sky. Each was shod with a brown wingtip and a sock, but otherwise nude. They were so long, he'd had to fold them at the knees to fit them in the sack.

"I guess I don't need to tell you I'm a little upset," said Sy, jamming the blade of the pick into the ice below the floor. "I mean, it's just like you, I should have expected it. You've always just hurled yourself at the world, without much regard for it, as if it were a trampoline or something." The blade of the pick punctured the ice, the loop of rope snagged his wrist. Green water gurgled up through the tiny one-inch hole and filled the rectangular gully he'd outlined. "Is that what you thought? That you'd bounce back?"

"Sy, my daddy molded steel into train parts. I told you the story about being a kid and cutting my thumb on the wheel of a standing locomotive."

"That's about the only story you ever told me, Wallace."

"Let's just say, my family and I, we were like oil and water."

"You were the oil?"

"You could say that." Sy jammed the pick into the ice and threw his jacket and shirt onto the little fishing stool. The stove cooked the air inside the shack to a hundred and ten degrees because the valve didn't have an adjustment on it, just on and off, open or closed. In his undershirt, Sy returned to his labor as sweat beaded on his forehead and neck and stung the corners of his eyes. "To this day, I don't know where you're really from. You show up, you've got nothing but a wired-together Mustang. I introduce you to some people, my Uncle Ned, my Uncle Ensign Wilder Powell, and suddenly, like water gushing through a busted-up beaver dam, the money's coming in, we're buying and selling, we're rich, you hear me?! we're unbelievably, incredibly rich!"

"I told you. I'm from north of here."

"Canada?"

"North, Sy."

"The arctic then?"

"North of there even."

"Right, you're from the north pole, Wallace."

"I told you, but you've forgotten. The night I met you. I held your hand. I told you I had grown lovesick and refused to dance."

"And that you came here, to northern Minnesota, to the iron range."

"I came for you, Sy."

"And splattered yourself over the whole northwoods. You know something, collecting you this morning, I had this crazy thought, that at the moment of impact, when the blood must've exploded out your legs and chest, that little bits of you dropped from the sky into people's yards like shrapnel, like meteor dust, and became the waddling plastic ducks we sold, the artificial rocks, the bird-baths."

"In a sense, that *is* what happened."

"It was garish and awful and tasteless."

"Tasteless?"

"I can't believe I was so completely suckered." Now the fat slab of ice floated freely in the water beneath the floor of the shack. With the blade of the pick, Sy pushed it under the water away from the hole and stationed it under the ice. Into the open rectangle he peered, into the shafts of refraction and the blackening depths.

"I love you, Sy Johnson."

Coated with sweat, Sy lifted the dripping gunnysack from the corner of the shack and held it over the opening with both arms as if it were a huge swinging pendulum. "Kawasachong. Lujinida. Wantonwah," he said. "Wisisi. Kivandeba. Ashigan." The weight pulled in his shoulders, arms, and neck, but he held the sack outward, so that it hung over the hole. "Gabimichigami. Kekekabic. Bingshick." He lifted it above his shoulders, so that the blood that had once united them might drain onto his neck and chest in fluid strings, strings that might continue to unite them. The coarse jute cut his palms, the weight pulled in his lower back, hamstrings, and thighs, but the moment of submergence, of departure and loss, had to be borne fully or not at all. At last, he was able to say it: "Good riddance, Wallace Triangle."

"A lie."

"What is?"

"Riddance."

He released the sack and it hit the water with a boulder-sized splash. It rested for a time amid the myriad floating chunks of ice, then sank straight and fast to the bottom of the lake—a ghost wizening into a mirror. Sy knelt on the floor of the shack. He peered into the water at his own eyes. The bottom was twenty feet below him, all rocks and crevices, which in the spring and summer snipped fishing line better than a razor. He saw nothing save his own reflection, no shade of beige, willowed and disjointed by the depths, nothing. With the pick, he pried the fat slab out from underneath the ice, and it buoyed back into place as snugly as a bar of soap into a soapdish. He scooped some slush and snow into the corner where Wallace had rested and scrubbed the blood from the boards with his hands. Then he washed his hands with some fresh slush and laid each of the removed boards neatly into place over the hole. When he had hammered each board back to the crossbeams, he grabbed the pick and went outside onto the ice.

The sun shone down blindingly now. In view of the plexiglass window, Sy chopped four fishing holes in a rectangle approximately

four by eight feet. From each of the four Fish-N-Flags, he un-
raveled three and a half arm lengths of line and secured two two-
ounce sinkers six inches from each hook. To each of the four lines,
he hooked a minnow, neatly, just below the spine. He let each line
drop until the sinkers pulled it taut to the spool, then he tested each
of the four spring-loaded flags. He tugged a little at each line, and
when the flag popped up, he pressed it back down and set it over the
hole. Then he went back inside the shack, sat down on the little
fishing stool, and watched the flags through the window.

It wasn't long before a flag popped up. Sy rushed onto the ice and,
pinching the line between his thumb and finger, set the hook into
the mouth of a fish. He felt a static resistance, like a loose board. He
pulled the line up hand over fist until the fish came through the hole
and lay there, breathing on the snow. It was a walleye pike, big but
not overly so, with pupils as white as the ice. It flipped itself several
times with its tail, as if only then aware of the dimension of air into
which it had ascended. He stationed it with his boot and tugged on
the line until its gills showed in its mouth. Then he gave the line a
quick yank and they dislodged onto the ice, useless as wax lips.

Inside the shack, he lay the fish on a cutting board on the counter
next to the sink. While it still breathed, he placed the long, thin
blade of the fillet knife on its scales, as close to its pectoral fin as he
could, then in a smooth sawing stroke, cut until he felt the firmness
of its spine under the knife. He angled the knife then, trimming the
meat from the fish's flank. When he came to the tail, he pressed the
fillet back as if breaking in the binding of a book and took off the
skin. He turned the fish over and did the same thing to its other
side. Then he cut the two fillets, which were about eight inches
long and three quarters of an inch thick, into as many bite-sized
pieces as he had No. 2 barbed hooks and into each of the soft, white
wedges, he lodged one of the curled, sharp pieces of metal. He
turned on a burner on the range, daubed a spoonful of lard into a
pan, and set it over the circle of blue flame. When the lard was
sizzling, he scooped up the pieces of fish and dumped them onto the
pan to fry. The grease spattered and popped. He turned the pieces
of fish over with a fork until they were cooked through and brown
on both sides. He salted and peppered them while they were still in
the pan, then he forked them all onto his plate. "No riddance, eh,
Wallace?" He sat back down on the little fishing stool and stared out

the window with his plate of hot fish. One of the flags wafted in the cold, but he didn't care. He forked each morsel into his mouth and swallowed it, hook and all, without chewing. Then he washed the plate off in the sink, lay down on the floor of the shack, softly, as if in expectation of love, and began doing sit-ups. This was how he had determined to take himself out of the world.

Sy passed an hour suffering quietly. With each contraction, the barbs hooked deeper into the wall of his stomach. Clots formed, a hundred holes tried to heal, but with each contraction, he felt the blood stream into his stomach like liquid through a colander. When it was full, he would force the blood up his esophagus into his lungs and drown himself from the inside. Fingers locked behind his head, knees bent, eyes shut in an exercise of self-mastery, he had swallowed seeds of his own destruction, like Niswi, Wagosh, Eskwagama, con men of legend who had swallowed seeds of the water hemlock, petals of the deadly nightshade, rhizomes of the blue flag iris, and saving their many faces, had become gods of the spring, summer, and fall. The seeds he had swallowed were those of the long-spined rose. With each contraction, he watered its roots. With each contraction, he felt its stalk thickening and pushing upward, its thorned limbs uncoiling and probing for breathable air and space to blossom.

He thought of spring, its tepid gusts warming the world above and below the division of ice. The frozen plate on which he and the tiny fishing shack rested would wizen into a sheet, a membrane, through which the cinder blocks would plummet. Then, perhaps a day or two later, the fishing shack itself would begin to fill up with water, through pores in the sheeting, through holes in the floor and ceiling, through vents. A day or two later, there'd be no sign at all of his undoing, save for an occasional bubbling, a lure snagged from a passing canoe, a bit of flotsam. Through the planking, tall weeds would rise, drawing spawn-bloated fish through the windows and door. As the roof fell, the stalks would force themselves through the tiny perforations, or make perforations where there were none, like sidewalk dandelions, like trees rooted in rock. The tank of propane would settle into the mud, as all boulders eventually did, becoming a pocket of marsh gas, sealed for eternity in sediment. His body was hardly worth considering. The muscles, tendons, ligaments, heart, spleen, lungs, cornea, penis, brains would be nibbled on by fish and turned into thin coils of excrement. In time, when his bones and teeth had decalcified and spread through the lake like spores of cottonweed borne on the wind, perhaps then, then, his two gold fillings would lie there for a time and shimmer back at the sun.

"Sy! You in there?" The voice belonged to his Auntie Barto. He recognized her shrill tremor. "I've come for my birdseed. I paid for it. It's mine by right." When her voice first came to him, he was halfway between sitting up and lying down, his abdomen like bread dough wrapped around a roller of nails. He lay back and felt the muscles stretch out and drain like wet sponges. "Heck's out here with me. You and Wallace make yourselves decent now. If you don't come to the door on the count of three, Heck here's gonna bust it down. You can't go breaking promises to people. Hello? One."

"I'm here, Barto," he said.

"I know it," she said. "Two."

He stood up, half expecting the door to burst open and the old man to be lying on the floor before him, crumpled up in his army-issue trench coat, beady eyed behind his three-inch thick lenses with the thick, black frames. "Three."

He swallowed the paste that thickened in the back of his throat. "I'm serious," said his aunt. "You boys put some clothes on. Lord knows I'm not one to shy away from a naked man, but Heck's here."

He opened the door and met his auntie's mufflered face, pink from the cold, a quarter inch of rouge, and her undeniable health. Beyond her, toeing the gills over the snow with his boot, stood Heck Miller in his glasses and coat. "Hey, Sy," he said, "looks like you caught one." He motioned at the popped-up flag. "Looks like you've got another on the line."

"I saw Wallace's car," said Barto. "I was worried about you two." Sy blocked her entrance with his chest. To her, his undershirt looked stained with fish blood, nothing more.

"Here," he said. He handed her the keys to the Mustang. "Your order's in the trunk."

Barto sized him like an owl. "Is it sacked? I don't want it if it isn't sacked."

The question stunned him—her birdseed always came in sacks. She curled her neck around the jamb of the door. "Where's Wallace?" she asked. "I expected him to be here with you." As she nudged him out of the way, he coughed up a little flower of blood over her shoulder onto the snow. Heck examined him quizzically, then strode up to the entrance and to the propped-up ice pick. Sy unsheathed the fillet knife and held it in the air within a whisker of the old man's throat.

"Stay outside," he said. "This is family." The old man's eyes receded and turned inward. Through the thick lenses, they told nothing, like eclipsed planets. Sy jerked the thin, tempered steel away from the old man's neck and sheathed it out of view of his aunt. Then he bolted the door from the inside.

"It's all right," said his aunt. "Heck likes the outdoors. Sometimes it's all you can do to get him to come inside to eat. It's nothing personal. He likes you. He told me so on the way up. He'd just rather fish than do anything else." She sat down on the little fishing stool, her auburn hair to the window. Her strong, wide knees made a perfect little table for a cup of tea and perhaps a brownie on a napkin. "Sy," she said, "how are you? How is Wallace?"

Her eyes pleaded with him as if for the latest gossip. Brown, fire-lit, her eyes would still be playful when she turned one hundred. "Wallace is all right, I guess. He laid down on the tracks last night and let a train run over him."

Sy watched the breath leave her, saw her eyes reach out from behind her strawberry-tinted lenses like strange, temperate suns. "He was sick, Auntie."

"How sick?"

"What he had a person doesn't live through." Sy saw her shock and sorrow turn to anger. "He gave it to me, Auntie." Lifting up his undershirt, Sy showed her the blemishes that seemed to float above the surface of his skin like curled, red petals.

"Well let's get you to a doctor. Heck sees someone in Isabella. Says he's awfully good. Says he's the only doctor who can make the—"

"Wallace went. The doctor only made him sicker." The doctor, in fact, had phoned to tell him that Wallace had left the hospital. When the night nurse had discovered Wallace's vacant bed, the IV needle removed from his arm and pressed into the mattress, the doctor had gotten right on the phone. More paste collected in the back of Sy's throat and he coughed a little of it into his hand. Barto watched him press the blood into his undershirt. The stain made a

depot for the long, red tracks Wallace had made through the gunnysack. His aunt blushed, but she did not turn away from nakedness
or suffering. "It's only a matter of time," said Sy. The compassion he
saw in her eyes now only embarrassed him, and he wished he had
dropped off her birdseed before he ever went looking for Wallace.
He could have wrapped the body parts in tar paper and looped it
together with jumper cables from the car.

"Can you walk, Sy?"

"Sure I can walk, walk twenty-five miles if need be." He hadn't
realized it until then, but he was feeling better and better, as if he
had lived his whole life in a state of hunger, a hunger that was only
now, for the first time, being properly fed. His contentment differed
from any Thanksgiving dinner he'd ever experienced. It was as if
his stomach were filled to the hilt with breast meat and rice pud-
ding, corn chowder and mashed potatoes, but he felt light, as if a
walk of fifty miles might wear him down as little as an after-dinner
traipse through the woods to Barto's boat dock.

"You're coming with Heck and me back to the car, Sy."

"No, Auntie."

"Then there's nothing I can do. You and Dean. You were the
spitting image of each another. There are remedies I know how to
make, with water from this lake. Every autumn, I dry out leaves of
the mayapple, fruits of the skunk cabbage, petals of the marsh
marigold. I could've helped Dean. I could've applied a paste to his
temples. But he wouldn't let me because he'd given up the will to
live. I could help you too, if you'd let me."

"There was nothing physically wrong with Dean," Sy said. He
caught himself against the wall of the shack, where in 1979,
married and with kids, Dean had scratched with the point of a
knife, I AM HAPPY AND GAY, HAPPY AND GAY, HAPPY AND GAY.
"Dean left the world because he was unfulfilled. That's the difference, Auntie. I'm leaving a world Dean could only dream of. I'm
leaving a world that has made me very, very happy."

"Then I'll take the Mustang to the dump and just leave it there."
He watched her strong hands unbolt the door. "If it's your wish to
vanish without a sign, I'll simply tell people I don't remember you.
They will think it's Alzheimer's. And in time, I probably will."

"Will what?"

"Forget you."

As she opened the door, Sy saw the old man leaning against the ice pick. He waved at them. "Looks like I caught me a dead body." Sy stepped out onto the ice and saw the pale, blue arm. It extended from the fishing hole as if from a rolled-up sleeve. Heck had turned the palm to the snow and stationed it to the ice with a jackknife. The dark cherry handle protruded the nexus of hand bones and knuckles like the grip of an ink stamp. Sy knelt beside it as the old man chopped, his thick hair jerking like a raven at kill. "It's too wide. It won't fit through the hole." Heck had almost connected the four holes. A few chops more and the rectangular slab of ice would be floating on the surface of the lake. Sy pressed two of his fingers into the cold, wet wound the knife had made. He saw, through the tip of the ring finger, the hook that had snagged it, and the loops of thin, aqua-colored monofilament. The minnow huffed for air, though it was skewered to Wallace's blue, perfectly-manicured nail. Sy tugged at the wrist, but Wallace's shoulder, some eighteen inches below the ice, kept it from coming up through the hole.

"I think we should leave it there," Barto said. "We've got no business exhuming the dead."

"Give me that," said Sy. He grabbed the ice pick from underneath Heck Miller's heaving neck.

"Heck, I think we should go."

"No, we can't go," said the old man. "There's a body down there. It might belong to someone we know."

"I don't think so," Barto said and looked longingly at the path of boot marks they had made in the snow. Sy drove the ice pick through the last few inches of the outline Heck had made on the frozen lake. His body no longer pained him. With each chop, more water gurgled up onto the slab. When the slab floated freely, he pushed it under the ice with the pick and saw the body of his lover lurking below the surface like a huge, fleshy fish. Then he moved the slab of ice under the body of Wallace Triangle and slowly, the slab of ice raised it into the cold air. He was nude, his limbs blue-veined and tendinous. In his hair, long weeds were entwined. For a time, the three of them stared at the pockets of silt his mouth and eyes had become, as if in his face they expected to see the first signs of returned life. Then Sy removed his shirt and let it fall to the ice.

He removed his boots and socks so that he stood barefoot in the snow. Then he unbuckled his belt and let his trousers and under-shorts fall to his feet.

"Look at the son of a bitch!"

"We've got to let him, Heck."

Sy crawled onto the slab of ice and cleaved himself to the base of Wallace's trunk. As ice and water crested the slab, Wallace's face and shoulders went under, and Sy felt the sting, then the numbing, of water closing over his shoulders, back, and buttocks. "Kawa-sachong," said Barto. "Lujinida. Wantonwah." Under water, Sy found Wallace's tongue and took it in his mouth, clammy and hard as a root. "Wisini. Kivandeba. Ashigan." He wrapped his arms around Wallace's head and kissed his lover as deeply as he could, then he rolled his lover's body on top of him, dislodging the pin in his hand, and through the closing waters saw, beyond the face of Heck Miller, beyond the face of his own Auntie Barto, beyond the tin roof of the fishing shack, the exposed rock of Baskatong Hump, golden against the sky. "Gabmichigami. Kekekabic. Bingshick." Through the depths he and Wallace plummeted, sideling fish, sideling weeds, until one of the sharp-pointed rocks underneath the lake touched Sy's back and Wallace pressed it into his spine.

What remained of the day Heck Miller spent pulling up fish through the tiny fishing holes. Each one he unhooked he gave to Barto to clean inside the shack. As the afternoon passed, the slab of ice on which the two boys had rested froze again into place, so that now, as the sun disappeared behind the sheer cliff of the island, there was hardly a seam left of the rectangle that had been. Barto would have the fish cleaned by now, he thought, as he reeled the lines into the spools of the Fish-N-Flags. He snapped the flags into place and set them on the red plastic shed. He didn't have many years left, he knew, but in those that remained, he would put the equipment to good use.

Inside the shack, Barto handed him his plate of hot fish. As the world outside the window darkened, he and Barto ate in silence. Later, when they had finished and were sipping their coffee in the light of one candle, she said, "Heck, I remember when Sy's mother used to bring him to the cottage. The men would be out fishing. I'd strip him down to his bare skin and stand him on the picnic table out back. I'd fill up a bucket of water from the pump. It had a huge, red handle. Then I'd scrub him down until his body glistened and he smelled as sweet as the balsams."

"I had a nephew," said Heck then. "But he went to Rupholding, Germany, to raise sheep, and I haven't heard from him since. You know, it's a shame, I can't even remember his name."

"Heck, did I ever tell you my mother was Swedish. My father, he was full-blood Indian, but my mother, she used to talk on and on of the fjords."

"No, Barto, you never told me that." Heck watched the eyes he loved glisten and turn inward, and then his own vision, which had never been very good, also turned inward, and he remembered all the gigantic fish he had ever pulled up through the ice.

Perhaps an hour passed. Barto looked at him and said, "Come lie with me on the floor, Heck."

He crouched to the floor despite the pain in his brittle joints. He put his old, dry lips to her ear, his hand on her breast. In this manner, he drifted to sleep. Sometime close to three, as was his way, he woke up. He picked himself up off the planks, lit the range, and set a pan of water to boil. Then he stepped outside onto the frozen lake. The sky was starry and clear. To the north, beyond the silhouette of pine tops, lights of many colors leapt and spiraled. "Barto!" he called. "Come and see!"

His love stepped through the open door and he put his arm around her. "It's a rare sight. You don't normally see them this time of year."

"What?" she asked, as if still in a dream.

"The northern lights." He looked at her and he saw her see them.

"You know what I read?"

"What, Barto?"

"That the northern lights have been around as long as the Earth itself, but what makes those beautiful colors—"

He felt her wrap her arm around his side. "Pollution, Heck. It's the sun shining through a bunch of toxic fumes, car exhaust, and chemical debris."

"They sure are gorgeous."

"Yes," she said, "they surely are." Then, as two lonely old figures, they watched the garish pinks, yellows, and blues dance like savages above the world.

THOMAS McGONIGLE

Dance of the Dead Puppets

(from the novel *To Forget the Future*)

> *Bury the flower and put a man on its grave.*
> —Paul Celan

. . . and the story wasn't there when I went to look for it. I had been away from thinking about it for a long time.

Fall, winter, and spring had taken it away. The weather is always a splendid alibi so why not use the passing of seasons to talk about what had happened to James Thomson and the story I had been assembling about his life and what came after that passage upon the earth.

Of course, I wasn't thinking about Thomson, the eighteenth century poet who is associated with "The Seasons" and "The Castle of Indolence."

That is all part of the story.

One thing led to another; one day merged with the next. The fall of leaves, slush in the gutters, the return of the leaves: my mind was abused by memories.

There had been some sort of plan to get the story assembled, locked away inside manila folders and brown envelopes.

I don't know if I was particularly upset at finding out that the story was missing.

One less story. Who cares. No one will miss one more story. The hardy ones will go on about there always being room for another story.

Sorry, we missed that one, but time goes on, doesn't it?

They're the same customers lined up halfway around the block just waiting to tell their own part of the march into the cemetery.

We all got a story to tell so shouldn't you be telling our story?

We were here first and we have a right to have our story told.

Who are you anyway?

Who gave you this power?

Who asked you to go about telling stories about a guy who has been dead for a hundred years?

We are the living. Don't we have a right to have our story told before you go on about some dumb poet who got shoveled into a grave that wasn't even his?

A well-informed objection is always worth overlooking. It drives that sort of nut to even higher refinements of anger. We can always hope for a burst blood vessel and the sudden appearance of the street sweepers.

So. This one is about James Thomson. The other Thomson. "The City of Dreadful Night" man, to adopt the vulgar description from the library porch.

By careful actuarial calculation I was able to come to the conclusion: Thomson was my great-grandfather. He had a short life, by some standards, but what came after Thomson lived on for more years than he was due. At least Thomson didn't drag out the disease. He knew what the poetry could bear.

Biographical futilities.

Why me?

Having gone through this life once should have been payment enough. And now to be dragged, again, down the muddy path, shouldered in the rain as when George Eliot was sent away or just the remains of her and finally to be eased (how much more to the point it would have been if dropped without ceremony, someone tripping) into the earth, *two rows over from where we used to keep Karl Marx.*

Which wouldn't be so bad if this resurrection was just for the purposes of the final scene, in the rain, and the using of the borrowed grave.

But no, I am supposed to be on call for the whole wretched show of the life. All of that which should have been done with is again to be summoned to mind, again, as if this guy is thinking: if he shouts up, in all its glorious detail, the life that led me through my years, he in turn will know that he is alive as he teases out this life of mine, my story, now that it too has been packaged up in the dates enclosed with a neat parenthesis, as I thought when they entered George Eliot into the earth.

Of course he is free to do as he wishes and he will do so. I have gone beyond, finally, the worry and doubt of the moment but why couldn't he have latched on to some other slice of meat, gone and done with and happy at that, brought through the wheel and strained down on so many previous pages and surely he would have felt far more comfortable walking along a well-trod path and the accompanying comfort of such a well-abused familiar journey. Instead, this: an exercise in obscurity.

For a few moments the life wavered, there was a hesitation, it could have gone either way, I could feel it, I am sure I did and you are free to believe or disbelieve as is your wont; but I did feel that it might be . . . and it was only for a moment, that there might be some possible respite, some detour before the rush into oblivion, accompanied by the dusty feathering angels of my own creation—but do not worry that was no mistake: the cards were drawn before I was born and I did do my frail little bit of rebellion and then was cast down as was fit and proper.

If any of us knew anything, really, would we allow our self to continue, to stay on in this world, with the possibility of allowing our self to become meat for machines such as you?

Does it matter, but of course it does.

Doesn't it matter is more like it, since there is no way to flee the words fastened upon me, who thought I had escaped, though I suppose I might have suspected that someone like himself would come looking for me, drag me from my box of the years, done with as sure as a New Year's greeting from Doctor Karl, ceaselessly repeats itself: As the years go by we are again moved to reassure one and all that our passage is but sure evidence that someday . . .

Makes me want to vomit.

To be yanked out of the room that I have carefully locked even when a night such as this has filled my hands with the horror of the coming morning.

To be dragged to the New World, again, to be either the salt or the wound.

The salt or the wound.

Again, another is drawn to my story and he too will get his just desserts. Taken in by my story or at least the story that was passed along by Dobell and Salt and every one of them a talkative sot even if he wasn't by the letter of the drunk shop.

Poor me.

Does not do justice. It fails to cross my lips.

Of course it is possible. People are thinking I should be able to be saying this about myself, while in fact it is closer to how he thinks about himself, and he would like to drag my life along into the room as a witness to his own life and have the two lives merge into some . . . monster of egoistic creation. And of course better known than his own paltry existence.

Left to think, it is actually me doing the talking with my life on the leash and out for a walk in the late twentieth century.

Of course, it is possible, I was never aware of what I was to be thinking about in my life.

I had to be dead and gone from it, in order for this man to come along merging our two lives.

And who do I get stuck with! Frail of course . . . as frail as we both are and the two of us admitting and knowing it is better in this day when the map leaks roads across lands in conquest, when the better and better mousetrap is being built, all the time, not to even talk about the railroads, factories, bridges: a wonder to the eye— prisons, a wonder to the humanistic imagination; insane asylums for those who have lost their minds, how careless, a wit is known to always say.

Poor me. But unlike him I never expected anything to be different. The iron laws were clamped down and it was not a matter of a mere change of policy.

I am not stupid. I have not given up my mind to a peculiar esoteric philosophy. Many could be excused for thus thinking. I took up a convenient mask (what a cliché, even then) took it out of the bottle . . . nay, better than a mask . . . a whole life for the asking, at the touch of lip to the mouth of the bottle and with a gentle heaving to the stars, knowing the counterpoint hours later.

Regret is the driest fuck within my imagination and that is claiming a great deal when compared to the trade on the street.

I have gone cap in hand. As I should. One or two times. There has been no need since.

I was thinking, I detect a slight warming in the day. I was sad. A not unusual condition. There should be a little laughter or at least a smile. He does know who he is, now, doesn't he? This change of weather: I am not affected by the facts of heat or chill; just the passage of seasons and knowing that summer is followed by winter and then . . . or the other way round, as you want.

Summer is surely on its way. The smiles will grow on faces like ivy upon a wall, to mix metaphors into an impossible, though poetic stew, for those who like such dishes—inedible, on top of it, but that's the charm, some say.

How the sun clogs my ability to think.

A good thing! The less thinking you do, the better for all those around you, she had said.

But not enough to stop me from being aware of it and the roadway, along which, again . . .

The futility of experience.

Now! That man is on to something. He is on to . . .

I have gone hat in hand. Yes, one or two times yet I am not trying to conceal the fault of my going. I did go, yet I have no taste for fingertips or boot caps.

> August 1, 1993. Today has been the Day of the Rope—a grim
> and bloody day, but an unavoidable one. Tonight, for the first time
> in weeks it is quiet and peaceful throughout all of southern Cali-
> fornia. But the night is filled with silent horrors; from tens of
> thousands of lampposts, power poles, and trees throughout this
> vast metropolitan area the grisly forms hang.
> In the lighted areas one sees them everywhere. Even the street
> signs at the intersections have been pressed into service, and at
> practically every street corner I passed this evening on my way to
> HQ there was a dangling corpse, four at every intersection.
> Hanging from a single overpass only about a mile from here is
> a group of about 30, each with an identical placard around its
> neck bearing the printed legend, "I betrayed my race." Two or
> three of that group had been decked out in academic robes before
> they were strung up, and the whole batch are apparently faculty

members from the nearby UCLA campus. . . . The System had already paid them their 30 pieces of silver. Today we paid them.

The passage had been copied out of a book. It's the sort of book he ordered through the mail using a phony name. "They" had his address but at least they didn't have his name. As to who this "they" is—depended on who was being talked to.

Everybody's convinced someone or something was keeping tabs against the day when . . .

My attention span is shot to shit. There are too many forks up my ass and each one is turning in a different direction.

I should probably be worried about my reading matter. Enough of a certain type of book and I wouldn't be fit for polite society. As if I ever was or had been or am found fit to be mingled by the self-appointed best which this society has to offer. Here express an exclamation point: fist to the table top, jab of finger into air in the immediate vicinity

A Sunday in March

Dear Thomas,

You write asking me to explain you to you, and as you put it, what do you think of me, my actions and of how the years have delivered me up to the situation I find myself in now.

I will admit, I am probably better able than most to describe you, to situate you in a specific time and place—at your convenience, as the dualist of old may phrase it.

On the field of honour, no less, and where, like yourself, I can sniff the flowers with the best of them. That's about the only place on this God's earth where this personal geographical problem can be teased out.

Who was it, when walking in a shop found written on the flyleaf of the anthology, *New Directions 27*:

Marc
Someday I hope to be fluent in your language and perhaps then I will be more able to express my gratitude for your kindness. Until then all that I dare write (humbly) is:

Merci beaucoup, mon ami. Perhaps fate will be kind and
we will meet again.
Enjoy your vacation.
Enjoy your life.
Jocelyn

The name of this adventurer has to remain hidden. A temper
tantrum won't produce his or her name from the memory bank.

I am serious, sadly, about this matter. It is often pleasant to
please though the face gets tired of the view of the earth that is
the constant object of the gaze for the eyes. No longer being a
child I am not waiting for a worm to dare the sunlight and the
teeth.

And I *do know* who you are! In spite of what you are thinking as
you read this near fable writing, the sort of writing you hate with
the passion of an inquisitorial angel who seeks the truth hidden
by the absence of nouns and decent manly verbs.

Yours truly,

Such a life: to end up with a drone of my own creation.

How in all that is holy in the world could I have found Van
Buren.

On the other hand, well, that is part of the search.

Van Buren is tall and skinny or short and fat depending on the
mood necessary to the story of what is about to happen or has
happened. He could have been the long-lost brother or misplaced
friend. He is created by the moment, much in the manner that we
newly fashion the street as we walk along it, because to know
beforehand what we are to see, each and every day, the same
damn thing, would eventually walk us in front of an oncoming
truck.

He is not happy with the situation. He has his rights. Like any
other breathing creature stuck within the borders of this country.
But he doesn't have his complaint worked up into some grand
scheme of things. He would like to have a last name. He would like
to have a country different from the one that I am part of. He would

like to be getting on with his life. He has miles to go and places to see.

A loose end has been created, a lot of loose ends. More paths to wander down.

At your leisure, sir, please, at your leisure, when you are good and ready.

Final Vinyl Days

I'll never forget the day Betts moved in. How could I? Open the apartment door and there she was with two suitcases, a purple futon, and two milk crates full of albums. It was 1984, the day after Marvin Gaye died. That's how I remember so well. I had just gotten home from my job at Any Old Way You Choose It Music, where the Marvin Gaye bin had emptied within a couple of hours. I'd spent the afternoon marveling at what happens when somebody kicks. For years, other than the Motown faithfuls and a brief flurry after *The Big Chill*, that bin was neglected; I had even *dusted* it back when everybody was BeeGee Disco Crap Berserk. Now Marvin is dead and there's a run on his music. Same thing happened with Elvis and John Lennon, always good sellers, but incredibly so when they died.

"You want me here don't you?" Betts asked, her thick dark hair hitting her shoulders. Her eyes were always wide open as if she were seeing the world for the first time, every object catching her attention. She was staring at me; *I* was the object of her attention for the moment. "I mean I've been staying every night so I might as well have my things, right? And by the way," she was saying, "I could use some help." The purple futon was unrolled and halfway in the apartment. "We don't need this but Helen said she didn't want it." Helen was the roommate, a physics major who liked to test all the physical properties during sex. Betts had said (before she started coming to my place) that it was driving her crazy (the shaking plaster and peculiar sounds). I didn't tell her but it was driving me *crazy,* for different reasons, the main one being that I was a wee bit curious about what took place on the other side of that wall. Betts' side was pretty tame: a bulletin board covered in little notes and photos and ticket stubs, a huge poster of a skeleton. She was majoring in physical therapy and was taking it all real seriously (too seriously if you ask me) or depending, *not* seriously enough. "I am not a masseuse," she said often enough with no smile what-soever. Short on sense of humor but long on legs. Sometimes you have to pick and choose. Sometimes you buy an album for just one song thinking that the others will start to grow on you. When she finally got that futon in, she pulled out her Duran Duran album and that's when I put my foot down. We were from different time zones. She had a whole list of favorite *good old songs:* "Afternoon Delight" and "Muskrat Love" to name two.

I played Marvin: "Stubborn Kind of Fella," "It Takes Two," "Mercy Mercy Me." She just shrugged and went back in my room to arrange her little junk all over the top of my dresser and all over the back of the commode. I just sat there with Marvin, tried to image what it must feel like to know that your old man is about to kill you like Marvin did.

"Why did he wear that hat all the time?" Betts asked looking the same way she did when she asked me why I still wore my hair long enough to pull back in a ponytail. "IS he the guy who sings that 'Sexual Healing' song?" She was standing in the kitchen with a two-liter Diet Coke in one hand and a handful of Cheetos in the other. She's the healthy one. She's the one bitching about an occasional joint. It's okay for her to go downtown and pound down beer with her girlfriends but for godssakes don't do anything illegal. "We've got to fix this place," she was saying. "And did you say you were going back to graduate school in the fall?"

"No." I shook my head and watched her peek under a dishcloth like she expected a six-foot snake to pop out. She sounded just like my mother, asking me if I just said what she knows I never in the hell did. Those were her words, *graduate school.* When my mom does it, the secret words are *electrical appliance store.* My old man owns one in a town so big it actually has two gas stations, and he'd rather pull his nose off of his face with a wrench or beat up a new

Maytag washer than to have me in his employment. Mom says things like, "Didn't you say you were looking for a job where you can advance in the business?" That's when I always click the phone up and down or flip on the blender and plead bad connection. It's a real bad connection, Mom. And there stood Betts, swigging her Nutrasweet, eating her fluorescent cheese, waiting for an answer.

"You know that night we first met you said you had been in law school and were thinking about going back."

"I said that?" I asked and she nodded. "Did I tell you I quit law school and joined VISTA? Spent a year in the Appalachian mountains with diarrhea?" She nodded a bored affirmative. "Did I tell you I loved it?"

"No."

"Well, that's because I didn't. But what I learned in that year is that I could do anything I wanted to do, you know?"

"So?" She took a big swallow of Nutrasyrup, then wiped her mouth and hands with enough paper towels to equal a small redwood. "What are you going to do?"

"I'm doing it." I lifted the stylus off of Marvin and cleaned the album, my hand steady as I watched that Motown label spin. She was still staring in disbelief. It was a real bad connection. As good-looking as she was, it was a real bad connection. I left for five seconds, long enough to go pee and see her little ceramic eggs filled with perfumed cedar shavings on the back of the john, and in that brief five minutes, she put on Boy George. What we prided ourselves on most at Any Old Way You Choose It Music then was that we did just that, *chose it* without regards to sells and top tens and who's who. Like if I was in one mood, I might play the Beatles all day long, might play "Rubber Soul" two times in a row. I had whole weekends where all I played were the Stones, Dylan, or the Doors and then followed it with a Motown Monday, a Woodstock Wednesday. Some days I just went for somebody like Buffy St. Marie or Joan Baez, which always surprised the younger clientele, people like Betts, people who might say who's that? Screw them.

"You mean you're going to work there forever?" Betts asked, Boy George staring up at me from the floor. Her fingers were tapping along to "Do You Really Want to Hurt Me?"

"I'm buying in," I told her, which was not entirely a lie. The owner, a guy my age who had already made it big in the local business scene, was considering it. He graduated with a *D* average from a small second-rate junior college, and found a small empire already carved out by his old man. I graduated from the University with a 3.7 in English and philosophy, highest honors for some old paper I wrote about Samuel Coleridge, and what I got was one of those little leather kits for your toiletries. *What toiletries?* I had wanted to ask my mom, who said she remembered me saying I needed one of those. Yeah right. I *need* a toiletries kit.

"I'm doing okay," I said and lifted the stylus from Boy George, searched in earnest for The Kinks so Betts could ask some more dumb questions. She came over and knelt beside me, put her head close to mine, little orange Cheeto sparkles above her lip.

"I know you're doing okay," she whispered and pressed her mouth against my neck. "You're better than okay," she said. "My friends all think you're interesting in a kind of weird way, you know, mysterious." Though her knowledge of gross anatomy was limited at that stage of the game, her own anatomy was doing quite nicely. Too nicely really because it made me a dishonest person. I was thinking *bad connection, bad connection,* and yet I let her play her albums and pull me to the floor. "Isn't it great I've moved in?" she asked ten minutes later, the needle hugging the wide smooth grooves of the last song, a long silent begging for the needle to be lifted. "Isn't it going to be wonderful?" she asked, but all I could think about when I closed my eyes was Marvin standing there in his hat, his old man with pistol aimed. Betts moved in the day after he died and he hadn't been dead three months when she moved out; she pled guilty to not *truly* loving me and I turned on the somber brokenhearted look long enough to pack up her books and hand them out to the squat-bodied pathology resident who she had taken up with and who was waiting for her. "Here's a live one for you," I told him and patted her on the back.

I didn't really miss *her* so much as I just missed. The young jerky store owner was still dangling his carrots about *maybe* letting me buy in. I told him he was getting too far away from the old stuff, the good stuff, but he insisted that we *go with the flow.* He didn't want me monopolizing the sound system with too much of the old stuff; he said Neil Young made his skin crawl. He was just sick all over

that he hadn't kept his Rick Nelson stock up to date. I figured what
the hell, did I *really* want to be in business with such a sleaze? I took
a little vacation to get myself feeling up, to get Betts out of my
bones, and then I was back full force, nothing on the back of my
john, no album that never should have been on my shelves. But
before too long there I was hanging up T-shirts of the Butthole
Surfers. Things were getting bad.

I thought things couldn't get any worse but let a couple of years
spin by and they did. There were prepubescent girls with jewelry
store names running around shopping malls singing songs they
didn't deserve to sing. It was plagiarism; it was distasteful. Where
were the *real* women? Where was Grace Slick? Then there was a
run on Roy Orbison's music and once again my jerk of a boss was in
a state of panic that he'd missed yet another good-time oldie post-
mortem sale. He was eating cocaine for breakfast by then and had a
bad case of the DBCs (Dead Brain Cells). I might sleep around now
and then; I might even end up with somebody who was born after
1968, but at least I'm moral about it. He gets them tanked and
snorted and then goes for the prize. One step above being a necro if
you ask me. And what really pisses me off is that society sees me as
the loser, the social misfit who's living in the past. The guy drives a
BMW and owns a condo and a business, stuffs all his money up his
nose, pokes teenage coeds who don't remember that he did it, and
he's successful.

I was just about to the point where I couldn't tune it all out when
I landed up with a bad hangover that turned into the flu and landed
me in one of those fast-food medicine places. You know, a Doc in the
Box, planted right beside Revco so you can rush right over and fill
your prescription. I felt like hell and I was about to stretch out on
their green vinyl couch and snooze when I saw someone familiar. It
was Marlene Adams, a girl from home, a woman of my time, no ring
on her hand, good-looking as ever. I sat straight up and was about to
say something when she turned calmly and called my name. "I was
wondering when you'd recognize me," she said and laughed, her
eyes as blue as the crisp autumn sky. "I had heard you were still
living around here. Who told me that? Somebody I saw at a wedding
not too long ago." For a split second I was feeling better, felt like

grabbing a bucket of chicken and sitting in the park, throwing a Frisbee, going to some open-air concert. "You haven't changed a bit," she said, and I felt her gaze from head to toe. It was the first time in years that I was *worried* about how I looked.

"Neither have you." I sat up straight, smoothed back my hair. God, why hadn't I taken a shower? "Why're you here?" I asked and glanced to the side where there was a cloudy aquarium with one goldfish swimming around. "I thought you were some place like California or Colorado or North Dakota. I thought you were married." I thought that fish must feel like the only son of a bitch on the planet, thirty gallons of water and nobody to swim over and talk to.

"Divorced. I'm back in graduate school, psychology," she said and laughed. "And I'm in this office because I tripped down some steps." I turned back from the dismal fish to see her holding out her right foot, her ankle blue and swollen. She had on a little white sock, the kind my mother always wore with her tennis shoes, little colored pompom balls hanging off the back.

"Can you believe it?" She shook her head back and forth. "It was really embarrassing. There were loads of people in the library when it happened." She leaned back, her thick hair fanning behind her as she stared up at the ceiling. I kept expecting her to say something really stupid and mundane and patronizing like *so, you say that you're living here but not in graduate school, you sell albums and tapes to coeds who you occasionally sleep with, you say that you have a hangover, what I'm hearing from you is that you are in search of a sex partner who has possibly heard of some of the songs of your youth.*

"I'm just as clumsy as I was the time we went camping," she said, her voice light and far removed from that psychological monotone I'd just imagined. "Remember? You swore you'd never take me again?"

"And I didn't," I said. "I never got the chance." I turned back to the fish. It was an awkward moment. You don't often get to discuss breaking up years after the fact but we were doing it. She dumped me, and now that I had reminded her of that fact, she was talking in high gear to cover the tracks. *Why does it take so long to get seen in this place?* and *When have you ever been home? Does your dad still have the refrigerator store and is your mom well?*

I was relieved when the door opened and the nurse called me in. "See you around," I said politely, half hoping that she'd disappear while I was gone. Marlene and I were the same age from the same small town, the same neighborhood even. I had known her since my family moved to that town when I was in the fifth grade and we had all run around screaming the words to "I Want to Hold Your Hand" and crossing our eyes like Ringo. That was the common ground that had brought us together that month in college to begin with.

I thought about it all while they stuck a thermometer in my mouth and instructed me to undress. Marlene had been pretty goofy as a kid, and though I considered her a friend, I never would have ridden my bike over to her house to *visit*. She had this dog named Alfie who smelled like crap, thus leaving Marlene and her wet-dog-smelling jeans rather undesirable. In junior high, Matt Walker and I had suggested we put Alfie in front of a firing squad and Marlene didn't speak to me for weeks after. No big deal, but then in high school we got to be pals just sort of hanging outside in the breezeway where you were allowed to smoke in between classes. Can you believe they *let* us smoke at school? That *they*, the administrators, those lopsided adults had *designated* an area? I spent a lot of time there and so did Marlene. She was on the Student Council which most of us thought was a bunch of crap, but still, she was forever circulating some kind of petition. She was really into womanhood, which I found kind of titillating in a strange way, don't ask me why, though I never did anything about it at the time. She was a hard worker, a smart girl. That's the kind of shit people wrote in her yearbook if they wrote anything at all. Nineteen-seventy was not a big year for yearbook signing. But then, get the girl off to college and there was major metamorphosis; it was like I could watch it happen there in poli sci lecture, blonde streaks in her hair that hung to her waist, little cropped T-shirts and cutoff jeans, her tinted wire-rim glasses (aviator style like Gloria Steinem) always pushed up on her head. Guys waited to see where she was going to sit and then clustered around her. God, she was beautiful, and then I had to take a turn just sitting and *listening* to all that was going on in her life just as she had *listened* to me there in the smoking area. I had a girlfriend here and there along the way, but I guess I was really waiting for Marlene to come around. Her boyfriend had been drafted, and though she told me how lucky I was not to have been taken (lucky break, legal blindness; my brother winged me in the left eye with a sharp rock when I was seven), I could tell that I was somehow weakened in her eyes. There would have been much more admiration had I had 20-20 vision and fled to Canada. It was a brief affair, the consummation of any likes we'd had for each other since adolescence, and then it was over, one fiasco of a camping trip, pouring down rain, Marlene spraining her thumb when she tripped over a tree limb and landed face down in the mud. It amazed me the things that that damn thumb *hindered* her from doing. It was a loss of a weekend.

"You have the flu," the nurse told me after I'd waited forever in my underwear, and I made my way back out to the lone-fish lobby to find her still there, though now her ankle was all neatly bound in an ace bandage.

"You don't look so great," she said. "Why don't I go home with you and fix something for lunch." I just shrugged, thinking about what was in my kitchen cabinet, a moldy loaf of bread, a couple of cans of tomato soup, one can of tuna. If she could turn it into something, I'd beg her to never leave me.

"What about your car?" I asked, and again she pointed to her ankle.

"I can't drive. My ankle." For a minute she sounded just like she had years before, *I can't do that, my thumb,* and I should have listened to the warning but I was too taken by her features, a face that needed no makeup of any kind, a girl who *looked* like she *ought* to be a perfect camper. "I rode the bus here," she said and extended her hand for me to help her up. "It'll be fun to catch up on things."

Marlene and I picked up with each other like we'd never been apart. It was like we could read each other's mind, and so we carefully avoided talking about the time we broke up. Instead we focused on all the good times, things we had in common just by being the same age and from the same town. Like I might say, "Remember when Tim Oates cut off the top of his finger in shop?" and she'd say, "Yeah, he was making a TV table for his Mama." Things like that. We had things in common that might *seem* absolutely stupid to an outsider. After three glorious months, tripling our first time together, Marlene and I finally came around to talking out all the things that ruined us before. She was starting to kind of hint about how she was going to be a professional and how maybe I

would want to be a *professional* too. I started singing that song, "I see
by your outfit that you are a cowboy, you see by my outfit that I'm a
cowboy, too."

"C'mon," she said and wrapped her arms around my neck, "I
don't mean to give you a hard time, it's just I've heard you say how
you really want . . ." Bad connection, bad connection.

"So get you an outfit and let's all be cowboys." I finished the song
and she went to take her exam in a real pissed-off state. I did what I
always do when I'm feeling lousy, which is to sort through my
albums and play all of my favorite cuts. I should have been a deejay,
the lone jockey on the late-night waves, rather than employee to a
squat coked-to-the-gills little rich shit. I thought of Marlene writing some little spiel about *composure; heal thyself.* I was playing Ten
Years After full blast, Sly and the Family Stone on deck. And then
all in one second I felt mad as hell, as mad as I'd been on that
pouring-rain camping trip when Marlene told me that it was hard
for her to think of me as anything except a *friend.* She actually said
that. It all came back to me when I saw that old Black Sabbath
album, which is what she had left behind that other time she moved
out. Thanks a whole helluva lot. Warms my heart to see a green-
faced chick draped in scarves wandering around what looks like a
mausoleum. She had said *all* the routine things you can think of to
say. "I know you don't really care about *me,*" she had said. "I could
be *anybody.*"

"Yeah, right," I told her. "I could cuddle up with Pat Paulsen and
not care. I'm just that kind of insensitive jerk."

"But you don't care about *me,*" she had said and pounded her
chest with her hand, which was wrapped in a bath towel to protect
the sprained thumb which had left her an absolute invalid. "I need
to be my own person, have my own life." I found out a day later that
she already had all the info on all these schools in the west; she had
been looking for a good time to bale out and it seemed camping out in
a monsoon was as good as any. It was hard to remember but it
seemed I said something like "And I don't need to have my own
life?" and then the insults got thicker until before long I was told
that I was apathetic and chauvinistic and my brain was stuck
between my legs.

"So, that's why you're always asking what I'm thinking," I said in
response. By time we were soaking wet and driving back *down*

the rest of this mountain in a piece-of-crap car I had at the time, an orange Pinto, with a Jimi Hendrix tape playing full blast (eight track of course). "And what kind of stupid question is that anyway and yet you always ask it. *What are you thinking?*" Yeah, that was how the whole ride home went and of course any time I had a good line, any time I scored, then she got to cry and say what an ass I was.

By the time she got home from her lousy test, I was as mad as if I was there in the pouring rain, jacking that screwed-up Pinto to change a flat while she sat in the passenger side and stared straight ahead at that long stretch of road we had to travel before I could put her out. Apparently she had been thinking through it all as well because she walked into my apartment looking just as she had when I dumped her out in front of her dorm years before. We had both played over the old stuff enough that we had independently been furious and now were simply exhausted and ready to have it all end, admit the truth. Nothing in common other than walking the planet at the same time. She was barely over her divorce, she rationalized (he had dumped her I was delighted to find). I handed her that Black Sabbath album on her way out and we made polite promises about keeping in touch.

And now I've come to this: Final Vinyl Days, the end of an era. Perfectly round black vinyl discs, their jackets faded, sit on the small table before my checkout and await extinction. I stare across the street, the black asphalt made shiny by the drizzling rain, the traffic light blinking red and green puddles in the gray light where a mammoth parking deck is under construction. There I see the lights in the store we compete with, Record City, and I can't help but wonder when they'll change their name: CD Metropolis. But what can I say about names? Any Old Way You Choose It ain't exactly true either.

"Record City doesn't have *these*," my boss had said just last week and began putting this crap all over the place, you know, life-size cutouts of Marilyn Monroe and Elvis, little replicas of the old tabletop jukeboxes that are *really* CD houses, piñatas and big plastic blowup dinosaurs. I work nights now, not as much business and I don't have to argue with the owner about what I play overhead. As

far as I'm concerned the new kids on the block are still Bruce
Springsteen and Jackson Browne. My boss said it was a promotion,
but I know better. Janis Joplin's singing now, "Me and Bobby
McGee" and the Stones are on deck with "Jumping Jack Flash."
The Stones are the cockroaches of rock. They'll be around when
civilization starts over, and I cling to this bit of optimism.

I had no choice but to give in to CDs. And yeah, they sound great,
that's true. It's just the principle of the thing, your hand forced to
change. Not to even mention the dreaded task of *replacing*. It's
impossible. Think of what's *not* available. I'm just taking my time is
all. I figure if I just go from the year of my birth to the year I
graduated from college, it'll take the rest of my life. I'm going
alphabetically so that I don't miss anything and it's a real boring
calculated way to approach life. I mean what if that's how I dealt
with women. Imagine it: Betts, Erica, Gail, Marlene, Nancy, that
one who always wore black either Pat or Pam, Susie, Xanadu. Yeah
right, Xanadu. I thought it was kinda cute that she had gone and
renamed herself. Then I learned that she had never even heard of
Coleridge, but rather had some vivid childhood memory of Olivia
Newton John. Scary. We were in a bar and it was very very late so
what could I expect? "Let's get physical," I suggested and she raised
her pencil-thin eyebrows as if trying to remember where she'd
heard *that* line before. "Can I call you Xan?"
    "Oh sure," she said, "everybody does." And when she walked
ahead of me to the door, I noticed her spiderweb stockings complete
with rhinestone spider. She wore a black spandex miniskirt and I
realized that my knowledge of women's fashions had come full
circle. I looked at myself in the beer-can-lined mirror to affirm that,
yes, I had hit bottom. Xan and I had *nothing* in common except
cotton mouth and body hair.

Now Del Shannon has gone and shot himself and no one has even
asked about his music. I hear the song "Runaway" and I see myself,
a typical nine-year-old slouch, stretched out on my bed with a stack
of comic books and the plug of my transistor radio wedged in my ear.
My mom made me a bedspread that looked like a race car, the
headlights down at the end facing into the hallway where my dad
was standing in his undershirt, his face coated in lather. "C'mon,

honey," my mom said. "We've got to get down to the store," and
then there we all were in front of this little cinder-block store at the
edge of town, our last name painted in big red letters on the
window. There must have been at least ten people gathered for the
event which my dad later said (while we waited for our foot-long hot
dogs to be delivered to the window of the car) was just about the
proudest moment of his life. He said it was second only to marrying
my mother (she had a ring of vanilla shake around her mouth as she
smiled back at him) and having my younger brother and me. My
brother was in a french-fry frenzy, bathing in the pool of catsup
he'd poured in the little checkered cardboard container, but he
stopped to take in the seriousness of my dad's announcement. I was
wondering even then how you *know* when it's the happiest moment.
I was dumbfounded that anyone could build a life on refrigerators
and stoves and be happy about it. It amazes me now to think that I
had ever sat in the backseat of that old Chevrolet and looked at my
parents (younger then than I am now) and thought how ridiculously
outdated they were.

Now this coed comes in. Tie-dye is *back*, torn jeans, leather
sandals. If her hair wasn't purple and aimed at the ceiling, I could
just about console my grief. "Can I help?" I ask, totally unprepared
for the high squeak of a voice that comes out. She sounds like she
just inhaled a balloon full of helium.

"I want *The Little Mermaid*," she said, a high school ring still on
her finger. "You know, the video? It's for my little brother."

"Yeah right. Over there." I point to the far wall, the latest
addition to any record/CD/video store, a menagerie of colorful
piñatas swinging overhead. "We got 'em all."

Oh yeah. We've got a two-foot table boasting the end of my youth,
leftover albums, the bottom of the barrel. It's all that's left and
nobody even stops to look, to mourn, to pay respect. I arranged them
such that Joni Mitchell is the one looking out on the dreary day. I
imagine someone coming in from the street and saying, "Oh I get it,
paved paradise and put up a parking lot," but no such luck; there is no
joy in Mudville.

I try to make myself feel better. I think of the positive factors in
my life. I recycle my cans and glass and paper. I ride a bike instead

of driving a car. Though my old man and I don't always see eye to eye, I know that I'll never turn to find him with a gun pointed my way like Mr. Gaye did to Marvin. I sleep peacefully, all bills paid, no TV blasting MTV like the one across the street in the cinder-block house where a couple of girls come and go. One of them is real nice looking in a kind of Marlene way, wears gym clothes all the time, no makeup, hair long and loose. Though I know sure as hell if I slept with her she'd get up and put on lipstick and control-top panty hose and ask me why I don't cut my hair and get a real job. It's the luck of the draw and my luck is lousy. "Give up the Diet Coke," I had told Betts. "Give up the fluorescent foods." I had told Marlene to give up the self-pity; if she wanted to be somebody, then to stop talking about it and be it. I had suggested to Xan that she give up the body hair. I told the boss to be *different,* not to cave in to all this new crap. The bottom line? Nobody likes suggestions. So why am I supposed to be different?

"What can you tell me about the Byrds?" My heart leaps up and I turn to face the purple-haired, squeaky-voiced girl who has placed *The Little Mermaid* on the counter and has a twenty clutched in her fist.

"Yeah? The Byrds? Like turn, turn, turn?"

She looked around, first one way then the other. Then she looked back at me, face young and smooth and absolutely blank. "The pink ones," she squeaks and points upward where flamingo piñatas swing on an invisible cord. "How much?"

I watch her walk off now, her pilgrim-looking shoes mud splat-tered as she heads through the construction area, her pink bird clutched to her chest along with *The Little Mermaid.* It's times like this when I start thinking that I might give my dad a call and say, "I know you've been saying how you want me to take over your business some day . . ." It's times like this when I start thinking about Marlene, when I start forgetting how bad it all got. I do crazy things like start to imagine us meeting again, one more try at this perfect 1970 romance. Like maybe I *will* go to work for my dad and in my off-hours maybe I'll get out the old power saw and make my mom a TV table (just like you've been saying you wanted, mom) and maybe I'll circumcise the old index finger and end up in an emer-gency room and I'll look down that row of vinyl chairs and there she'll be. It's not the *perfect* fantasy but it's one I have. It's one that more and more starts looking good after I watch Marvin's music revived by a bunch of fat raisins dancing around on the tube, or after I see a series of women getting younger and younger, arriving at my door in their spider hose and stiff neon hair, their arms filled with little plastic squares, a mountain of CD covers dumped on my floor.

RICHARD McCANN

Hôtel du Roi,
Nôtre Dame

(from the novel *Our Mother of the Late Movies,*
Our Mother of Sorrows)

When I left home, I made up this lie: I said my father was
French.

Français.

I said he was the last son of a prominent French family which, for
obscure reasons, had settled itself in Rabat, Morocco. *Une famille
du haut monde. Une famille de fortune aisée.* I said I was born in
Rabat, too.

I said I was born of an American mother, a divorced socialite,
whom my father had met and married during a brief sojourn in
New York City. Her name was Maria Dolores, which, translated,
means "Mother of Sorrows." She had what people called "Spanish
eyes," like Gene Tierney in *Leave Her to Heaven. C'est amusant,
n'est-ce pas?*

In fact, I have never been to Rabat. But I have been to Ceuta—I
was thirty-five, and running away from the life I still hadn't made.
And from Ceuta, I traveled onward in a broken-down Mercedes
taxi, the driver smuggling Dior bed sheets beneath the backseat, to
Tetuan and Tangiers. By the time we reached Tangiers, I was so
fatigued by the assault of newness, and by my constant wariness
amidst the unfamiliar, that I could no longer fend off the local
Arab guides who loitered everywhere—bus stations, markets, hotel
lobbies—attempting to catch the eyes of frightened and befuddled
tourists, to whom they then bound themselves for days, and so, the
second I stepped from the taxi, I was taken up at once by one of

them, Mohammed, a muscular boy of seventeen, who, in what seemed a quick moment of cunning, grabbed my suitcase from my hand, vowed his loyalty and his services, and walked promptly up an alleyway dead-ending at a shabby pink stucco palace, the Hôtel du Roi. I followed.

Each morning after that, when I emerged from the hotel, I found him sitting at the curb, as though he'd been waiting since daybreak: whether his patience derived from his promised loyalty, or whether he was leary that I'd try to ditch him, I could not tell. In any case, as we toured Tangiers, he told me how much he hoped to visit New York, or how much he like the Motown sound, and sometimes, at lunch, he showed me airmail letters he'd received from American and German tourists he'd once guided around his city. They were short letters, written on aerogrammes and onionskin paper. In a kind of simple and hesitant language hinting at the stilted syntax they'd used with Mohammed, their authors assured him of the quality of his company, telling him how in their fond memories it was he, Mohammed, dear Mohammed, who stood for the large heart of Morocco. Sometimes there were photos enclosed—a heavy German blonde in a swimsuit, posed by her emptied pool; an angular, pockmarked man standing on a sun-bleached concrete driveway, holding a chihuahua. "I am hoping," Mohammed said, carefully refolding the fragile paper, "that you shall one day write me such a letter."

And then at night, after he steered me back through the narrow streets of the medina and toward the Hôtel du Roi, there was an awkward parting at the door. Seen from a distance—by the veiled woman who once watched us from an upstairs window, perhaps— we must have looked like strangers pausing to give the time or to buy hashish, or like paramours shyly parting. "You are really so tired?" he asked, standing half within the building's shadow, desultorily picking at the pink stucco wall until paint chips fell to his shoes. Then he touched me on the elbow, as though he meant to take my arm, the way Moroccan men did as they walked with one another, and his touch so exhilarated me—*He is beautiful*, I thought, *and nothing like me*—that I instantly imagined its possible intention as being some ludicrous and sad contrivance of my own. Certainly he was simply attempting to negotiate whether or not I'd value his presence at the hotel door the next morning. But why should he?—certainly his presence was a fait accompli, for if there was one thing people said of all these guides, it was that they simply couldn't be shaken. In this way, the debate I conducted within myself wore down my own desire. "Good-night," I said. "I'm very tired. Very tired." Truly, I could not figure how to tell him just how tired I was.

That is, I could not figure how to tell him I wanted him to come to my room. My room was preposterously simple, if not in its execution, then in its mentality. On the right was a plasticized orange valet chair, presumably for *monsieur*. On the left was a bidet concealed behind a tattered pink curtain, presumably for *madame*. In the middle was a sagging bed, presumably for pleasure. *Une chambre trés bon confort. Un hôtel trés agréeable.* In retrospect, of course, I see he would have fucked me, if that was really what I wanted, or, perhaps, he might even have allowed himself to be fucked, modestly preparing himself in the bidet behind the tattered curtain. In retrospect I see there was a way of telling him what I wanted, and telling him quite simply—words, for instance, or money, preferably in dollars or deutsch marks, although, if necessary, pesetas would also have been accepted.

In retrospect I even see that Mohammed himself had wanted this—I don't just mean the money—for on my fifth day in Tangiers, we argued, and he stormed off like an angry lover, abandoning me in the medina. On my behalf, he'd been haggling in Arabic with a rug merchant. They must have haggled for half an hour; in any case, they haggled so long that I felt the way I felt when we occasionally ran into a gang of his teenaged friends—jealous for the earnestness of his attention. But when at last they settled upon a price, I saw both the merchant and Mohammed smile, as if in concert, and at that instant, my jealousy came forward, as did my wary doubts. I hesitated, and Mohammed saw in my expression that I feared I was being cheated. At first he looked embarrassed, as though he held himself responsible for having invented some affection he'd imagined was quite mutual. For a moment, he looked at me directly, seeking some confirmation, or, more precisely, some denial of the reality my hesitation had created. But I looked away: after all, there was certainly no reason for him to be upset; my caution was hardly personal.

He was furious. He picked up a bag of oranges he himself had bought and shoved his way past me into the street. Then he turned and threw the oranges to the ground, and the bag split, and the fruit ruptured, and its bright juice puddled on the cobblestones. He shouted that I should keep them, they were his gift, *un souvenir trés symbolique,* surely I could appreciate *that,* even if there was little else about him I seemed to understand. *"Evidemment, monsieur,"* he said, *"vous ne savez rien de Maroc. Ni des hommes. Ni de moi."* My god, I thought as he walked away, *he's practically flouncing.*

Then I saw the medina merchants were watching me, and I imagined they found me at fault, as though I had made some untoward suggestion which Mohammed had naturally and justly rebuffed in the clearest and most necessary manner, and to show them how unperturbed I was—it was nothing, *nothing* like they imagined—I turned toward one of them, the one who seemed the least successful, the most wretched and most needy, and I said, "I *assume* those rugs are handmade. I *assume* they are *originals."*

I made my way back to the Hôtel du Roi, to the lobby with its dirty banquettes and its caged reception desk, where the concierge presided over the room keys as though they were racks of pawnshop watches. I hated him: each night when I came in, leaving Mohammed at the curb, I hated finding him in his steel cage, regarding me steadily as he sipped his mint tea; I hated asking him for my room key, whose number by then he surely must have memorized; I hated the way he dropped the key onto the counter, as though indeed it were something he were selling to me, an undiscerning customer, who had chosen an utterly unattractive item of the poorest quality; and I hated they way, as he pushed it forward, he smiled unctuously, as though to tell me my bad choice would surely cost me, but if that was what I wanted, then, *alors,* what could he do but oblige me?—*Caveat emptor.* That is, each night after I left Mohammed at the curb, I imagined the concierge had witnessed my desire, and that he'd disapproved of it, and of me, and of all my kind—My kind! What kind was that?—although, in retrospect, I see that if he was angry it was because I'd denied him the small bribe it would have taken to get Mohammed past his desk.

"Peut-être monsieur désire autres choses? Perhaps monsieur desires a newspaper? A nightcap? Anything at all?"

"*Non,*" I said, "*monsieur ne désire rien.*" Nothing, that is, except to get past you, past you and into that elevator that will lift me upward, shaking on its loose cables as it rises.

I went to my room and lay down. It was then I thought to go to Rabat. After all, it had a reputation quite different from Tangiers: in the scheme of Morocco, in fact, Rabat was often considered somewhat quiet, even disappointing, though such opinions tended toward the highly touristic, formed by those least well-equipped to get the feel of a place. When it came right down to it, of course, Tangiers was really a bit more like Tijuana than anywhere: one could hardly judge a whole country by the chaos of its borders.

This was a good plan. But first I would get a good sleep, a very good sleep, and when I got up, I'd probably find Mohammed sitting at the curb outside the hotel, as he always did, and I'd explain that I was headed to Rabat, and, if he liked, and had the time as well as inclination, I'd be pleased if he'd be my guest for a glass of tea before I headed for the station. While we had the tea, I'd find an inoffensive way to settle up, for he had as yet received no money, which was quite unfair, since, after all, he had shown me around almost the entire city, and had done it quite intelligently. Not that it was rare, the thing about the money; indeed, it was the custom, I had heard, to present the money at the parting, so that it seemed like more of what it was, a deeply felt and well-intentioned gift, and not a series of demeaning tips individually awarded for specific services satisfactorily performed.

But when I came down the next morning, there was of course no Mohammed.

There was only the concierge—and beside him, also locked within the metal cage, was an Arab child, a boy. The boy was crying. The concierge was punishing him. I could not make out the offense. What carries us to places which express us better than we might express ourselves, so that were someone to ask, "What's the matter?" we might point mutely—"This. . . ."

The concierge looked up at me. "There's no message from your friend," he said, "if that's what you're waiting for."

By then, I don't think I expected a message from Mohammed.

The concierge unlocked the cage and pushed the boy, still crying, through the door. "Go," he said. "Get out of here."

The boy hurried into the street. The concierge sat down again

and busied himself, copying sums from one black ledger into another. I simply stood there. I was trying to make up my mind. There
was a hydrofoil leaving for the Spanish coast at 11:00 A.M.

The concierge put down his pencil. "Is there something else?" he
asked. He was impatient, annoyed. "Look, if it's about the kid, he'll
come back. He always does. He's my son."

So, he was his son.

And then I was crossing the Spanish frontier at Tarifa, its beach
lined with army tanks. And then I was in Torremolinos, and from
Torremolinos I hitched a ride with a drunken countess—"*Le Roi est
mort!*" she kept shouting from her Fiat's open window—to Alicante, where she lived, and from Alicante I took a bus to Barcelona,
and from Barcelona I boarded a train for the border at Port Bou, and
at midnight in Port Bou, waiting on the concrete quay for the Paris
Express, a blonde kept staring at me, as though she might have
known me, until at last she came up and asked, "*Sind Sie auch
Deutsch?*" "No, not German," I said, turning away. "I'm something
else." And then I was drunk, and I was in Paris, and I was at the
Cinema Marotte, on rue Vivienne, sitting beside a Vietnamese man
who rubbed my crotch as we stared in silence at a movie of two men
fucking, one with his legs raised, slavish and demanding, and the
other, mounting him, brutal and apologetic. The men were mus-
cled like Americans. "*C'est amusant, n'est-ce pas?*" the Vietnamese
man whispered; he smelled faintly of the restaurant he must have
worked in. Then he withdrew a handkerchief, which he fluttered
briefly in the dark before dropping it to my lap, where he held it—
"*Vite, ça viens*"—as I came. On screen the actors exchanged roles,
and the one who'd been on the bottom became wildly angry, unbelievably so, like a furious cartoon character, or maybe the movie
itself changed, I don't remember—*Séances continuelles.*

And then I was alone again, and drunker still, and standing on
the pavement, staring into a shop window filled with dusty stuffed
iguanas and dying cacti, and in the rear of the shop, I could see five
small lighted clocks that told the time in major cities around the
world, and beneath them a banner: *Agence de voyages. Traversez par
tôut l'univers.* In New York, it was late; in Paris, later still. I hailed a
taxi.

And then I realized I could go anywhere, turn right, turn left,
drive dead-on for a million miles, *traversez par tôut l'univers,* and I

threw my cigarette to the gutter, for at that moment I realized I could give up anything, even smoking. I had no more dependencies.

A taxi stopped and I climbed in. The driver was a corpulent, middle-aged woman with a German shepherd sitting on the front seat beside her.

"Hôtel Saint-Severin," I told her. But this isn't what I wanted. I simply did not know how to say in French that I wanted her to drive on forever. Where could I find a phrase book, an emergency lexicon?—*farther, farther, anywhere but here.*

I must have scared her with my drunkenness, for as she drove she watched me in her rearview mirror, watched me so long and so intently, in fact, that I began talking. I talked so much I couldn't stop. "I've always wanted to be in Paris," I said. "It is all I've ever wanted, to be here. All of my life. Since I was a child, studying French. Or most of my life then. Since hearing Edith Piaf."

When I said *Piaf,* she studied me yet more narrowly. She sped up.

"Yes," I rattled on, "Edith Piaf. I know all those songs. I memorized them. '*Mon Dieu.*' '*Je Ne Regrette Rien.*' '*La Vie en Rose.*' When I was a child I listened to Edith Piaf. I listened to Piaf in our basement rec room. I lip-synched to her records. I pretended I was Piaf, and when I was done singing, I rapidly flicked the switch of the ceiling light on and off, on and off, as though it were applause calling me back onstage. I have always wanted to come to Paris. To Paris. It is all I ever wanted. It is what I dreamed of all that time."

We were crossing Pont Neuf. Suddenly, the driver slammed on her brakes, and her German shepherd lurched forward against the dashboard. We stopped in the middle of the bridge.

The driver turned to face me. "*Mais monsieur,*" she said, "*vous êtes à Paris. Voilà, Nôtre Dame!*" And indeed, when I looked to my left, there it was, Nôtre Dame.

I felt sober. How long had I been traveling, and how far away, and from what fixed point outside myself, from what decimated blast crater? But I had fled nowhere, nowhere at all. I was drunk, and sitting in a taxi stopped on a bridge, watching the driver pet her German shepherd. They had brought me to the deep interior. Nôtre Dame.

Nôtre Dame. No matter what I said when I left home, I never lied about my mother, not once, not ever, unless it was to say I hated her.

Natural Bridge Collapses

At the Visitor's Center
the brunette selling tickets
feels a vague queasiness
while
in the nearby Wax Museum
the sequined effigy
of Elvis shudders
imperceptibly.

ROBERT BESS

Oswald Fell, into a Comma and Died*

Our keen young scholar fires one fingertip
at random into World Book—Volume O:
shot of Lee Harvey Oswald in the grip
of twin marshals.

                    A Pentel rises slow
as smoke. The bright eyes soften to a sage
boredom as Oswald tumbles, and the flow
of words clots into puddles on the page.

---

*found in a freshman paper

IRV BROUGHTON

A Dream of Sinkholes:
Winter Park

Certainly, Fairbanks was
Predisposed, or disposed
Though its residents know
Things go
Down.
       But, in houses
Across the posh flanks
Of Central Florida,
Or on old Ivanhoe
Drive, a renovator
Stirs uneasily, shaving
The bottom of doors
Above a newly laid
Green carpet, as if
The subversive
Earth had this
Time risen—
Like the polite dead—
To meet him.

AMANDA B. BULLINS

Grief

You give away first the instant
oatmeal you never could stand,
use the toothbrush left behind
to polish your few pieces of silver.
You put tape over a name
you don't want to see on books
and hide everything else
in hatboxes in the attic.
You learn tricks. You act fast.
Of course, your neighbors watch you
and are not so easily fooled.
They ask whether you have thought
of doing anything about your lawn.
You realize you've been inside,
forgetting the grass that's out there
flowering like sea oats,
though it isn't dunes that encroach
on your house. Your hillside is
tangled in wire grass, tough-rooted
weeds your neighbors warn you
will take over everything if
you forget and let them go to seed.

ROSANNE COGGESHALL

"Moving in Memory"

For Julia Randall

From Hartley Mill you name and number proofs:
resiliencies, earth's tenses, celebrations
of earth's sense—bloodroot, jack pine, mayapple,
birch—light tinder for a tracker's fire
against dark traces.

What you never taught me long enough
for sentences to end I find again
to recognize as real—
Dead Man or Furness Fell,
all conjugations clinch to spell horizons
to the listening eye,
remaker with new alphabets of blues and grays,
reds, lilacs, golds.
No flower holds as long as trees and mountains;
even transients need rest.
You resolve each wilderness
in increments; syllabic structures
piece the plain flawed swoop of sense.
Over where the light turns dark
we look for words
to tell us where we are
or where we were,
maybe in an August night,

with stars like milkweed blowing
down the sky, the moon in its blue satchel,
silver semaphore whose signals try
our torn intentions, our common *why*.

To till best your own unleavened field
you work against those obstacles
to fallen nature's weave;
light lifts each metaphor,
swung barriers to grief,
to grave.

On Eight Mile

She appears as if at the edge
Of a screen, her brown hair black
In this light, her legs moving the way

She wants you to want them to move.
It's hard to see the woman you loved
Dance naked in a room of men

And come up to your table after
And ask for a light, and the light
In her eyes is still the same,

Only her job has changed. She changes
Into clothes and we cross the street
To a tamer place of food and talk,

And the talk turns to me, to what
I do that makes me think I'm better
Than her. I'm not and I know it,

But she won't be convinced. Nothing
I can say will sway her the way
She sways on stage. And nothing

Can make me look away.

—for R. L. W.

House of the Lord

for Alvin Ailey
with love

I

A tree splits from a crysalis of light:
branches shattering the patient
repose of the spirit.
Fall, turn, harrow the air,
the heart, turn, and then return
to that stillness, that mouth of joy.

II

Water pulled out of the dark,
waves falling up in blind ascent:
break the rock and shout,
break the rock and feed the desert.
Dance on the scalding sand.

III

Bones of clay, body of sand:
stand, and move.
Caress me with your right hand
and your left.
Rise and bless the air.
Turn and turn and turn in an arc of longing.
Bend back and touch the water.

IV

You hear the water?
It's moving like ribbons across the ground.
Touch it. Your hands to your face,
your face to the water. Touch it.
Under the umbrella, you turn to water.
Turning under the umbrella, your feet
flow into the ribbons. In the ribbons,
your arms are waves.
Breathe. Water is air.
Air is water.

V

Curve up and fall back.
Curve up and fall back.
Pull me up in this air.
Lay me down in this earth.
I breathe in.
I breathe out.
Mother, where are your arms?

VI

Fire on the rock.
Fire in the sea.
Spread your arms, turn,
Spin through the flames.
Run to water, earth, and air,
wrestling in their single element.
Your bones are brass melting,
Your arms, your legs, are glass.
Now you are the river,
the river turning to ash.

VII

The day is past and gone, o Lord.
The evening falls like a fan.
What she said to you was how the world began.
What you said to her was time rolling on.

We are all here:
the neighbor's wife, the neighbor's son,
Uncles, cousins, enemies, friends.
We are the house, building itself
from bare wood,
pulled up plank on plank,
shouting in the shingles,
shaking in the walls,
rocked in time and out of time,
in Your endless arms.

Void and Compensation

Early August. The churlish day gives itself over as a gift, hands
itself to night like a gilt-edged plate on which sits not the head
of John the Baptist but his just-cut steaming heart,
glittering like a tiny ocean dissecting a tiny land—
His just-cut heart, as I said, which is like the bell
of darkness the day becomes as it grows less and less light.

And it is this we move to, isn't it, not simply light
but its reduction, its absence. & the possibility of our hearts
loosing that light, of it pouring like balm from our hands,
from our lips, spurting from our unruined heads
like a volcano. We look at each other steadily—the silence a bell
between us, and we become the same country, the same land.

I dreamed of you again last night. We were in Virginia
     and the land
as we crossed it gave way to lakes, and the light
rose and fell over the water the way a tolling bell
sounds closer or farther, depending on the direction of the head.
And the landscape was mythic, and we were mythic: our hands
were strong and calloused, and our clean-swept hearts

felt as if they'd been scourged: That we'd never known
     other hearts,

or wanted to, and our dreams held nothing of desire. And I
        was able
to know that this was what I wanted. —The simple work
        of the hands,
good bread, the sun through the window just *light*
& not an emblem, an elegy for a higher order. The land
spread out beneath us like the great head

of a bull whose snort-mist curled like horns around his own
        shaggy head.
Simplicity and an end to needing to know the end. To be handed
certainty. Sometimes when we moved together I could hear
        my own heart
beating like a bird that cries its own name, or a bell
that takes as its name its tone. —& then the light
broke like glass & I woke fast in your arms, my head

pillowed against your heart. It was your heart beating in my head
like a longed-for, sonorous, light-tipped bell.
Let everything between us be a falling away, an ascent
        to this land
we have made: I want the light
to spill from our hands like mercury, that our hands
together hold nothing but each other. Listen: a heart

that understands void rings like a bell in compensation;
& that heart plumbs its own depth like light glimmers down
the land-crusted sides of a hand-dug well, heading deeper,
        ever deeper.

The Whale

Purple, languid, content, cruising
the ocean bottom, land without light;
behemoth fuelled by a cumulus shifting breath
rolled in its lungs delicious as smoke
in the addict's mouth, but having at last
to break the membrane of the surface to take
air. So while I peel potatoes, or bend
to pick up a tennis ball, or when I lean
to switch the channel on the car radio, grief
may without warning break my face,
my everyday skin. Because there was
a summer day when the clouds overhead
like magic slates rewrote themselves in silence,
because the falling chatter of the chimney swifts
at twilight sank tighter and tighter into circles
of darkness, I know that the world does speak,
but in all its tongues each word means good-bye.

Surfing

Picture a large room.
The largest you have yet to see
without walls and
tiny flecks of color
splash-dashing into the sea.

If all the colors
decided all at once
to move toward the sea,
picture the quiet
and the little stretch of green.

MARGARET GIBSON

Sarah

Before I enter, at the door
alone and secret, I pause
for balance at the threshold,
and for breath.
I breathe slowly, a scale
of muted notes that rise, and fall,
and rise. Smells, immaculate
and sterile, tinged with
salt and medicine and oil,
swell, recede.
How bare it is—window, chair,
and the bed where my father
sleeps, his body a faint
ridge of white beneath
the cover, his head
tilted, mouth
open, hardly a stir of air
going in, out.
And the hole that is his mouth
(that used to blow a kiss, or swear
or grin, telling stories)
that liminal hollow of breath
barely felt,
is the naught that draws me, here.

I release the will to be home,
fire rising in the kiln.
I release my will to find Kate,
or stay with Brook. To hold them.
Through tears I wait until
again I can enter
the unknown matrix of water and sun,
letting myself be drawn
beyond own will—to a movement
that, silent, seems flame
and emptiness, and promise.
I let disperse
all will but this—
I have come to be with my father.
This man who has made me burn
with terror and anger. This man.
My father. I cross the room,
open the window, find a pitcher
for water. I've brought
yellow chrysanthemums,
as acrid and bright
as the lie I could tell for comfort—
but won't—

that Lila and Jennie come tomorrow.
They won't, and the yellow
bough of maple, leaves
about to curl at the edges,
is from only Brook.
Quietly: to resist the lie.
Quietly: to accept
what the moment, infinitive, gives.
I run water, let it
splash about the sink.
The water chills, the water grieves.
I want water softly to wake
this man who has gone from his family
so often, that the sound
of water running, gone by,

says more aptly
"Father—father good-bye"
than anything Jennie might say,
or Lila, too numb, too hurt.
I think of the flat stone I have
in my studio, a round
O in its center where water sank,
drop by drop, and hollowed.
And for the will to receive

the power of water
into the stone of my grief,
without asking to achieve
anything by my being here,
but being here,
for that will-be-done
I ask. "Your father
wears his motives on his sleeve."
My mother's voice weaves
in and out of the leaves, as if
alive only by wanting to relive
what's as bitter as the smell
of these blowsy flowers,
heavy-heads
that shudder as I move
the pitcher over to his bedside.
I laugh softly at myself—
voices in flowers? absurd.
"That's better." A raspy whisper
meets my laugh.
A slow turn of his head.
"The news of my death has been
greatly exaggerated."
"Aha," I say. "Mark Twain—"

let us now quote famous men—
I know the game, a favorite
of his, and it's my turn.
"Let me think," I say, but I can't.

Though he turns his head
towards me, he can't lift it.
Beside his mouth, a white
smear has dried, the medicine
he drinks to soothe, to coat,
to cloak the ravaged
linings burned by acid,
blood and gall, and alcohol,
years of it, his recent
abstinence too late.
All I can think of is Twain
again, "Do not bring your dog,"
the first line in a monologue
on funerals and etiquette—
just his wit. A special
defiance he'd call
giving necessity the guise,
graceful or raucous, of rigmarole.
But then I see his eyes.

They hold mine steadily,
a careful stealth,
as if to inquire
beneath anything said openly
whether I know what he knows.
What I see takes my breath—
There's death
in his eyes, a fact the social poise
of his manner denies—the gesture
of a hand graciously
extended—still the host of the party
who cares, if not to please,
then somehow to amuse.
I take his hand and hold on—
not too tightly,
though I want him to say
it, let death
be spoken between us, energy
summoned consciously, agon or koan,

claimed, used—*this is mine,*
and let go of, the gift given.
And not this guarded non sequitur,
this detour—the truth
of the moment deemed improper.

No matter what death I'd opt
for, myself—this is his
to shape and honor, or not—
and so love, that profound
courtesy, has me respond
simply, "How are you?"
"Tired," he whispers. "Tired."
Then he winks. The rake returns.
"I'm what they say, *in and out.*"
He likes the phrase.
He croons it as he sinks
into the lull drugs make
of his body, medicine
his merciful angel, his retreat.
In and out, the quick
trip he always promised, into
the gin mill and out—just one.
I hear the surface pattern
of excuse, *in and out,* the taboo
rhythm of the afternoon affair, a sunrise
swim—a slantwise
permission for pleasure and guilt,
wry refreshment, and no
sense of the pattern his pain makes.

How can I tell him what he ought
to do, or feel, or be? He is.
He is asleep.
Again, his mouth falls open,
tensely open.
His breath spins wide, spins down.
He's lonely as a tunnel.
His breath barely rises, falls.

I breathe with him, for his
sake, and mine—*we are not*
separate, no one is—
but these words taste hollow, false.
Someone's missing, and the shape
of the emptiness between us
is a door, opening. Yet here
in the room with my father,
I find I'm grateful
for the gift of spoken
truth he spilled, pouring out
a family wine turned vinegar.
Perhaps now I will no longer
be compelled to go off to the wheel
to find respite in the cool
control of clay. Nor hope

to purchase my innocence
in good works and a silence
that would unify everyone
around me, whether they want it
or not. And so . . . grateful.
But my God this is hard.
To my children I have said
accept what unfolds as meant,
and be grateful. But this small
gratitude I feel
is not the point—and I don't
know anymore what is meant.
I go over to the sink to rinse
hands and face—
if I am to enter the unknown
pattern each moment
gives, at least I can
enter also the comfort of water
as it takes the shape of whatever
form surrounds it
briefly, cup water to my face,
rinse its outline, bone and skin,

and feel how water
lightly makes sorrow's trace

or joy's, then goes.
I let an open brook run over
the rim of my hands.
I let water race
through my fingers, as spring
rain on a mountain
ridge, down
hard in all directions, diverse
channels through rock and rubble
and spume, finds
neither bound nor obstacle
enough to contain
its onrush. I still the water,
fitting the stopper
in the sink, floating
one gold leaf there on water—
and I remember
floating, just inside
me the first baby Comfort also floating,
and I'm teaching young
Kate to trust the water,
to trust her body, to lie back in
the flow of the sky's unbounded
openness, and feel it present within

a watersilk of cattails,
clouds, and a green maple rooting upside
down in ripples,
billowing—even the redwing's nest
turned shimmer,
turned spiral and meander,
each thing around us
softening, passive to a wider
will. This holy
art, father,
may we know it, breathing quietly,

sinking with the sun's last ember.
And if it's deathwatch,
as it was once in Charlottesville
(I remember the slope of the bowl
inward, how I fell
through the dark, not so much
forgiven as released from the clutter
of an intense resistance)
may we not cling to any
feeling that's aggrieved, confused—
may we have peace together—
and no word, not a touch, unless touch
means lightly

letting go. Now I pull the stop,
and the water swirls down,
leaf in a spiral
following—then, guttural
a sound like *botch,* and the bright
leaf, sucked down,
comes to rest on the dark gape
of the sink. I look up—
the room's blank, white,
sublittoral as a shell, clean as salt.
Symmetry, order, repose—
all the laws
he believed in and never,
faithful to, brought home, hover here.
Little by little,
what we really are, we learn
by subtraction—less than we thought.
What's left is light—
or the wild refusal of light.
My father's hand flutters open,
grasps air, shuts.
Eyes closed, wincing hard—
now only this pain
left to believe in.

I sit down now, finally
with him. And he says, clearly—
though he doesn't open his eyes
or give any sign
that he feels my hand on his—
"After all this, what do I know?"
Out the window, far
from the misted shore, an ease
of sea horn, low,
gives itself to the sea,
and the night sea gathers.
Again, low. And in the pause
between two notes, I whisper
to him. How every night
as a child I looked for the light,
late, beneath his door,
or opened the front
door, wishing him home with us.
If he wants the release
this shyly offered truth tries
to give, I trust—I feel
I must trust—him to take it.
Does he? I can't tell. But the yellow
chrysanthemums seem more yellow—

the flowers deepen,
as if they might transmit more
light from sources beyond
what we know. I feel
our lonely honesty
as if it were color. And I remember
the single most vivid memory
I have of him alone—in the stern
of his craft, the line
lightly held as he waits
for wind that rises with the sun,
wind that settles east, where
the lighthouse is a bright

needle, and the wind threads
round—a ripple,
ripples—and now wind takes the ready
modesty of the sail—
and yes, the joyous
shout he gives as he goes
running with the morning wind,
one with that motion.
I feel my pain, and his, subside.
Wind and sun come to meet my father,
and I hold that brightness close.

The door opens, and a nurse comes
with a basin, a towel folded
underneath it, and a smile
that wants to be tactful, but isn't.
She wants me to leave while
she washes him.
Well, of course. I begin to defer—
but here's my father curled
away like a child from the cold,
from the dark, from the blind
sources of pain without name.
"I'll be glad to do it," I say
quickly. "I'm his daughter."
And the guile of that non sequitur
combines with the docile
truth of the offer to surprise her.
"I'll just turn him,"
she replies, but looks strangely
at me, handing over the towel
and the oil, her look reminiscent
of Lila's disapproval, wary.
I'm to see my own father naked.
I'm to touch the body

that, younger, got me here,
yoked sweetly to flesh, to clay.
I'm to touch armpit, shoulders,

thighs and the curve of his belly,
the limp sack of his sex,
taboo or not.
I'm to touch this stranger
who gulps air
and paws the pillows, who kicks
the covers fretfully like a child
who would bully illness.
I'm to take him as he is,
a man, like most, who let
flesh be fate,
be compass and trespass,
be rubric and sleepless
dream. I'm to let him be
or cease to be, as he chooses.
As for the nurse, I try to reassure
her, my gestures
(filling the basin, testing the water
for warmth) efficient.
She turns him from one side
to the other, careful to tilt

his head back. She spoons
chalky stuff down his throat.
He swallows, submissive,
though he rucks up his mouth,
the folds of skin
beneath his jaw so loose
they crease like a ruche.
She checks the level of his urine
in the plastic bag, undoes
tubes taped tightly to his wrist,
and leaves. Acrid,
the odor of urine weaves
about us. "I hate the smell of piss,"
he whispers. "I'm afraid."
I shiver—this is what it means
to be naked, exposed
utterly, the first and last

pulse of each primitive
moment a death, a death, a death,
and still the ruse
of dignity, though it grows thin,
thinner, finally transparent.
Carefully I place my hand
around the curve of his chin,

my cheek to his forehead,
pressing gently. "Afraid?—don't be."
I ask him to think of the sea
he loved to glimpse
just ahead as the path of beach plum
narrowed in the dunes, the rim
of the tide line rising,
the presage of a fine sail
felt in the frail
billow of a web held
taut in the salt wind
that skiffs up the steep sand—
and once again I'm a child
with my father's enthusiasm
for the sun to buoy me,
and nothing harsh has come
into this paradise—
though it will,
and how shall I say *be grateful*
no matter what unmeasured
passion flames or chills?—
so I rock him until the rousing
sea slides still,
and he sleeps in the measure of my arms,

neither father nor lover.
He slips past my hands
into an eclipse of consciousness
too deep for me,
past the image of the sea
I gave him, for courage,

to follow. I loosen
the knot of the blue hospital gown
and slip my hand inside,
his skin dry as paper.
His flesh feels hot, he shivers,
and sighs with the fire inside
him—an emptiness
in the shape of a flame, a whisper
of the intensity of his solitude.
My role here is to tend—
what little I know transferred
to the work of tenderness
this work is. Forgive us
(I murmur) this
day (and yesterday's doors, hard
edges that opened, closed,
and kept us separate). I massage
his shoulders lightly—remember

the basin, now cool, and the oil.
I resume the pattern of tasks—
nothing special,
renewing the water, soaking the cloth
and smoothing it, more quiet
than warm breath, across
the gray hair of an armpit,
down fallen muscle—
wiping smoothly the rough
burl of an elbow, a slow progress
down the bend of the back's
long bone, his skin a bisque
yellow and gray—the slack cheeks
of his buttocks, and the crease
between them, his legs,
the long plainsong
of thighs and calves, the cradlesong
of belly and scrotum, and the idle
penis, an afterthought,
limp as a curl.

My hands take on the heat
of him, traveling the thin lathe
of the ribs, over heartbeat
and slack breath—the unsung

history of his soul somehow held
in the hover of breath I feel
moving across my hand
as I wipe the stain of medicine
from his chin. I use the oil
where skin blazes from
the pressure of the bed, then cover
and sit with him,
my hand over the one of his he still
holds in a fist. I remember
my childhood angel,
abundantly light, abundantly color.
Light gathers and turns in my hand,
over the burning ground,
here—light brims
in the room. Light brims.
Nothing's lost, this is home.
The light sings *I am, I am.*
And in the quiet
after, I feel
how round and clear the moment,
how fragile—light
reconciled with light, only this moment
world without beginning, or end. And Amen.

Providence

i like to learn the way of things
how they fit or break apart
how a bit tears into steel;
the glory of a lock

i like to learn the way of things
and not just the tool and die
but how a bass fans out a nest
how a man will die

then live

to fly on rainbow wings
and sail beyond the dark
as if it were a certainty
that the way of things is art

SUSAN HARKNESS

We Are Tillers

> *No race can prosper until it learns*
> *that there is as much dignity in tilling a field*
> *as in writing a poem.*
> —Booker T. Washington

Stubborn mud resists your plowshare's chide
to fall away in easy chunks and bits;
wet grasses cling to harrow's spikes, and side
with every force of nature that resists
your efforts. Into soil's inborn pull
you lean against a gravity which calls
ground home. Your harvester and barn are full
of corn; your sweat and labor strains the walls.

Wrestle with the pig then slit its throat:
the pink nose squeals, the blood flows warm and bright.
Upside down the last drops spill and float
back down to hay cleaned at the day's first light.
    You live the stuff of which I try to speak:
    I turn to you for detail, food, technique.

Elvis in Oz: Pondering Wild at Heart

Oh, yes, we know that Sailor is Elvis,
    Lula a depraved Dorothy
whose dancing feet fill stiletto heels.
    While Sailor's leopard skin jacket is
"an expression of my individuality"
    and he's willing to fight for it—
we could not have guessed
    at the degree of violence,
his eager fists could have frightened
    the Wicked Witch of the East—
more than the swirling house
    which fell on her, if she saw it at all—
more than the ferocity of his high kicks
    on the dance floor,
or the wild way he makes love to Lula.

When Sailor is enraged, the failed assassin's
    brains resemble liver on the floor,
and the cheerful spray of his blood
    on the oaken walls of the ballroom
prefigures the red rain
    of Bobby Peru's decapitation.

Lula's mama is the witch here,
                         Lula sees her on a broomstick.
But Johnny the detective, who's sweet
                         on Lula's mama, can't imagine it
for her red fingernails, which gently rake him
                         into chasing Sailor and Lula.
And when faithful Johnny gets tortured
                         by those voodoo deadbeats
from another movie we wish
                         they were flying monkeys
with clipped wings and bad breath.

Bad breath is the ill wind of Bobby Peru
                         with his brain of spittle,
his heart of a rapist.
                         He loses his head in the Texas heat
and who could have missed it—
                         the grotesquerie of flying entrails,
the stray Toto who steals,
                         not Bobby's head, but the severed hand
of one of the hapless feed-store guards.

Bobby's head: the stocking cap much
                         improves his baby-toothed, large-gummed,
fat-lipped self—with his head he pays for
                         the hand he places on Lula,
the words he makes her say,
                         our greatest agony.

Why doesn't Lula confront her Mama
                         about her Daddy's burning death?
Each close-up of the curling ash
                         of somebody's cigarette
reminds us how he went.
                         When her Mama smears her face
with bloodred lipstick,
                         we know whose blood she wears.

We want Lula and Sailor to arrive somewhere—
                when over the rainbow is not enough—
where he can sing "Love Me Tender"—
                thank their lucky stars
there's no place like home—
                where Lula's heart is,
where her mama's heart turned
                murderous and lipstick stained—
the size of a closed fist
                holding a lit match.

When at last Sailor sings to Lula
                on top of the convertible,
he has become Elvis: Elvis in heaven,
                Elvis in a musical—
he is tenderly loving Lula,
                as if for the first time.

Agoraphobia

From my window
I can see the wasp
is a dog's nose

sniffing the dead
azalea. It is not
spring

yet, but the sun
has tricked some color
out of the landscape.

Already, the forsythia
is a yellow fountain
and green

moths blink
like eyes
in the flowering

quince. For a moment
the winter wind
dies

and the black leaves
   quit scratching
      across the roof.

I remember
   there is a trellis
      nailed to the lattice

porch where my rose-
   bush bloomed red,
      orange and pink.

It was a ladder
   of mouths,
      each one kissed

by frost.
   The petals fell
      and crumbled

like ashes
   from the vine. Now
      it is a white

skeleton,
   a net of bones
      clinging to the house.

JULIA JOHNSON

Memoir of a Woman of Pleasure

These clocks, handy clocks. Six
and the last finger slipped
slightly from my eye edge. Insight
I don't even know. The measure
to this certain pleasure I took
like an alleyway or rusted train
over swollen creeks and he,
with a stomach of ball bearings,
a rope with becket around his neck,
we wore the same crown.
Five, the clocks wound tight
their rickety bones,
pointed sharp pin-needles.
The clocks, face on face, pleasured
woman in the face of each.
Four, chimes fell like steel throats
and he was bound. At three, the birds
fiddled with their wirey heads
and the minute, thrown like a discus,
split down our hands
before the last gesture.

Blood Bank

The click of the counter in the turnstile
Woke me up out of that dream I have while
Walking: the war between the heels and
Soles of my shoes. I had stopped at the blood
Bank earlier to make a deposit and still feel
Subcutaneous, the false euphoria of sugared
Doughnuts dropping like the downramp in
The parking garage. A fleet of bloodmobiles
In the side lot is dunked red, the cots
Inside still hot. My car clock has stopped
In nearly the exact spot as my father's car
Clock, a quarter to four, whether A.M. or P.M.
I don't know. My eyes are bloodshot in
The mirror on the underside of the visor. On his,
My father has six plastic drops of blood, one
For each gallon he has given. He believed
In bloodletting and now his blood pressure is
Higher than the bell ringing at the carnival,
Hit hard with the shot from the mallet.
He hasn't won prizes. He eats less red meat,
Although he grew up on *czernina,* soup
Thickened with duck's blood, and has got
A blood count that won't quit. I'd rather
Be driving away from the blood bank than

Driving towards the blood shed, where
My brother worked for four summers, squeegeeing
Turkey blood into a hole in the middle of
The floor. He got paid in blood money.
He was called a bloodsucker. He is not
The end of his bloodline, is holding on so
Hard that his hands are white. I have lain
On the table with a tube in my arm, watched
The plastic sack fill up with drops, fill
Out with a thickness that is always viscous
Inside me, the art of the artery, veins
Of gold, struck, bleeding colors, split and splitting.

The Small You Control

I pull my fortune from its cookie,
bend the pink paper around my third finger,
drop it like egg into broth.
The typed words float away like noodles.

> Everything is small here:
> black mushrooms with hot and sour soup,
> cups of oolong, grains of fried rice.
> Chopsticks are finger stilts,
> and waitresses wear children's shoes.
> Tiny golden dragons
> fly across the red ceiling of happiness.
> They land on walls
> and hide under starched napkins.

Outside the restaurant, the hotel elevator
catapults me to a high angle.
I read Atlanta's largest love letter:
"Steve Luvs Linda" spelled
out in spare tires across
the recapper's roof next door.

> Two blocks from the graffiti, strands
> of Peachtree folk braid themselves into a vast

welcome mat weaving through the gates
and carpeting Atlanta's new Taj Mahal:
High Museum, High Tech alabaster.
People pigment the ramps
and stare at canvases from Rococo to Rothko,
that painter who wants
"to say something about large pictures":

The small you control,
the large you are in.

Intercepting a Solar Eclipse

She traced the blindness back to then,
to those moments when she refused to blink.
Even after itch spread to fire, she watched
a dark hole deposing all
but an outer edge of daylight. That false night
rubbed stars on the tops of her eyelids.
She tracked their dying or taking flight,
as if blips and flashes might fill in
where the world was missing.
The universe faded around her. She waned to scale,
evaporating like vapor off water, casting
a shadow's shadow. Her face skimmed off mirrors.

Whether it was how soon the moon came out—
the sun shorting midway through that afternoon—
or how the planets collaborated,
this looniness melded to her reason.
(Still she believes she came deliriously close
to figuring out everything once-and-for-all.)
She prayed, when she wasn't thinking,
for one perfect memory: her irises spinning,
spools on a reel,
her personal clip of God, uncloaking himself.

Her vision kept the world out of kilter,
rocked her side-to-side, until she imagined
she was always falling skyward or dreaming,
one inside another.
If only she weren't so afraid
of roadside astrology and the devil, she's certain
she could make do with even this,
the bare bones of nearly nothing.

What drove her wholly mad
was a slender aperture of milky light,
the sign of her sight returning.
Senseless, she kept quarantined to her bedroom
for weeks. The blinds, like vague bars,
clamped her world to its revolution
as she held guard. How blackness elevated sound:
People laughing behind the walls
only when the toilet flushed;
secrets tapped at her door past midnight;
the compound whistles and hisses of running water.
She went wild believing how deaf she grew in daylight,
how that, too, would pass, leaving her soon
an ordinary maniac with no revelation.

She took to the streets finally,
stark naked except for the weight of original sin
and a 14 kt ankle bracelet
she'd ordered from TV, a name engraved in script
she only pretended was hers.
That landed her a chair in this dayroom,
a bunk in the ward, surefire sleep.
She's swollen as a blowfish now,
but restored to order.
Though once-removed, she can see again; the gospel,
vast as she'd pictured it, unfolds in living color.
Everything under the sun
grows wider on the big screen.

She's cable-ready
for signs and wonders, examines
every forehead to a fault. Once, she says,
she found a beastly mark overlaying the weather map.
She's always hoping
she'll discover logic or kindness. She believes
all things somehow work for good.

And even as words hide through the alphabet,
she persists, expecting a rush, a snapback,
the settling of facts into rightful places.
Ask her anything. She considers every question,
keeping faith there is an end to this.
Hold on, she thinks, wait,
it'll come to me any second.

CHARLES MOLESWORTH

Sue's Poem

I

War news leaks from the media:
sorties, target-rich environments, ground force:
the whole lumpy terrain of a new vocabulary,
and the constant search for a new way
to bring it home, to make it new for the first
and last time:
this evening
they show us
some marine's videotape
that he'd sent to his mother
in Houston, Texas: the kid,
muscular, tan, well-spoken,
keen to show how normal and settled he was:
the dishes he had to wash,
the cookies from home,
some reading matter—
and his buddy pans the videocam
over the two paperbacks, only one
name visible: L. Ron Hubbard,
which he hadn't had time to read yet,
like a late assignment, his failure
well excused by the "extraordinary circumstances"—
yet there it is: the unreal book in the real place,

or is it just the opposite: the total falsity of the book
so true to life, so correctly dumb, it's hard to think
of the desert vast enough to make such nonsense human.

II

Questions dumb and otherwise:

    How many angels can dance on the head of a pin?
      Can you tell me what music is playing?

    Don't you know there's a war on?
      Who called off the peace?

It's all there before us, in the opening pages
of Dewey's *Experience and Nature*:
how mistakes and confusions are forms of knowledge,
how everything ends or begins, and most of it is in between:
termini: why would a philosopher talk about how ends
never cease, and yet the world is thick with consummations:
we need to reconstruct, to tear apart the habitual
even while we almost pray to it,
to something like the god of sequence, of events
holding onto one another like shipwrecked travelers
who must claim a community of truth, must have
community in their hearts before they claim anything—
As if all we can know is what we can call a stop to,
all we love is what we can continue—

III

Never enough: to list someone's qualities:
instead to appreciate the combinations,
the balances that overtake the melody:
instead to see them dance together:
hard work and a sense of humor:
"Stop laughing," you'd say, when there
was work to be done, and with one last
swallowed guffaw we'd set to it.
Sunlight through a lace curtain:
the light is filigreed,
the curtain made palpably reticulate.

The monody of the visible draws us out
and the pathos of the apparent sends us back:
you could always tell the real virtue
from the assumed: what a virtue that is.

IV

We shared a poem that day:
I leapt at you with my remembered line,
its words thick, dense as cheese from the farmhouse,
then we were both possessed by one word
but knew it escaped us: "frowsty."
We went to look it up in separate places,
half hoping not to find it, and so keep it special,
and so we did—
its insistent moist English country-laneness
almost shook a mildewed finger at us:
be lowly wise, it said, the words that grow
unto themselves, shunning the common
coin of boredom, anger, or gossip,
will carry with them a damp nutrient
slippery presence. Oh singularity, oh the thrill
of pointing it out, then watching it fall back
into the possessions, the things that hold.

V

The day you entered the hospital
for the last time
I heard on the radio an exquisite rendition of
Chopin's etudes: as if the man's fingers
had answered every claim of poverty, had abandoned all
they could remember to do except measure this labyrinth
of pause and echo and the rushing on
one last time:
how that rushing on takes us, how lost we'd be without its call
and our dutiful answers.
Good-bye sweet and smiling Sue:
how like a mumbled curse such a valediction might sound,
how completely unfair it is.

Honest enough to curse what was unfair, yet
you never lost the train of each day's melody:
and so I owe you something I may never pay.
Such impossible debts we accumulate all the time,
and would have no way at all to even any account
if we didn't know—and want to know—that some law
governs and even leads us far beyond any tally, back
simply to the fact of the world and all the people in it.

Daphne's Blues

Apollo saw her hunting, "her hair in wild disarray. . . .
Apollo thought 'what would she look like properly
dressed and with her hair nicely arranged?' The idea
made the fire that was devouring his heart blaze up
even more fiercely."
                                                    —from Ovid

Didn't you hear him Daddy
Hear him say
Didn't you hear him Daddy
What he'd say—

She's a fine lookin woman
but she'd look finer *my* way

You taught me how to hunt Daddy
and leave alone my hair
and wear these boy clothes
Apollo couldn't bear—

Didn't you hear me Daddy
Hear me say
Didn't you hear me Daddy
Hear me say

Daddy Daddy I just want to be free
Daddy oh Daddy just let me be

And you were glad I didn't love him
'cause now you had your tree
Now you've got your river and your tree
Yeah, Daddy, you both got your laurel tree.

The Canoes

The canoes slept upside down on the wooden racks
at the end of the beach where the volleyball court
and the picnic tables were, and the good climbing tree—
the long line of bright canoes—
red, yellow, green, white, orange, blue, light blue—
only one in those days aluminum's dull silver.
It was good to see the curves of the prows lined up,
one after another, and the colors, a pleasure
like opening a new box of crayons in the first grade.

It took two of us to flip a canoe over on the rack
and carry it down to the lake, trying not to let it scrape
the gravelly sand and rocks in the shallows.
Only Harold Riley, three or four years older,
who returned one summer with a body
I had seen before only in *Strength and Health* magazine,
would hoist a canoe alone, carry it down,
and set it, without a splash, in the water.
Then he would paddle away and not come back for hours.
We didn't know where he went, but there were Girl Scout
    camps,
with counselors, stuck in the woods all summer,
at the far end of the lake.

In the morning, before eleven, it was permitted
to take a canoe into the swimming area and swamp it.
This was luxury—leaning, leaning too far,
the moment just before going over, going over,
plunging sideways into the chilly water,
the canoe flipping to make a floating cave,
wood and water echoes, strange smiles
and conversations in there.
And trying to push the canoe down,
to get it vertical in the water,
to make it touch bottom, never succeeding
against the slow, whalelike rising of the canoe.

But what tinged the canoes most
was the story Kevin, another older kid, told,
of going to the beach at night with Chris,
who was tall, and good-looking, and impossibly distant,
whose straight blonde hair hung down on her shoulder blades
and brushed across them when she walked—
of how they spread a blanket under the canoes
and she took off her clothes.
"All of them?" I asked. "All of them," he said,
with a smile that should have been hers.

After that, whenever I walked past the canoes
I would think of her, and whenever I knelt
to pick a stray volleyball out of their shade
I would glance around, wondering
under which canoe
was that spot of fortunate, haunted ground.
It is night, her skin glows
as white skin does on a warm summer night,
the katydids are rattling,
and she is beautiful, and merciful,
lying out naked under the canoes' dark arcs.

First Birthday

Like bags of light, my child's birthday balloons
circle the room. Silver animals,
weightless as dust particles, floating.
She crawls after them, tugging their ribbons.
She wants to lick their shiny, mylar faces.
"Balloon, balloon," we tell her, again and again.

For weeks seizures have lit her small brain.
I picture them as lightning which strikes
repeated paths, hitting the same tree, barn, or home.
No one knows why. We force sticky elixirs
smelling of alcohol down her throat.
The doctors will do anything to stop them—
make her sleepless, give injections that can kill.

They tell us her retardation could be severe,
but today, on her first birthday, she places
one foot deliberately in front of the other,
following the silver, gleaming globes about the house.

She tugs on a ribbon, pulls one down
into her fat hands, squeals as she touches
its shiny surface to her tongue. "Ba ba,"
she says clearly as it rises, "Ba ba."

My birthday wish is to cut away this piece
of time, tape it like a child's drawing
to the wall. The afternoon floats away
like the elusive silver balls. Later,
I'll tug at its ribbon, reach
high as I have to for the luminous sphere.

MICHAEL PETTIT

Mozart and Kama

Big flowers red as the plush
bodies of exotic bees,

on their long stems the geraniums
are dancing, swaying

like bees would sway
or hummingbirds

above the red stars of bee balm,
above the blue columbine.

Sway geraniums, to the Mozart
to which I lift my face.

Music has entered my heart.
Is this what the flower feels

as the bee plunges
its tongue deep inside?

Is this how it feels
when Kama comes riding his parrot,

carrying his bow of sugarcane,
his bowstring of bees?

How it feels when Kama shoots
his arrow tipped with a flower

and then and then and then
we begin dancing, dancing for love?

A Critical Assessment of Faulkner by a Boardhead Who Isn't Like into Academics Big Time but Thinks Faulkner Is Way Cool

Faulkner was like this way cool dude who wrote some totally awesome books about the South which were all cool and trippy and different, despite being into booze, big time (especially because he was seriously stressed out by the job he had writing movies in Hollywood), so he was like getting totally wasted on moonshine—and moonshine is even more toxic than Ripple—all the time when he was writing and his sentences got real long and confusing like yours would too if you tried writing after a kegger without even puking first to sober up like I did before writing my term paper for this lit class I flunked last semester, but even totally wasted he wrote some killer novels like Sanctuary in which this dude Popeye can't get it on with this babe Temple so

he uses a corncob which was pretty gnarly and then Temple ends
up in a whorehouse except this totally clueless dweeb Benbow
gets her out and she ends up going to Paris with her father which
must of been way lame because there's like no snowboarding
there and parents are way lame anyway and he wrote some other
bitchin stories about drinking and fighting but didn't have alot to
say about sex because after pounding that many brews you're like
not really able to do much even if there are all these babes around
and besides he was married.

A Fear of High Places

for Dara Wier

Imagine the Japanese tourist
at Grand Canyon, just arrived.
Exuberant, happy to be here,
his gesture to the woman
seated in his car is to leap
onto the low wall that marks
the parking lot's perimeter.

Imagine his surprise
when he finds himself
on the canyon rim, nothing
but air rising to meet him.
He wavers an awful instant
on the edge. His arms outstretched,
he looks like some madcap diver
readying for flight.

Who knows
what he's thinking?
But when he regains
his balance, he steps down
from the wall on legs
that are new and strange.

He turns to the woman
still seated in the car.
Fumbling with her seat belt,
her handbag, a map
that won't fold, she's missed
one of the important moments
of his life.

A middle-aged couple
stands a few yards away.
Out of their element, the safe
green of the east, they step
tentatively toward what
they recognize as the abyss.
They lock hands and look down,
seeing for the first time
what they had been up against.

The young man they had caught
with their breath, held
in their lungs, kept
from falling until the canyon
gave up, smiles at them.
This is our honeymoon, he says,
as if in apology.
The three of them look
toward his wife, who is just now
getting out of the car,
and the couple smiles back at him,
softening his fear, calling it
their own.

Train from Budapest, 1944

Grandmother, when you go
you'll struggle off over loose stones,
a yellowing stack of untranslated stories
clutched to your tiny coat.

What you don't know is this:
You can not disinherit us.
In my sleep a train hungers
up a snowy hill. Wheels grind
so slowly I can see needles
on the pines. Onward, onward,
to the dark center.

Eve Out of Season

What roses remain stretch tangled and issue
a few crooked blooms. Little of the world
entrusted to us is left. Once a garden,
clear paths, gentle order where we sat among
grasses and on that carved bench, cracked
through now, thrown over, under branches
grown twisted, adapted, as we.

Long now since we shared the fruit of that
perfect tree that taught us. I still don't know—
was it put there to ensure this
dissolution, or to offer us
choice? What's good, what is not.
I never could tell.

What's left is this burnt-out summer place,
bounded by dark corroding streams,
ancient grounds, ancient plots once known to us
as heaven; through all the thousand troubled years,
it still surrounds us. We've learned that
what dies dies repeatedly. How often
have I lost, and how often replaced you?
Yet each instance of love was the first,
each moment the one when I knew you
naked, knew my lust, knew you as beautiful.

First-time lonely guy?

The hero of this film is a big guy
Who lost weight just for the role, I tell you
He looks great.
The audience will not know
His third wife already dreams of Stacy Keach.
But Jeez the look in his eyes
Is there for all with a ticket to see,
Splattering right through the screen,
Bouncing right off the walls in time with
The brassy entr'acte score.

The Oldest Story in the World—so
What has been left at home
To make it all so new
And confusing? Men pause to search their jackets,
Women check that handbags are
"Securely on their laps" and still

His confession drills all of them through
Like an injury perfectly felt
Yet dimly understood, inflicted upon the soul
Without the kiss of the fist.

He is reaching through time
and the meaningless script—

Whose actions, whatever he tries,
Produce terror:
Terror in place of travel,
Of charm,
Terror in fancy clothes
And laughter.
Terror in touch that is real
But not present. Terror trapped in this poster
For something patently
Not as promoted.

Naked Ladies

Jean-Jacques wanted: a cottage on the Swiss shore,
a cow and a rowboat.

Wallace wanted a crate from Ceylon full of jam
and statuettes.

My neighbors are not ashamed of their poverty
but would love to be able to buy a white horse,
a stallion that would transfigure the lot.

Darwin was dying by inches from not having anyone to talk to
about worms, and the vireo outside my window wants nothing
     less
than a bit of cigarette-wool for her nest.

The unattainable is apparently rising on the tips of forks
the world over . . .

So-and-so is wearing shoes for the first time

and Emin Pasha, in the deepest acreage of the Congo,
wanted so badly to catch a red mouse! Catch one he did
shortly before he died, cut in the throat by slavers who
wanted to kill him. *At last!* runs the diary

and it is just this *at last* we powder up and call progress.

So the boys chipped in and bought Bohr a gram of radium
for his 50th birthday.

Pissarro wanted white frames for his paintings
as early as 1882, and three francs for postage, heaven-sent.

Who wants to hear once more the sound of their mother
        throwing
Brussels sprouts into the tin bowl?

Was it *ping* or was it *ting*?

What would you give to smell again the black sweet peas
choking the chain link fence?

Because somebody wants your money.

The medallions of monkfish in a champagne sauce . . .

The long kiss conjured up by your body in a cast?

The paradisiacal vehicle of the sweet-trolley rolling in
again, as cumulous meringue is piled on your tongue
and your eye eats the amber glaze of a crème brûlée.

The forgiveness of sins, a new wife, another passport,
the swimming pool, the rice bowl

full of rice, the teenage mutant ninja turtles escaping
as you turn the page . . .

Oh brazen sex at the barbecue party!
Desire is a principle of selection. Who wanted *feet* in the first
        place?

Who wanted to stand up? Who felt like walking?

Enrichetta Is Singing

Enrichetta is singing
and night falls through a window
open at her back.

It is the moment between dusk
and light; it is the light
that stops where the song begins.

Enrichetta is singing
with Mirko on her lap,
her torso grown round
as a moon-cradled cloud.

All the artists have been deceived.
There is not one anywhere
in this town. Enrichetta is singing,
and the child that once wrestled
now looks peacefully from her lap.

Wide doors leave the balcony
empty, and all the streets
are bare
as families sit down to eat.

Even the dogs
have left no trace,
not one howling or lapping
in the air. Chickens hold profiles
and wait for night to click
but wait a bit longer today
while Enrichetta sings.

Song for Billie Holiday, Song for the Rain

The daughters of men are the seeds of death,
hull, husk, flesh, pulp,
  arsenic at the pit, not sweet,
      bitter root.

A cloud of birds escapes through the attic window.
  Soot and ashes, black leaves,
        they settle blank branches.
  Rain soaks their feathers.

      They shelter in the red cave
  of your mouth, peck at the tongue root,
        warble with your breath.

A man bathes a woman's feet.
  She belonged to him, limbs divided,
sparrow tangled in her hair,
      wet bird, red root, stone fruit.

Flight is the prophecy of rain,
  song the promise of the torn tongue.
      What separates leave and forsake?
A tongue pierced with thistles,
a tongue pierced with thorns.

The daughters of men house the seeds of death.
A woman washes perfume from her dress,
the breath of flowers suggesting grief.

A scarlet bird inhabits your mouth, a bird
drinking water, carrying its burden of crumbs,
a bird of mirrors, drumming
this joy is all I can bear.

Remythologizing the Fisher King

In a cold March, fishermen
stand hip-deep. Roots of trees

reaching into the river
are rimmed with ice.

The pain of the cold
is a knife in the thigh

while the shapes of things sought for
glide silently past.

Overhead a kingfisher perches
on a telephone wire, gray and loud.

MATTIE QUESENBERRY SMITH

Cosmonauts Return to Earth Safely

*Two cosmonauts whose mission was plagued by a perilous
spacewalk and technical problems returned to Earth
yesterday with a multimillion dollar payload of space-
grown crystals. . . . "Back in the landing spaceship, we
felt the slightly bitter smell of absinthe in the Kazakh
Steppe," Mr. Solovyev told reporters. "I also dreamed
that my wife would bring me fresh, delicious apples when
I was back on Earth."*
            —Washington Times, August 10, 1990

Starry-eyed Cosmonaut, catapulted through
that sequined ceiling of our Cosmos,
turns his face toward Earth.
He is anticipating the fall

and falling every second of the day
towards the Kazakh Steppe, rough home
where men gather to drink dark absinthe
and grow wild thoughts in their heads.

She opens the shutters and leans
across the wooden windowsill,
eyes the road to town.
She is still there, handing apples to him.

She pushes them across the windowsill,
beckons him to come in and rest the day,

renourish with sweet apples.
Their flesh cracks and juice jets in air.

He takes the plunge, packing a payload
reaped from the top of Earth's head.
He falls through her space, his hot halo
kicking flames behind into cold dark.

MATTHEW J. SPIRENG

Fence and Maple

It begins
with a curling over, as if the wire
were just

sinking in
beneath the maple's bark, as if it
were soft

as skin is,
supple as mud. For years the hard scars
remain

where the wire
was and now emerges from within
as if

growing out
in three low rows. Time is the scars are gone,
the wire,

once as taut
as taut is, rusted, sagging, broken,
not a

fence at all
now, but deeper in the tree, drawn nearer
the heart.

Nightwork

Supper's over, cleared from the porch,
swallows thread and rethread the sky.
Bats will be out soon to finish the job,
hemming crazily the whole skirt of night.

I'm eleven or twelve, still in hand-me-downs,
on my hands and knees in the garden,
searching the iris beds for roots to divide.

Behind me the barn leans into deep light,
one unshuttered eye looking off
past the railroad tracks to the hills.

In the half-light my father looks, too,
and hauls the boat from the pond to mend.

Another year gone,
and the old pear tree by the house
holds out its fruit to my mother.
She fills her apron heavy, accepting each
when the light goes, by touch.

Night Search for Lost Dog

Not yet midnight, but late, and in through the window
the sound of a fox barking often and not far away
made me sit up and strain for something else, a clue
to the disappearance, two days before, of a silly old dog;

maybe they were out there in some kind of standoff.
High whining under the odd crystalline barking
made me think she was caught on the fence through the woods.
So up, into clothes, the hickory walking stick Larry Higgins

whittled for me, and I went out into the late winter night,
the sky high overcast and giving back from somewhere
more light than I would have believed possible this time
of night and year, easy walking down the hill to the woods,

and there it was again, out the driveway and down
to the left, where I went then, onto gravel and clay
packed almost to pavement, not hard to walk quietly,
and the drive stretched down through the trees

as it seems to have done once in an old illustration
in a book my grandparents had. It was something like that,
since the sight of it made me stop and go soft at the center
that a landscape so long gone could still be there

under my feet, winding out to the clearing
where the fox barked again, just there where the drive
comes out of the trees. Quicker then, still quiet,
I took one step at a time, stopping once at a sound,

a faint rhythmic thumping that turned out, probably,
to be a wrinkle in the nylon parka working against
my own pulse beating somewhere inside it, so I went on
to the big field on the right, past the woods,

to the place in the fence where the barbed wire
will hold a climber with a stout stick to prop him,
and the fox galloped freely away over the hill.
After a while it was just myself standing there,

hearing for the first time the racket from the house
on the opposite hill, young hounds maybe sensing
someone walking and climbing as quietly as his age
and a noisy down parka would allow, but not knowing,

maybe, that he was looking for a dog who was born here
and stayed for eleven years, learning little, but loved,
then one day was simply not there. No sign of a fight
or the hoped-for standoff with the fox, or a coon,

rabid or not, the thought of which had prompted the stick
now supporting two folded hands, my chin resting on them,
my eyes going in and out of focus on a world that right then
it was good, after all, to be in, mystified though I was, and sad.

BURN THOMPSON

The Way

Woods ring the Center where I may get a better gait—
their trees forbidden to visitors,
forbidden to patients and staff,
patrolled by security.
I had never seen grown men fight
or billy sticks hard against backs.
Still, *I spoke out with my tongue.*

I begin in my clumsy way to hang up my shirt.
Nurse Samantha, beside me, shakes
to the heavy metal music she hears inside.
She knocks me on the bed with one hand
and jerks the hanger away with the other.
As she dances, she screams.

Out the rec-room window, I see the field filled with goldenrod.
Still I have studied plants enough
to know goldenrod can bloom in the worst of soils.
My body does not get rigid with tears of rage.
Just droplets of water,
no one sees, slip down my cheek.

Through shower curtains, I see Samantha
with a woman in a wheelchair. When the woman insists
on wearing white in September, I feel Samantha shake.
In the wild dance, I feel
the woman knocked from her wheelchair,
her hipbone vibrate against tile.

NATASHA TRETHEWEY

Warming

for GTG, 1944–1985

Someone thought to take
this last picture—you
smiling, looking beyond us.
It was a good thing.
We needed it when you were gone
to put on the program
and in the paper.

I remember your grave site,
cold rain falling, soaking
us through. We lowered you
then, not into dry sand
or dust, but into slow mud
that seemed to suck you in.

April, forsythia blazes
on the hillside, mountains
green in the new breeze,
willows reach down, drag
the stream with leafy fingers,

and this warmth flows through me
into hallowed ground, touching
the roots of living things.

Summer Night with Storm Cloud

The wind is rising now, bending trees
out in the darkness, and the first drops
stutter on the tin before
they thicken to the howl of rain.
In here the air is still a burden,
so close the bare bulb wallows
in the haze, shadows falter,
the intricate world is rendered
into simple shapes.
I too am changing, breaking myself down
to words, arranging
and rearranging their syllables,
turning them, searching for
their combinations. I am trying
to crack my code the way
they used to crack safes in the movies:
fingers turning the sensitive dial,
the dark mind seeing
through steel, and the ear pressed
hard against the inscrutable door,
listening for the tumblers in the lock,
the soft oiled clicking,
the falling into place.

EDWARD WESTON

A girl hiding under the bed and a girl hiding in the closet

In [the suspect's] bedroom, the inspectors reported finding a girl hiding under the bed, a girl hiding in the closet, a hypodermic needle under the mattress, and a large pet rat in a cage.
        —Item from the *Malden Evening News*

Girls are hiding everywhere you bend to look,
crouch, stretch, or through a locked door's keyhole peek.
Turn back curtains, rugs, and covers, seek them
in cupboards and rafters,
under bolted basement bulkheads out in back.

How ever did she end up mixed up
with such rats?

Authorities know for certain.

That she is here and everywhere hidden,
we can always count on: girls, girls,
stashed like paraphernalia, crouched or flat,
muffled by mattresses and shirt sleeves.

Nightly stashed at the knock on the door:
Midnight! Police!

S. LAUDERDALE WHITE

The Raccoon

From beauty, the knowledge
of which no one is certain yet
everyone learns, what beauty?
　　Distracted, he went back
to the place he had been born—
an aging beauty released
and took him in.
　　The field's new growth
strains and lifts against the wind,
sleek as the frozen fur of the animal—
and his eyes are open, confiding.

JAMIE YATES

Chaplin

More than most who flicked past in scratches
and splices, yours was the one face that mastered
exits, even then we knew you could not stay.

So, when I heard on the radio
that your body was missing from the grave
I wasn't surprised.

Always in silence you stole the scene,
and now you've left the town
in a last misty reel.
Who, but you, could have died as he lived:
a train-bound tramp of lights
somehow misplaced.

I see you now sitting in first grade,
the kid who stole a box of gold stars,
and wherever you walked thereafter
—stars fell from your trousers.

GEORGE BUTLER. *Laying the Waves, 1970*

GEORGE BUTLER.   *Mr. & Mrs. Reid & Grandson Leon, 1971*

George Butler. *Officer Tidwell, 1971*

GEORGE BUTLER.   *Deborah, 1971*

SALLY MANN.   *Listening to Madonna by the Tadpole Jar, 1990*

SALLY MANN. *Odalisque, 1989*

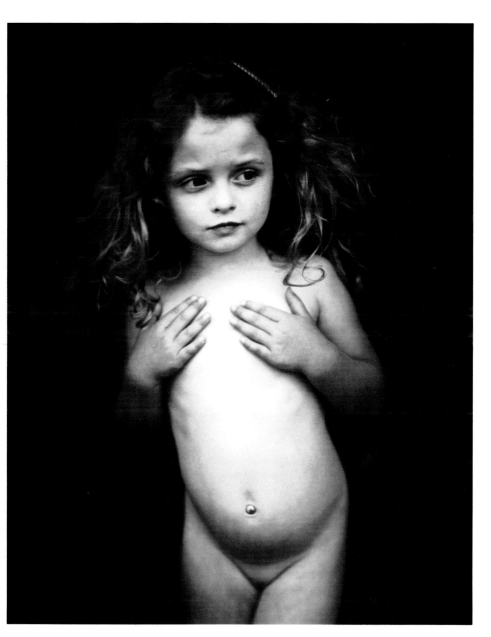

SALLY MANN. *The Modest Child, 1988*

SALLY MANN. *The Hot Dog, 1989*

KATIE LETCHER LYLE

Venturi

Things are kind of tense at the moment: my son Freddie has dropped out of his rich prep school and come home to the country high school to finish—in the middle of junior year. Kelly, my daughter, his half sister, is acting spacey in school, and they want me to have her tested for epilepsy. I said, What fifteen-year-old isn't spacey, tell me that. One of the cats, Violet, actually my favorite one, is missing. This is the third day. We've called the Addlers, down the road, who graze their cows on our farm, and the radio station. And my ex-mother-in-law slugged a black babysitter, for God's sakes, the same one she bit last month, at the nursing home; only this time the babysitter hauled off and knocked her down, and they had to take Gaga to the hospital, where she may have a concussion. Then Elrod, my ex-husband, sold my soul to this witch out in the mountains, in payment, as he explained it, for some kind of interview he needs for this anthropology course he's involved with. My soul! He acted like it was just a big joke when he told me, but I don't know. And the kids won't drink the milk because it has onions in it.

I tell them it's a sign of spring, for God's sakes, and that it means it's real, and to add Hershey's, but they won't touch it. "It's always tasted like that in the spring," I say. "When I was little—"

"You're not drinking it," Kelly says.

I change the subject. I tell them their bones will all dissolve. Kelly says, "Oh, Mom! That's just so gross!" and Freddie says, eating two pieces of bacon at one time, "That might be interesting. There's a character in English history, Ivan the Boneless. He just had gristle instead. No bones."

"You made that up," Kelly says, which is just what I've been thinking.

"I did not," Freddie says. I try another bite of doughnut, but like the first, this one will barely squeeze through my gullet.

After they've left for school, I take their untouched milk out to the barn. The cats don't mind the onion; they drink lakes and ponds of onion milk and don't complain. I think about the severed wasp—there's some story about how it goes on eating jam even after its body has been cut in half. You have to go on, no matter what happens. Every day, I sit down like a real writer and things come out, but then I read them and it's all the most terrible drivel.

When I head out for the grocery, having sat for my two hours at the computer, my car starts making this awful racket, so I take it over to see what's wrong, and this guy I went to high school with, Sevvie, tells me, he says, "Sounds like it's the transmission."

I don't mean to laugh like a madwoman, but see the irony? So I say, "That's the problem? That's always the problem. For a writer, the problem is always transmission. Get it?"

And Sevvie, because he is a gentleman, chuckles politely.

I was once in love with Sevvie, but that was back when I believed he would have gotten a joke like that. I mean, I had a crush on him. Last year out of the blue once he asked me in the late spring, "Have you found a lot of morels this year?"

I'd already enjoyed watching him, just looking, no harm in that. He has a nice mushy, comfy body, tousled brown curly hair, and a nice unassuming moustache. He wears red plaid flannel work shirts that look soft and are faded from washing. I used to think that if I could call his house, a woman plump and kind would answer. He's always pleasant and cheerful, and I had no idea he remembered me, we only doubled once in high school, and that was fine. But then he asked me about the morels, and that told me he knew exactly who I was, and even read my columns in the paper. I began to fantasize about meeting him in the woods, maybe accidentally, maybe not. I wondered what a bright guy like him with a jacket that says "Sev" was doing working in a service station.

It was harmless in the extreme; I have always felt that brain-lust was safe, static, and probably in the end more satisfying than any messy reality. I enjoyed his nice smile whenever I drove the car up to get serviced, and it is good to have a friend in the automotive business.

After we had gotten to the chatting stage, and used each other's names when we talked, one day I had summer on my mind, and asked Sev if he was getting any vacation time. He beamed and said he sure was, once school was out. School? He went to school?

I asked, because I couldn't imagine, "What are you going to do?" And he stopped wiping my windshield, and held the grimy cloth in both his hands as if it was a ball, and said, or pronounced, "I wish I was going to the Caribbean, Maggie, that's what I wish I was doing. Instead, I'm staying here, and hoeing my own half acre. Reckon I'll be substituting tomatoes for tan."

I could almost hear sound-track music. I really couldn't decide if it was the corniest comment I'd ever heard, or the wisest. When he asked me in return what I was going to do over the summer, I mumbled, "I'm working on a book about interesting food facts."

"Then I'll bring you some tomatoes to practice on," he said. I went on to tell him about an oyster recorded in 1629 at Jamestown that was thirteen inches in diameter, a lobster taken from Plymouth Bay in 1622 that fed forty men, but Sevvie only hmmed and nodded, and I could tell he wasn't knocked out by my fascinating facts.

Today I have to leave the car, so Sev says when Rick comes in he'll take a look at it with him and give me a call.

Walking home, I suddenly notice my legs flashing out from under my fur coat—still in turquoise tights and red leg weights from aerobics class. I thought I'd remembered to change into jeans, but I guess I forgot. Along the way, people wave and I wave back.

At home the flag is up, and in the mailbox there's a letter saying I have definitely won one million dollars, and one from sister Sarie, no letter from Josh, but he's called twice in the last week. A couple of bills. In the kitchen, I turn the stove on, and the kettle begins to hiss as the heat burns off the water drops. Outside I can hear the Peter Peter Peter of a titmouse, and the Turtle Turtle Turtle of a Carolina wren in counterpoint. Wanita told me one day while cutting my hair that she knows a woman who has quit eating, herself, but has taken to feeding birds. If she finds a baby bird fallen out of a nest, she chews worms up and feeds it, just as a mother bird would do. Now every time I hear a bird, I think of that woman, denying herself, scattering birdseed in the wind. Wanita has some fascinating story or other about everyone in town.

I open Sarie's letter. She says one of her friends reported that she saw me last week. She's right, I was on a panel discussion at this big convention of where literature is going, as if I had any idea myself, but it always amuses me to find that watchdogging can occur between Milwaukee (where my sister lives) and New Orleans (where the convention was) and here (where my ex-husband's farm is).

I can't believe the next thing: Sarah's friend says I was drunk and blowing bubbles, you know, with one of those wands and liquid soap, while other people were talking. I go call her up right away.

"I can't believe someone told you that," I say, indignant. "How rude! You know I'd never be drunk at a talk!"

"It sounded like you," Sarah says, "tall, short curly-red hair, even to the fur coat and fuschia Nikes. Did you really wear fuschia Nikes?"

I sigh, glancing down at my feet. "I guess so, but—"

Then she says, "I thought it was kind of strange."

"You should have defended me," I say. "We were raised better than that, and you know I'd never—oh, it's pure fabrication! Whole cloth. People love to invent stories about writers. They think all of us are alcoholics and sex maniacs. Are you sure she didn't say I took off all my clothes?"

"Well, I'm glad if it isn't true," my sister says, her voice doubtful and ghostly—which is probably the way telephones work anyway— you can't make me believe that there are really 800 miles of wire between my ear and hers out there in Milwaukee, Wisconsin.

"If?" I say. "There's not one single drop of truth to it. No one on the panel was either drunk or blowing bubbles. It was a perfectly respectable, boring panel. Three men, two women, one of whom was me. Your friend should be a novelist."

"She is," Sarah says. "I was going to say I think you'd like her. She's still writing on her first novel. Travis says she's been working on it for twenty years, and that she'll die the day it's finished. He says it's what keeps her alive."

My sister, who is the marrying kind, is always quoting her current spouse or one of her four exes. She collects their sayings the way she used to collect things, anything, in her diapers. The summer she began to walk and I was babysitting a lot with her, at diaper-changing time I might find anything at all in her pouch: rocks, blocks, flowers, earrings filched from Mama's dresser, wallets. As she grew, her thievery became more sophisticated. One time after a dinner party it was clear that she'd raided the guests' pocketbooks, for her draggy saggy diaper next morning revealed lipsticks, combs, a tiny vial of perfume, and a set of car keys. She is, I think, still a collector of small things. "Nick always said—" she starts, but I don't listen. Nick took her for half of everything she owned when they split up, even though she supported him the entire two years of their marriage. Daddy said her lawyer must have been crazy, out there in Ohio, to make her do that. Of course you could say that Fred, my first husband, took me for everything because we didn't have insurance, but he couldn't help it that he was the youngest man on record to ever die of a certain kind of pineal tumor. A fluke, they said, I don't have to worry about Freddie anymore than if his father had died of snakebite.

We end the conversation with me saying, "Well, whoever it was, it wasn't me."

When Sevvie calls, he says it isn't as bad as he thought, and that Rick will check something in the carburetor called a *venturi* and maybe replace a gasket, and it will be ready in two hours, and do I want them to deliver it? I say no, I'll walk out and get it, that I need the fresh air. "A what?" I ask, but the only answer is a buzz.

I call the nursing home. They have got Gaga back now, and she doesn't have a concussion. I'm not sure how they could tell. As the children say, Gaga is gaga, and her senility is as bizarre as anything a concussion could do. She sneaks out, sometimes dressed in four dresses and as many coats as she can get on, but sometimes in only a nightgown. One time she took a cab to the airport and insisted that her son was coming there to take her to Japan. Finally the authorities connected her with the elegant nursing home, though why it took them so long is a mystery to me, and they came to fetch her. On any given day, she might put on twenty different outfits, planning social engagements with everyone from Teddy Roosevelt to her husband, Elrod the First, who has been dead for thirty years.

"Did she ever *know* Teddy Roosevelt?" I once asked Elrod.

"Sure," he said.

The only part of her left is her southern veneer of manners, but whenever anyone frustrates whatever plan is in her head at the moment, she grows absolutely furious and no one ever knows what will happen. Some of the sitters do fine with her; others she can't stand. For instance, she calls Rosa "that black girl," right where she can hear, but Rosa, who is Italian, is good-natured about it. Right now, they are worried that we might sue them because Kishia knocked Gaga down. They always call me, since Elrod is in school. I reassure them: we know it wasn't Kishia's fault. Of course it isn't Gaga's fault either; she's long gone.

I stand in the back door and call Violet over and over, but instead three of the others show up, and a few of the barn cats, to sing me an impromptu chorus. "No free brunch," I tell them. "Where's Violet?"

I decide to walk to Sevvie's the long way. As I'm struggling into my fur coat, which is a full-length sheared beaver I got for thirty-five dollars from the thrift shop, Josh calls. He thinks my life is bizarre, and wonders why I don't write about it.

"Oh, Josh, if you didn't have a soul, you wouldn't be able to write either."

"Mags, for God's sakes, you—"

"Laugh all you want. But ever since he did it, I haven't been able to write a word!"

"You weren't writing before, either. Margaret, that is so stupid. In the first place, you're an atheist. You—"

"I know. But can you believe the nerve? That bastard would do anything. 'Well, I'll give you my ex-wife's soul.' I mean, we kid around about selling our souls, but Josh, Elrod *did* it. And to some stupid witch—I mean, you know, she *says* she's a witch—I don't think people his age should be allowed back in school—"

"Come on," says Josh, his voice sinuous as a snake, "you don't believe that stuff. Come to New York, Darling. We'll find your soul. A couple of martinis, some fettucine Alfredo at Pappini's—your soul will come skulking back trying to make up, you'll see. Besides, look at it this way—better your soul than your jewelry."

"And now poor Freddie's back too, wondering how come the school is all full of rednecks. I mean, Kelly warned him, we talked and talked for two months about all this, and he still insisted on coming home. He loves his home, he says. He really said that."

Josh laughs softly, at the other end of that impossibly thin wire all the way from here to New York City, "So—did he get the interview?"

"Elrod? With the witch? I don't know. What difference does it—? all I know is that I cannot write one goddamned word. Just drivel. Two or three new beginnings every day, and every one of them bad. He showed up here last night to get me to cut his hair. 'Nobody cuts it the way I like it except you . . .' he said."

"Elrod? You didn't cut it, did you?"

I sigh. "Sure. I didn't have anything else to do. Besides, Kelly loves him. You'd think he was her father. Art never calls her. Oh— and my most favorite cat's disappeared. Violet."

Josh laughs softly again. "Art is envious of life," he says. "How many cats do you have left now?"

"Maybe twenty," I say. "But I don't mind about Elrod, since he's letting us live here. I mean, I know they have the money, but he's really decent most of the time—anyway, Josh, I cut it too short, probably on purpose, now I think of it. He's so vain. God, he's vain. It really upset him. He stomped around for an hour, making mournful, suffering noises every time he went to the bathroom mirror and looked at himself. So I told him why didn't he see if the witch would restore it? I mean, I presume he still has *his* soul. I don't know if it's worth a haircut."

"Anthropologists are crazy," Josh says. "I'd never represent an anthropologist."

"He's not an anthropologist. He's a damned community college commuting student, who lives with his aunt and screws around with some blond boy named Michael he met in one of his classes. But this is interesting: the guy is born-again, and has Elrod going to church!"

"Maggie, don't write about your life. No one would believe it. Mags?" he says. "I miss you, Sweetheart. Come play with me?"

When he says that, it makes my throat tighten. He sounds pathetic, but he has a wife. And *four* kids. "Josh," I say, "Will I ever write again? What if I had never won the AmNat Award? Could I write then?"

I told Josh way back in the beginning that I never have a martini until after five o'clock. And he said, "That doesn't prove—" something. I forget what it didn't prove.

I thought I would like it back here. All the time in the world to write, I told them. I had to get out of the city. Elrod offered us his mother's house. Coming back to Sweetwater seemed such a simple solution. The dream of ease, that's what I had: wildflowers in a jar, blue-checked tablecloth and curtains to match, in that dear little house overlooking the old family graveyard. "Josh," I say, "I thought nobody would pay any attention, but the other women in the Presbyterian basement aerobics class act as if I'm some Famous Person, and the schoolteachers all call me for visits to their classes, where the children all sit as if they needed to have their adenoids out, staring at me as if I were something other than their species."

Now Josh tells me, "What you ought to be writing—"

What I ought to be writing? I know he's dumping a gift in my lap, and I can't even pick it up. He knows he can sell anything I write, and most writers can't even get an agent. I manage to grind out my weekly column like sausage, on things that grow, and/or how to prepare them to eat. Twenty dollars a week I get, to say anything I want. It seems to be the only thing I can manage to do.

Then he says, "Listen, Sweetheart, everyone gets blocked, maybe you ought to be back in the city. Forty is younger in the city. It's like the old rope game, you know, where the teams pull on both ends of the rope? Down there in the wooly-by-gods, you've collapsed because you don't have anyone else pulling at you, see?"

"Josh, I don't have the energy to go to the grocery store, much less haul Kelly out of school, and try to find somewhere to live in some city. And now there's Freddie to think about too—"

It pleases him to think of me as only forty. From this window, I can see out to the highway, and a new scattering of color that wasn't there yesterday: it is the crocuses: yellow, white, purple, a bright scatter right by the ditch at the end of the drive. "Where did I find that book in me?" I said to Josh, a long time ago, in a hotel room in Boston. "Tell me that." I didn't expect him to know. Sometimes I flip through it, and am astonished. Someone else, not me, wrote it. I couldn't write that well. It's a phony. A million copies out there, and me talking about the direction of American letters, when I can't do any better than the Fair County *Gazetteer*.

That hotel had a sunken bathtub, with a jacuzzi. "Oh, Josh," I say, "come down this weekend, or whenever. Just come soon!"

All he says is, "I'm sorry. Gotta get the other line, Sweetheart.

Cheer up. When spring comes, you'll feel better. I'll be in touch soon. And don't hang your age on Kelly, hear?"

—And then the line clicks. He could do better.

"What?" I ask, too late. What does he mean? Did he say my age, or my rage? It can't have been rage. I have to ask him what—but there is only a maddening buzz.

Now I'm all sweaty underneath the fur coat. But I'll cool off outside. I'll walk by and admire the crocus, the first of the year!

But there, just at the edge of the sudden bright splurge of blossoms, her blue-gray stripes dull and dusty, already fading, is Violet, lying on her side, stiff and cold and dead as Robert E. Lee.

I pick her up, and she's chilly and stiff. She was coming home, and a car hit her, I think, and a thin stream of blood is dried against her cheek and down onto her soft white bib. I stand there by the road staring down at her little body, unable to blink away the tears. She feels broken, and already seems lighter, as if her soul has left and gone floating up to Heaven, and I'm left here crying like a fool.

I think of her quintessential catness, of how she came nights and made her sleep-nest right by me, leaning against my leg or my arm or side, and purring until the bed vibrated.

Two cars pass, one slows down but neither stops. When I get back to the house with Violet, the phone is ringing. It's Elrod, and I can hardly talk but he understands. He's very sweet, and says he'll bring steaks out for supper, steaks the size of Rhode Island. I agree to type his term paper for psychology.

I do a few deep breaths, sniff, blow my nose several tissues' worth, and pat cold water on my eyes. I look in the mirror at my splotchy face, and say to it, out loud, "I'm going after my car. I can't bring Violet back, and it's better knowing than not knowing." I turn off the water, and add, "And every gift is complete." I find a shoe box, Dan-dees, 9M, dump the shoes out on my bed, and put her in it. When the kids get home, we will bury her in the field near the road, near the crocus, so we can remember her whenever they bloom again. I want her to have her own spot. Cats are more territorial than we are.

And I'm walking down the road just crying to beat the band. By the time I finally get to Sevvie's, I've turned down half a dozen lifts and my head aches, but I'm okay.

My car's wedged in between an old red GMC truck with rust

patches for decoration, and a sleek new silver Mercury. Sev's garage smells like gasoline and new rubber tires. I love the smell, and take that excuse to go inside, where he is on a dolly under someone else's car by now. His red shirt is just visible under the edge. He gets milk from the Addlers, too. "Sev," I say, sitting down by his legs, "will your kids drink the milk this time of year?"

"Kids these days won't drink milk," he says. "They won't drink anything but soda pop. They won't drink anything that's good for them."

"What'd you say that part was?"

"What part?"

"You know, in my carburetor." It occurs that he can't see me. "Oh—I'm Maggie."

"Sure," he says. "I'd know those shoes anywhere."

"Doesn't anyone else wear Nikes?" I ask.

"Well," he says, "not that exact color." From under the car, his voice floats out disembodied. "I gotta quit this business. Go back to full-time teaching. Or find me something else to do."

"What'd you say that part Rick had to look at was called?"

"Oh, a venturi."

"It sounds like good-bye in Italian."

He doesn't say anything. "What is it?" I ask again.

"Uh, kind of a funnel—kind of like a throat. They get stopped up."

"Sev," I say, "my cat got hit. My favorite one."

"You poor soul," he says. Poor soul? I think souls are like cats: you can give one away, but if it has a mind to, it will come home again.

Then, underneath the big car, Sev swears softly. At me? "I hate making my living off other folks' mistakes," he says.

"But it's so nice here," I say, listening to the gentle metal-on-metal sounds of Sev's surgery.

"You really think so?" his voice is surprised.

"Yes," I say. Then I don't say anything else, just close my eyes and swallow, and practice deep breathing while I wait for Sev to roll out and give me my bill and keys and all.

I guess I'll have to go see Gaga soon. Whenever I visit her, she always holds my hand tight and says, "Haven't we had a wonderful life?" She doesn't even know me, doesn't have a clue who I am, but I always squeeze her hand and say, "Yes, haven't we?"

~~~~~~

Places Where Men Live

I

The first place I have seen only on the outside, and that is quite enough to make my point. It's all there, right up front; it is the cover of a book I need not open to get the gist of the statement being made. They live just up the road from me, the part that climbs towards the best view of the rugged Worchester Range before it goes down and out of the Hollow.

As a matter of fact, it occurs to me now that they probably bagged those three gutted deer that hang head-down from the large pine at their front door in that range, which shelters my back door from the coldest winds. The bright yellow synthetic twine that they have used to display their trophies is not cut off, but draped to the ground ominously, as if the string is not yet complete. I see them at warmer times of the year walking home along my road with a shimmering cluster of rainbows strung nonchalantly from their belts, as if the trout were as unmiraculous as their well-worn carpentry tools.

Now mind you, I haven't been crossed by these men, and don't mind them much except for the time the nephew, the one abandoned with them by his mother, their sister, shot my doe right in my meadow in front of my house. He dragged it across the white, frosted morning, trailing wavering threads of crimson that froze there and could then again be found in the spring thaw. Evidence, I call it, of their insistent clinging to things that no longer matter to contemporary manhood.

Their house, the sad, mottled brown of wet dirt, is down off the

side of the road not more than twenty-five feet, but dropped below it
a good twenty more so that they must feel the traffic in erratic
vibrations that run through their no-doubt vermin-filled walls.
Beneath the delicate, soft-eyed deer's heads, above which the poor
animals' recently warm flesh is spread wide and partially frozen in
the November wind, lies a gaggle of lablike dogs, chewing at themselves and sleeping in piles of blue-black fur like the litter of
puppies they were last spring. The dogs are fat and oblivious to the
sweet flesh dangling just out of reach above them, which tastes, if
cooked fresh, of last summer's fragrant meadows. A six- and an
eight-pointer hang with this year's doe, and I wonder how they
manage not to sicken of that much rich meat by midwinter. They
probably don't taste much though, just keep the stewpot going all
the time, adding chunks of the dark, wild meat periodically to cook
the life out of it when their bellies get low. I could leave some of my
root vegetables on their stoop some evening on my walk to add to the
stew, just to lighten up their characters a bit and balance out the
wildness they consume.

The stoop is worn swaybacked and bare in the center of each step
by their gritty boots, and though I have never been that close to it
because of those dogs, I imagine the threshold worn down similarly,
so that on cold nights the wind roars through the bowed spaces to
freeze the floor close to it by morning into a nimbus of white.

There's a garage, full, of course, of rusting body parts of the
many trucks, in every degree imaginable of disrepair, that occupy
the rest of their lot. Sometimes, in the late afternoon when it is
already dark, the lights they attach to the open hood and the inside
of the engine of whatever they are working on glow and throb like
the beating of a heart. Their silhouettes look boyish against the
heavy, illuminated guts of the engine, and, despite the cold, their
muscular arms are usually bare, as though the opened bodies of the
trucks shed warmth.

On a warm day, even at this time of year, you can see the younger
ones playing Horse around the old, netless hoop on the garage, and
in the spring, they throw a baseball between them across the length
of the narrow yard as straight and lethally fast as an arrow.

Once I gave the abandoned nephew a ride home up the long hill
into the Hollow. Neither of us spoke, for although we know each
other well enough, we have nothing much to say. Years ago, when

my son and he were on the same Little League team, I made a scene with the coach because he had benched my son and others of the younger boys for missing a makeup game scheduled on the same night of the elementary school graduation. The boy, a couple of years older, had laughed to humiliate my son further, as if I hadn't done a good enough job of that myself, asking how old I was, and saying that women of "that age" get like that. When my son related the boy's comment to me I was enraged. How would *that* boy know, living in a house of men, what women "get" like at *any* age?

They are hard-skinned beasts, mules, or rhinos. I see the boys and even the men on a soft winter day sometimes standing around in the mud by their stoop with their heavy wool jackets opened and their bare bellies exposed to the breeze. Imagine, bare belly skin against those thick wool jackets! Or, think of the wool chafing hard against their naked, grimy necks as they work on their trucks or play their manly games. No different, maybe, than a man's beard against tender skin, but if the timing is wrong, it chafes. Men like that sort of thing, rough wool, cold winds, immutable winter stew.

2

The second place is a tepee perched in a poached clearing on a ridge of land high above a privately owned trout stream. To get there you park your car at the side of the road, preferably in the weeds so that it doesn't draw attention. Then, you walk across an old, arched bridge over the stream and follow a narrow, steep path up along the ridge. The path is solidly railed alongside the drop by the tall, bare trunks of maple and cherry trees. These will someday become someone's heirloom furniture, but now their weather-broken branches are carefully chopped away, cut into lengths and stored by my lover nearby, to use for cooking and heat in the old wood stove he has installed dead center of the tepee, just below the hole at the crossed poles that is open to the sky. In the winter, snowflakes drift down through this hole as the fragrant cherry and maple smoke drifts up, and in the summer, starlight drifts down in much the same way as the snow.

My lover sleeps on a mat covered with rough rugs and blankets women have given him over the years. At night he sleeps naked, pillowless, with the stove pushing the cold back to the sloped canvas walls. By morning the musty smell of the canvas creeps back in with the cold, and he'll cover himself, head and all, with a woolen blanket or an old sleeping bag he keeps piled at the foot of the mat. Sometimes, when the heat and the fragrance of the burning wood get too seductive, he will take the sleeping bag out to a hammock he has strung between two ice-bowed birches right on the edge of the ridge and sleep there under the stars, with the snowflakes or starlight drifting down on him all night. In the morning his dark skin glows warm against the pale light, and his black beard delineates his jaw and the cleft of his chin.

His outhouse stores his Telemark skis, and when he is using the seat he props the door open with a pole and watches the birds flicker through the stand of birches along the ridge. In the summer the birch leaves dangle in the breeze like ornaments, like a flock of tiny birds passing through. I have watched him bathe under the bridge in the icy stream, his graceful, dark body submerged face up as he rinses the soap from his hair. His eyes beneath the rushing water are the frigid green of winter ice.

But although this is the place my lover lives, he lives really with me, or with another woman, and piles his belongings by the door, or in a large basket he has rigged to carry like a backpack. I offer him closet space and a corner of my house as his own, but he will never take them, saying he is afraid to get too comfortable. Were he to let himself be cared for, he would lose his Spartan conditioning, which is the foundation of his soul.

When I get tired of his leaving every morning and returning every night as if he changed his mind, he goes to the other woman, bringing his friend Matt, a forty-five year old man who lives in a borrowed deer camp with no running water, but with a large stereo and an even larger television. Matt has no outhouse, so he keeps his daily bowel movements in an empty joint compound bucket outside his back door. How they all live together is a mystery to me, but there is affection between the three of them that he cannot find here. I love the tepee, but she loves the bums.

3

The third place is a hundred-year-old barn converted into a home and an architect's studio. The entry is so well hidden that newcomers must stand bewildered outside until they are recognized from within, that is, if they don't know dogs well enough to realize that their welcoming yelps are an invitation to follow them inside. The entry makes a visitor sure there has been a mistake, as the old stalls and cast-off objects that are found around barns are intact. But the dogs lead visitors up an open staircase to a large, two-story room heated by a gleaming porcelain stove and lit by strings of white Christmas lights.

The dogs have mats under a table at the top of the stairs, and they go immediately there and collapse, tails flopping on the varnished, wide-board floors and faces scrunched into facsimiles of my bachelor friend's wide smile. The furniture is large in scale and handmade by my friend, all by himself. The kitchen is cabineted in warm wood and well stocked with cooking implements and spices. The studio is above the living space in the half-loft: three drafting tables with work in progress, filing shelves, a computer, and speakers for the elaborate stereo system. Above the studio is a sleeping loft for guests and relatives. The entire end wall opens out on chains like a drawbridge to form a deck overlooking the volleyball court. On warm evenings, friends gather to play and watch the sun setting over the line of dark pines at the edge of the meadow, and then, the gradual slow-blooming of the summer stars.

The sleeping loft of my bachelor friend is apart from the business, guest, and living areas, perched atop a narrow, steep ladder on a tower within the barn that houses the bathroom and sauna below. I have never seen this loft, but imagine it furnished with a large futon wrapped in tasteful, crisp, pin-striped sheets and flat pillows. No lamps, no books, no photographs line its half-walls, for only solitary sleeping is done there.

Once or twice my bachelor friend has climbed into my big, cozy bed when the hour has gotten too late and the weather too bad and slept there, restlessly, amongst my pillows and quilts, animals, books, and children until the first crack of dawn could light his way home again, where his smiling dogs wait to show him the door and his gleaming stove is getting cool. I imagine him racing the dogs up the narrow staircase, throwing a few logs into the stove, flicking on the Christmas lights and stereo and wandering into his cool, smooth-surfaced kitchen for his daily dose of oatmeal, "gruel," he calls it with great relish and conviction. As he stirs, he sighs relief at his narrow escape from a woman's nest and the fragrant, fruity pancakes which we are just about to sit down and eat at my breakfast table, which he says vibrates too'hotly with the hungry life-forms that hover there.

4, 5 and 6

There are others, like the bare cabin where my young carpenter friend lives as he waits for a wife. Two rooms, one with a cot and a table covered with books and receipts in disintegrating piles, the other a kitchen with nothing except a refrigerator and a stove. The closet has no rod and no hangers, just some hooks on the wall, the windows no curtains or shades, the cot only a thin army blanket belonging to his father and one of those flat pillows that men seem to like. To get to this cabin you park on the road below and climb up a path over some large, protruding rocks. You can grab hold of a stringy pine for a boost here and there, but it doesn't matter much since he is young and strong and will not be there for long. Soon he will have a wife to make a home for him and she can do whatever she wants with wherever they live, as his own needs are as bare as his temporary cabin.

And there is also the rent-controlled apartment of the graphic artist with whom I fled home once and stayed for a year, children, dogs, and all. A sagging, king-size bed covered with treasured quilts and blankets, each a souvenir of a past experience, a drafting table littered with varying tools and objects of his trade, movable goose-necked lamps never where needed, and a small, bare Buddhist altar and thin mat for daily meditation. All intruding insects, no matter how terrifying or dangerous, are carefully carried down the stairs and outside to be released by the Buddhist, who cooks vegetables and rice in his wok and eats with chopsticks. When he goes on his month-long retreats each summer, his windowsill garden of herbs is attended to by the current lady in his life, and his belongings are not arranged neatly for his absence, but left as though his return is imminent. Once, when we were driving home to visit his ailing father on a winter evening, the northern lights were so alluring we pulled off the highway and lay side by side on a bank for hours watching them. Our imaginings intertwined as the hot breath of giants frosted the chilly, moonlit pane of the sky.

Last, there is the room of my son, just a teenager; a young man who has always lived with women—his sisters, his mother—in the hot heart of a woman's house. Although the house now has central heating, his room remains cooler than the rest, and slightly damp, like the tepee over the stream or the mud-colored cabin with the hole under the door. His clothes are hung by me in his closet, but eventually even the clean ones seem to slither to the floor to collect lint and wrinkles which he never seems to notice or try to correct. Damp towels are wadded behind the towel bars in the bathroom until rescued by me and either refolded or laundered and put away on the bathroom shelf. He and his dog sleep on a mattress on top of a platform bed of his own design with drawers he never uses beneath the platform. I have put an open bookcase in his room where his treasured toys are as I have arranged them, untouched in several years. His skis are saved from year to year as souvenirs, for each fall he purchases a new pair with money he earns himself by working in the summer.

I have placed deep, soft pillows on his hard bed, but he always rescues his favorite from the closet, a flat, shapeless one that does not even fill a pillowcase. His computer is in a cabinet of his design, and behind the closed doors the disks are arranged in a haphazard pattern that only he can decipher. Once a week I go in and flush the toilet, water his plants, change the sheets, hang the clothes back up in his closet and dust the favorite untouched toys on his shelves. Each time I enter his room, a refreshed sense of mystery envelopes me. As each day passes, my son lives more and more apart.

Still, on blustery winter nights I wake, thinking of the cold blowing through the threshold of the hunters' door, the snow falling into the tepee through the hole in the top, the cold, comfortless sheets in the converted barn's solitary sleeping loft, the thinness of the army blanket covering the sagging cot in the bare cabin, or the tender herb leaves turning to mush against the rent-controlled apartment's windowpanes. I rise out of my cozy bed and go into the cold to cover my son, who lies unencumbered in a T-shirt and shorts on his hard, bare bed. I cover him and his dog as they sleep. Surely, my thick, soft quilts could keep them all warm on such a long, lonely night.

ANDREA LASLEY

~~~~~~

Indiana

Indiana is a very flat state. Lonely white houses stare at the highway across any stretch of black soil. In a flat state things can be seen coming from a long way off. In other words, it's hard to take anyone by surprise in Indiana.

The wind is the only exception. The wind always bothers flat-state residents, because no matter how long you look, you can never see the wind coming. One might innocently stand on a cleared acre, only to be assaulted by the molestations of the midwestern wind.

Other than the wind, surprise, in flat states, is generally associated with birthdays and Christmas. Even then, the sensation is dulled, so that one living in Indiana might spend his or her entire life never experiencing the delicious terror of the unexpected.

Sometimes, though, it does happen. Someone in Indiana turns around and, with a look of horror, lets out an exclamation. This is just what happened to Catherine one day. Catherine got taken by surprise.

Winter smells smoky. I won't pretend that this characteristic is unique to flat states. Winter smells smoky in mountainous states, also. Nevertheless, it was a smoky-smelling winter morning, but this wasn't what surprised Catherine.

The wind was speeding across the field, the front yard, then slicing through the crevices in the house, causing a sensational draft in Catherine's room. The wind took a lot of people by surprise this particular morning, but not Catherine.

It was Saturday. Catherine liked to sleep late on Saturdays. Catherine wasn't actually asleep. She was just lying in bed with two blankets, a quilt, and three feather pillows listening to the wind whistle through the gaps in the window.

Catherine lived in an old farmhouse. There are two rules about old farmhouses: (1) an old farmhouse must be drafty and cold and (2) sleeping late in any farmhouse is a priceless luxury. So, it goes without saying that Catherine was both cold and lucky on Saturday mornings.

Catherine looked at the alarm clock beside her bed and read 9:30. She always made it a rule not to get up before 10:00 A.M. on Saturdays. So when she pushed back the warm mountain of covers and put both feet on the cold hardwood floor, it surprised her.

"That's unusual," Catherine whispered. She tugged off her nightgown, stood very still, and closed her eyes, ignoring everything except the soles of her feet and the floor's iciness. She thought, "I am out of bed before 10:00 A.M. on a Saturday."

Catherine walked over to the birdcage suspended by a twisted coat hanger from a hook on the ceiling. She picked up a box of seed and slid the little door open, all the while suspecting that something wasn't quite right. She took out the tray and poured in a little pile of seed. The tiny canary hopped over and cracked shells in his beak.

Catherine watched the yellow bird for a minute. She walked to the bathroom, where she loosened the hot water from the pipes. She sat on the edge of the tub and watched steam rise, then mixed in cold.

Just as she eased in, pinned up her dark brown hair ("I dream of Jeannie with the light brown hair," she thought), and soaked the washcloth, the telephone rang. Her hands and the washcloth suspended above the bathwater, she looked at the bathroom door.

The phone was ringing for the third time when she ran out wrapped in a towel. The bird twittered nervously at the sudden opening of the door. Even birds, with eyes on the sides of their heads, can be surprised. "Hello," she said, while water formed puddles on the floor and on the plastic of the telephone.

"Are you alone?" asked a husky voice on the other end of the line.

Catherine was twenty-two. This was not her first obscene phone call, so she started to hang up, but heard the voice say, "Wait."

Catherine brought the phone slowly back to her head. She clutched the towel to her chest.

"Yes," she whispered.

"Yes," the voice repeated. "What are you wearing?"

Catherine answered, "A towel."

"Yes," said the voice again. "Are your breasts wet?"

"Yes," said Catherine. Her daze was interrupted by a familiar beep that meant she had a call on the other line. She clicked to the other call.

"Can I come over now?" It was Catherine's best friend, Molly Maguire. Molly worked at the convenience store about ten miles from Catherine's house. Sometimes when Molly's shift was finished she would stop by.

"Yes," said Catherine. She put the phone back on the cradle.

The bath that had been steamy a conversation ago was now lukewarm. Catherine finished quickly. The coolish water made her anticipate the feel of her white terry-cloth robe. She wrapped her hair in a towel then descended the surprisingly cold stairs.

Sunlight greeted her in the kitchen. Catherine put on the water to make some coffee. She had poured herself a cup and was sitting at the table when Molly opened the screen door and walked into the kitchen.

"What a night," Molly said as she opened a cabinet and got a cup and saucer. Molly helped herself to some coffee and turned around to Catherine. "I think we made about fifty dollars last night. For the life of me, I don't know why we stay open for twenty-four hours."

Molly sat down. "Bobby McMillan came in at about two this morning and I told him that if he didn't stop harassing me, I would tell my father and he said he didn't care but I told him he better care because my father is a state trooper and he said that maybe he ought to be going and I said I thought maybe he ought to be going, too."

Catherine looked at Molly and hoped she'd made decaffeinated coffee.

Molly asked Catherine how her morning had been. Catherine said, "I got an obscene phone call."

"I hope you hung up. I got one of those at the store a couple of nights ago and was scared to death that someone was going to bust into the store and rape me or something. Did you?"

Catherine looked surprised. "Did I what?"

"Did you hang up?"

"Yes," said Catherine for the fourth time since she got out of bed. She stood up for another cup of coffee.

As Catherine was walking over to the counter, Molly said, in an amused, almost surprised tone, "I think that this is the first time I've ever seen you barefoot. Are you feeling brave today, Catherine?"

Catherine smiled. The coffee was hot, the house was cold, and Molly had asked her if she was feeling brave. Catherine took a sip of coffee and burned her tongue. She pulled the towel off her head.

Molly let the screen door slam as she left. Catherine surveyed Molly's departure from an upstairs window. "There is certainly nothing unusual about Molly today," thought Catherine, as she watched the tan Maverick pull out of the driveway and dart down the road.

Catherine sat down in front of her mirror. She began tugging a red plastic comb through her wet hair. Then she got up, walked over to the closet and opened its creaky door. She selected a pair of old jeans and a white button-down from way in the back, also a pair of boots.

"Socks first, then jeans, shirt, and boots," thought Catherine, as she dressed. She pulled the front part of her straight hair back and secured it with a rubber band. "There," she said. Catherine grabbed her purse and heavy coat and headed out to her car.

Catherine drove on the highway for a while. On this highway, she passed many farmhouses. She paid them no attention. Their familiarity, along with the wind and other elements of scenery, wiped the windows of the car. Catherine drove with the radio turned off.

A fact: Sometimes when one is driving, especially on a familiar road like the one on which Catherine was driving, he or she will begin to daydream and arrive somewhere thinking, "How did I get here?"

Catherine listened to the wind. It reminded her of a song she knew. This in turn made her think of the band that sang the song. She imagined meeting this band.

Catherine looks incredible. She and the members of the band

click immediately, become the best of friends. No, one of the members becomes infatuated with her. He must have her. He wants to spend the rest of his life with her, or just the night.

A sign moved closer outside the car. It read "Lafayette 10." Catherine thought, "How did I . . . ?" But before she could complete her thought, it happened. Catherine was surprised by a rooster leading a group of hens across the road.

The rooster strutted shiny red, a green tail pouring from his hind end. His dirty yellow legs and clean head floated in time together. His bloodred comb crowned him the stately leader of a strange parade.

Catherine hit the rooster with her car. Chickens are lightweight animals. Cars are heavy machines. Two tires of the car, one half the car's weight, brought the rooster down. The hens squawked and fluttered. They had all been surprised.

Catherine pulled off the road and turned off the car. Her first thought was "Why were the chickens cross . . . ?" Catherine began laughing. She loved birds, but she'd always thought that line about chickens crossing the road had been a joke.

She walked toward the nearest farmhouse. A deserted chicken coop stood in the yard next to the white farmhouse. She knocked on the door and hoped it was the right one. Catherine tried to stifle a snicker.

A middle-aged woman in a housecoat, who had probably been up since daybreak, answered the door. Catherine explained what had happened. The woman immediately began cursing. She followed Catherine to the group of hens pecking around in the road. Catherine apologized, paid the woman for the rooster, then turned her car back home because she simply couldn't remember where she had been going.

As Catherine started back down the highway, she turned on the radio. She thought about how beautiful this stretch of country was, the way that her dashboard lined up parallel to the horizon. There was something about living on land that had been smeared flat by glaciers, a majesty opposite that of the mountains.

The surprise had been good for Catherine's mood. So good, in fact, that on her way back down that wondrously flat highway, she picked up a hitchhiker (Are you feeling brave today, Catherine?) standing on the side of the road next to a black pickup truck.

The hitchhiker slid in and asked where she was headed. Catherine told him and mentioned that she would pass a gas station where she could drop him off. He said, "Great. My name is Tom, by the way." Tom was blondish, wearing a flannel jacket and jeans.

Catherine introduced herself and pulled back onto the highway.

Tom began talking. "I graduated from I.U. three years ago. Now I work for this fertilizer company, only they sent me out here because I guess there have been some complaints about cattle and sheep getting sick from drinking the water. So I came out to get some samples. Wouldn't want any lawsuits on our hands, you know."

Catherine nodded.

"When I was at I.U., I knew this girl who had lived in this town where everybody had gotten sick, like cancer or something, from chemicals getting into the water and it turned out that it was the result of some fertilizer company who had known about it the whole time. I guess they went out of business when the survivors sued the pants off of them. I think this is the gas station you mentioned. Isn't it? Thanks a lot. I really appreciate this."

As Tom was getting out of the car, Catherine thought that perhaps this guy and Molly should get together. She waved good-bye and drove home with only the sane radio playing for company.

When Catherine got to the front door she could hear the phone ringing. She fumbled with the keys, jiggled the lock, and ran to the phone. "Hello," she gasped.

"Are you alone?" a deep voice asked.

Catherine hung up the phone.

It rang again almost immediately. Catherine just let it ring and walked upstairs. If it wasn't her prank phone caller, it was just Molly wanting to talk about getting raped by Bobby McMillan.

Brave Catherine slipped off her shoes while listening to the phone ring. She stood in front of the birdcage and whistled at her canary. He twittered back from inside his cage. Catherine was content with the knowledge that if he ever escaped, her canary would fly. He certainly wouldn't be crushed under the tires of a car in the middle of the highway.

Catherine padded to the bathroom, where she splashed her face and got a glass of water. She walked back to her big bed, lay herself down on top of all those covers. She put her head in a square of sun that had been warming one of the pillows, and fell asleep, probably tired from getting up earlier than usual on a Saturday.

While Catherine napped, the wind continued to speed past her house, crossing the highway and invisible state lines. On the highway to Lafayette, the wind tickled the feathers of the dead rooster, then pressed past on its way to jingle chimes, erode topsoil, and surprise other flat-state residents.

Banshee

Okay, Mickey, I tell myself. *Maybe if you pretended she's dead, or something.*

But how can I? Five days a week I see her, Monday through Friday, nine o'clock till sometime after six. Except on Tuesday mornings when I'm out, and Wednesdays when, believe me, I'm grateful that Kate leaves at noon.

She used to stick around then, get her case notes written up. We'd go out for coffee, flirt a little, swap tales of neurotic clients, the genuine psychotics, the heartbreak and boredom of listening, listening all day long. Now she sneaks back evenings, weekends, rushes past my office if the light's turned on. "Mickey!" she'll say if I happen to meet her in the hall. "You're here."

Unable to stop myself—she smiles up at me as if we were in love, what a joke, her whole face shines, her eyes latch onto mine, *cut it out,* I think and smile right back—unable to stop myself I say say, "Kate. Want to go have coffee?" It's always me that asks, these days, and the conversation's strictly decorous. We still laugh a lot and sometimes she forgets herself, leans close, but I wish she'd say *no* instead.

Here's what else I think about. Tuesdays I put in half a day at the maximum-security prison up in Troutvale. Seems the least I can do, let the attorneys' seventy-dollar-an-hour midlife crises subsidize a group for incarcerated adult survivors of abuse. Funny, how it all pays backhand tribute to my father: respectable Judge Reilly could slap his son around some when he got a snootful, that's for sure. (And you can spare me the smart remarks about why people go into psychology. I've heard them before, made half of them up personally, in fact. Big, funny Mickey Reilly, always good for a laugh, especially a shot at himself. So what? I do what I do, that's all. Besides, I hear plenty of stories about parents considerably worse than mine.)

So I think about LeRoy Booker. I'm sure he's innocent. He's also smart and sensitive, despite a little brain damage from some random beating when he was a kid. And if rehabilitation counts for anything at all—well, killing LeRoy's not going to bring that girl back.

Still, even if I didn't know that LeRoy (I'm talking about LeRoy the way he used to be, fifteen years ago, trashed out on booze and reds and speed and bad self-loathing) would have said anything, that's how scared and confused he was when he came to in the blood-splashed apartment, even if it didn't make perfect psychological sense that LeRoy confessed and confessed and confessed again, telling a different story each time, yet careful each time not to implicate poor Sonja's crazy mother or her dealer-boyfriend, there's the simple fact of the physical evidence. Wrong semen, according to the retest. He's right-handed, not left. And it took a strong man to finish up that job.

LeRoy's five foot four, so frail you know no one ever fed him right. In my dreams, he shakes his head and mumbles, "I'll never remember that night, Mickey. But thanks for the sandwich. I'm going to file another brief." Papers flurry like wet snow off the north Atlantic. A gavel bangs. Outside the window, the window of a stone cottage, Kate's white white face peers from the cave of a great black shawl. Her hair hangs loose. She wails, a banshee announcing death to come.

Death in the family—that's what a banshee sees. It's an election year. The governor's a good man, by and large, but he's got ambitions. It's an election year and the crime rate's soaring, an election year and LeRoy's innocent.

What changed things with Kate: three months ago, she cooked dinner for me in her apartment, first time, and then I lost my head.

Surprised her. Pushed it. Made her nervous. When she finally started yelling, I stopped. Just in time, I guess—the idea of rape turns my stomach—but I couldn't make the damage go away. We sat there on her flowered couch and cried together, after she told me about what her stepfather used to do. She brushed damp hair out of her dark-lashed, bright-blue eyes and swore we'd always be friends.

What can I say? She seemed as eager as I was: she'd been touching my hand, throwing her head back when she cracked up at my jokes. We'd both had a lot of wine with dinner. Since then, I've been watching what I drink.

In my professional opinion, there's hardly any chance she'll ever sleep with me. If I were my own client, I'd ask me my reasons for clinging to this impossible longing, would name for me all the interesting, attractive, available women at the edges of my life. I'd relight my pipe—yes, I really do that—and wait while a meaningful silence shrieked anguished warning somewhere nearby.

Between appointments, I slouch behind my desk, stare at the bookcase, listen for Kate's footsteps in the creaky hall. Sometimes I hear my grandmother's brogue, spinning out tales of spectral visitation and lingering heartsick love.

"You done a lot for me, Mickey," says LeRoy. "I ain't—I'm not going to forget that." He nods, pasty-faced, hollow-cheeked, eyes alive with some vision I'll never see.

We're talking by phone, though only a plate of glass and a foot or two of empty air separate his mouth from mine. If I didn't know better, I'd think I could punch that fragile-looking pane, smash it like an empty bottle, cup my heavy hands around LeRoy's shoulders and guide him gently past the lethal shards.

The guard thumps me on the back. Time's up. Anyway, I've got a staff meeting back at the office at one. I like to get there after Kate does, but not so late I have to sit directly across the circle from her, where I keep seeing her slender legs, her bare arms carefully folded across her chest. Still, today I would stay longer if I could.

As I pass the guardroom, a muffled lunch siren moans. "I'll be there Friday night," I told LeRoy when I left. "Outside, waiting. There'll be a whole lot of us, remember. Not just the media people. Unless of course the governor—"

"Stop," said LeRoy. "I do appreciate what you're saying, Mickey. But I don't believe I care to talk about the governor right now."

Late Friday afternoon, Kate hovers just inside my office door, stepping forward, stepping back. She wants to go with me to the vigil. Her face gleams pale and grave. She catches her lower lip, damp between her teeth. My chest tightens at the sight. *That does it,* I think. *I can't stand any more of this.* But of course I tell her I'll be glad to pick her up. She's not a tease, not deliberately, and none of it is her fault, after all.

Dawn comes on windy-cold. We stamp our feet, stand close together to keep warm. And for some kind of animal comfort: LeRoy's death isn't the only one we're mourning, I suppose. People sing, make speeches, sniffle in dark corners. Kate's eyes glow like the ghostly candles we shelter behind curved palms. If she hadn't come along, I'd feel only misery.

Inside my head, Gram's reedy quaver keeps repeating an old ballad she used to sing to me after I'd been punished, a song about cruel and faithful love. Kate smiles wanly as I hum it, rasping, beneath my breath. I look at her straight on. She looks away.

The execution's set for six. Eventually a spokeswoman in a crisp blue suit comes out to tell us LeRoy was pronounced dead at 6:19. A voice booms from a bullhorn. A chant begins. Off to the side, I mutter some stupid crack about the mess from the candle wax. Kate starts to giggle. She laughs out loud.

She doesn't stop. The laughter turns to sobbing, to narrow howls of lamentation. My stiff, parka-fat arms wrap awkwardly around her. "Mickey," she says. "I'm sorry. I'm so sorry." After a while, the keening ends. She quiets, her face still buried in my chest.

Now what? If this were a made-for-TV movie, Kate would shyly take my hand, ask me if I wanted to go for coffee. Music would swell and the audience would know that in a couple of hours we'd lie down together in her bed, making tender, wet-cheeked love. In a different kind of film, the last scene would show how all hope, all desire, had died with LeRoy. Maybe it would close with a shot of Kate's face, bleak and frozen as the face of a faery-woman bearing a knowledge too awful to put into words.

But this is life, my life. Maybe I'll stop wanting her, stop loving

her, in time. Probably we'll keep on making each other miserable—
and happy—in the same way. Right now, I can only think how a
man has been killed, how I have no choice, really, about what I feel.
Still, holding her for just a moment longer, I think I see it all a little
differently, think it might go a little easier after this.

BRETT LAIDLAW

center & circumference

Dad was a manufacturer's representative, traveling salesman. We lived on the far fringe of the Minneapolis suburbs, in
the township of Eden Prairie, where Purgatory Creek meandered
through the Eden Views and Eden Vales and Paradise Valleys, a
country utterly new and in hope and vision redeemed. Dad covered
most of the Upper Midwest, handling a dozen lines of over-the-
counter pharmaceuticals and sundries. On local calls and around
the state he drove, a legendary driver he was, having cut his teeth
drumming for drug firms in the prairie provinces when he and my
mother were first married and still lived in Winnipeg. The vastness
of Saskatchewan negated motion. You drove and drove, a day, and a
night, and then where were you? Still in Saskatchewan. Assiniboia,
Moose Jaw, Prince Albert, Saskatoon, what did it mattter? He still
drove the car that had carried him on those long prairie calls, a great
square Ford Galaxy 500, grainy gold and weathered. Dust storms
had pitted the windshield—you couldn't see it but could feel the
rough texture under your fingertips. Hail had pocked the hood, hail
from thunderstorms that came boiling purple-black out of the West,
while the grain was still golden bright, and a silo or elevator in the
middle ground floated in refracted light. Once, on a trip to the
northwest part of Minnesota and the North Dakota border towns,
he ran off the road in a tremendous storm. Just north of Fargo, the
storm clouds had come out of nowhere, and in a blink the highway

was a river, and he had just floated off into the ditch and hit hard. There was nothing to do in rain like that so he had waited it out, and when it cleared he got out and stood by the highway and waited for help. Someone came along soon enough, a nice fellow who traveled from Duluth for a woolens concern. The two of them managed to pull the Galaxy out, and then they met down the road for a cup of coffee, and then went on their ways. On his return Dad rolled into the drive with a clod of North Dakota soil still wedged between the car's bumper and frame. He called my brother and me out to see it.

—That's Red River gumbo, he said.

We regarded it with awe. A relic, this was, a piece of the true cross. As a young man in Winnipeg Dad had worked on the Red River Floodway. All the able young men of Winnipeg had toiled under the prairie sun, moving by hand the acres and tons of clayey red earth, Red River gumbo. Sometimes you would put your spade in, and there it would stay, it took two or three men to pull it out. This piece of earth, neatly squared as if Fords were built for cutting gumbo, was heavy and damp, a thick ruddy brown, and even in the bright afternoon, hundreds of miles from its source, it carried its own river coolness. My brother and I lay on our backs on the gravel drive to see it. It still had grass attached, the blades wide and coarse, not like our grass. It seems impossible that Dad just kicked that clump of gumbo loose and threw it away, but he did it, with even a kind of prideful disregard, as if the wonders you could take for granted or dismiss were a measure of the fullness of life, and of resignation to time.

On road maps he showed us where he had been, described the condition of the highways and narrated unexpected detours. He had tricked out all the fastest, most direct routes, where the county roads were actually quicker than the trunk highway, where an unmapped lane would save twenty minutes. If there was romance in this, in the highway numbers, names of towns, and in the precise black lines that joined and crossed and parted, it was mainly a romance of competence and mastery, of tools and knowing how to use them. Still, didn't a portion of wonder remain in, say, the town of Hallock, even though he had just been there, even though it sat flat in the middle of soybeans? Something in the way he revealed to us the intricacies of the maps and helped us to imagine his real journeys in this ideal world described a love of his territory which he couldn't otherwise speak.

If Dad ever got lost he made the being lost into a finding—that was how you discovered the twenty-minute cutoff, or a better, cheaper diner or motel, or maybe even a new account, an unknown drugstore hiding out there on the prairie. Dad did everything as if he meant to do it.

And he could fold up maps like there was nothing to it, even though they did not all fold the same way.

On longer sales calls or meetings, out of state to the flat-sounding cities of the Midwest—Omaha, Grand Forks, Sioux City, Des Moines—Dad flew. We all went with him to the airport if we could. On a summer afternoon Mom made us put on school clothes, and combed back our hair with one of the tonics Dad sold. (Our basement was a dark jumbled drugstore with shelves piled with boxes of samples of the varied lot Dad peddled: bobby pins; all manner of arcane vitamins; a portable hair dryer in a case that looked like a ladybug, even to two springy antennae with wooden balls on the ends; dietetic candy that my brother and I and our friends devoured in spite of ourselves; tampons, fascinating, the cottony batons and their plastic cases endlessly adaptable in projects and make-believe, but slightly sinister, since their actual purpose was unclear, and no one seemed willing to explain.)

While Dad shaved and showered and Mom packed his suitcase, my brother and I sat in the living room, where we, or anyone, hardly ever sat, and dangled our legs from the upholstered chairs. Dad came from the steamy bathroom, his tan face redly shaven, clean, cologned. He put his face down to mine, wide planks of cheek, smelling sharply sweet, the skin smooth and leathery, with here and there a square of tissue on a nick. He wore suit pants and a sleeveless undershirt, and when we had seen how clean he'd shaved, and smelled how he smelled, he went into the bedroom to finish dressing.

He came out of the bedroom blue-suited (he owned two suits, the other brown), white-shirted, trimly tied, listing to correct for the big gray suitcase in his hand, and then we three went down and waited by the car while Mom finished dressing. When she came down the steps in the billowing smell of going-out Mom—acid scent of hair spray, sweet powder, thick perfume—then we were off.

This part I don't remember well. Dad drove, the route is vague. The freeway that now loops the city south was not yet built. At the airport we parked in the ramp, saw Dad through baggage check and to the gate, where he smoked and told us about the planes, and to take good care of Your Mother. And he boarded, and we waited, and never left until he was well aloft, and then we walked away down the suddenly desolate concourse in the sense of something ended and something begun. In the main terminal the flags of all the countries hung flat in the air of departure.

The day was bright and still, late afternoon in summer, as we walked in cool concrete shade of the parking ramp to the car with some feeling of adventure and some small dread. Mom plumbed her purse for keys half the way to the car. Dad had told us many things to do and not to do besides take care of your mother, but they are hard to remember. Mom found the keys, and the car (the latter feat far from routine—I have traveled many miles with her in parking lots where not a single car was ours). In the car she discovered the parking ticket wherever Dad had secreted it, behind the visor, up on the dash, in the glove box—it seemed almost like a game. No one spoke as Mom negotiated the mazy rows of cars, found the exit, jangled out change for the attendant, crawled through the gate and gained speed toward the highway. Dad was somewhere high above the plains; there was more danger, more excitement of discovery, here, in the Galaxy's wide backseat, where my brother and I sat straight and tense and Mom alone in the front aimed us down the road to we never knew where.

Mom always got lost driving home from the airport. Here is the central point, arrived at by a way Mom would approve, though somewhat too directly, and then, in her way, all points are central. Her sense of direction has never been keen; more than that, destination holds for her little urgency. When she told a story, all particulars tended to distract her. Plots, intrigues, and sentimentalia emerged in the telling and drew her attention away from the supposed point of the tale. Just because she had started with one thing in mind, what reason not to change her mind, to develop richness and meaning and a whole wide connected world? An anecdote beginning unpromisingly at the local shopping center, purportedly concerned with why we were eating plain hamburger buns instead of the crusty kaiser rolls that Dad preferred, would wind up in Missoula, Montana (Mom always gave city and state, or province, for locales outside of Minnesota or Manitoba), with her hairdresser's estranged husband, an itinerant baker, who had run off with a beauty school student and a lot of his wife's money (the short version: Mom had been kept waiting at the beauty parlor because her hairdresser, who usually worked briskly while recounting gossip and personal tragedies, had to stop, and gain her audience's fullest attention, to relate this ultimate tale of betrayal, and to each and every customer, so she fell farther and farther behind; thus Mom had been late getting to the bakery, and the kaiser rolls were gone; the baker husband had no connection to the bakery with no kaiser rolls; the hairdresser did not know the beauty school student; these were merely interesting coincidences). Her stories were like Dad's maps, where lives branched and parted and joined and crossed, but there were no towns, and all the ways led on to all the others. Something of this same ethic seemed to rule her driving.

Perhaps if Mom had driven *to* the airport, instead of Dad, she would have known better how to take us home. But more likely not. She had no trouble getting to the airport when we went to pick Dad up. And a journey's return is never a simple mirror image; things seen from one side take on new life when turned around. Invariably, sometime shortly after leaving the airport, she exited awrong, followed some tangent too appealing to resist, even as she must have known that this narrow vista of houses and stores was one she had never encountered before. It was as if all familiar context dissolved the moment we turned from the straight way home, and there was no turning back.

As we came away from the airport, my attention was diverted for a time from Mom's doomed determined driving. Ahead, to the right, the Mendota Bridge stretched from bluff to bluff across the wide forested bottoms of the Minnesota River near its confluence with the Mississippi at Fort Snelling. The bridge's stone arches step among islands and narrow channels in its looping march to the southeast. The bridge is flat on top, two lanes and lampposts all across. On the other side is a tall round hill, a cemetery among trees on the hill, all greenness and distance and promise. A white church steeple emerges from the treetops in a town below and on the far side of the bridge. A river; a bridge; a hill. What was over there, across the bridge, behind the hill? Mendota, and Mendota Heights, and farming towns to the south, places that were no place to me, I didn't even know their names; the only logic was that of desire for the other side, the where-you-are-not, that comes on with a drowning wash of want.

The Mendota Bridge still is the shape of my dreams and desire. We were going to get lost, so why not over there? But Mom's ways were more subtle, and we never crossed the bridge. The left-hand veer away from the river was the single certainty in our ever-uncertain return.

In the first few miles down presumably the proper road Mom steered stiffly, hunched behind the big wheel, kerchiefed, sunglassed. Once we were lost she relaxed. Looking out the back windows my brother and I knew without anyone's saying a word that here we were again. Mom seemed to consider losing one's way as some sort of natural phenomenon (the old-fashioned "Act of God" has perhaps a more appropriate resonance), something one could not combat or control. She looked around curiously, cheerful and resigned and with mild motherly concern, as this calm fate unfurled. She was only its conduit. Just for show, I think, she eventually said:

—Oh shoot—pardon my French. How'd we get here?

As if she knew where *here* was.

—Mummy, are we lost?

—Yes, I think so, dear.

—Where are we?

—Well, I think we're, well, but maybe not. . . .

We rolled through flat and treeless suburban tracts, like where we lived, though the houses were closer together here. The lawns looked freshly laid, the drives jet black and scarcely tracked. The house scrolled by, clad in pallid siding that only hinted at nameable colors (our house at least had real wood shakes, Dad painted it, and it was yellow). The houses were ramblers, but modest, compact, and they seemed to settle slowly through the unrealness of the new.

In the yards were bright swing sets and slides; bikes on their sides; bats and balls and gloves. But where were the kids? Nowhere to be seen, as the yellow light pressed down and we drove through this strange and strangely familiar terrain. Mom turned here or there, through streets of more of the same. This being lost had its own organic shape which Mom felt through the light, or vibrations of the steering wheel, I couldn't begin to guess.

We turned a corner. Ahead, a shopping center, beckoning.

—Well for pete's sake is that . . . No. Dash. Wouldn't you know it.

The shopping center, so like one she knew, betrayed her, and on we went.

No one has ever been back to the places we visited in these digressive returns from the airport. The eccentricity of Mom's way insured their uniqueness in the instant we encountered them with no idea at all of where we were or where we were going or where we had been. At any time we might have been within minutes of home, might have crossed a familiar road from an unfamiliar direction and never known it, and wandered again into the shadeless wilderness of orderly streets. And then, we might have strayed farther than we could have imagined. The center was wherever we went, and circumference traveled with us; since we were the only known point, this world shaped itself around us. And if consequently we could go nowhere but where we were, then that was in Mom's way, as well. To her a road map was a ridiculously involved riddle in a dead language. If she stopped to ask directions—rarely, and only because at certain moments it must have fulfilled her sense of what one does when lost—she drove away with thanks and smiles, more bewildered than before.

At some point, a moment or two short of real despair, some landmark appeared (that shopping center whose sinister twin had nearly duped her before), and things fell into place in their usual order—where we were and where we wanted to be. Or, after all our windings on quiet residential streets, we came upon a broad trafficked avenue. The purling logic of this trip dictated that Mom now decide, and she turned onto the avenue, one way or the other, and drove it till the wrong way turned to right.

The wrong way was the wrong way because it was never the same way twice, and it digressed and meandered and brought us to the edge of despair, and while we were in it we never knew exactly where it would lead us. Just the same it always brought us home.

By the time we got home it was early evening, and in the long light we climbed out of the car, my brother and me with tired excitement, Mom with sighs and conspiratorial looks. With weary relief she unknotted the kerchief and removed her sunglasses, and her eyes seemed to shrink from the sudden brightness, and they gave her face an odd look as she said to us:

—Here we are, home again. Your father won't believe it. I just don't know. . . .

By now Dad had probably arrived at his destination, hundreds of miles through the straight clear air, and if he took a cab from the airport to his hotel he would know if the driver was trying a circuitous route to plump the fare, and he would speak to him.

Mom never got lost driving *to* the airport. We arrived there well ahead of Dad's flight, Mom instructing us to remember the ramp level and row where she had parked, and went and waited at the gate for Dad's plane. He came off smiling, tired, hugged Mom and tousled our cropped heads. Had we taken good care of our mother? Of course we had. Well then there might be something in his suitcase for us. Of course there was.

As Dad drove home, sitting in his solid easy way behind the wheel, guiding the car with one palm while the other arm rested out the window, checking the mirrors and from time to time making adjustments so fine that less practiced drivers would not even have seen the need, Mom told him with comic exasperation how we'd been lost again on the way home (though she always made us promise to *not say a word about this to your father!*). He was amused or annoyed depending on his mood and how the trip had gone.

We came on to the highway with certainty and speed. There was the bridge, arching away to the green invitation of the other side. But with Dad driving the other side was impossible to consider, and I felt strange at how its appeal could be tarnished, how I felt bad for wanting to go there.

Dad lectured and critiqued Mom's driving as we went, pointing out the pitfalls this route presented, and how to avoid them, while she carefully listened and repeated things to fix them in her mind, but her attention seemed more taken with the many wrong ways than with how to maintain the right one. Pointing:

—Now is that where I should have . . . ? Oh, I don't know.

—That's going to take you right downtown, Grace. You'll wind up on Lake Street.

—So I should have . . .

—Bear left and left again. You can't go wrong.

—Oh of course. I see where we are. How stupid. Boys, will you help me remember this? We bear left here. Was it left, Bill? Yes, left. Have you got that?

We looked and nodded, and whispered *left*, full of responsibility. Next time we would take good care of Mom.

Once, and only once, we found our way out of, or through, or beyond the neat subdivisions, and came upon a rising road that overpassed a highway at the foot of a hill and curved out of sight behind the hill. The car slowed as we came on to the overpass, and stopped in the middle. Below us the cars went this way and that, straight, and fast. We looked in both directions, parked there in the middle of the road, in the middle of the overpass. Up on the hill there were houses, windows glinting up among the big trees, and if you lived up there you might have a fine view, of the highway, of the cars going this way and that, and you could have seen my mom and my brother and me and our car, stopped on the overpass for a minute or two, looking both ways down the highway, and down the road that curved around the hill, wondering where these roads went, or maybe just looking, and not saying anything.

After this minute or two Mom put the car in reverse, backed off the overpass, and after several backings and frontings from shoulder to shoulder, got us turned around and headed back the way we had come.

The Short Flight

She must have noticed my eyes, too, because all the while we're sitting in the waiting area, we're sneaking looks at each other. Or she sees what I'm looking at—some grandly decked-out dude gliding down the corridor or a kid picking his nose and wiping it on somebody's carry-on luggage—then our eyes meet for a flurry of conversation about how I see it, too, and I know how funny it is, but you and I are the only ones who are getting this, and what does it mean? and so on, the whole thing occurring in the catch of our eyes. She looks away, and I do, too.

Sure, everybody has this kind of thing happen to them, but what makes this communication unusual is that there's a terrific reluctance to it, as if she and I have both just renewed our wedding vows and we're doing our damndest not to send any inviting signals to anybody, but in spite of our best intentions, here our eyes are playing that old game of peek-a-boo, I-see-you-naked, don't-you-wanta-see-me?

What else sets this experience apart from your basic airport flirtation is that in the game of age, the woman and I are advanced intermediates. Maybe we've got eighth-grade eyes, but we're both mature citizens. Neither one of us is checking into a nursing home tomorrow, but I'd guess her to be mid-forties and I know exactly how close I am to fifty.

I'm no Don Juan. Since I got married this last time I haven't gone looking to get involved with any woman. I've even taken some pains to avoid taking up with some that wanted to get involved with me. But I have this vulnerability. I don't know what else to call it. When a woman wants to be touched, I can sense it even if she and I have never met and we're in a room with fifty other people. Sometimes I can sense exactly where she'd like me to put my hand.

Call this vanity or male ego or whatever you want, the terrifying data is that there are women, attractive and unattractive, walking around everywhere who want to be touched, not necessarily by me but by some man they wish had the gumption to do it. A lot of them wouldn't admit this desire even to Satan on a dirt road late at night, and some of them would have you in a court of law early the next morning if you set that hand on her too quick or too hard or on the wrong spot. Nevertheless.

What I mean to say is that I bring a certain amount of unwilling expertise to the situation, enough so that you'd think—I'd certainly think!—that I'd be able to evade a little swirl of trouble like this. The part you can never figure, though, is old Mr. Fickle. Losing each other in the crowd, the woman and I pass through the gate and walk on board, only to find that there we are, 11A and 11B, on the two-seat side of the aisle. In the old days, if I'd been hot to start up something with her, they'd have had her in first class and me back in the tail-feather seats. But now here we are, buckling up together, the two of us fighting our natural inclinations on a sold-out commuter flight up to Albany.

How intimate you have to get on an airplane has always been a shock to me. I live in dread of some fat guy plunking his big butt down next to me, and there I'll be, snuggled up closer to him than some honeymoon couples sleep with each other. This woman isn't fat, but I get an odd notion that she has been fat—maybe until just a few months ago. She still has a few extra pounds in the middle of her body, though the cut of this very tasteful pant suit she has on under her trench coat is doing all right by way of directing my attention away from her middle up toward her chest where she's got some extra that looks just fine.

Something else I notice now that I'm right up beside her, there's a slight scar just along and underneath her jawbone, as if she's recently had cosmetic surgery. I'm a little clairvoyant, and I get a flash: this woman has been down; right now she's making a hell of an attempt to put herself back together.

Sometimes nowadays I surprise myself. I realize that I like her for these scars and for the weight she's lost and for the pant suit she's picked out that makes her look good for this trip to visit her old Aunt Velveeta, or whatever. I like her for not being a suntanned blond eighteen year old with a smooth face, a turned-up nose, great legs and a miniskirt that barely covers her Victoria's Secret bikini underpants. I might not want to know the details, but I like her for having lived through whatever she's lived through.

Here's what else I'm grateful for: she isn't wearing any perfume. What scent there is around her is just regular human being— clean, female, with maybe a touch of soap, deodorant, and nervous sweat. The olfactory assault of perfume always intimidates me even though I know that most women, when they're traveling, find it necessary to splash it on.

However much an expert I am on *what* women do, I'm usually as mystified as the next guy about *why* they do it. But at least in this case I know why this woman isn't wearing any perfume: she isn't looking for company. I appreciate that. I'm not either. She's window, I'm aisle, and while we're settling in, stowing our coats and her carryon and my briefcase above and below us, we're not saying anything. We know we'll get to the conversation soon enough. Our eyes have told us we've got some things to say to each other. Whether or not we get them said is, I guess, the little buzz that has my blood pressure up about a notch and a half.

Quicker than you'd think, the plane casts away from the gate and taxis out to the runway. This, too, is unusual; I'm accustomed to sitting on airplanes waiting for takeoff so long that I always start thinking of concentration camps and how all this regimented behavior and noise and machinery must be something like what kept the Jews from resisting the Nazis. You don't find any of us airline passengers unbuckling and standing up and saying, "Let me off of this thing, you sons of bitches, I've had enough of this shit!" We'd probably keep sitting still, with our trays fastened and our seats in the upright position, until the flames started licking up outside the windows.

The woman and I don't say a word, though our eyes continue their subtle conversation. Even in the plane's crazy sprint down the runway and heaving itself up off the tarmac, she and I have our faces turned toward each other but our mouths shut tight. The look on her face has me wanting to put my head down in her lap.

This silence we're keeping is a cocoon we've pulled around ourselves, a private room where we're exploring each other with daring intimacy. I'll swear, it feels to me about as naughty as any act I've ever committed, and all I'm actually doing is looking at a woman who's had the good sense not to dye the gray out of her hair.

What's passing between us also has this depth to it. It's like what I imagine a lapsed Catholic must feel when he comes back to the church and confesses all his sins for the past twenty-five years. She's telling me that there was this man who brought some major-league pain down into her life, and I'm telling her that I've gone through more women than cards in a canasta deck, and until my present wife I haven't been able to find the one I've been looking for. This telling is sad as hell for both of us but all right, too, because now at least we're telling it—except that we aren't even having to say anything out loud, our stories are just flowing out of us while the aircraft rips up through the clouds toward cruising altitude.

I've lost track of time, though I guess my watch would tell me what's passed if I wanted to break the spell and look at it. But all of a sudden, there's a lurch downward of our side of the plane, we're tilted over in that direction, the plane is curving around in some spiral-like pattern, and there's a noticeable loss of power. There's also a scary quiet. The flight attendant who's coming down the aisle toward us, catches herself against a seat back and keeps her balance, then turns and heads back to the front of the cabin, bracing herself from one seat back to the next. I turn again to the woman beside me, her face telling me what I already know—what everybody on board must be figuring out right this minute: this plane's in trouble!

What comes into me is awful, as if my vital organs are failing in unison, but there's also this curiosity about what I'm actually going to do. My third wife used to tell me she'd never run into anybody as scared of death as I am. I've never attended a funeral in my life. When my relatives and friends get sick, I don't go visit them in the hospital—I call them up and send flowers; I tell them quite frankly that just the thought of serious illness slides the backbone right out of me.

The specific occasion of my third wife's observation was this time we were on vacation, she was driving in a thunderstorm in the

Poconos, and a Mayflower moving van bullied us off the shoulder and damn near over the side of the mountain. When she got the car stopped and looked over at me, I was whimpering like a four-year-old. At first she was furious—she was moody that way. "I'm scared, too," she spat out, as if I'd claimed she wasn't. Then she felt sorry for me and reached over. Her hands moving toward me released whatever inhibitions I had left: I shoved my head into her chest—she also had the most distinguished breasts of my personal acquaintance—and before either of us quite knew what we were doing, there I was tugging at her shirt, her hand wiping the tears off the top side of my face, and her voice whispering down to me, "What has gotten into you?"

"Attendants, please carry out procedure number 3. Procedure number 3," comes the captain's voice over the intercom, calm enough to be informing us that we're flying over Cleveland, while beside me, the woman's face is as full of meaning as a Tolstoy novel. What she's telling me is that she sees what's in my face, which I know must be this god-awful vision of groveling cowardice.

Here's what's funny: I am aware that I ought to be strong for this woman, that she has suffered and fought despair and that she deserves someone to give her comfort in these dreadful circumstances. I lift my hands. I don't know why; it's like I want to describe the shape of something I'm about to give her, or more likely it's the gesture a frightened person makes to fend off something. Maybe you just lift your hands when you understand you're truly helpless.

Whatever my reason for doing it, it provokes the woman beside me to act. It surprises me that I'm not surprised by what she does; her face has been telling me she's going to do exactly this. With her left hand, she catches my right hand, pulls it toward her and sets it on her breast. Doesn't do it lightly or shyly. Sets my hand right there on the front of her jacket, where anybody who wants to can see it, and keeps looking me straight in the face. The plane has been eerily quiet, but now it begins generating this low whistling noise.

My hand has had its own education. My first wife, who was only modestly endowed, used to say that if anything could have increased the size of her breasts, it would have been the palm of my right hand. She used to swear that my hands were always whispering to her chest, "Grow, grow!" So even though it seems an indecent gesture in this circumstance, my hand, of its own volition, seeks properly to grasp what it has been offered.

That movement of my fingers—and whatever else my face is telling her provokes the woman once more. In moves that demonstrate her hands to have had some education of their own, she undoes one button of her jacket, two of her blouse, and the front clasp of her bra. She sets my hand right inside there where it wants to go. Then she rests her arm along mine, lightly pressing me against her.

There we sit, looking each other in the face and waiting. I figure we can't be that far away from what's coming to us. Up front there are a couple of women crying, and behind us there's a guy saying in this Alabama accent, "I ain't goddamn ready for this! I tell you, I just ain't goddamn ready!" The whistling noise seems to come from outside the plane and rises in volume and pitch.

Like a lock with a key turning in it, some essential part of myself moves. All of a sudden—I don't know why—I'm not afraid. I feel my face relax. "What's your name?" I ask her.

"Elaine," she says. When she smiles, I know that I haven't seen her do that until this instant. "What's yours?" she asks.

First, of course, I start to tell her my name, but then something stops me, and I start to explain to her that crazy as it may sound I don't want to give her my name because this is how it has gotten started between me and a lifetime of women. I seem to be able to hear this very same exchange in all these women's voices echoing down a huge corridor, "What's yours?" and my rasping little testosterone croak, "Wayne Wilson."

I have my mouth open, and it looks like I'm going to tell her this even though I know it's going to ruin everything, but in this circumstance I'm helpless to say anything else to her.

I've gone as far as saying, "Please forgive me, but I don't want—" when the aircraft seems to catch itself and start angling upward again. It feels like when you're a kid on a swing and you've gone as far back as you can go, back to that point of weightless suspension and falling straight down, then the chains catch, you start forward and down, but now you can feel the swing underneath you and you know you're going to be all right.

And it's like suddenly finding yourself frozen into a photograph of yourself doing exactly what you're doing. The plane is gaining altitude; the woman and I are sitting right there with her holding my arm close to her and my hand inside her blouse holding onto her breast like it's something precious that I'm not about to let go of. She smiles again, but I don't seem to be able to read her face the way I have been up until now. But when she makes the slightest shrug of her shoulder, I understand that well enough.

Taking my hand away, I turn in my seat and become aware of a tall blond stewardess standing in the aisle over us, trying to give us a grin. Her nametag says "Carleen." She moves on, and my seatmate very deftly reassembles her clothing. The captain's voice comes on the intercom again, still so calm that I suspect him of being a recording; he's explaining how we've just recovered from a freak loss of power, not something that's likely to happen again in another fifty years of aviation.

With my now-free hand, I touch my forehead and realize I'm sweating. As much as I don't want to, I think of my second wife, the only one of them that I never did understand why I married. Late one night while she and I were watching an American League playoff game on TV, she went completely cuckoo over the sight of Roger Clemens wiping the sweat off his brow and rubbing it into the baseball. "Why does he do that?" she asked me in a voice so shrill it was like she'd just witnessed Clemens biting a baby's wrist. I tried to explain it to her as a pitcher's ritual to bring himself good luck or something, but the truth was that even though I'd played a little baseball in high school, I didn't know why a pitcher rubbed his sweat into the ball. They just do that; I hadn't thought about it before. My explanations put her off even more. She excused herself and went to bed before the inning was over, and when I showed up a half hour or so later, she wouldn't even turn over to give me a goodnight kiss.

So I'm sitting there looking at my sweat-slicked fingers and grinning to myself over that little harridan of a second wife I had, when Elaine's hand comes over and takes those fingers; she puts her palm right on top of the sweat. I give her a quick glance and see not a smile but something better, a look that tells me she wants me to know I'm all right with her no matter what comes next. What she does next is pretty startling: she rubs hands with me, rubbing that sweat from my brow into both our hands. When she's done with that, she gives my hand a little squeeze and lets go, gives me about five percent of a smile, then turns her face toward the window.

And that's it for Elaine and me. We don't speak, we don't touch, we don't let our eyes meet again, even after we've set down in Albany. Actually, this is Elaine's decision more than it is mine, because while we're gathering up our coats and her carryon and my briefcase and climbing up out of our seats, my eyes are still flicking over in her direction every now and then. But now she might as well be somebody else. Just by the way she moves her body, a woman can tell you things, and Elaine's posture is definitely declaring, "I don't know you, pal."

That's OK by me, of course, because Albany is where my wife is picking me up. With a record like mine and a wife who's intensely aware of that record, I don't need even the hint of a romantic complication. I let Elaine get well ahead of me in that weird zigzag portable corridor you have to walk through to get from the plane to the gate. From far enough back, in her trench coat and with her head bowed forward, she looks like Ms. Middle-aged Anybody, from Anywhere, USA, and I'm relieved about that because when I greet my wife I don't want my eyes betraying me by sneaking off to the side for one last look at Elaine.

Coming out into the public area, I don't immediately see my wife the way I'd expected to. It's a little disconcerting because there are lots of husbands and wives and sweethearts and children and parents and grandparents and friends all around waving at people coming along behind me or hugging people up ahead of me in that way people do at airports, as if they're determined to get as close as they can to somebody. I worry a second that maybe my wife has changed her hair or something and I'm just not recognizing her. I'm looking into all these women's faces, even the ones who are young enough to be my daughters, but I'm not seeing her. She'll show up, though, I'm certain of that. When I set my briefcase down in the place where I'm going to stand and wait for her, I think I hear a voice calling out my name. But then I turn and see it's just somebody else moving into the arms of his loved one.

Ponytail

The girl is my age, sixteen or seventeen, obviously deranged. She's talking loudly to a blond couple in white beach pants who sit, carefully, like scolded children. They're from L.A.—I know because they sat next to me on the plane and told me—but you can tell. His and her Evian bottles, no-nonsense watches that measure milliseconds. Sleek and photogenic and brimming with aerobic fitness. You know.

"So, my Dad stuck me in rehab, right? But the minute I got out, I started doin' horse again, so he threw me out and I hitched to Sunset and started turnin' tricks, you know, to support my habit . . ."

The couple, wearing frozen, polite smiles, suddenly realize their expressions are inappropriate. In perfect synchronicity, they manufacture looks of shock and dismay.

"Oh, that's awful, isn't it, honey?" The woman glances frantically at the man.

"Terrible," he agrees, gazing sadly at the Walkman in his lap.

"Well, ya gotta do what ya gotta do, you know, to survive." The girl lights a long, thin cigarette and exhales like Bette Davis. "I got beat up plenty by those johns . . . God, know what one of em did to me?" The girl settles back comfortably in a cloud of smoke.

The chair I'm sitting in is like an enormous, halved grape, bulbous and violently purple. O'Hare's color scheme is as alarming as Miami's. I don't like this chair, so I work a pen into the prickly seat cushion, boring an ink-stained hole and watching it tear. It passes the time. So does listening to this crackpot Hitler Teen whose story—in content and vocabulary—is very familiar. It sounded familiar when I heard it twenty minutes ago, when she was telling it to a grandmotherly type who clutched a lapful of embroidery and looked fearful, who pressed a dollar bill in her hand and hurried off to hide. It's like those Young Adult novels, precautionary tales about hitchhiking and drug use. Plus a liberal smattering of terse, *Miami Vice* dialogue.

"Most johns don't like junkies, so I had to start shootin' up in some pretty weird places," the girl tells the couple. "Don't worry, I won't tell ya where." She brays. The couple sighs.

Airport lounges are supposed to counter fatigue and jet lag, but this one makes you feel like you're coming off a three-day Dexedrine high. The furniture is so loud it hums—acid-green, sunshine yellow, neon grape—a large rainbow is painted on the partition that hides the rest rooms. It's tackier than a mall in Florida, which is where I'll be going in two hours. Well, almost. Our housing development is behind the Shady Grove Mall in West Palm Beach.

My father has a ponytail. I can't believe it. It's symbolic to me, it makes me want to die. Almost. It's a middle-aged ponytail, dark, flecked with silver, grown by desperate men. Wanna-be hipsters. The kind of ponytail that screams identity crisis, male menopause. An impotent squiggle of hair, insubstantial and ridiculous, a lot of silver strands escaping at the sides. You've seen them.

My father—one of my last memories of him as my mother's husband: he's standing in the kitchen of our old house in Baltimore, choked in a tie and Brooks Brothers' jacket, stalking on thin, hairy legs. He sips coffee, paces, and jabs at his pants on the ironing board. "Wrinkle," he says, pointing. A muscle in my mother's jaw ripples, and she pushes the iron back and forth. The creases aren't the creases of a high-powered Baltimore exec.

Of course, I know that happened a couple years before the divorce. Birthday presents, a camping trip, good times were sandwiched in between. To my mind, though, he put his pants on that day, grabbed his wine-colored attaché case, and drove straight to the airport, straight to California. It just seems that way. That man in the kitchen was my father. The fifty-year-old whom I've spent the last two weeks with, who says "Just smell that air!" and "Just look at the sunset!" who wears that ponytail and quotes his shrink on "salvaging bonds"—he's my father now. He went to L.A. to find himself, and did, in the form of a woman who can best be described as "nubile."

Yes, cringe away, that's what I do every time I think about it. And prepare yourselves, because it gets worse, more clichéd and stereo-typical, more like a bad TV movie. He lives in an oceanfront cottage in Venice Beach with, you guessed it, a blond girlfriend. Her name isn't Candee or Cindee, thank God, but Joan. And thank God again that she's nowhere near my age. She's thirty-four and talks about it all the time. "It's not easy," she'll say, leaning between her legs to lace her Nikes, "keeping this tired, thirty-four-year-old bod in shape," and, on her way up, she'll slap a cement-hard thigh for emphasis. The first two phrases that come to mind when I think of Joan are "nubile blond" and "perky breasts." I don't even know what nubile means, but I'll bet you anything it's what Joan is. She and my father bustle around their small, white kitchen, cranking the pasta machine and throwing raw string beans at each other, getting in each other's way and laughing about it. They go to STOP GENTRIFICATION meetings, they're in an aerobics class for couples. It's sick. It's sicker than this fat girl here in O'Hare, sicker than her tight, VIRGINIA IS FOR LOVERS T-shirt and her words.

"There are two kinds of johns, okay? There are the ones who like seeing girls doin' it to each other, and there are ones into pain. Course, I'd go for the lesbian stuff any day . . ."

My parents' marriage and divorce were nothing new. If you've grown up on TV and Judy Blume, you've heard it all before. She was tight-lipped and silent, pretended great fascination in house-work or *Ladies Home Journal* whenever he was around. He worked late. He'd spend hours manicuring the lawn, practically trimming the hedges and driveway blade by blade, to avoid coming in the house on weekends. Inside, he'd gulp Scotch and watch wok-cooking demonstrations on TV. She even threw things at him, sometimes, but they were soft things, like packages of Wonder bread. It was boring. "Why don't they get a divorce?" my brothers and I used to say glumly, after one parent had snapped at us, or denied a request. As we knew from all the Afternoon Specials we watched on channel 7, fighting and divorce were normal. It was the happy people, like the Williamsons who kissed and clung and did tandem somersaults in their backyard, who were weird. And we were right, because Mrs. Williamson had breakdowns and was institutionalized every year for a few weeks, usually in March. Once my brothers and I saw Mr. Williamson carrying his wife to their Buick. She sat stiffly in his arms, pulling her earlobes, giggling. I found out later that she was manic, and didn't like taking her medication.

"Smack's the coolest thing," the fat girl confides to the blond people, who are now holding hands, their eyes glazed. "It's, like, better than dying."

"Smack" is the word they used in the Seventies, isn't it? Smack, horse, H. You know that book, *Dinky Somebody Shoots Smack.* Nowadays they use "junk" or the all-purpose "dope." Or they're casual and indifferent to hip terminology, like Lou Reed, and say simply "heroin."

Even the dialogue, two years ago, was lifted from a sentimental movie: "Your father won't be coming home this time." We sat soberly on our mauve couch in Baltimore as my mother explained what "irreconcilable differences" meant, even though we knew. We'd seen that dumb cable show with smarmy little Drew Barrymore. And it didn't have anything to do with us, that sometimes these things happen, they still loved us just the same, they had been too young and didn't know what they wanted . . . we knew all that. Oh, yes.

That part about visitation and "You'll probably see a lot more of your father now than before . . ."—that was a lie. Read—Dramatic effect! Tension! Conflict! We didn't see him for two and a half years. He wrote us letters. Letters that began "Dear kids." He used to refer to himself as "your old dad." He'd write things like "your old dad is having a rough time adjusting to bachelorhood." After a year, he adjusted, started writing postcards. He started writing "I" to conserve space.

The blond couple is making their getaway. She suddenly remembers that she needs to buy some duty-free cigarettes before their flight. What a lame excuse. If there ever was a nonsmoking couple, it's these two. The man is mystified, and then catches on. "Oh, right. Good thinking, honey." They smile at each other and collect their matching pastel tote bags.

The girl is disappointed. "Nice talkin' to you guys," she says forlornly.

The man turns around and reaches into his pocket and thumbs through his wallet. You can tell the bills are ordered by denominations. He thumbs past the singles, and pulls out a five. What generous people we are! is written on their faces. You can see them preening, inside.

"Buy yourself a magazine, or something," he says tenderly.

The woman flashes him a tender smile, and tells the girl, tenderly, "Now, you take care of yourself."

"Good luck," they chorus, and flee. Probably to the cocktail lounge to sip a few Perriers and lime, where underagers aren't allowed.

"Wow, thanks a lot!" the girl says. "Nice meetin' you guys!" she sings to their backs.

Definitely a money-making scheme, I think. Not bad, though I've seen better. Last spring, my mother and I made the College Interview Trip to New York City. She spent a day visiting friends in Brooklyn Heights, and I smoked a joint in our hotel room and rode subways for the next five hours, all over Manhattan, Queens, and the Bronx, a captive audience to the spiels of panhandlers. Many of them were remarkably imaginative. A group of college-age people in tattered black clothes and combat boots played complex riffs on guitars and sang a song called "Give Us Your Money." Others played accordions, harmonicas, and teeth; some tap-danced or break-danced or shuffled down the aisles, displaying chancres and amputated limbs. The best stepped in our car at Rockefeller Center.

"Ladies and gentlemen," he announced, and begged for a moment of our attention. "No doubt you have witnessed many victims of suffering here on the IRT line," he said in a trained voice. "But few, I assure you, can equal the suffering I've endured." He held up a glossy picture, ripped and uneven on one side, of a toothless hillbilly in overalls. You couldn't tell if it was man or woman.

"Allow me to introduce . . . my wife." He looked around meaningfully. "Need I say more?" He bowed to the applause.

"And, if I may, I'd like to show you some family snapshots of the kids . . ." He lurched down the aisle, holding the strap with one hand and showing pictures with the other, walleyed midgets and burned Japanese children running. All glossy and tattered on one side, page numbers in the corners.

"So my lovely wife and I would greatly appreciate any financial assistance . . ." He passed around a roomy Rastafarian cap, even though he was white, and most people dropped bills. He bowed again, and proceeded into the next subway car. Over the train's clattering, we listened to the same words, muffled.

This girl's performance is nothing compared to his; still, it's better than average. I realize she's looking directly at me, so I quickly bury my face in *Mademoiselle*. She stares hard and cranes her neck, trying to get my attention, and then wanders towards the snack bar, wedging the bill into her jeans with one finger. Her bra carves ridges into her back, under the tight cotton T-shirt. Her bikini underwear digs a deep triangle in the seat of her jeans.

My father probably wears tight bikini underwear now; I'm sure he abandoned his Fruit-of-the-Loom diapers long ago. Black bikini underwear, maybe leather, on days when he's feeling particularly studlike. Joan buys it for him and leaves it on the king-sized futon, with a note saying "For you because you're you." Or they buy it together in Frederick's of Hollywood. I can see Joan, unzipping a peekaboo crotch, looking through it, past her blue mascara, squealing "Peekaboo!" And my father laughs and throws his arm, his heavily tanned and newly muscular arm, around her neck. She makes him feel so young, so alive.

My parents got joint custody of the house, my mother full custody of us. With her settlement, she bought a furnished condo in West Palm Beach. (In, not on, we're nowhere near the ocean.) She works at the mall we live behind, Assistant Marketing Director. She wears white miniskirts now, and has cut and streaked and permed her hair. I don't hold it against her, she looks great. She's started to date, and the man she sees most often is named Elvis—that, I hold against her. He's bald, has a goatee—trimmed within an inch of its life—and resembles Yul Brynner in a Nehru shirt. My brothers and I call him "Uncle Elvis" and snicker behind his back. It makes my mother angry, we can tell, but she pretends not to hear. She is giving us Time to Get Used to the Idea.

The girl ambles back and forth, between the gift shop and the snack bar, trying to catch my eye. I hide behind my magazine and stare at a long, slim, female thigh, fascinated by a depillatory cream ad.

I was prepared, or thought I was, for California. My brothers had visited several months before, one at a time. My father's not stupid, and he helped us with our history homework once. He knows military strategy, divide and conquer. My fourteen-year-old brother, Jeff, was first, and he reported the existence of Joan, whom he called the Blond Bombshell. Or, in a falsetto imitation of my mother, "That Shameless Home-Wrecking Hussy." (Of course, my mother would never say that. She calls Joan, matter-of-factly, Your Father's Girlfriend.)

"Man, she's stacked!" Jeff had leered at my twelve-year-old brother, Eric. "Tits out to here!" he said, holding his arms straight out in front of him. Eric looked troubled, but laughed, macho and loud, along with Jeff. After Eric returned from California, he called Joan "Dad's Piece of Ass." He and Jeff locked themselves in their room for hours, sucking noisily on their bong and discussing Joan's anatomy, which grew to astronomical proportions. Stoned, they giggled and discussed the "stuff she did" to my father, the sexual props she wielded, cries of passion she howled. They didn't have much to say about my father, and never mentioned the ponytail.

They blame her.

"Hi, I'm Lisa." The fat girl flops into the chair beside me. "Don't you fuckin' hate airports?"

She says "fuckin'" because she's my age, and it forges a bond. We are teenagers, this is our language.

"No, I like them." I study my magazine.

I do. I like airports, Greyhound bus stations, IRT subways. Noise, excitement, weird things to look at, people rushing off to exciting places. Not today, but usually.

"Oh. Well, I hate them. I fuckin' hate them." She emphasizes the *k* sound spittingly. "I guess it's cuz I spent a lotta my life in 'em."

I'm careful to remain expressionless, but she takes this as an urging to elaborate.

"I been a runaway since—fuck!" She runs a pudgy hand and four turquoise rings through her frizzy shag cut. "Since nine?" she asks me. "Maybe eight. Smack does lousy stuff to your memory. Anyway, I hung out in bus stations at first, since the pimps lookin' for kids usually go there. But after a few years, I switched to airports." She glances sideways, to gauge my reaction, and sighs explosively. "An I been to all of em, doin' sick things you can't even imagine. Cuz a junkie'll do anything for her fix. Lemme tell ya somethin." She hangs in my face. "Never trust a junkie."

Oh my God! "Okay," I say. I've seen *Sid and Nancy,* too, you dumb twat. I rip to another page.

She launches into an explanation of heroin usage, warning me of air bubbles and overused veins. She uses words and phrases like "mainers," "the candyman," "cookin up." She speaks out of the side of her mouth and squints through cigarette smoke, a 1930s bad girl of the silver screen. I curl my lip, somewhere between a sneer and a smirk, but it's lost on her.

I spent the two weeks at my father's in Venice like my brothers did, refusing opportunities for exercise, looking disgusted at the healthy concoctions my father and Joan "whipped up." I found the baggie of Thai stick my brothers had raved about and helped myself to a liberal fistful; my ponytailed father was far too hip to comment. I looked through the drawers of their bureau (careful to avoid the top one, where my father always kept his underwear) and noted with revulsion the array of Spandex sportswear, his and her, matching, side by side.

I filled my father and Joan in about Elvis, except his name was Julian, and he was tall and twenty-seven and a part-time model. He also did free-lance work for NASA, I told them. I don't know why I said that. They sat on the couch, knees touching, and agreed how wonderful it was my mother had found somebody. They must have known I was lying.

I wince.

"Oh, yeah!" The girl nods her head vigorously. "All the time!

Sometimes he'd even tie me up. You can still see the bloodstains on our carpet in the living room . . ."

Last night, my father and Joan went to a Fleetwood Mac concert. They bought a ticket for me.

"Fleetwood Mac?" I said incredulously. "God, are they still around?" I reattached my headphones, shaking my head. "God! Fleetwood Mac!" So they took Joan's friend from the boutique.

They returned, shortly after midnight. I was sprawled on the couch, watching an awful movie on HBO, one of those celluloid excuses to show a lot of naked women. *Hollywood Hustlers* or something like that. Joan cha-chaed through the living room, pumping her arms and bouncing on her espadrilles, and boogied into the bedroom. My father collapsed onto the couch, next to me.

"Your old dad is too old for rock concerts," he said ruefully, rubbing the back of his neck and tweaking his ponytail. Making sure it was still there. "Listening to Frank on the hi-fi is more my speed."

Hi-fi. I rolled my eyes. He and Joan own a CD and stereo, with every possible accoutrement. What the TV advertises as a 21st Century State of the Art Home Music Center.

"Fleetwood Mac's not rock music," I said, staring at the *Hollywood Hustlers*. "It's Muzak. Bad seventies elevator tunes."

"Yes, well." My father laughed. "I guess I don't like them any more than you do."

"They suck."

"Yes, they do." A few minutes dragged by. "I sure wish we could have spent more time together, these last couple weeks," he said finally.

"Enough time for me," I said.

Undaunted, my father stretched his legs out on the coffee table and put his hands behind his ponytail. "So," he said, looking at the TV set with interest. "What are we watching?"

What a coincidence. A bad TV-movie kind of coincidence. I warned you, this is full of them. The movie was perfect and wonderfully apropos for my last night in California. Three aging men from Houston journeyed to Los Angeles for the sole purpose of "scrounging for snatch." They strode jauntily, Stetsons perched on liver-spotted pates, through malls, bikini stores, and discos, on the prowl for nymphomaniac mud wrestlers. Failing miserably, they hired a local surfer to give them lessons in "babe-snagging." When one paunchy Texan, the one who introduced himself as the Rhinestone Cowboy, broke a vertebra and was next seen, desperately disco-dancing in a back brace, I laughed. Derisively. My father turned to look at me.

"You don't like me much anymore, do you." It was not a question.

"I hate your ponytail. It's pathetic and desperate and ridiculous. It makes you worse than these guys," I said through clenched teeth, gesturing furiously at the TV screen. "Trust me, the entire boardwalk is cracking up, after you jog past in your California sportswear."

God, it sounded so stupid out loud. It made perfect sense until it hit the air, and turned into some more bad TV dialogue. "Grow up, for God's sake," you tell the sniveling kid on the screen, watching the Confrontation Scene.

"In that case, I'll cut it off," my father said blandly. "It makes my neck itch, anyway."

I crossed my arms and stared stonily ahead.

"Tired, babe?" Joan hung sexily in the doorway—actually, she was leaning—in a short terry-cloth robe. She had purple veins in the insides of her knees, but it didn't make me feel any better. "Or could you go for a little jacuzzi action?"

My father sucked in his breath, tantalized. "Hey, now that's an idea!" He lightly tapped my leg with the side of his hand. "You haven't set foot in the hot tub yet. Why don't you suit up? I think we might even have a little California bubbly left . . ."

"Oh, God!" I exploded, and rolled my eyes to their limits. California bubbly! "Right."

"No one's forcing you," Joan said, throwing me A Look. "It's just an invitation." She disappeared into the bedroom.

He made a move as if to touch me, changed his mind, and clasped his hands on his knees to stand up. "I hope you change your mind," he said. "You know where we are." He walked out to the patio.

Can you believe, this girl is still talking to me? And finding new lines to deliver, an inexhaustible supply.

"Listen—I think you're telling all this to the wrong person," I say, interrupting a lurid description of a detox center in Milwaukee.

"I have no pity for you. I'm the kind of person who has a lot of fun, pulling the legs off insects," I say pleasantly. "Homelessness—I love it. And there's nothing I like better than laughing at handicapped and retarded people."

The girl's eyes are like cow's eyes.

"I've really enjoyed your story, it's been very entertaining. I especially liked the part about the horsewhip. But I don't have any money, so this is sort of a waste of your time."

She blinks.

"Just thought I should let you know," I say, returning to *Mademoiselle*. "But," I add helpfully. "That guy over there looks pretty gullible. Compassionate, you know? And look at his luggage—he's got lots of money."

I flip a page, study another ad.

Then she balls her fists and screams at me. I smile and admire a jar of Noxzema. People stare. She offers to show me her track marks, enraged. I decline. She screams some more, kicks my knapsack and tells me where to ram it, and stalks off, making shrill, philosophical comments on the human race. I look at recipes for avocado facials.

A jacuzzi, a CD player, a ponytail—I hate these things more than nubile blonds. Actually, he didn't acquire Joan until afterwards. He didn't leave us because of her, so I don't really hate Joan. She's another prop, another part of the interior. My father's beach cottage, my mother's condo, even this airport and its fluorescent glare, stages. She's a piece of furniture on the set, a walk-on character with a couple lines.

My first few days in California, I made a whirlwind tour of Los Angeles landmarks: Grauman's, the La Brea tar pits, where John Belushi died. On a studio tour with a group of Saudi Arabian tourists, I trouped across the sets of prime-time TV shows. The tourists snapped their cameras furiously, immortalizing every second, as we paraded past endless couches and kitchen tables. Even though each set was identical, indistinguishable from the last: the same plaid, lived-in couch, the same geometric patterns of family photographs on the wall. When you see the sets up close, you marvel at the illusion—how could you have been fooled—for the walls are flimsy cardboard, and the books painted on.

JUDITH HAWKES

Switcheroo

It all begins the night the three of them decide to switch heads.

They're walking along, it's raining a little, and one of them (afterwards they can never remember who it was) notices that each of their heads actually matches one of the other bodies better than its own. Dee's dark-blue baseball cap seems more appropriate to Marty's body in its green nylon anorak; Ellen's yellow sou'wester obviously belongs with Dee's yellow slicker, and Marty's red ski cap is clearly the mate to Ellen's army fatigue jacket. But it's more than just a question of hats and coats. Ellen's long frizzy hair, Marty's mustache, and Dee's tinted glasses are a part of it too; and in the light of streetlamps reflected in wet black asphalt it seems to make perfect sense. They'll just switch heads. Naturally it's the most radical for Dee and Marty, but Ellen ends up having the worst of it.

One of the first things that comes up when they notice, later that night or in the small hours of the morning, that it's actually happened, is just how they're going to define who each of them is now. Is it going to be bodies or heads? Heads or tails? Surprisingly it's Dee (now wearing Marty's body) and Marty (now wearing Ellen's) who vote for heads—surprisingly because in doing so they're abandoning their respective sexual identities and so forth, less surprisingly perhaps because Marty is a computer programmer and Dee has an office job and they are both oriented, so to speak, in the head. They also point out that it's going to be a lot easier to pass their new bodies off as the old than it would be their new heads (here Ellen's hand fingers Marty's mustache), and that's a strong point. In fact there seems to be no question whatsoever that it's the heads who are running the show. Except that Ellen, divided as she is between Dee's body and Marty's head, has her doubts.

Ellen is a free-lance artist, and from the very first moment—or at least the first moment she becomes aware of the switch, for somehow it happens without their noticing—she has a feeling, or her head does, that this business of switching isn't going to work out, at least not for her. For one thing Dee, whose body she has inherited, is just a glorified secretary with about as much artistic sense as a doughnut. Ellen never thought much about it before, but now it seems very clear that artistic sense is located not in your head but somewhere in your body, somewhere around the stomach or possibly a little higher. For another thing Dee is quite a lot heavier than Ellen, and—although one of the other things they decide right off is not to make complaints or recriminations—it's like having to drive a big luxury car when she's used to a small sporty model. Dee, on the other hand, is busy inventing the crash diet that's supposed to have trimmed her down to Marty's shape over a single weekend (it's Saturday night, or early Sunday morning, when it happens)—"Watercress," she keeps saying. "No, bean sprouts. Bean sprouts."

But what's bothering Ellen most of all is what's going to happen to her and Marty. The three of them have been friends for a long time, but recently she and Marty have become lovers. And now here she is with Dee's body, which is bad enough—but there he is with hers, which is worse. She doesn't think she's narcissistic enough to want to make love to her own body just because Marty's head is on it, but she isn't at all sure she loves Marty's body enough to take it in conjunction with Dee's head. The more she thinks about it the more it seems that, in this game of musical bodies or heads, the music has stopped and she's been left out. Because there they are: her body and Marty's, probably not caring a bit whose heads they're wearing—that's just the way bodies are. As the feeling grows she begins to have a sense that she doesn't even like Dee, although before she might have said they were best friends. "Sunflower seeds?" Dee is saying. "Sunflower seeds."

It turns out even worse than Ellen expects. There's no teaching Dee's body to draw; it can't make a straight line even with a ruler; it keeps tidying up the drafting table, and worst of all, it has cravings. Ellen has been a vegetarian since she was thirteen; she's still a vegetarian, however separated from herself she may have become; and to have Dee's stomach craving baloney which will have to pass through her mouth is about the worst she can imagine. Dee also has flat feet. In any case their resolution not to complain to each other's heads about their bodies falls apart almost at once. It seems that Ellen's hands doodle incessantly in the margins of Marty's computer printouts, and Marty's feet are too big for all of Dee's shoes.

"I had to go out at lunch and buy a new pair," Dee says. "Size eleven. Your feet were killing me."

Marty looks under the table at his feet (they're sitting in Ellen's kitchen the following night). "God," he says. "You shaved my legs."

"I had to."

"God," says Marty. He snickers. Dee giggles. Ellen stirs her coffee. She hates coffee, but Dee's body is addicted to it. She doesn't know how they can laugh. Her hostility culminates in curiosity about how they are handling the sex change (it seems that here, at least, she's come out ahead in not having to make that particular adjustment), but she's shy about starting a discussion in which her own body is intimately concerned. After all, Marty might say something embarrassing. "Your feet can't be the biggest change, Dee," she says significantly.

"Huh?" says Dee, and then purses her mouth. "Oh. Them. Well, I have to watch how I sit."

"You'd better," Marty says, and they're off laughing again.

Later on, when Dee leaves, Ellen asks Marty how he likes being a girl.

"It's great," he says with such a broad grin that she gets the feeling he's enjoying himself—that is, her—in some kind of perverted way that will give her an unpleasant shock when she finally gets herself back. For somehow they're all assuming, with a sort of blind trust, that they will get themselves back.

"Sure we will," he says when she asks him what he thinks. They're sitting on the couch; they're alone, and Ellen is wondering a little nervously what's going to happen next. "Why shouldn't we?"

"Why should we?" says Ellen, depressed by her craving for baloney (she has not yet given in).

Marty looks at her. "What's the matter with you?" he says. "You've done nothing but mope since we switched."

"I hate it," she says. "I hate Dee's body. I want my own back. I miss it."

"What do you mean?" says Marty. He chuckles. "It's right here."

The tears start in Ellen's eyes. "Stop it," she says. "Stop acting like it's some kind of big joke."

Marty stops being horrible when he sees she's really upset. He pats her knee and leans over to kiss her cheek. His mustache tickles in the old way. Ellen turns her head; they kiss; she goes limp. Marty strokes her hair and she leans against him and they kiss again. Marty mumbles against her mouth. "Mmmm," says Ellen in response. He mumbles again; it sounds urgent this time. She pulls her head back.

"What?"

"I said you're crushing me."

Ellen realizes she's quite a lot bigger than he is. The thought is chilling. She sits up.

"It's okay," Marty says. "We'll just have to be careful, that's all." Ellen doesn't answer.

Marty strokes her back. "Okay?" he says.

"Don't." Ellen shrugs his hand off.

"What's the matter?" he says.

"I don't want to," she says. "It's disgusting."

Marty looks surprised. "Come on," he says. "It'll be fun."

"Fun?" Ellen says. "Yuk."

Marty assumes a serious expression. "You know," he says, "I think there's something wrong, seriously wrong, if you find me, I mean you, so unappealing."

"It's not me," Ellen tries to explain. "It's Dee. The idea of my body and hers together—"

"Why don't you let me worry about your body?" Marty says. "After all, it's mine now."

"Like hell it is," Ellen says. She scowls at him. "Don't go thinking you can do whatever you want with it."

Marty glares back. "What the hell kind of attitude is that?" he says. "Don't you trust me?"

"No," Ellen says. In such moments the facts are often crystal clear. When Marty leaves he slams the door so hard that the drafting table tilts and all the pencils roll off onto the floor. Dee's fingers itch to pick them up, but Ellen lets them lie there.

The next night she goes over to her mother's for supper. Her sister Millie is there too; Millie and her mother are having a fight about Millie's boyfriend, who has invited Millie to lunch tomorrow after ignoring her for four months. "He's a bum," their mother keeps saying. "The guy's a bum." Millie, who has been crying, tries to defend herself. "I just want my shirts back," she says. "Mom, he has six of my shirts." Ellen tries to remember if Marty has any of her clothes. Right now it would make sense: they'd fit him a lot better than they would her, Dee that is. She realizes she's eating a lot. Why don't Millie and her mother say anything about how big she is? Don't they even see her? During a lull in the fight about the shirts her mother gives her a searching glance. "You don't look so good, honey," she says. Ellen's heart leaps. "You look pale," her mother says. "There's flu going around. Are you eating right?"

A week goes by in which Ellen doesn't see or hear from Marty at all. She misses him, although she tries to squelch the feeling by revving her anger like an engine whenever the blues get too bad. "That bastard," she finds herself muttering in the grocery store between cliffs of cans. "That son of a bitch." Unfortunately even in her anger she finds herself frustrated by the situation; for instance, is it still accurate to call Marty a son of a bitch? "That bitch," she adds just for good measure. But it doesn't feel right.

By the end of the second week she's given up on her anger. It's worse than a car on a cold day: just gives a tired cough and dies. By now she's missing him—their jokes, his mustache. But what can she do? Apologizing is out of the question. It wasn't her fault. This stage passes too, and she's thinking reluctantly but seriously about calling him when there's a miracle: she runs into him one rainy Saturday afternoon in the cafeteria of their favorite museum. It's fate, or something better. Even the mob of pint-sized Cub Scouts has been sent by fate or God to set off their reunion like something in a movie, and she fights her way through the turbulent waist-deep blue throng to the table where Marty sits reading the paper, a cup of coffee in front of him.

She reaches him, breathless, and he looks up from his paper. He looks surprised. "Ellen," he says. ". . . Hi."

"Hi," Ellen says. Even though she's forgiven him and everything is going to be okay now, it's still necessary to get through the preliminaries. She smiles at him. He seems dazzled, or maybe dazed. She sits down.

"Hi," he says again. He heaves a big sigh. Ellen looks into his eyes. She's glad his eyes are still the same.

"Hi," she says.

His eyes shift and drop. "Ellen," he says.

But she wants to be the generous one, the one to say it first; she wants to forgive him, not make him crawl. "Marty," she says, "listen, Marty—"

He shifts in his chair and looks up, not at her but over her shoulder, across the room. He makes a little grimace so eloquent of misery that she turns and looks too. The Cub Scouts have started a jello fight; so what? It's all part of their romantic reunion. Then she sees Dee.

Dee looks terrific. There are raindrops covering her hair in a fine sparkly mist; her cheeks are pink. She's halfway across the cafeteria when she sees Ellen, and the sight makes her falter, but she gives a little shrug and comes ahead anyway. "Hi," she says when she gets to the table. The scouts are making an ungodly racket. Dee pulls out a chair and sits down. Ellen sees the look that passes between her and Marty and suddenly it's too late: she doesn't want to know but she can't stop herself now, can't stop knowing that it's happened the way she knew it would all along. They're having an affair, those stupid bodies of Marty's and hers, wanting each other and nothing else mattering, just the way bodies always are. But she's been left out and it hurts, and she gets up, indignant at finding herself crying, the scouts staring at her. Dee and Marty get up too, both talking at once. "Ellen—" "Listen, Ellen—" and she tries to push past them, but Marty is in her way. Below his unhappy face, arms reach out for her; and her own body, that betrayer, that beloved now lost perhaps forever, wordlessly clasps her close.

LIZ HAHN

Trailing Shadows

Before I enter the rooms of your solitude
in my living form, trailing my shadow,
I shall have come unseen.
—Denise Levertov, "The Presence"

Tonight, because it is April and the moon glows full, I lie awake restless—moonlight heavy on my skin—and think about men I know, men I love. I have finally been able to throw open the dusty window, so I can smell the hyacinths that line my walk. Their fragrance weighs on me like my covers, which I kick off. If I could throw my leg over my extra pillow and sleep, I would scrutinize the dark of my own slumber until I found the man whose eyes smolder at me in my dream life. He slinks into my nights wearing a slouch hat and hiding behind a tree. He is aging. He assumes the form of a coyote and prowls into my nights. He howls at me from the hill above my pond out back and I walk out to him. When I trip and fall on the soft dirt by my pond's edge, he pounces and begins to feed on my flesh. I wake, and wipe away the sweat that has gathered between my breasts.

Perhaps I will give up on sleep. I'll get up, slip on jeans and a sweater, put on sneakers, light a cigarette. I'll drive through the valley from my farm, through the silent mountains and up the hill to a bar in town. I'll sit by myself and order bourbon, neat. The plan is to revel in my solitude, wallow in my spring fever, my obsessions. But there, too, I'll find a man I love. All eyes turn toward him, a professional musician in the lighted corner who plays his guitar with his body angled slightly away from the crowd, looking vulnerable. He appears disarmingly boyish. As I watch him play, I smoke cigarettes, attempting to breathe my fire back into myself. I want to offer him a cigarette with a graceful gesture, light it for him, place it between his lips for him as if he were an invalid. He will smile at me tenderly, work his mouth, and move through the progressions.

The phone by my bed rings, startling me home. I pick it up and hear my father's voice.

"Hey, baby," he says. "I'm in London at the Stafford Hotel."

He is calling to give me his number there in case I need anything. Do I ever.

"Are you all right?" he asks me, but I know it is a rhetorical question, not to be truthfully answered in good taste. What I want to tell him is about a man I love, a man afraid to love me because I am the daughter of a very powerful father. He fears you, I silently mouth into the phone, fears your money and power, fears your gleaming white Learjet.

"What did you say?" my father asks.

I don't say, "he wants to live like you—fast planes, expensive cars—so he talks to me about complexes he perceives in me, calling my love for my father an Electra complex, something he learned about studying psychology in college. He identifies with you, although he has no gleaming Learjet, no phone in his ancient Cadillac."

"Nothing," I say.

"I thought you did say something, honey. Is something wrong?"

"No, Daddy, it's only static. Yeah, talk to you later. Bye."

I want to call my father right back in London and tell him I love him. I want to call a man I love and scream my love over wires, long distance. But my legacy, along with the leather furniture and the family portraits and the diamond earrings and the trust fund, is repression. I have learned more devious approaches.

It will be different with my children, I tell myself, pouring water from the bottle beside my bed. I will swoop them up and kiss them at any moment. I will explain myself to them. I will introduce them to a man I love who wants to meet my children. He wants to see the miracles of flesh I produced with my body, the body he used to know so well, the body now too flawed for his taste by the miracles who are my children.

My children stir in the spring night, made restless, I'm sure, by my restlessness. I breathe in the fragrance of hyacinths at my window and then go to their room to cover my son who feels cool, uncover my daughter who feels warm. They sigh as I touch their heads. One child of mine I cannot cover, cannot touch her head. I may not smooth her hair, although at times I still long to do so. I did not allow her to come to me, because her father did not want her or me at the time. I want her father to come to me now, but he sprawls in his ancient car snorting cocaine with his friends. If they see me walking by dressed for the dentist, the lawyer, the stockbroker, his friends smirk. They advise him: divest, high risk; a lemon, they say. They kick my tires in the parking lot, pick at my paint job.

In my April room, I breathe the cloyingly fragrant air, sip water through a thick tongue, and think about a trip away from here. Manhattan, maybe, or Cozumel. Santa Fe, or Baltimore. I know a man from Baltimore, a musician. Now there's an elegant man. I have a long past with a man from Baltimore, far longer than he remembers. Sometimes, I seek him out. I talk to him about incarnations, and it sounds trite, although he finds it cute when he considers me well dressed.

If I tell him what I only recently envisioned, well, in fact feel sure I remember although it took place before I was born—that once upon a time he was my driver, that he used to chauffeur my Dusenberg for me once upon a time—he will swirl his vodka in its glass and tell ME to lighten up on the juice. He will squeeze his lime and tell me that such talk arouses him, tell me how he recently saw a B-grade movie on TV about a woman like me, rich, beautiful, crazy like me, with crazy ideas like mine. "I masturbated," he will tell me, "watching this movie and thinking about you."

But I do remember these men, this man. In truth, they are one man, a man as multifaceted as my granny's diamonds I inherited, this man who enters my dreams wearing a slouch hat, who wore a low cap when he drove my Dusenberg. He glanced at me in the rearview mirror, eyes smoldering while he drove. I mouthed a kiss at him, my servant, my penniless lover, tossed my furs and returned to my bootleg whiskey, MY cocaine, My friends in the richly upholstered leather seat.

Beyond my bedroom window, the moon flares. I hear my children breathing rhythmically. I glance around my room at my books, my talismans, the crow wing, the deer skull. The crystals I find on my farm. Juju is what he calls it, this man I love. Juju, he says, laughing, even though he knows we all walk only a thread of what can be called reality.

I feel heavy in my body, weighted with desire. The sheets on my bed are twisted and sweaty. Suddenly, though, on a sweet breeze that lifts the curtain, comes a knowledge that makes me weightless. Tonight I will clothe myself in different furs than the sort that heiresses wear. I will wear the fur of a night creature. I choose the cougar: nocturnal, secretive, stealthy, elusive. I stretch, arch up in bed. My skin ripples over my spine, loosening. I am ready. I will run to him. I will run to the next county.

Outside in the cool April night, my nostrils flare. I switch my tail, leap the fence, and begin to run. I set out running at an even, steady lope, the pace of my children's breathing, soundless, unswerving. I run up the hill by the pond, into the woods, and through the trees along the ridgeline. In a clearing by the old orchard, a herd of resting deer scatters. When I sniff after them, I smell their peppery fear and the juice rises in my mouth. Tonight, though, my hunger is of a different sort, so I run on, following the ridge along Parris Mountain.

Gradually now, the mountain begins to slope downward. On the hillside, I can see phlox blooming. I see it in the moonlight, and smell it, along with redbud, dogwood, and the wild strawberry blooms I am crushing beneath my feet.

I smell another smell, too, something anxious, slightly synthetic. It is the smell of the people who live down in the valley below where I am running. I see the lights of their houses around the golf course at the country club. Inside the houses, a few of the more intuitive women vaguely sense my presence. They press up tightly against their husbands' backs in bed, slightly fearful but also aroused as I pass on the hillside above them. They will make love and moan like cats after I am gone.

Now I pass more houses. I am approaching the rough, trashy places that lie outside a town I must cross, the county seat. I am forced to slow down, to slide silently past the junked cars, the garden plows, the stink of outhouses behind the shacks. I cross the railroad tracks and then I am in town. The acrid odor of fundamen-

talism rises from a Baptist church I pass, where in the parking lot a
pickup truck idles noisily, burning oil. I hear raucous laughter, a
bottle breaking on pavement. Three men slouch in the truck drinking whiskey. As I lower my body and move into the shadows of the
church, the men shift their testicles. They reach over their shoulders to touch cold steel, the reassurance of their guns on a rack
behind them in the truck.

This is the most dangerous part of my journey now, for I must
cross the main road that runs through town in order to reach the
mountain to which I am bound. In the darkness of an alley, I pause.
I peer out, watch the stoplight change, several cars pass. Then, my
feet whispering on asphalt, I slip across the street. Past the court-
house, past the feedstore, through the cemetery. The lights fade
and I run out of town.

After stopping long enough to sip some water from an old quarry,
I run on, picking up speed, sprinting up Walker Mountain. I have
picked up his scent now; I savor the mix of smoke, salt, sweat, and
expensive cologne. I sniff the marijuana he is lighting, one more
smoke before bed. Some clouds have blown up, hiding the moon,
but I am following my nose. I require no light. Sniffing, panting,
striding like this, I reach his farm.

A possum lurches down his lane. It bares its teeth at me, receiv-
ing in return a sharp swat. I could kill it easily, of course, but I don't
care to do so. My time runs short. The bloody possum staggers
away, and I ease myself down the lane toward his house.

Ah. There he is, walking past a window. I watch silently from
behind a tree next to the house, see him glance up at the moon
which has reappeared, see him shiver slightly. He moves out of
sight, then I hear him in the bathroom urinating, splashing in the
sink, brushing his teeth. Naked, he comes to the porch to call in his
dog for the night.

"Here, Stevie, here old boy," he calls. The fuzzy Airedale
bounces past the man, who then shuts the door. The lock clicks into
place.

I breathe his scent deeply, circle the house twice, and spring to
the roof. From where I lie beneath his bedroom window on the
porch roof, I can hear him rustling around his room, opening a
drawer, turning the pages of a magazine. Finally, he flicks out his

light. I wait until, at last, his breathing levels off. The man I love is sleeping.

In my bed, under my satin comforter, I sit awake reading. When cougars mate, I read, the female behaves aggressively. Although the male seeks her out during her receptive times, he stays back from her, hovering by, approaching, backing off. When he retreats, if she is interested, she will chase after him. She likes to swat him hard to get him to notice her. Then, irritated and aroused, he will swat back, and they will tumble together.

In the morning, a man I love will oversleep, because his sleep has been restless. Was it the sleep of the haunted? When he finally wakes, the sun will sit high in the sky. The man will pop up in bed, smile to himself, perhaps even chuckle out loud when he thinks of the dream he had. There will be dirt on the rug, and he will notice that his guitar case has fallen over from where it usually leans against his desk. A strong wind in the night, he will speculate. He will feel good, this man I love, he will feel rested and alert in spite of his fitful sleep. Downstairs, drinking coffee in his warm spring kitchen wearing only his boxer shorts, he will pick at a scratch on his leg, idly wondering how he got such a long deep scratch without realizing it at the time that it happened.

Back home, I lie in my bed in the dark. The moon has gone down. The wind has risen, and I smell the sweet fragrance of the hyacinths again. I stretch, arching my back, feeling good. I will go to sleep now. My silk robe brushes my thigh like a touch.

SUSAN HANKLA

Chief White Tower

In the country where the stone lions in front of each house get bigger and bigger the farther in you retreat, Chief White Tower plotted a raid upon a city. He was hungry, and sick of field peas and withered carrots he stole from rabbit hutches out in yards with satellite dishes, where skinny dogs barked incessantly, baring their fangs, but so far none had molested him. So far, no one knew he was there, as he trespassed from house to house, sneaking in sometimes, if the coast was clear, doing what he needed to do to stay healthy, then keeping moving again, which was his strength.

The Chief ran through the backyards and the fields. He was only fourteen. He was about five-feet four-inches tall, and his white skin glowed like the moon at mystical dusk when he ran, and his shoulder-length flaxen hair flew out from his head like a pony's mane. He had been running so long, he had run through his entire wardrobe, so that now he was naked, but despite excellent muscle tone acquired from his trials, he was still plump and round looking, like the moon, his skin pearly white, like roll dough, which suggested a previous existence of staying inside somewhere, possibly watching a lot of TV and snacking.

White Tower, the name, was something remembered from the life he could no longer recall, except in confusing fragments of dream, when he dared to fall asleep. He had amnesia about himself, so he ran, eating whenever he could.

The Chief ran through the backyards and the fields.

He had gotten filthy with time and his smell was becoming rank. It could give him away. He saw a lady in her backyard hanging laundry out to dry on one of those metal-spoked contraptions, like an umbrella missing cloth, so he made his way around her house to the front door, and testing it, discovered it to be unlocked.

He headed through a tiny foyer of philodendrons, into a carpeted living room containing a baby grand piano, which he could not resist running one hand over, and in doing so remembered part of a song he found he still knew how to play—"Heart and Soul"—so that for a minute or two, he nearly forgot himself.

Through a cool, wooden hall, fragrant with shiny wax, the Chief wandered. That feeling he had felt in other houses he had been inside that made him want to cry was particularly strong here. At the end of the hall, he found her kitchen. On a table was a wooden bowl of beautiful bananas. He peeled one and ate it in one bite.

The kitchen sink had several inches of lukewarm dishwater in it, so the Chief hoisted himself up into the porcelain basin, like a child taking a bird bath, scrubbing with a scratchy square of green which he squirted liberally with New Dawn, keeping an eye out the window above the sink at the lady outside. When he had finished, he dried himself on some handy paper towels.

Cold air from the open refrigerator gave him goose flesh when he stood in its light, selecting his food carefully, taking his time. He took out a jar of three-bean salad and half a pound cake that sat on a china plate. He got out a pint of milk, too. These he put into a plastic Safeway sack he found on a doorknob to savor more thoroughly later.

Wrapped in a white pinafore apron trimmed in red rickrack, the Chief ran through the fields, through the twilit dusk light, traveling through the pines, like the moon, plump and full, with no feet. A Safeway sack slung over one of his shoulders, the big S of its logo thumped like the S on Superman's chest.

As the Chief ran, he thought about food and about eating some, and about the possibility of some day not having any, and it made him grow hungrier and hungrier, which, in turn, slowed him down. But food thoughts, those pleasant fantasies, were what kept him running, and blocked out the other, extremely confusing thoughts, which were unfathomable, dark and nagging. In fact, everywhere he had been he left behind clues.

The banana peel he threw down for that lady to possibly fall upon when she finished hanging out her laundry to find her kitchen ransacked, and stand in the middle of the room in his wake of soggy wadded paper towels, crumbs, and puddles, startled by the brown ring around the sink, the muddied water with his long, light signature hairs trailing through it. The pound cake missing, a distinct scent of flesh in the air—what was it—a nostalgic smell, reminding her of tow-headed children who do not smell bad, but melony and grassy, rainy and elemental like the worms, but then they have to grow older, glands going haywire, full strength and pungent with rebellion and blackmail for those who have raised them.

The lady, who lived in an empty nest and sniffed all these memories, immediately sat down at her kitchen table, pushing aside the bowl of fruit, and wept aloud for all these things that seemed over and gone, then bravely began a letter to her only son, guiltily writing him out a check for one-hundred dollars, and in just thinking of him, she could feel his presence tangibly in the room, though it was just the Chief leaving spirit where he wandered.

Outside, Chief White Tower ran, stopping only for another promising dining experience, numb to the hungry pull of hearts. He was just too tired to think *Who am I?*

At the edge of a suburban settlement he found a mimosa tree with a child's neat tree house, not much bigger than a fruit crate, nestled in its low limbs which drooped onto a covered carport in someone's perfect lawn. While outside night fell, inside this secret place, hidden behind boards with KEEP OUT painted on them in Day-Glo orange and green, the Chief devoured the contents of his Safeway sack, then fell immediately asleep, dreaming of wonderful things: of vines loaded with ripe concord grapes falling into his open mouth, of a salad bar, mile-long, supplied with large chilled pewter plates, of an unattended picnic hamper, open and precariously resting on a station wagon's back hatch, which seemed so real, he even heard the music of the car radio and could identify the song.

It was real. A family, preparing to get away for a vacation early in the morning, were packing their car perilously close to the Chief, who hunkered down, peering out through chinks in his hideout, impatient that they all go back inside and stay, so he could more thoroughly investigate the food.

Soon he got his wish, for the mother from inside the house called for the little boy and the father to come back in. It seemed they were trying to eat all the leftovers in their refrigerator.

"Come back in here, Jimmy, and eat this seafood salad!" called the mother.

"But Mom, I just ate three hot dogs and a blueberry popsicle!"

"Well, somebody's got to finish this pasta. We can't just let it go to waste. Tom?"

"Barbara, it is seven in the morning. Give me a break!"

Coming down from his tree house and lifting the lid of the enormous straw hamper finally convenient to his reach, the Chief was met by the familiar aromas of mustard, pickle relish, swiss cheese, tangy ham, rye bread, peanut butter and jelly sandwiches, and potato chips—the perfect picnic. Underneath some paper plates in the hamper the Chief unearthed a fresh new bag of Oreo cookies, which he had just enough time to slip into the generous pocket of his apron then duck behind the car, before the family came outdoors again.

They made several trips in and out, except for the little boy, Jimmy, intent on following the erratic path of the tabby cat, Winks, who was trying to lose herself at the last minute. But the boy was determined and caught Winks by her tail and pulled her in, gripping her to his chest, so the Chief relaxed.

Then, the family decided to take a picture. The man, Tom, positioned a tripod skillfully to get a shot of the three of them, standing in front of the car. He set the timer, then ran to take his place before it clicked. He did this three or four times, until his son said, "Can't we quit, Dad? I hate smiling."

"So do I," Barbara agreed. "Let's get going, Tom."

But the Chief had thoroughly enjoyed smiling when he came and stood barely breathing behind Jimmy and Winks.

By the time Barbara, Jimmy, and Tom were finally in the car with their seat belts fastened, they were so overloaded Tom could only see what was behind them from the side mirrors, so he missed the hazy spectacle of a smiling blonde-headed boy wearing what looked like a toga and holding to the car tightly with one hand, the big fat tabby cat in his other hand and his dirty and blistered bare feet hooked with loyalty under their bumper.

When only a few miles into the drive and they had cleared the fieldstone pillars marking the entrance to their suburban settlement, Tanglewood, and were about to turn onto a real highway, Jimmy suddenly realized he had let the cat slip out of his grasp somehow during the picture-taking session, so they had to retrace their route.

Somewhere just short of their yard, the Chief sadly dismounted, and with a silent benediction let Winks go. The cat was immediately barked at and pursued by a large Doberman standing about five hands tall, but the Chief got away.

And the Chief ran, breathing in hot pollen, Chem-lawn fertilizer, and the eternal melancholy of humid flowers. The neighborhood was awake, and construction workers stood at the tops of ladders propped against new roofs of split-level houses being built, which the Chief as he ran made a note to possibly inhabit sometime.

Now nakedly aboveground, visible and vulnerable in these manicured lawns, he had to hide.

Inside another house in this same settlement, a lady sat indoors watching the weather. She read *House and Garden,* a beautiful, expensive magazine about people making atmosphere indoors . . . homes where it is okay to stay in, and spurred by the hope of a brand new world, a person could at first tentatively organize a room in tones of peach and brown, then gradually expand these limits and move toward dangerous awakening, rooms bursting into restless bloom.

This lady, Maureen, wintering on a crewel divan, was nearly disappearing into floral ground, her dreams reembroidering its shams. She was so recently a widow, that she was now afraid of everything. Her doctor told her to walk two miles a day, but scared to go out, she walked inside her house, vacationing by the hand-painted china punch bowl, and the collection of silver teaspoons and the lovebirds on twigs, and the lead-crystal animals.

Sometimes her dead husband, Colonel Wyrick, visited her, leaving a trail in the hallway, or glowing blur in the mirror above the living room mantel, which was what she believed she now saw, so she welcomed him.

"Come in, Doug. I've been thinking about you."

The Chief, who had entered through her basement and up the stairs, had been invisible for so long, he nearly came apart when spoken to.

"Are you lonely?" asked the lady.

Yes I am, thought the Chief as he sank numbly into the big wing chair across the lady who patiently waited to speak.

"Good, you're Here," she said. "While you were away, I have had time to think of all the things I've been wanting to know. Well, Doug, I guess the first thing is, Do you live in Heaven now, and if so, what's it like?"

The Chief sat in his chair, staring at the lady from the vast distance of someone who has fully accepted invisibility.

"I didn't expect you to answer, Doug. Of course you are There, when not Here seeing me. I'm sorry if I pried."

"Well, to continue, this line of questioning is rather trivial, and please don't be offended, but there is something I just have to know. Is this the official costume Up There? I mean, does everyone wear the same thing, or does it come in different colors?"

The Chief squirmed uncomfortably in his chair, staring at his rickrack.

"Well, I sure do wish we could eat supper together. Could you possibly stay, just this once?"

At the mention of food, the Chief grew more attentive, and his face brightened, which Maureen took to be a yes. She stood and the hungry Chief followed at her heels into the spotless kitchen, where a table was set for one.

"Now Doug, if you would just sit down at your usual place there," she said, pointing to the head of the table, where she had set her own place, "and I will move my things over to my old place there, where I used to sit. Sorry, Doug. I didn't mean to bring up a depressing subject. I guess we both have had to do some adjusting."

To the Chief's dismay, the lady took his china and cutlery and white linen napkin in a silver ring from in front of him, moving them to her place, then she began giving herself large helpings from steaming pans on the stove.

"Seeing you has given me such an appetite!"

Then the Chief watched her eat two helpings of each thing, then he watched her clear. He watched her get out a large fresh cocoanut cake with thick icing and set it between them on the table, but when he saw her give only herself an enormous slice of it, he could not stand it anymore. He put his head down on the table and sobbed. He felt the lady hovering near, but he could not stop crying. He cried about so many things, that it was a blankness rising up in him like a big dark ghost, because he knew who he wasn't.

The lady was stroking his hair. "I didn't know I could touch you," she was saying. "This is all so new."

So Chief White Tower went to bed that night without any supper and had an experience he would never forget for as long as he lived, which was a very long time, as it turned out.

Late in the afternoon of the very next day, dressed in baggy khaki slacks too long for him, and a bright red sweatshirt that said "BEST HUSBAND ON EARTH," the hungry Chief ran.

When he had been absent from her house for almost an hour, Maureen came down from the attic, where she had been unpacking things, and began looking for him, starting in the kitchen. When it was nearly sundown and he was still not to be found, she, for the first time in a year, went outside and walked down the road. She was just in time to see the big orange fiery ball drop like the yolk of an egg behind the blue mountains.

"He's gone," she told a woman in wrist sweatbands, wheezing 'round the bend.

"He's gone," she told three teenaged boys on bicycles, as they sped by.

"He's gone," she told the big black Doberman, coming toward her to lick her outstretched hand.

CATHRYN HANKLA

Etch A Sketch

Six years old, she woke, cold in the night, fearing fire. Summer, yet here, visiting her godparents, it was always cold, because they were old, and she was here to make them happy. Jessica jumped on the furniture, on chairs, footstools, beds. She demanded ice cream on sticks and other extravagances of summer. She hated going to the grocery store with them, hated how much time it took Mr. Wilson to write a check, and the way he, in his silk ties and shirts, muttered "highway robbery" when he finally handed the money over to the clerk.

She woke in that night, fearing fire, knowing fire was possible because she had seen a house burn up with a child inside. And her godparents' house was heavy with dark wood paneling. Real, solid paneling, not the kind builders tack up now. The dark wood encased the foyer, entombed it, and the parlor, living room, and dining room, as high up the walls as the wainscoting. Polished wood, smelling of oil, oily darkness.

She thought she smelled fire, could see flames licking the staircase, tonguing for her room at the top, the way she probed a space where a tooth was missing, the very first room, to the right. Every night she climbed those stairs, counted steps slowly after her godmother, until she reached the landing and skipped to the other side, skittered like a water bug, to finish the flight in a rush, because the grandfather clock squatted on the landing, and she knew in her

heart that it wanted to fall on her, to knock her down the way
Dorothy's house buried that bad witch's sister.

Hickory, dickory, dock—Jessica was the mouse sneaking past the
clock, the clock with an infinitude of minutes already tocked,
because it was a grandfather clock and very old and wise and mean.
She raced in split seconds too fast for it to count. This clock did not
like children; it would topple for all time just to crush one of them
on the stairs. It had already fallen on her father.

When the clock lived alone with her godparents, it ticked to fill
silences, bellowed down the stairwell into the lapses that filled up
their latter years. But when Jessica visited she stole its thunder,
with leapfrogs, skips, shouts, with tapping her shoes in the house,
and hopscotching on the porch. She liked to balance on the curb,
pretend disaster when one foot dangled over the edge.

Grandfather clock, she knew, meant to catch her, trip her up.
Morning and night she fled past it, trying as if in a dream to work
paralyzed limbs. She held her pee all day to avoid passing the clock
more than twice. Give the clock too many chances it might just get
lucky. Chinese checkers on the stairs. Ready your hoe, Farmer
McGregor, she's almost there.

One day in a quiet mood she sat hour after hour painstakingly
drawing lines on the Etch A Sketch Magic Screen. Turning the
knobs carefully, she traced away as much aluminum powder as the
stylus could reach, until she could study the silver drawing stylus
poised at the intersection of two metal rods that moved back and
forth, up and down, in a configuration of pulleys. For days, Jessica
studied the exposed magic of the Etch A Sketch. She peered into
the screen many times, but she was also fascinated by the gold globe
banded by the words "Ohio Art" embossed in the red plastic frame.
Her fingers worried that raised world, touching its braille.

Mrs. Wilson had kept, from her childhood, a giant set of domi-
noes that she would unwrap from shiny black shoe boxes for Jessica.
Since no children had lived in their neighborhood for years, there
was no one to match dot to dot. Jessica invented her own games that
skirted math for architecture, her godfather's trade. Jessica would
snake the tiles through the parlor, regardless of the match. Beaded
water at her Adam's apple, she was good at concentrating on her
game. Little mouse, though, would go up in a blaze. Only one way
down, and windows painted shut. When she looked up, she'd

reached the arch between parlor and dining room, and there, she finished the curving walkway, then stacked the rest of the black tiles into a polka-dotted house, crossing *T*'s to open spaces for as many windows as her structure could support without falling down.

Her breath caught and mounted, collected in a fist that pounded against her throat. The black and white house teeter-tottered, while she hung as if upside down from monkey bars, afraid to skin the cat. If she tried to copy that embossed world onto the magic screen in a picture of her own, she knew she would have to sacrifice seeing the secret works. Of whatever "Ohio Art" might mean, she was unsure, but she must duplicate that little, perfect world. She must, must lie awake until she can almost feel herself burning, from the inside out. To be drawn in, to kindle her own dreaded dreams, she lay fitful, in a summer swelter, and the walls collapsed into dark. Her godfather snored loud as a freight train to punctuate her terror.

If Jessica called out in that dark, burning house, no one would ever hear. Jessica felt for the Etch A Sketch on the bedside table, and shook it hard with both hands. In the dark, she twisted both knobs at once, beginning to draw a wobbly curve.

DENNIS GIOVANETTI

My Life Destroyed by Vanna White

My brother-in-law stumbled in from the guest room, tucking in the tail of his flannel shirt and wiping sleep from his eyes. It was after six, my wife and I unpacking groceries as she began reheating last night's dinner. "Dolores," he said, this after grunting past me. "Dolores, it's time."

"Honey," she smiled at me, "will you watch the stove? Just stir everything." Television voices rose in the background. She brought her lips to a tight pucker, winked, and turned away, leaving a delinquent kiss in midair. I snapped at it with a dish towel as the television audience called out the name of the show.

"I feel lucky tonight," my brother-in-law said, adjusting the recliner, settling into a supine position. The recliner was a present from my wife, after I was hired at the college last year. Her brother settled into it, like natural habitat.

"I know this one! I know this one!" he hollered. Through the serving window I saw his arms flailing above his head as the recliner shot forward. "It's—It's 'The thrill of victory,' ummmmm!" He snapped his fingers, "It's from that show! uhhh . . ."

I closed the serving window and shut off the burners. Not long ago, no more than two months, that show seemed to exist only in idle classroom chatter. "What's that?" I would ask, my question answered with stares of disbelief. Not long ago, my wife and I spent our time before dinner watching the news, taking in the seriousness of a reporter's purpose, the tone of the anchorperson as she

patted the papers in front of her, and the smile of the weathergirl
pointing to sunny skies, the sway of her dress indicating approaching storms.

Then he came. During his first weeks I would spend this time in
the bedroom skimming reports and watching the news on the color
portable. But soon the channels wandered, and, keeping the sound
low, I would watch her in her gowns and dresses as she clapped and
turned the letters, and clapped again. At times I wondered if, in
another time, she might have given aid to flood victims and service-
men, offering a word of encouragement and a fresh plate of donuts.
"Oh," she might have said. "Things'll get better. Just you wait and
see."

I leaned across the bed and adjusted the tint, bringing out the red
of her lips. In the bottom of my sock drawer I have the photograph
the show sent to my post office box across town. I've written her
twice, once admiring her poise and the ability to do so much with so
small a role, and then, later, to thank her for the photograph. The
studio sent a biographical sheet. That's in the small envelope atop
the magazine clipping about how she's to be the goddess of love in a
television movie, a letter stamped with her signature—that atop
the photograph stamped with her friendly schoolgirl penmanship,
"All the best . . ."

After dinner my brother-in-law walked to the convenience store
for a six-pack. My wife and I crawled under the covers. "Oh, Jackson," she sighed, her back arching, her holding me tight as I rub my
hands across the swell of her thighs, her mouth wet against my ear.

Her feet began to feel warm against mine when I heard the
refrigerator door slam. My wife was up on cue. From the living
room I heard the announcement of the winning lottery number, and
my wife telling her brother, "It's okay. Maybe next time," in that
voice that consoles the lost puppy or the halfhearted job seeker.

I closed the door, sat back, and lit a cigarette.

In the morning I turned off the television as my wife gently woke
her brother and helped him off the recliner. The toaster stuck and I
spent my breakfast time airing out the kitchen and jamming the
four charred slices of bread into the disposal. My wife carried a
bundle of her brother's clothes toward the laundry room, her feet
scuffing across the linoleum. As I leaned over the bundle to say
good-bye, she pecked at my cheek in mid shuffle.

Over coffee I heard discussions of upcoming conferences and topics for presentations. When Mitchell asked about a popular television comedy they split, raving or muttering until I mentioned my brother-in-law unable to figure out "To be or not to be." Mitchell raised his eyebrows and pointed his finger saying, *"That show?"* Roberts, the reference librarian, crumpled up a styrofoam cup and smiled. "He looks guilty," he said. I backed away, denying the charge as they circled my chair, accusing me of polluting my life, destroying the minds of my students, telling me it's wrong, a sham, a mindless parlor game. Looking out the window, I imagined her legs disappearing into a spangled dress, joining at her sweet deliquescence.

I dismissed my morning class early, filled up the tank, cleaned the windshield and made the six-hour trip at seventy-five, pushing eighty, past billboards for retirement villages, gambling on the Colorado, the sixty-four ounce steak for seven ninety-five—"One to a customer"—guiding the Buick into the desert, past tourists admiring alkaline flats, creosote bushes, these citizens reaching some understanding with dry lakes, coyotes, and military ranges, past an old bus settling beneath crates and boxes and the petroglyphs of a new age, its owners milling around in casual attitude, waiting for a change in fortune, then the thick tufted golf courses of Palm Springs, and, by twilight, into the basin, the Hollywood sign showing dimly through the smog.

I eased the car into the parking space at the Motel 6, filled the ice bucket, and poured a polite two fingers of Canadian Mist. I set the double lock, and hung the "Do Not Disturb" sign turned to the side in Spanish—the loving tongue. Now, my wife and her brother are seated at their TV trays, idly spooning heated leftovers in the television glare. I remember the correspondence in my drawer, and recall, from one newspaper clipping, that she lives nearby. Turning to the darkened screen, I imagine her mouth forming a sweet exclamation. It's almost time to buy a vowel.

Dusk

Somebody must hav sense a miracle comin on w/them twin sister.

I feed th fire glossy magazine & it make green, blu & yello flame. Somethin happenin.

Nothin similar bout them twin sister. They bout lak as spagetti noodle & red ripe tomato. This b th 8th wonder o th world, I convince o it, all I have to do is contac th proper authoritees fo verification.

This day I don know what happenin to me.

Them sister hav th proof o identicle twinship: they placenta—one, jus one—b stor upstair in a sealed bell-shape jar. They say it move back & forth between they bedroom as tho by it own steam, as tho they have nothin to do w/it. Th baby doctor sign th bottle lable. Them nurses did too as witness. I thing this th most curious part o all: why did they save & mark that placenta? Not only was they only one placenta, but them sister look exact alike as babes. Nobody had no question o twinship back then.

Somebody must hav sense a miracle comin on.

Th flames n th fireplace lickin green/orange now.

Them twin liv in my hous now a year & a day.

When I put th upstair fo rent I specify women. I would have taken men if I were desprit. It would have been nothin but trouble. Men r messy & opinionate & dont know how to express they emotion. That only my opinion. It base on personal experience, tho. I know that th way I use to b.

How to explain what exactly Im doin housbound at th ripish ol age o 30 is somethin I probly cant. So I dont.

If I were th parents I wouldn't have name both twin Mary. Mary Munro & Mary Emma. I skip th problem tho by callin em Munro & Emma. But they—& everbody else so far as I kin tell—hail each as Mary. It seem lak identity would b enuff o a problem in twinhood w/out this name doublin. But parently not.

I guess th fact they no longer favor each other make th difference nowaday. Munro th one who genetically correct—they say. She tall & thin & have white blon curlin hair fallin down her back. Her skin pale as newish cream & she have develop a religion o keepin it safe from th sun.

Emma smallish & dark. They say sh th victim o girlhood dis-eases which change her chromasome. She not above five feet. Her hair all fall out once & when it come back n it b brown. It gone browner thru th year. I seen picture o th two as babes—Emma were light & blindingly blon jus lak Munro.

Them twin not clear to me on what ail Emma—I get snippet o infomation here & there. Somethin erase all th print on Emma finger (as tho them finger trap in a spy movie). She canna say Rs correctly. She canna remember certin important incident o th twin chilehood which Munro swear b true.

All along I takin picture o them twin w/my 35mm camra. They look lak statue n th grainy black & white. I develop these picture & hang em roun the downstair o th hous.

Munro teachin englis at th University th way I use to do back b-4 thang happen to me. She a medievilist. She speak latin. She sing latin to me. I never hear her stumble on a word in any language. She not around yet when I were dancin n them class-room. I got th twin to move in later w/a note on th community bulltin board.

Emma b a waitress in a diner down University Avenue. It th coolish place after midnite. Emma try only to pull day shift. Emma alway wear white. She never spill food on herself o th customer.

Munro say Emma speak french & german fluent. I cant say becuz I don't hear Emma speak even much o englis.

They a bond between Emma & me. Often it tangible as th

fireplace logs. I thing sometime it that we knew each other n another life. Mayhem we was angels waitin to be born together. Mebbe it jus cuz we lovers. It one o those imponderables.

They was a time when we were not together. I fine this hard to remember. I canna even remember th first time we was together. I still not sure why it happen. Somethin they is about the language o skin.

Munro & me are lak th autumn trees & sky at dusk. I th black sticks & she th forever expanse o dark blue beyond them, stupefyinly calm.

Munro behavin strange these day. For some reason she quote Horace time & again. "Otium sine litteras mors est" b her favorite. "Lesure w/out litrature b death." Munro never spend her lesure w/litrature. She off on th nod o out w/some o her wild girlfriend.

O both.

Emma have a concern about Munro. Emma never know Munro to use drug b-4, she say. Emma glad Munro only snortin th horse, not injectin it. I thing it make no diffrence. Th road to addiction may not b pave w/AIDS, but it still addiction. Heroin b heroin.

Th fire have leapin flame now. Downstair everythin but th fire b brown & red. It seem we r out n th country, but really they is just an acre o tree in front & behine th hous. Th hous b on a dead end. I own th lots both sides too—few more acre.

Somethin happenin. I canna do nothin.

I never go upstair. It th women place. They have hot plate & mini frigerator. I not sure when they use em—Emma alway cook & eat w/me. Munro dont seem to eat atall. She take a lot o asprin, tho.

Emma & me alway make love downstair in my big bedroom. I afraid o heights. Theys all them mirror in my bedroom, anyway. & pitures o them twin. Sometime I thing ghost o spirit hauntin upstair. Most lakly it only th ol radiators clangin.

I make a poem. Munro & Emma both read it.

MARY

She tole me she had a baby
Lock n th trunk   I wuz spinnin

Toward th Milkaway n red shoes
They was Lepercons lak hairpins

Fillin my dresser drawer   I say
It live?   She say   What u thing?

A Brown Recluse crawl it big web
To th left o her pretty head

I thing it a kitty o pup
I say   She say   Well it yourn trunk

She had hip little as a boy
Her lipstick were peachfizz & smear

If I look then I knew I'd seen
Pee streamin down my wooden leg

So I move to th blue kitchen
Et a bowl o yellow corn flake

She set it n a blanket on th table
I know from th way her thin hair
Stick up she goin backa Kalamazoo

They was silence fo a while after they red it seprately. Both o them twin thing it bout th other. Munro ask me private if Emma w/child. I sez How should I know. Emma ask me private if Munro w/child. I sez How should I know. Munro dont know I do it w/Emma. Then them twin wonder aloud—seprate—if th other goin to Kalamazoo. Munro even knock on my leg, testin fo wood.

They intellgent young women & it annoy me that they take thang so literal.

I didna use to take pitures til I stay indoor. In fact, it all start when them twin move in.

I thing I m n love w/Munro.

Emma dont know this.

I thing Munro suspect.

I know becuz o th way Munro flirt w/me. I certinly never tell her Emma my lover. Munro egg me on. Munro bring me thang: picture, chocolate, flower. She set on the floor next my rockin chair & tell me bout her latest wittiness n th classroom. I fine it fascinatin she can b funny in modern englis, medievil englis & medievil latin. I hav to take her word on th last one.

Munro have no real interest n me whatsoever. I believe she a thru & thru dyke. She merely gettin attention off my attention on her. My lap get hard when Munro come roun. I have to cover it w/somethang. Munro move th way I imagine a spirit would. Munro toss that blon hair & I want to take it & hold it n my mouth. It would taste lak sugarcane.

Munro hear storie roun the englis department bout why I dont teach no more. She dont tell me em, but Emma do. Emma report that Munro hear that one day I walk inna class & lose my voice. I fall on th floor n a fit.

Munro hear that one day I walk inna class on th 20th C novel & start yakkin about John Donne—& didna know th diffrence.

Munro hear that one day I get nekked n front o a class.

I wonder if any o this b tru.

I dont remember much. They say that common w/a condition lak mine.

Emma dont ask if none o it b true: she jus makin reports. I dont get hard w/Emma until she kiss me. Her tongue drive me wild. I know this & not englis b her true language.

Somethin happenin.

I thing them twin have incest when they was young. Mayhem now, too. They sleep n th same bed. I know becuz one footstep go to th other room & dont leave all nite. I listen all nite to make sure o it. Many time. Mebbe this when th placenta make it move. Emma admit they sleep n th same bed. She claim it habit. Habit b leavin th toilet seat up. Beds a diffrent story.

I pretty sure Munro never ever date men. & o course now she only ever bring women to th hous.

Emma might see other men, she might see other women. It really not my business to ask. Specially, I thing, when I dont leave th hous.

It were somethin that happen late last nite.

Peoples use to phone th hous & ask fo Mary. When I say Mary who? they hang up. I try to remember to say Mary which? but that make em hang up too. I dont answer th phone no mo.

Th days pass slow but before I know it, it dusk. Then night. I thing I take afternoon naps. I thing they gettin longer & longer. Sometime I wake up & fine Emma in th bed w/me. I canna remember if we make love or not so we do it—mebbe fo th second o third time. I lak it when she leave her work cloth on becuz they smell lak steak & egg & fresh bred. Often she bring bred home, but it not only fo me. Emma dont bring present to me th way Munro do.

Emma bring me a 8mm movie projector once, tho. Th Marys giv me hom movie o them to watch.

Emma lak me to photo r lovemakin. Sometime she bring th film & load th camra. She never look at them picture after. I look at some everday. Evernite.

Everday I watch home movie o th Mary twins when they was babes. I watch em alone & cant pick out which Mary is which Mary. They was alway dress alike. They b movies o them n they crib: they n th same position & they change position at th exact same moment. They father get this time lapse. That th only fact I know bout they parent. Them parent never n th films.

Then they b a stretch o years—from age nine to 15. This th time Mary Emma sick. No movie. When th movie come back at 15 th Marys look entirely diffrent. It as tho they traded one in fo a new model. I suspect this but never ask.

Th only proof that they twin anymore is that placenta n th jar.

Emma due home soon now.

She goin tell me what happen last night.

I only know little bit.

This b what I know: Somebody come n from a gable on th roof. It were a friend o Munro. She & Munro do something. Mebbe they snort. Mebbe they mek love. Whatever it were, they do mo & mo. & th somebody else disappear.

Then Munro tie bedsheets onto her bed & leg & clamb down th side o th hous. She was ravin.

Emma drop th alumnum fire ladder out her window & follow Munro.

I hear all th noise, but they was nothin I could do becuz they was outdoor. I pace my room, I take pitures o th mirrors, th flash blind me.

I hear them twin shoutin Mary! Mary! Mary! at each other. Then they was screamin it. Mary! Mary! Mary! They was screamin they name th way other people scream rape o fire.

Munro didna go on th nod. I don know what she snort, but parently it not heroin. Mebbe she didna snort nothin. She were runnin & screamin & jumpin inta th trees & stompin on th gardin. She rip her clothe off. She eat dirt. She beat herself w/rocks.

Mary Emma call fo an ambulance.

Mary Munro taken away.

Mary Emma follow.

Emma phone late, but I dont speak on th phone. Emma tell th answerin machine she & Munro stayin overnite at hospital.

I look at piture o me & Emma, lovemakin, far inta th nite. Theys 100 of pitures & I never see th same 1 twice.

Im wonderin now lots o thang.

What do them Mary twin look lak.

Is Munro k.

Is Emma th new era.

Is they such a thang.

It dusk now. Th colored flame leapin high n th fireplace.

Mo & mo I have only sighs.

GARRETT EPPS

The Heart Operation

These days a strange airport is as foreign as the moon. Even the names of the carriers differ from city to city, from week to week. He was confused and disheartened to find himself in a strange industrial city in midweek, a place that seemed forgotten by time, too primitive even to have covered jetways, so that he had to leave the airplane in a soaking rain, scanning the faces pressed against the terminal windows for his wife's, wondering what emergency could have led her to ask him to break off his travels and meet her on a few hours' notice in a city neither had ever visited.

He tightened his worn gray raincoat, shouldered his garment bag, picked up his briefcase, and trudged, head down, to the terminal. He saw her through the glass door, and in the instant before she saw him, he reflected simultaneously, as if realizing two incompatible parts of an overarching truth, how tired she looked and how young she still seemed—how much, well launched into middle age, she still looked like a Smith girl on a blind date, well turned out, serious, intelligent, but a trifle uncertain. Then she saw him and waved once, an anxious, tentative motion, before rushing over to gather him in an embrace so fierce it suggested he had reappeared miraculously after being lost in an Arctic storm.

"I'm so glad to see you," she said. "How do you feel? Was your flight hard?"

"I'm fine," he said. The force of her concern was so great that he began to wonder whether she knew more about how he felt than he did—whether he in fact did not feel fine at all. Mentally he rummaged his body like a man searching for wallet and keys; he felt as well as he usually did. Not that that was so well: he was overworked, there were worries, bad meals on the road, angry customers, shipping delays, new sales quotas. He was no child. He didn't expect praise, appreciation, or the bloom of health, but just to get through the days and weeks, to meet his obligations and get home from time to time.

"Thank you," she said irrelevantly as she led him away by the arm. She was talking to an airline official, who touched his hat and gravely said, "Good luck to you folks."

"What's wrong?" he asked. "Why did I have to meet you here?" They passed into the main lobby, a low, gray-walled dirty room that smelled of disinfectant and sleepless nights. Sheets of rain slid down the picture windows, casting strange moving watery shadows on the walls.

"The doctor called," she said. "Those test results came back. You need an operation right away."

"Test results?" He could just remember taking tests in the doctor's office; it seemed months ago, but perhaps had been last week. It was hard to remember how long he had been on the road—all days between the first and the last blurred together into a gray timeless dream. "What kind of operation?"

"On your heart. They'll explain it at the hospital."

"What hospital?"

"There's a clinic here that's famous for this operation. The doctor set it up. We have a bed reserved for tonight. The operation is set for tomorrow."

He had a feeling that reality had begun to melt, pool, and flow like the wet shadows on the walls. This was moving too fast. Again he checked his body for signs of danger. What could be wrong? He felt no chest pain: nothing at all. "This must be a mistake," he said.

"No, I don't think so," she said. "The doctor was quite sure. I didn't tell you on the phone, because he said not to upset you. But he says it's urgent. You need the surgery right away."

"Or else what will happen?"

She fixed him mutely with her clear gray eyes, and in them he could read a ruthless tenderness for him, a willingness to drag herself across the country in the rain, to face uncertainty alone, to make decisions for the two of them. The question answered itself.

"They'll explain at the hospital," she said. "We have an appointment there soon. Let's get a cab."

There was a long line at the cab stand. They huddled under his umbrella. The rain showed no sign of relenting. A stocky black dispatcher in muddy gray rain slickers herded the travelers into cabs; many of them seemed to be going to suburban destinations— communities with Indian names that he had never heard of— requiring the dispatcher to match customer with type of cab. The drivers were an unruly lot, trying over and over to bend the rules, to get fares for cities they were not licensed for, to jump ahead in line, to snatch customers out of the line without the approval of the dispatcher. Each attempted transgression seemed to bring the group close to violence until the dispatcher's authority was restored.

He could feel her making an effort to suppress her nervousness, standing quietly and not wringing her hands, pretending, in a way she had that he sometimes found maddening and sometimes bewitching, that it was not raining, that they were not in a hurry, that she was not frightened, that he was not confused.

At length they were directed to a yellow cab, a squat Checker model that seemed, in the line of battered cabs, oddly old-fashioned, as if it had been waiting in the line many years just for them. The driver was a tall man with a shaven head and a salt-and-pepper stubble of beard. She told him the destination and they set off in the choking traffic, the drive of the rain muffling the sound of horns and brakes. He shivered, and she quietly took his hand.

He felt his hand lying against the worn fabric of the seat, chilled by the cold unfamiliar air of this drab city, with faint points of heat where her fingers touched it; her fingers felt warm but faint, as if the sensation were reaching him through some barrier. The cab was crossing a suspension bridge over an oily river; he looked down at the cold surface of the water and imagined a swimmer plunging into the frigid currents, feeling the shock of cold, the instant of fear, the spreading numbness, consciousness fading forever. These imaginary sensations came to him with the force of memory, as if he had felt and refelt them hundreds of times before, while the cab, his wife, the traffic, and the winter day around him seemed as gauzy as a dream.

He felt her watching him. But before he could speak, the driver said deferentially, "You folks visiting somebody at the clinic?"

"No," he said.

From where he sat, the driver's head was a square hairless block of flesh, with the button of a hearing aid protruding from the right ear. Perhaps the hearing aid softened his initial determination to cut off the conversation, or perhaps he simply welcomed the escape from thoughts of what would happen when the trip was over. "I'm going in for treatment," he added in a more conversational tone.

"You're going to have the operation?" the driver asked. His English was thickly accented but confident.

"The operation? Is there just one?"

"Oh, sure," said the driver. "I had it done myself."

He felt a sudden internal lurch, a rush of hope. This solid man had lived through whatever ordeal awaited him, and seemed as rude and healthy as one could ask. True, he was no longer young, but none of them were young any more; the question wasn't any more whether illness and mortality would strike but whether the blow could be borne with dignity and strength.

The cab had pulled down an exit ramp into a waterfront district of warehouses and grimy, secretive-looking lunch counters. The rain was still falling, sometimes straight down in disheartened-looking streams, sometimes billowing in sudden gusts of wind. They pulled up to a stoplight and the driver turned to face them. He had a broad face, wary and intelligent looking, with a light in his eyes of some unspoken passion. His two front teeth were gold, and he wore a white moustache that curled down around his mouth. Though it was still morning, he needed a shave. "Look, folks," he said, "maybe it's none of my business, but are you sure this is the right step for you to take?"

His wife answered as if desperate to forestall some disaster. "Please drive us to the clinic now," she said. "We have an appointment with the doctors there. If there are any questions, they'll answer them. I don't want to offend you—"

"Oh, sure, sure," the driver said, with a sagely cynical nod. "I know this clinic, lady. I drive people there all the time. They do this operation, they're very famous for it. *Time* magazine, *Donahue*, 60 *Minutes*. Do they ever advise *against* the operation? I never heard of it." The driver fixed her with a disapproving stare. "Back home, did you get a second opinion about this?"

The man felt conflicting impulses: one told him to protect his wife, to rebuke the driver for his odd behavior and tell him sharply to drive on; but a countervailing impulse welled up to know the answer, to rebel against the decision she had reached without him. Silently, he turned to look at her.

"Our doctor is a very fine doctor," she said. "He's a family friend. He told us they'd review the case at the clinic and advise us there. I think the doctor said something about more tests."

"Sure, sure," said the driver. "First the tests, then the operation, why not? That way they bill you for both. Listen, I know what I'm talking about, I had this operation. There's a lot of people in this town had it. Okay, I'm not complaining, I needed it, I would have died. But it was tough, there was pain. I couldn't work for a couple months. Cost me plenty, too, and I'm not a rich man. All I'm saying is, you want to be sure. What about a real second opinion? Call somebody you trust. Am I getting out of line? Is that really so much to ask? Believe me, I got nothing to gain from this."

"We need to go. We have an appointment in just a few minutes," she said. "If we miss it, we'll lose our bed."

"Oh, come on, lady," said the driver. He was hanging over the back of the seat, as relaxed as a family friend. "They always say that stuff. Believe me, that place is a regular factory. They got lots of beds. If you got to, you could always say your plane was late, couldn't you?"

Behind them a car horn shrilled, a long angry blast. "Okay, okay," the driver muttered absently. The cab moved forward, then turned onto a wide avenue of stores and restaurants.

The rain seemed to lighten, and at that moment he felt he was awakening from a dream. It was his life, his body, it was his decision. "Driver," he said, "would you pull over here? I need to make a call."

The driver nodded to himself, a sober, companionable nod, as if of one wise man saluting another. His wife put her hand on his arm. "We can call from the clinic," she said. "Or from the hotel. I have a room reserved."

"Let me handle it," he said. The cab pulled up in a bus zone next to a phone booth. "You wait here with the bags. I have a friend in cardiology in Boston. He can talk it over with me, refer me to someone here if need be."

"You trust this guy?" the driver asked.

"Absolutely. We were in school together."

"That's the way to go! Just check it out with somebody *you* trust. That doesn't seem too much to ask, does it?"

"You wait with the bags," he said to his wife. Climbing out in the rain, he still felt nothing inside but a deep weariness from days on the road. His heart seemed to be beating fine—perhaps a little faster than normal, but surely that was not surprising.

The phone booth was leaky and cold and faintly smelled of urine. Entering his credit-card number, his fingers slipped and he began again. The neighborhood they had stopped in seemed to belong to some new Asian population: Korean, Laotian, Mongolian, who knew anymore? Unfamiliar ideograms, curved and dotted in surprising ways, decorated the windows of stores and restaurants. Old men in worn vinyl jackets walked past the booth, carrying bulging shopping bags. The number was busy; he dialed again and got an answer. His friend was at another number; he dialed, but that number did not answer; he called the first number back; his friend was out of town, he was told, another doctor was taking his calls. He held.

The rain drummed monotonously against the booth. It was the kind of day to sit by a fire and doze. From an upper story came a burst of military Asian music, then the sound of voices chanting in unison. He heard a dial tone; he had been cut off.

Even in the chill, he was sweating now. Certainty seemed so close, if only he could complete this call. His fingers slipped. He felt a touch on his sleeve and whirled in alarm, heart hammering. It was his wife. "Dear, please come on now," she said. "It's cold here. We can ask the doctors at the clinic."

"One more minute," he said. "I'm about to get through." The busy signal sounded. He depressed the switch and began again.

"You shouldn't be standing in the rain like this," she said. "They'll let you call when we get there."

"Oh, sure!" he said furiously. "If we go there, I'll find myself on a gurney with a drip in my arm in no time flat! I just want to talk to somebody I trust—is that so unreasonable? Now listen to me—you go wait in the damned cab. I'll be there in a minute."

With a shaking hand he pointed to the bus zone. He saw the rain drumming on the asphalt, rolling into the gutter in tiny waves. But the cab had disappeared.

LINDA DUNN

Healing with Herbs

Serial killers and roundworm: these became my obsessions. Symbolic, certainly, of all that means us harm—danger from the outside, and then danger from the inside. But within the boundaries of my first and only semester at Majestic Herbal College, serial killers and roundworm were tangible fears, devoid of any abstract qualities or symbolism for me, at least until much later.

It's hard to pin down what set this strange segment of my life in motion. Every time I try to establish the source, cause and effect squirm backwards, everything contingent on something else. I'd like to pin it on Jack. That's as good a place as any to start. I left Jack, then I took him back after he followed me halfway across the country. We'd only been apart for a couple of weeks. Which one of us is weaker? A flip of the coin.

Herbal College: another likely suspect in the case of the temporary wrecking of my life. Ignorance is bliss; we draw dangers to us simply by learning of their existence. We really do. But, back to the question of blame. Herbal College is the best place to pin the guilt. At least I made myself believe this, as good a criterion for the truth as any.

God knows, I didn't want to be attending Herbal College; it was forced upon me. When I was seventeen, my father, an intellectually lopsided college professor of forty years had died and left me a fairly large inheritance (old family money). My mother had died when I was a baby, and I barely knew my father, really. I'd been

375

shipped off to high-class boarding schools since I was old enough to walk.

It wasn't enough money to make me fabulously wealthy or anything, but I could live off the interest comfortably for the rest of my life if I didn't get carried away. The trouble was, I couldn't touch a red cent unless I was enrolled as a full-time student. That was the stipulation in Dad's will. Furthermore, this stipulation would be in effect until I turned thirty-five, when the full fat sum would revert to me.

Dad had, no doubt, envisioned me at Smith, or Wellesley, or even Bryn Mawr, going on to endless graduate years at big universities, but I outsmarted him. The quality or even type of school was not stipulated in the will. So, I just went to live wherever I wanted to, picked the most pathetic, low-key, bogus school I could find, and enrolled myself. By the age of twenty-three I had attended the Crandell Institute of Ornamental Ceramics in Tacoma, Washington, the Madame Adama Academy for Channelers and Psychics in Boston, the Pots 'n' Pans Culinary College in Spartanburg, South Carolina, and the Diver Down Scuba School in Dunn, North Carolina. In short, I would not even consider attending a school unless it had a display ad in the yellow pages.

The driving force that moved me around the country from school to school was Jack Montague. We met when we were both in prep school, we both wanted to get out of the academic grind, etc. I've never claimed to have some new and different life story. Anyway, Jack wanted to be, and eventually became, a dog trainer. We had lived together since my father died. Our relationship was never particularly smooth, but dysplasia afflicted it in North Carolina when I practice-permed two of his prize Afghan hounds. There was nothing left for me to do but move to another town and pick another school, only this time I would be on my own. In keeping with the self-defined purpose of my life, my decision regarding place of residence had to be made on purely anti-intellectual principles—no museums, art centers, dance companies, or educational perks could inform my choice. Boulder, Colorado. Plenty of culture there, to be sure, but what attracted me was the idea of living in Mork and Mindy's old stomping ground. Upon arriving in Boulder, I was delighted to have the opportunity of enrolling in Majestic Herbal College.

Orientation day included a tour of the campus, which consisted of a two-story brick building, three greenhouses, and five acres of land, divided up among the student body for individual herb plots; besides learning the ins and outs of herb lore, we were expected to become proficient in growing our own materials. Later in the afternoon, we were all shepherded into an auditorium to listen to the dean make a speech.

Dean Ellison was a short puffy-looking man with pasty white skin and thick glasses. His voice, however, was surprisingly deep and resonant. "Our philosophy here at Majestic Herbal College is a simple one," he said, nervously running his fingers over the edge of the lectern. "We want to return to the natural methods of healing human disorders by using herbs. Many people see this approach as unscientific, even medieval. Well, let me assure you, homeopathy is not a return to the Dark Ages. Many modern medicines are made from the extracts of herbs, merely mimicking so-called home remedies, the same home remedies that have fallen out of favor with the medical community. Here at Majestic you will learn that herbs are not only a viable substitute for chemicals and man-made medicines, but are a more effective and healthier alternative."

I signed up for four classes my first semester, which was the minimum load for a full-time student. Three of these were required intro courses, while the fourth was an elective: "Herbal Treatment of Human-host Worms." Not that I had an interest in the subject, but it was the only elective class that didn't meet at some ungodly hour of the morning.

I missed the first week of classes. Jack had tracked me down, and I spent six days alternately unpacking and arguing. Ultimately I had to take him back; how could I not? He'd sold all but one of his prize dogs just to get the money to follow me. If that isn't love I don't know what is. Maybe I just don't know what is. Anyway, the only dog he'd kept was a half-chow half-German shepherd named Gremlin, who had no monetary value whatsoever. Obviously he was starting over, with a life of the heart in mind. Something like that.

We were lying in bed smoking cigarettes on the second night of our reconciliation when Jack suddenly smiled at me and said, "Hey, I forgot to ask you, what kind of school did you decide on out here?"

"Herbal College," I said.

He laughed. "You're starting to scrape the bottom of the barrel, Ellen. How much longer do you have to go? Ten years?"

"Twelve."

He leaned up on one elbow and reached across me to put his cigarette out in the ashtray on the floor next to my side of the bed. "You're running out of bullshit schools."

"How could anybody possibly run out of bullshit *anything?*"

"Well, you will. Bound to happen."

"I can always duplicate. I think I might do bartender next. Stay trashed for six months, or however long it takes."

"So where'd you find out about Herbal College?"

"Yellow pages."

"When do you start classes?"

"Last Monday," I said.

Jack lit another cigarette and smoked silently for a few minutes. He kept taking this short little breath, like he kept wanting to say something and then stopped himself at the last minute.

"What is it?" I finally asked.

"I was just going to say, I was just going to predict, I mean, you'll have to end up in a real college sooner or later, Ellen. You just will."

He brought this up every six months or so, I think just to piss me off or something.

"Why don't you go to a 'real' college if you're so hot on it?"

"I don't need to go to college to do what I like to do."

"Neither do I. 'Cause what I like to do is collect that damn money, and I don't need to go to a real college to do that."

"If you've got to be in school anyway, I think it's time you went to real school. Both us have spent a lot of time doing nothing, but now maybe it's time to really start on something."

I knew better than to answer him. But he still knew he'd hit a nerve. The truth was, I'd have been happier if I'd known what it was I did want to do with my life. Working my ass off studying to reach a thousand dead ends didn't appeal to me. With Herbal College and the like, at least the dead end was right out in the open. I had to do some degree of work, but they sure as hell weren't Vassar.

"You must have some ambition, Ellen. You just won't say. Isn't there anything you really want to do, even a little bit?"

"Now that you mention it, there is," I said. "I think I'm going to find an herbal cure for cancer."

Most of the students at Herbal College were what one might expect; not much different, at core, than the sixties throwback types I'd encountered at the new-age psychic school. The term *hippie* has been thrown out of common usage too soon; they are still with us. Mostly, these were people who worked really hard at making life harder for themselves. I was put with a small dark-haired woman named Doris in my intro to herbal agricultural class—they didn't trust the freshmen to solo on an herb garden until second semester.

Doris was pretty nice, a crunchy granola without a doubt, but amiable enough. The only thing really unusual about her was her hobby, if you can call it a hobby: she studied serial killers. As we dug in our assigned plot of land, I listened to her pontificate in her low, soft voice about the Hillside Strangler, the Zodiac Killer, Son of Sam, et al. I kind of ignored her at first, but I have to admit she drew me in after awhile.

"I hope this isn't too personal a question," I said one afternoon as I sliced open a bag of organic peat moss with a garden trowel, "but did somebody in your family get, you know, murdered by a serial killer or something? You seem really into this, and I just wondered . . ."

"No, thank God, I don't have any firsthand experience. I just got really interested in this stuff in the seventies."

"Why? I mean, what happened?"

"Nothing happened, at least not to me. But that was when I heard about Ted."

"Ted?"

"Bundy," she said, as if I'd asked her how many thumbs people usually have on one hand.

I nodded even though the name was only vaguely familiar to me, like a celebrity guest on an old syndicated game show.

"One of my best friends in college had a drink with him once," she continues. "Before he got caught, you know? Hell, she almost went out with him. Gave him her phone number. Said he was really cute and everything. When the whole story came out, I got really freaked about it. Any of us, you, me, any of us, could be dating a Ted Bundy."

I thought about Jack. Hardly a ripper. "At least I don't have to worry about that," I said, scattering moist handfuls of peat moss and patting it into the earth.

"You're not dating anybody, then?"

"Well, yeah, I am. But I've been living with him for years. Since high school." That in itself was probably pretty perverse, come to think of it, but not in the way Doris meant.

She shook her head and picked up a trowel. "Bundy had a girl-friend he practically lived with for, like, five years. She never knew, and he was butchering these girls right and left the whole time."

"What about you, then? How do you know you're not dating one?" I imagined she'd be a blast at a singles bar.

"No. I'm not dating anybody. I'm still working out a foolproof system, to ferret out the potential s. k.'s, you know? That's why, well partly why, I'm studying this stuff." She paused to take a deep breath. "I didn't mean to spook you about your boyfriend, Ellen. I just hope you're being careful, watching for the signs."

I didn't ask; I figured she'd subject me to a complete run-down sooner or later. As I spread the clumps of peat over the topsoil, my fingertips hit something cold and ropey. I pulled up a large pink earthworm, big enough to be a small snake.

"Son of a bitch!" I said, flinging it away from me instinctively.

Doris crawled after it and draped it over her fingers. "Oh, he won't hurt you. I love earthworms."

It was to be a long semester.

———

"So what did you do all day?" I asked Jack when I got home that afternoon. He was sitting on a packing crate reading a dog maga-zine.

He looked up and smiled. "I got a job."

"Where?"

"At this kennel about a mile from here." He put the magazine on the floor and started biting his nails.

"Are you sure you want to do that? Being a kennel hand's kind of a step down."

He stopped gnawing his thumbnail only long enough to answer me. "I just feel like doing something low-key for awhile. Easy work, you know. I don't want to get set up here as an independent yet. I need a little break from responsibility."

I sat down on the floor, up against the wall, and lit a cigarette. The only sounds were my exhalations and the steady, familiar click of Jack biting his nails, a chronic habit he'd had since I'd known him. It still annoyed me from time to time.

"Honey, why don't you let me file those for you. I know there's an emery board around here somewhere."

He waved me off and picked his dog magazine back up.

"When do you start?" I asked.

"Tomorrow. What are you going to do, go to class?"

"Yeah. I've got my first worm lecture."

"Herbal College," he declared flatly, as if that were some kind of universal explanation. At the moment, of course, it was.

I picked up my worm book, which I'd bought that afternoon. I'd planned to just skim the text and do my best to avoid the pictures entirely, but I got sucked in, so to speak, the way you can't stop yourself from pulling open a paper cut again and again. Gory compulsion.

The first chapter was titled "An Introduction to 'The Worm,'" *The Worm* being placed in condescending quotation marks because, as the author explained, "The name 'worm' is an indefinite though suggestive term popularly applied to any elongated creeping thing that is not obviously something else."

From there, I was confronted with parasitic worm after parasitic worm, each more heinous than the last, each attacking a progressively more vital part of the human anatomy. I had had no idea. And these were not tiny, characterless sorts of worms. These were worms that had actual *faces,* even personalities of sorts.

"Listen to this," I said, waiting for Jack to look up, ignoring the impatient look on his face. "'Hardly any organ or tissue is exempt from attack by worms of one kind or another.'"

"What the hell are you reading?"

I flipped to the title page. "*Introduction to Parasitology with Special Reference to the Parasites of Man.* Oh, and get this: 'by the late Asa C. Chandler.'"

"You're making that part up."

I turned the book around for him to see.

"That's really sick, Ellen."

"You think that's bad, you should take a look at some of these pictures."

"I'd rather not be subjected to it, if you don't mind."

I went back to reading. The horrible parade of parasites slithered past me. I'd expected tapeworm, I even vaguely remembered hearing about hookworm. But how could anyone ever be prepared for the terrible knowledge of the roundworm?

"Would you have ever believed," I said, ignoring Jack's annoyed rattling of his dog magazine, "a worm that lives in the human intestine that can be a fucking foot long? And it's self-limiting."

"So? What does that mean?"

"It crawls out of you when it gets too big."

"From where?"

"Where do you think? Or, in extreme cases, the nose or mouth."

"What's the name?"

"Roundworm."

He shrugged. "Yeah, dogs can get that sometimes."

"But Jesus, people? They crawl out at night and people find them in their damn beds."

"Romantic."

"This doesn't disturb you at all?"

"You ever know anybody that's had it? Come on."

I ran my finger down the page and felt the hair on my arms stand up. One out of four. One out of four *people* are hosts to roundworm at some point in their lives. It had to be a misprint.

Who knows what evil lurks in the hearts (to name but one locality) of men?

Schistosoma japonicum
C. inhabilis
Echinostoma revolutum
Opisthorchis felineus
Paragonimus westermanni
Leuchchlordium migranum
C. macrocerca
C. gorgonocephala
Australorbis glabrutus
Achistomsoma mansoni

This list does not begin to scratch the surface. And these are only the ones that never get big enough for us to see with the naked eye.

Fasciola hepatica
Dicrocoelium dendritucum
Eurytrema pancreaticum
Clonorchis sinesis
Opisthorichis felineus . . .

As it turned out, Doris was in my worm class. I sat down next to her and grimaced. "Didn't the reading just gross you out?" I asked.

She shrugged. "Parasites have been around as long as we have. They have as much right to exist as we do."

"All I want to know is if this class is going to teach us how to get rid of them."

She shrugged again. It was beyond me how she could be so casual about something this awful. "You missed the first lecture. The professor said herbs can be very helpful in coaxing parasites out of the body."

"Coaxing!? They're going to have to do a fuck of a lot better than that. What's this guy's name, anyway?"

She shuddered. "Berkowitz."

Now it was my turn to shrug. "Coincidence."

After class Doris and I went to work in our garden for a little while. I was so intent on steering our conversation away from worms that I left myself wide open for another discussion of serial killers.

"The Midwest is due for one," Doris said.

"Due for one what?"

"Serial killer. These things occur in patterns. I keep track of trends. On a map, you know? It's some kind of weird law of the universe or something; there's a pattern of serial killers. The Midwest is due for one."

"Where'd you hear about this pattern thing?"

"I do my own research. I subscribe to ten major newspapers. And two clippings services. So many people are murdered, or just disappear every year, it can take ages before agencies make enough connections to suspect a serial killer." She shook her head. "Bundy'd killed in three states at the very least, before they caught on it was one guy. I keep up with it, though."

I jerked my hand back; another earthworm. I slammed a handful of dirt over it before Doris could ask to fondle it.

"You don't seem particularly disturbed by any of this," she said. "I'm worried about you. You're wide open to an attack if you don't keep up with things."

"Well, Jesus, I mean, sure I'm disturbed by the, you know, prospect of a serial killer. But there's not a hell of a lot I can do about it."

She mumbled something under her breath.

"Now what is it?"

"You could be actually harboring one."

"A serial killer? I told you Doris, I've known Jack forever. We've been living together since I was eighteen."

"But that's not . . ."

"I know, I know. Bundy, right?"

She nodded. "Just watch for the signs, that's all. Sometimes you just can't tell, even then, but you can watch for the obvious signs."

"Such as?"

She didn't miss a beat, just launched right into them like she might be reciting multiplication tables. "First, does he disappear regularly for periods of three or four hours? Do you wake up in the middle of the night and he's out of the house? Does he have an obsession with cleanliness, like washing his hands over and over? Does he have a particularly noticeable or obsessive nervous tic? Does he try to limit the number of friends he has, or the number of people he is particularly close to? Does he become irrationally irritable when certain subjects are brought up, subjects that seem to you perfectly innocent? These don't have to be subjects that relate to murder or rape, by the way. I could just go on and on."

I had no doubt of that. "I'll keep a close watch on the situation," I said, inadvertently digging up the same earthworm. I chopped it in half with my trowel without thinking, and watched horrified as the two severed segments squirmed and writhed.

I was reading my worm book when Jack got home from the kennel that night. He walked in the door biting his nails furiously. "How were the dogs?" I asked.

"What do you mean?" he snapped.

"Christ, I just asked you about the dogs, that's all."

"They're fine. Why wouldn't they be?"

"You're acting very weird, Jack."

"Well, hell, Ellen. I walk in the door and you give me the third degree about the damn dogs. Why wouldn't they be just fine?" He softened up visibly. "Just forget it, OK? How was your day?"

"I learned more about the worms." I held the book up. "Do you want to hear?"

"No. No more about worms." He went into the kitchen and came back with a couple of beers. He opened one and handed it to me. "You're going to learn to cure these things?"

"Are you kidding? With herbs? If I even suspected I had worms I'd drink kerosene and swallow a lit match, and these fools are talking about pomegranate seeds. And this herb called wormseed. Wormseed! Does that sound like something to *cure* worms?"

He sat on the floor, alternately swigging his beer and biting his nails. Jack was not usually the irritable type, and I couldn't imagine why he'd been so touchy about the dogs. I caught myself eyeing him suspiciously over the top of my worm book. Ridiculous. Doris just had me spooked.

Suddenly he stood up. "I'm going out for awhile," he said.

"Where?"

"Out. Just out." Pissed again; what the hell was up his ass? "I'll be back in a couple of hours, I'm just going for a walk."

I shrugged and went back to my book. It was all very strange, but I've always believed we draw coincidence to us just by thinking about it. You find whatever you look for, generally, even symptoms of a serial killer's personality. That didn't mean someone was a serial killer.

I immersed myself in worm lore. My stomach churned. It was just because I hadn't eaten. Surely.

People speak of gut feelings. What can that mean, really?

> *Gastrodiscoides hominis*
> *Watsonius watsoni*
> *Fascialopsis buski*
> *Nanophyetus salmincola*
> *Echinostoma ilocanum*
> *Echinostoma lindoense*

Every last one of them living rent-free.

Echinochasmus japonicus
Euparyphium melis
Cotylurus flabelliformis
Prosthogonimus macrochis . . .

I would never have become so paranoid about the prospect of Jack being a serial killer had I not been emotionally weakened by my daily worm studies. I became convinced I was hostess to all manner of nematodes and flukes. Every little muscle twitch became larvae struggling to get out of my body. An upset stomach was translated into churning adult specimen. I suppose that everyone has a particular fear that they are not even aware of, something that lies dormant in them since birth, like a nest of sleeping cystoid eggs. I don't mean common fears; I mean the kind of terror that most people probably never even discover except by chance. I unwittingly found out, however, that my ultimate fear was of hosting parasites. It made no difference to me that most of the parasites I studied were only found in Third World countries, tropical locales, or the Great Barrier Reef. Further, most of them could only be contracted by eating rats or cockroaches, walking barefoot through animal feces, or snacking on raw pork. My fear was irrational, but knowing that didn't make it go away.

And then there was Jack. Doris's irrational obsession with serial killers had somehow wormed into my consciousness. I mean, I didn't actually believe Jack was a crazed killer, not deep down, but I worried about it in a vague way from time to time. Hearing all her horror stories day in, day out, had taken its toll. He had been acting so odd and jumpy ever since I'd started telling him about the worms, but then he'd be so casual and nonchalant about it. It didn't make sense.

He became a fiend for washing his hands. One of Doris's warning signs. He bit his nails down to the quick time after time, and though he'd had this habit as long as I'd known him, it had suddenly seemed to become more intense.

Trying to make myself stop worrying, I constantly tested him. A reluctance to form friendships or meet new people was at the top of Doris's list of telltale signs of dementia, so I suggested to Jack that we invite Doris over to dinner. It wasn't that I particularly liked

Doris, but she was the only person I had met in Boulder; I hadn't gotten out much.

"I really don't feel like playing host just now," Jack said when I asked him about it.

"It's just Doris," I said.

"You told me she was a freak." Jack had just gotten in from work, and was sitting on the bed unlacing his shoes.

"Well, she is, but she's the only person I know up here. You could invite some of the people from the kennel if you want."

He shook his head. "I just don't want to be around people, Ellen."

"Why not?"

"I just feel really shitty, is all. I've felt sick all week."

"You don't look sick. And you haven't said anything about it until now."

"I didn't want to worry you." He made a face. "Besides, with all your worm shit, I haven't been able to get a word in edgewise. If Doris comes over here, all you'll do is sit around and talk about that, and I've had enough of it."

"What's your problem? Where have you been going after work lately?"

"Huh? I've been working late."

"You don't have to work late at a kennel, Jack. The dogs are always there. You feed them and go home. I woke up last night and you weren't in."

"I couldn't sleep, and I went for a walk."

"Where?"

Jack flopped back on the bed and rubbed his eyes. "Let's just not fight, OK? We've both been acting weird as hell. Can't we just get back on some sort of even keel?" He sat back up and looked at me until I nodded. That's when I realized how stupid I'd been. Jack was no more a serial killer than I was a hostess for *Taenia solium*. It was all ridiculous. I put Doris's craziness out of my mind. Slack as it was, I started having doubts about Herbal College. Maybe I'd quit when the semester was finished. Bartending school was a possibility. At any rate, I felt I could put things in perspective.

Easier said than done. Once the worms had been pointed out to me, I couldn't get them out of my mind. Jack was off the hook;

that was chalked up to my own paranoia. But the worms were a different story.

From *Introduction to Parasitology: with Special Reference to the Parasites of Man,* by the late Asa C. Chandler, M.S., Ph.D., and Clark P. Read, M.A., Ph.D., John Eiley and Sons, Inc., New York and London, 1961:

"Like those of *Trichinella,* larvae of tapeworms are usually permanently sidetracked in man, and escape only if their hosts have the greater misfortune of being eaten by cannibals, leopards, or rats."

> *Taenia solium*
> *Taenia saginata*
> *Dipylidium caninum*
> *Hymenolepis diminuta*
> *Mesocestoides variabilis*
> *Diplogonoporus grandis*
> *Dibothriocephalus latus*
> *Gyrocotyle urna*
> *Sparganum mansoni*
> *Spirometra mansonoides*
> *Cysticercus cellulosae*
> *Echinococcus granulosus*
> *Echinococcus multilocularis* . . .

Against my better judgment I agreed to go to lunch with Doris after our worm class, just one day after my resolution to put things in perspective. She vetoed a cafe near campus because they used a microwave. "I feel it behind my eyes," she said in this really spooky voice. "The rays are dangerous."

We ended up in a little hole in the wall called Rikki's. Almost all of the customers were sipping from little cups of bottled water. They did have coffee, but only decaf. I couldn't smoke.

Doris's was obviously a familiar face at Rikki's; when she walked up to the counter, the guy at the cash register smiled at her and hollered to one of the waitresses to bring Doris her usual—a bottle of Evian and a bowl of some sort of brown goo.

"It's brown rice, yogurt, raw honey, organically grown raisins, chick-peas, and mashed tofu," she explained.

I tried to order a hot dog, to no avail. I stuck with coffee.

After we were seated, I noticed that the guy at the cash register kept looking over at Doris, as if he were trying to catch her eye.

"That guy over there seems really interested in you, Doris," I said.

She didn't even look up from her goo. "I know. He asks me out all the time."

"Have you ever gone?"

She shook her head. "No way."

"He seems nice enough," I offered. "And he's pretty cute." He had a scrubbed look, a short black ponytail, bright blue eyes, and wore baggy bohemian clothes. Not exactly my kind of Prince Charming, but he was probably right up Doris's alley.

"He's very cute," she said. "But I don't really know him. I mean, I've known him a little for about a year, but that's no guarantee of anything."

Serial killer bullshit, no doubt. I started to tell her how neurotic and unhealthy her obsession with this subject was, but I stopped myself when she looked up at me. Irrational fear: it makes no difference if you know how irrational it is, it still won't go away. If something in those killers' souls had been twisted and warped, then something just as vital had been broken in Doris's.

"I know you think it's crazy, Ellen," she said softly. "But I really can't help it. I envy you, I really do, but I can't let myself . . . *not* worry about it. It's like a reflex. How do you protect yourself against a Juan Corona, or a Starkweather? It's not so much immorality. It's amorality. Like you think about the worms, you know?"

"Doris, I hope this isn't too personal, but how did you get started? When did you get so . . . obsessed?"

"I don't really know for sure," she said, poking at her organic sludge, but not eating it. "I told you I heard about Bundy, all that. But then when I started studying the whole subject it seemed so overwhelming. You can't unknow something."

I didn't stop her as she explained the cases of killer after killer to me; who was I to judge? Me and my fine-segmented friends, after all.

———

Jack the Ripper:

Even children know this one. The grandfather of the whole business.

Juan Corona:
Twenty-five murders under his belt, a record he held until Bundy came along. Listed his victims and their belongings in a neatly kept ledger.

Herbert William Mullin:
Killed a series of thirteen people as human sacrifices to ward off earthquakes.

Edmund Emil Kemper:
Mass murderer and necrophiliac—often kept his victims for sexual purposes for periods of up to a week after their deaths.

Peter Kurten:
Killed dozens of victims in a series of sex crimes; when finally incarcerated, he became psychotic and writhed on the floor, convinced he had metamorphosed into a silkworm.

John Norman Collins:
Killed seven in a series of coed sex crimes.

Albert DeSalvo, a.k.a. the Boston Strangler:
Thirteen innocent victims, strangled to death in the safety and privacy of their own homes.

Melvin David Rees:
Piano salesman and multiple rapist and murderer; details of each crime were copiously set down in his diary.

Charlie Starkweather, a.k.a. the Nebraska Terror:
Self-styled James Dean disciple and killer of ten.

Edgar Herbert Smith:
Convicted of murder, incarcerated, later was released when he won an appeal largely through the intervention of William F. Buckley, and then killed again. He smashed his victim's skulls with a baseball bat when they refused to have sex with him.

David Berkowitz, a.k.a. Son of Sam:
Shot and killed six people after he was instructed to do so by a neighbor's dog, which was acting on behalf of a 5,000-year-old demon.

John Wayne Gacy, a.k.a. the Candy Man:
Raped and murdered at least thirty-two young boys.

Kenneth Bianci and Angelo Buono, a.k.a. the Hillside Stranglers:
Mass murderers and rapists, working as a team. Bianci was an ex–police officer.

Ted Bundy
Of course . . .
This is just a fraction of the killers we actually *know* about. And we only know about a fraction of the real total thereof.

"How can this not just scare the hell out of you?" Doris asked me after she'd finally wound down.

"Well, sure it does. But I can't live my life in terror. I can't do but so much to protect myself from it. You're pretty defenseless up to a certain point."

"Exactly."

"No, I mean, if there's not anything you can ultimately do about it, you might just as well forget about it."

"I just don't want to end up on some victim list, that's all. That's my biggest fear. And they don't even have a complete victim list for Bundy. There are thirty-some women they can trace to him for sure, but when they finally caught him, and asked him about the thirty-four murders they suspected him of, Christ, Ellen, do you know what he said?"

I shook my head.

"He told them to add one digit to it, and they'd have it. Hundreds. There are hundreds missing from that list and we'll never know who they are."

"So you're just going to live your life without men because of this?"

"I'm not a lesbian, either. Don't misunderstand me and think

this is all about men. I mean, think about Martha Beck, who
killed . . ."

"I know it's terrible, but don't you think you should just . . ."

"I can't help it, Ellen. I just can't." And that pretty much ended
the conversation, because I knew she was telling the truth.

———

A fraction of Bundy's victims:

Katherine Merry Devine
Brenda Baker
Joni Lenz
Lynda Ann Healy
Donna Manson
Susan Rancourt
Roberta Kathleen Parks
Brenda Ball
Georgeann Hawkins
Janice Ott
Denise Naslund
Melissa Smith
Laura Aime
Carol DaRonch Swenson
Debby Kent
Caryn Campbell
Julie Cunningham
Denise Oliverson
Shelley Robertson
Melanie Cooley
Lisa Levy
Margaret Bowman
Karen Chandler
Kathy Kleiner DeShields
Cheryl Thomas
Kimberly Leach . . .

Is Doris's name missing? Go back and check again. At any rate,
that doesn't guarantee anything; this is only a partial list.

———

I had a hard time falling asleep that night. Besides being disturbed by my conversation with Doris, Jack was tossing and turn-

ing, sleeping fitfully. He was still complaining of an upset stomach, and his face was a sickly white. At least it kept my mind off that serial-killer business.

I finally dozed off to horrible dreams of some faceless killer tracking me through an abandoned grocery store. I woke up with a start when I felt something unfamiliar against my leg. I turned to Jack but he was gone. Pulling back the covers to get out of bed, I saw something; there, feebly squirming and dying in the warm spot where Jack had been sleeping:

Ascaris lumbricoides.

———

Jack was throwing up violently in the bathroom. I put my hands on either side of his head and held his hair back. A smaller worm than the one in the bed was writhing in the toilet bowl. I didn't look at it as I flushed. When Jack was finished he sat back against the bathtub and looked at me, his eyes moist and weak.

"Jesus, Ellen, what am I going to do? You've got to help me." I could barely hear him. "What do I take to cure it? Have you got anything at school?"

"How the fuck did you get it?" I asked, trying to take charge, keep my cool. I was on the quiet shaky verge of hysteria, a state that allows you crystal clarity, albeit briefly.

Jack started talking so fast he bordered on babbling. "I didn't want to tell you, you were so freaked out by these goddamn worms in the first place. One of the guys at work was talking about roundworm. It was weird, Ellen, you'd just told me about it. One of the guys that worked there last year had it. He caught it from the dogs. It was fucking ridiculous, I mean I heard about this not two days after you started with your worm shit. I washed my hands all the time, and I thought that was enough." He grabbed his stomach and rocked back and forth. "You've got to help me," he said. "Can't we go to school and get some shit to cure it?"

"No, look, that won't do any good . . ."

"What am I going to fucking do? These goddamn things are *crawling* all through . . ."

"No, no, I meant the herbs won't do any good. There's real medicine that'll kill all of them. Let me get my worm book, it's got the drugs listed." Berkowitz scoffed at the drug lists. Well, screw

Berkowitz; let him have these things crawling through his body and listen to him scream bloody murder.

————

A partial arsenal:

> Tetrachlorethylene
> Chenopodium
> Phenothiazine
> Trichostrongylidae
> Ficin
> Papain
> Dithiazanine
> Hexylresorcinol . . .

————

I called the nearest hospital to see if they had a dose of Hexyl-resorcinol on hand. The nurse put me through to a tired-sounding doctor.

"A *what* infection?" he asked.

"*Ascaris lumbricoides* . . . roundworm."

He had the nerve to laugh. "It's not life-threatening if it just showed up, honey. Take him to the doctor in the morning."

"You think you could sleep with a thing like that crawling around in you?" I demanded. "We don't know how long he's had it. It just showed up, but it could have been in there for weeks. Liver, heart, lungs, brain . . . you want to have that on your conscience?"

"What are you, some kind of parasitologist?"

I supposed I was, though not by choice.

"Do you have the drug or not?" I was losing patience.

He sighed. "Bring him in. Ask for Dr. Bundy."

"What was the name?"

He spelled it for me: "B—U—N—T—I—N—G."

Good. One threat at a time, please.

————

Unless you have made the study of parasitology your life's work, as I eventually did, the scientific names will mean nothing to you. The Latin terminology pacifies and distances. These creatures, however, have other names:

> The Dragon Worm
> The Guinea Worm

The Hookworm
The Giant Kidney Worm
Medina
The Pinworm
The Roundworm
The Screw Worm
The African Eye Worm
The Serpent Worm
The Tongue Worm
The Tapeworm
The Whip Worm . . .

A partial list. A fraction.

———

I drove Jack to the emergency room, he drank down Dr. Bunting's evil-smelling medicine, and then we went back home.

"What if they don't die?" Jack asked, sitting on the floor, still rocking back and forth like he had in the bathroom.

"They'll die. One hundred percent cure with this medicine." I know now that it's more like 99 percent, but that's because I've read better books. I've done the lab tests. I've studied with the best. It was just as well that I didn't know about that then, though. As it turned out, the cure took, and Jack had no reason for worry.

"You probably never want to see me again," Jack said forlornly, later that night.

"Don't be stupid. You're going to be fine. I will not, however, ever sleep on those sheets again."

He began to bite his nails.

"That's how you got it," I said quietly.

He didn't understand at first, but then it dawned on him. He sat on his hands and stared at me helplessly.

"I can't believe you didn't go off the damn deep end," he said. "I'd have thought this would just make you snap."

"I don't understand it, either," I said. "I was thinking about that at the hospital. It's like . . . it's like when you see a horror movie, and you're just totally grossed out by the monster, you know? And these people are just being really clinical, trying to figure out ways to kill Godzilla, and you're thinking, 'Look, fools, just haul ass out of there.' But that's because you don't really believe this monster exists; it's all on a movie screen."

"Or in a book."

I smiled. "Or in a worm book. Right. But if you were in their shoes, you'd know the thing *really* existed, and running wouldn't help. You'd learn to kill it."

"I may never get over this."

"I know," I said. "Me neither."

———

I lasted through the semester at Herbal College. Just biding my time. In the spring I enrolled in Colorado State University. My declared major was biology. Within three years I had graduated summa cum laude. I didn't hear a peep out of Jack when I decided to go to Johns Hopkins School of Hygiene and Public Health for my graduate degrees in parasitology. He moved with me and set up his own kennel. He never bites his nails.

I don't know what I intend to do with my degrees. It doesn't matter, all that will take care of itself. I just need to learn these things. The chances of someone getting these worms in North America is relatively unlikely. But I know, as Doris knows, as Jack knows, that unlikeliness is no protection.

The odds may be in your favor, but we're all at the mercy of flukes.

ANNIE DILLARD

Hugh on the Train

(from the novel *The Living*)

In April 1893, Hugh Honer, seventeen years old, was crossing the country westward on the Union Pacific Railroad. He and his family had attended his grandfather's funeral in Baltimore. Now he was bound home—to a hop ranch on the Nooksack River, ninety miles north of Seattle, at the northwest edge of the United States. This evening the train was crossing southern Wyoming and boosting up the low slope towards South Pass.

Hugh Honer sat with the men in the smoker. He was curly-headed, thin, with a wooden, wide mouth and alert light eyes. He wore a jacket buttoned high against the soot, a white shirt and loose tie. Like all the men in the smoker, he had removed his hat; where the hat brim pressed his hair a slick ridge encircled his head. The smoker smelled of lamp oil and coal dust. It was an express coach. His mother and young brothers were forward in their sleeping car, a Pullman Palace.

Just in front of Hugh sat a long-eared, red-eyed young fellow who had the sporting look of an Eastern college boy. He had a piece of sticking plaster on the edge of one of his ears, where apparently a barber nicked him. Now the college boy folded his newspaper and addressed his neighbor, who wore a bowler hat and muttonchop whiskers like an old-timer.

"Tell me," the college boy said in a quavering voice, "Has a young man a better opportunity to secure wealth and preferment in the

West than in the East?" Hugh was impressed with the way he talked.

The old-timer rubbed his speckled nose. He said something Hugh did not hear. He said he personally knew of a waterfall in Oregon that was a good proposition. He said there was a good proposition in Port Townsend, and there were excellent propositions along the Great Northern route, where Jim Hill had granted the towns a clear thing. They were just coining money. Pretty work!

The college boy banged his thin knees together repeatedly, as if from excitement. "I have thought myself," he said, "that opportunity in the East was used up. The cities are unhealthy and ridden with vice. But the East has the capital." The car's swinging and bumping made a hash of his elocution. "I myself have been said to possess the needful application. Do you find me capable of making a good impression? In any case," he finished lamely, "I hope to be making a stir soon in something. What do you think of the proposition at Humboldt Bay?"

"Oh, that is a washout"—a shake of the muttonchop whiskers. "Dead in the shell. Some say business is falling off everywhere. Now Idlewild! There's a likely town. And Florence—"

In the aisle, standing by the porcelain cuspidor, a long-necked redhead, wearing spats and a rusty silk eye patch, boasted to the businessman behind Hugh. He had single-handedly bested whole railway trains full of immigrant farmers. In one instance he sold one fellow a hayrake for five dollars, he said. Sold him ten rolls of baling twine, a gold pan, and a fireproof safe. Sold him tools to build a barn.

He tilted his red head towards the heavens at the thought, then leaned into his audience, lurching with the train, and extended an arm to the back of Hugh's seat.

"—And he's bound straight for hardpan desert."

This same outfit had told the whole smoker yesterday, "Them mugwumps are not strictly by nature what you would call—men," and it looked to Hugh like the college boy made a note of it.

The prosperous Norwegians on the train played pangingi, starting after dinner. Hugh hoped someone would start a game of cooncan, so he could learn what it was. On the coach he rode East, two ranchers from Arizona played cooncan clean to Chicago. One of them won from the other 2,000 oranges, 5 gallons of wine, 17 buckskins, and 200 heifers, and they wrote it down. He had missed this famous event, night after night, by sitting back with a botany book after he settled his brothers. Hugh was smart enough to watch out for the pink cuffs—the cardsharps that rode the rails and fleeced sheep at three-card monte. They all wore pink shirts, he had heard—so perhaps they were not strictly needle sharp, after all.

That night, while the steam pipes clanked in the smoker and the salesman with the eye patch rubbed a hole in the sooty window to see the stars, Hugh fell to talking with the red-eyed college boy, whose name was Arthur Flockheart, and who was a hopeful, pompous, dreaming youth from Cleveland, bound to Portland, Oregon, to visit his grandmother. A barber had indeed nicked his ear; while he and Hugh talked, he scratched off the sticking plaster, and the nick bled a little. He was wearing a reasonably white shirt and collar, a blue neckerchief knotted at the ends, and a jacket too short for his wrists. He crossed and uncrossed his long legs, and banged his knees together.

Hugh moved to sit beside Arthur Flockheart. He listened to him soberly for an hour before he spoke to ask, "Do you happen to know about a game called cooncan?" Arthur did not. He owned he enjoyed a game of pinochle with his Phi Gamma Delta brothers. And his saintly grandmother, who was said to be failing now, had taught him to play three-card monte for two bits, which was first-rate fun for a little boy, but it palled. How do you play? With a monte deck. Sports called it the railroad Bible.

Two hours later, Hugh's luck had started to sour, and his column of silver winnings was down to a line of three coins, when the conductor Tommy Cahoon passed into the rattling smoker. Tommy Cahoon had already made a sensation with the passengers, because he had been scalped years ago by Sioux Indians near Cheyenne, and lived to tell it. Now he carried a yellow telegraph envelope in his hand. He stopped at the aisle by Hugh—Hugh Honer? He passed the yellow envelope across the table, with a respectful nod, and moved on. Hugh could see the pink streak below his cap all around the back of his head.

"Excuse me," he said to Arthur, whose red eyes looked mournfully sympathetic. He rose and made his way forward to the space by the door. Could something have happened to his sweetheart on

Bellingham Bay? Would her mother think to notify him? They would not know where he was. Could Kulshan Jim have telegraphed—did the barn burn up with the stock? He slit the yellow envelope carefully with his pocketknife. Inside he found no telegram, but only a small white card. It bore the engraved seal of the Union Pacific Railroad, and read, in engraved type, "Beware. You are in the hands of a professional gambler."

JOHN CURRIER

Going Crazy with the Telephone

Everyone wondered whether or not it was wise of Harold to get a phone. He had been going crazy ever since it was installed. He would call every number in the phone book and talk to total strangers. What was worse, he would call himself up and talk to himself, whether or not he was home. Sometimes he would call himself up and pretend he was someone else. Then he would tell himself he had the wrong number and hang up on himself. It wasn't long before he was making obscene phone calls to himself. Soon it got so bad, he wouldn't answer the phone.

The End

Offerings to Jackie O

Cicero took his turn at the battered Royal in the public library every Monday morning at nine. The bums who waited on the brick wall outside and clutched their Veterans Administration disability forms until somebody came to open the library door always let Cicero have first crack at the typewriter. He was big and serious. They were afraid of him.

He sat down and got the envelope out of the way first. Upper left-hand corner on Woolworth's cheapest stock: C. Smoot, 729 Jamison Ave., S.E., Apt. 3, Roanoke, Va. 24013. Then he put his sister's address halfway down the envelope and far to the left of center. He had run off the right side too many times. Stationery cost money. He punched hard with his index fingers: Mrs. Gilbert Pullin, P.O. Box 563, Martinsville, Va. 24112.

```
Birdy,,Got youre birth-day card, thanks.
You never forgat and i appreciate it.
seem like every nOv. 2d i remember youres
but too late to by you card I never
was as organised as you was. I hope you
had a god birth-day. No much news up
this a way..   Glad i finerly quit up at
the Night Watch Man job   guest ill just
it easy now &try to be like a retirred
man. you ever think of youre little baby
brother bein g retirred? i dont care
```

much about it i do miss that old railroad.
think i migt start goin to Church. bet
you cant believe thatneither you sweet
old gal. you been goin to that Baptist
Church all these yrs. i saw a nice
Church up by the last place I did
Night Watch Man work. mabe ill go
there one a these Sundays. i got all
this $ piled up at the Bank, might as
well go fore some good use. mabey
the Lord would like to see this old
sot a few more time before i croke.
Dont get mad Birdy but i aint goin
to give my $ to one a them preachers
on the tv. i want it to go some
respecterble religion thats got some
class to it. take care and tell
Gilbert hullo.   cicero.

Sometimes Cicero did his Birdy letters over if the first try was real rough, but he was satisfied enough with this one, so he folded it, half, half again, half again, into a small neat rectangle and slid it into the envelope. The bums and librarians were watching as Cicero licked the envelope flap and flattened the whole thing on the typewriter stand by rolling the end of his fist over it.

From his back pocket Cicero took a dilapidated wallet, more parchment now than leather. He fished around in a back corner of it and brought out a strip of four stamps. He folded one over, under and over once more and carefully tore at the perforation. He had ripped up plenty of stamps and Lord knows they cost money. He laid the stamp on his fat tongue and in a moment pried it off with his thick thumbnail. He squared the stamp in the envelope's right-hand corner. One press on it with his fist and he was done. He guided the envelope into his inside pocket and reached to the floor to pinch the peak of his worn gray fedora lying there. He stood, positioned the hat on his hand and, straight in the back, shaky in the knees, he walked out.

Cicero rarely spoke to the librarians, or the bums either. He didn't smile much. No one wanted to approach him. He was ugly and he wasn't very clean. Plus he picked his giant nose in between the typing. The nose had pores so deep you could drop a pinhead down in them. It was the nose of a drunk.

He strode up Jefferson Street, head up, long legs flying, his dusty size 14E wingtips smacking the sidewalk. He turned up Franklin Road to the main post office, ignoring mailboxes along the street. Too much chance one of those mailmen would drop his letter on the ground. He went inside the post office and slipped the letter in a chute that said "Stamped Mail/Out of Town."

Cicero's Social Security check had come on Saturday, so he headed down the hill to his bank. The bank had gone through several names lately. That irked Cicero. It was the same bank he had used for forty-eight years.

In the bank lobby, he brought out the Social Security check and, deeper in his coat pocket, his savings book. He would deposit all of the check. He only cashed one every two or three months. That was enough to keep him going. He opened the savings book as he waited in line and looked at the last figure in the right-hand column. $91,506.08. He ran the tip of his index finger over it. The bank kept sending him letters about certificates of deposit and other things, but Cicero wanted his money right where it was.

He always went to the last teller. Mrs. Cheatham. She'd been watching his money grow for the last twenty years, and as far as Cicero could tell, she'd never made a mistake.

"Hello, Mr. Smoot." She was cheerful even though he always seemed sour. He grunted at her and kept his eyes on the savings book and check as she picked them up. He signed the check at home so the transaction would take only a few seconds.

Mrs. Cheatham started to return the savings book to its plastic sleeve, dusty and greasy and the tan color of old cellophane tape. "Oh, let me get you a new one," she said, all singsongy. Cicero frowned. That one would last for years more. The bank was wasteful. He didn't say anything, though. He put the book and its new cover into his pocket and turned to leave before she could finish what she always said. "Have a ni——." Yeah, yeah. Crap.

On to the ABC store for a fifth of Canadian Club and then Cicero caught the bus back to his apartment. He liked his apartment building. Much better than his old place. That one was taken over by a bunch of weaselly boys selling dope and women. First, old Mrs. Humphries and her retarded boy got fed up with all the commotion and moved out. Then Amos Shockley, he was a school maintenance man, couldn't take the racket anymore. He had to get up for work at five in the morning and he wasn't getting any sleep, so he found another place. Cicero had little to say to those old neighbors, but he'd tip his hat to them on the stairs.

He missed them when they moved out. The place got worse. More no-counts moved in. One night coming in from the neighborhood bar, Cicero headed up the steps to his room. A pimply-faced man was sitting on the stairs with his pecker out. A fat girl had her jeans pulled down and her big spongy butt stuck out toward Cicero. It looked to him like the fish in jars that Jewish people eat. The girl was swinging her long breasts over the man's head as he tried to catch her nipples in his mouth. The pimply-faced man laughed when he saw Cicero's surprise. Cicero went outside and sat on the porch, fuming, cursing the white trash he was born into, until the man roared off in an old International Harvester truck.

The new apartment was better. It was on a busy street. No place for dope hunters and whore hunters to park. Upstairs next to Cicero was a kid in his first job at the PicQuik. A divorced woman who worked at Sue's Kutz 'n' Kurls was downstairs. The PicQuik boy came out of her door some mornings looking like he'd had a rough night, but Cicero pretended not to notice. An old lady from Saltville was the other one downstairs. Her son ran a Christian bookstore called the Lord's Library up the street. He moved her into Roanoke to look after her. Cicero saw the man bring TV dinners to her stacked in a grocery bag.

Cicero slid his key into his lock and heard the familiar kerchink that opened his one-room home to him. Under his arm with the brown-wrapped bottle was the newspaper that had been waiting for him in the downstairs hall. Cicero put them both on the porcelain drainboard next to the kitchen sink. He took a jelly glass from the open shelf and cracked open the bottle. He spread the front page out on the kitchen table. Nothing on page one. He flipped the page.

There she was. Jacqueline Onassis with Teddy Kennedy and the rest of them at John F's grave. Every year the day after the anniversary of Kennedy's assassination, Cicero looked for her picture in the paper.

He took a sip of whiskey and studied the photograph. Yep, the neck was as fine as ever. The full lower lip. The winglike eyebrows.

The round brown eyes like a doe caught out in a field. She had her hand on Teddy's arm.

Cicero pulled open a drawer in the kitchen table and took out his scissors. He cut out the picture and the caption under it, bending his face close to the newspaper to do it right. He went to a small bookcase near his bed and selected the last in a row of scrapbooks. This was the fifth Jackie book he had made.

He took it to the table and found the next free space on the plastic-covered pages. Cicero lined up the clipping under one from a few months ago of Jackie in *People* magazine with a new boyfriend. Cicero patted the plastic down over her. The last few years, he hadn't been clipping so much. He had plenty of pictures of Jackie.

Leaning back in his chair, he turned to the front of the book. Jackie at a Democratic dinner with Robert Kennedy in 1967. It looked like she had on diamond and ruby earrings. She was staring straight ahead. Robert was staring at her neck. There was one of her with her hair pulled straight back in a bun. No jewelry, maybe no makeup, just perfect. In another picture, she had on wrap-around sunglasses and jeans and a tight sweater. She was turned to the side and Cicero could see her childlike breasts. And there she was in a polka-dotted dress, walking beside Aristotle Onassis with her head down. Cicero examined the profile of her nose and mouth, then the greasy hair, thick glasses, and big nose of the short Onassis.

slimy Greek bastard no he didn't touch no his hairy paw no his tongue no his big belly flopping not even for money not even for money . . . . . come sweet lady queen baby doll wrap my big hand around your waist suck your white neck white smooth smell like rich feel like money taste like angels . . . . . my hand up silk leg cream arm long fingers soft rich never worked . . . . . put this in your hands girl make you work girl make you smell like a woman take it take it hold it like one a them things you hit the horse with hold it hard and hit it beat it beat it break it . . . . . little titties pull my head toward slobber on em chew on em like baby rabbits aw grab me hold on bite me suck me arms round me take me take me love me love . . . .

Cicero groaned. He stretched back in the chair and thought about sleeping a while but took a drink instead. He was sticky in his pants. He'd let himself dry. Nobody around to smell it anyway. Nobody knows about him and Jackie. He closed his eyes.

Love baby sit on papa lap stroke hair kiss cheek cool cheek my forehead smooth skirt smooth sweater sleep baby woman fall on me take care a you awright . . . .

Cicero's head fell against the back of the kitchen chair and he dreamed that he was in the woods and a snow-white owl with a woman's voice called to him from high in a tree. Ants and spiders crawled over his skin as he climbed toward her. The higher he got, the cooler the air and the younger his body became. He stepped from limb to limb without effort. There were no bugs anymore. His skin felt tight and his lungs were clear. The bird flew away, but in her nest Cicero found his savings book.

Cicero snorted awake. He put the book away. He read the newspaper, all about how his railroad was paying people a lot of money to quit. He wished that had happened to him. Then he'd have even more money in the bank. Then he wouldn't have thought about being a night watchman at the furniture store after he retired from the railroad. The long nights of sitting near the line of La-Z-Boys. He thought about Jackie. The streetlights sparkled in the chandeliers. The shiny wooden tables with the high-back chairs and the gold-framed pictures of men on horses chasing foxes reminded him of when he first loved Jackie.

It was when he was in his forties and living in a boardinghouse. On his little black and white TV one night he saw Jackie giving a tour of the White House. He liked the fancy furniture and the pictures on the walls. The way she talked about the pictures was like putting her honey tongue in his ear. Like Mrs. Alexander sounded, his teacher down in the coalfields when he was growing up. Mrs. Alexander came from up North and read poetry. Mrs. Alexander had big wide-open brown eyes and stood tall and never had runs in her stockings and never sounded like a hillbilly. Then Cicero's folks got killed when their buggy was hit by a coal train and Cicero got sent off to a foster home and Birdy to another foster home and Cicero never saw Mrs. Alexander or anybody like her again. Until he saw Jackie and heard her voice.

He used to talk about Jackie to the other men laying railroad lines down in the mountains, but they laughed at him. "You old coot," they jeered. "That woman wouldn't even piss on you. You crazy?" Those men wanted pigs like Mamie Van Doren and Jayne Mansfield. Cicero never liked slutty women, either in real life or in famous people. Maybe it was because of Mrs. Alexander, but Cicero never wanted the same things as other men around him.

Take the *Encyclopaedia Brittanicas*. Cicero read about them in *Reader's Digest* and started going to the library to see them. But school kids kept wanting to use them when he was reading them, so he asked a librarian where he could get some of his own. He never forgot how smart-alecky she talked to him. "You can't *buy* those," she said. He wanted to know why not. "Because they cost a lot of money, and I don't think you could afford them." He wanted to know how much. She started laughing.

"Quit laughing at me, lady," he said. She looked scared when he said it. He guessed he looked mean because people said that about him. He didn't mean to. It was just that he frowned when he was thinking and it made deep mean-looking creases over his nose. He wasn't going to hurt that lady. He just didn't like being laughed at.

The librarian went off and got him the address of the people who made the encyclopaedias. Cicero wrote to them on the library typewriter. A long time later, they sent him a phone number in Richmond. He called and they said they would send a salesman up to Roanoke. The man came on a hot day when Cicero was sleeping in his underwear with a fan blowing on him. The man looked around Cicero's room and asked if he really wanted *Encyclopaedia Brittanicas* and Cicero said he did. And the man asked if Cicero knew how much they were and Cicero said he didn't. The amount the man said was as much as five social security checks. But Cicero didn't flinch. He just told the man he'd have to go down to the bank to get the money. He got the man a stack of $100 bills and in a few weeks a truck driver came with the books.

Cicero never did learn how to write good, but he could read like nobody's business. When he got the encyclopaedias, he started with the first A volume at the very first thing, Accounting. He thought it was funny that the beginning of all those big books was money. He read about noncurrent assets and paid-in capital but most of it didn't make much sense. He read it anyway. He moved on to Afghanistan. Then he read about amphibians and Amsterdam and angiosperms and arachnids and most of that he understood. Cicero had the idea that he was putting together some kind of puzzle about the world, some stuff that he should have gotten in school. He couldn't make the pieces fit, but he figured if he kept on reading, maybe someday they would.

When Cicero finished reading the newspaper story about the railroad, he picked up the first *K* volume of his encyclopaedias. He'd been reading about Turkish rugs called Kazakhs. Cicero couldn't say a lot of the words and he didn't know what they meant, but he'd stopped using a dictionary a long time ago. Took too much time. He'd pick up what he could.

He'd been moving fast through the *K*s. He liked reading about the kamikaze pilots. He was bothered a little by the section on Paul Kammerer, a biologist who thought we get a lot of our ways from our kin. Cicero thought his grandpa was an ornery old cuss and ugly as hell. Cicero was real interested in kangaroos and in Kansas City. Made him want to go somewhere. He was disturbed to read about the kappa, these mean, horny little critters in Japanese stories. There was a picture of one riding on the back of a cucumber. The kappa had scaly skin and a hollow space on the top of its head that was full of water. Cicero felt the top of his head as he read about it. He lingered over the Boris Karloff part. He remembered seeing *The Old Dark House* when he was a boy. He'd been afraid he'd grow up to be a deaf-mute killer like Karloff. The writing about katydids made Cicero homesick for the mountains. Of course, Cicero had read the entry on John F. Kennedy when he first got the books, but he looked at it again. There was one thing he didn't like. It was the part that said people didn't love Jackie so much after she married Onassis. That wasn't true. Cicero forgave her. He knew she didn't love Onassis. She wasn't even with him when he died.

Cicero put down the encyclopaedia and changed his underwear. It was time to walk up to Myrtle's Lunch to eat supper and drink beer until he came home and fell into bed drunk, as he did every night. But he was always up clear as a bell at seven every morning and he was proud of that.

Most every day went like that. Up early. Toast, instant coffee. Do errands first thing. Read the paper. Snort a few. Start where he left off in the encyclopaedias. Sneak a peek at the Jackie books. . . . Jackie in pearls in Puerto Rico, clutching the hand of a little bald-headed man named Casals. Jackie in Vienna in long white gloves, smiling at Khrushchev. Jackie looking regal on top of a jeweled

elephant in India. Jackie in a black lace veil with Pope Paul VI in
Rome. . . . Over to Myrtle's. Listen to the other scum all night.
Don't talk to them though. He wasn't really there. The Budweisers
called him home to Jackie. To Rome, to Sun Valley, to the West
Indies.

Cicero took the bus downtown on Sunday to that church he had
seen when he guarded the furniture store. Grace Episcopal. Gray
stone with a big red door. Looked like a castle. Cicero wasn't
dressed up, so he didn't go inside. He just wanted to see what the
people looked like. The ladies reminded him of Jackie. They wore
soft wool coats. They had smooth legs and bony ankles Cicero
longed to close his hand around. The men in dark suits opened the
red door for the ladies. Cicero thought they might be nice to him if
they knew how much money he had. They went inside and Cicero
heard them singing. *Oh Lamb of God that taketh away the sins of the
world, have mercy upon us. . . .*

At nine Monday morning Cicero was at the library ready for the
typewriter. His first letter to Birdy was messy, so he folded it
carefully and laid it in the trash can and started over. He finished
the letter and walked out. But down the street, he realized he'd
forgotten two envelopes he'd left on the typing stand. He walked
back in and an old brown-haired librarian was standing by the trash
can reading his letter. She was the one who had laughed at Cicero
for wanting his own encyclopaedias.

> Birdy, how you doing my old girl?
> nothing goin on here as allways. youre
> letter ▨▨▨▨ was real nice and to here
> you still get a Thanks-Giving ham and
> t̶h̶e̶t̶ p̶i̶e̶l̶e̶ have that sweet pikle like
> our MOmmie used to make. i found that
> Church. Grace Episs. look like them
> Cathadralls i read about in my books.
> ▨▨▨ Lot a rich people go there, Birdy.
> The ladies wear expansive cloths and
> perls around there necks. All that $
> sitting around for nuthing, a waste
> for sommebody not to get it. dont
> know what theyll think of this old
> yokle . . . i̶t̶ll give them big shot people

a shock wont i?? sometime you gotto
take a chanced even if it scarey. ill
let you know how it goes .. hopt they
dont thro me in jail   love to both
of you.   cicero.

The librarian's mouth was hanging open as she read the letter. She jumped when Cicero yanked it out of her hand. He growled "Mind your own business" and headed out the door. She ran after him. "What are you going to do at my church?" she hollered as the door clicked behind Cicero.

Next Sunday morning, Cicero borrowed a steam iron from the Saltville lady and pressed his green gabardine suit on his bed. The suit was thin and shiny and too big for his bony frame. He Vasolined back his long, thin, graying blond strands of hair. His protruding forehead showed white above his red face. He wore a yellowed dress shirt, a narrow clip-on tie, and dark blue sneakers.

It was funny. When Cicero walked into the church, the people seemed to be expecting him, even though he was a stranger. He didn't know a soul there but he saw that brown-haired librarian sitting up front looking back at him kind of mean. A man led him to a pew in the back. Cicero sat with some men who were very friendly but seemed nervous. When the offering plate came around, Cicero put in $10. He wanted to start out giving small amounts of money. Cicero hardly had time to drop the money into the brass plate before the men jerked it away from him and moved it down the row. But for the most part, Cicero liked the church. The minister, they called him the rector, came up to Cicero after the service and shook his hand. The rector seemed kind of jumpy. Maybe he didn't like talking in public. Cicero could appreciate that.

The next Sunday was the same. They ushered Cicero to that back pew and the same men were sitting there. The rector talked about how the church was 100 years old. It gave Cicero goose bumps when they sang. *'Tis the gift to be simple, 'tis the gift to be free, 'tis the gift to come down where we ought to be, and when we find ourselves in the place just right, 'twill be in the valley of love and delight.*

Cicero felt big. He felt he was part of a powerful thing. He thought about Jackie and how she went to the opera and to hear that classic music. He read somewhere that she liked Mozart. The rector mentioned Mozart in his sermon. Cicero was with the big people now, the right people.

The church was raising money for a pipe organ. Cicero liked the little organ they were still using. It seemed good enough to him. He could feel it buzzing through his bones and he bet the men who sat beside him felt it too. When the organ played, he closed his eyes and thought how he'd seen Jackie on TV in memorial services in big churches for her dead husband, how calm and beautiful she looked sitting so tall and straight with a black veil over her face as the big organ boomed.

Another Sunday came and it was almost Christmas. The poinsettias and the candles and the carols made Cicero feel like a little boy again. One Sunday the rector said people weren't giving enough money for the new organ. It was going to cost $75,000 and they only had $10,000 so far. The organist played something they called a Bach chorale prelude on the old organ. Then they played a tape recording of the same thing played on a big pipe organ like the one they wanted. It was much better. The music flew up to the rafters and shimmied the stained-glass windows. Cicero thought of the churches he'd read about in France. He thought about St. John the Divine in New York. He thought of Jackie sitting in St. Patrick's looking way up into the ceiling as the music vibrated in her head.

Monday morning, Cicero skipped his letter to Birdy and headed straight for the bank. He asked Mrs. Cheatham for a check for $65,000. He thought her jaw would drop off. She stared at him a few seconds. Before she could ask, he whispered in a low growl, "Yes, ma'am. I said $65,000. I got it, ma'am. It says so right here." He tapped his savings book.

Mrs. Cheatham said she'd have to get approval from one of the bank officers for such a big withdrawal. She went to a phone and turned her back to Cicero as she talked softly to somebody. Shortly, a man in a suit walked up to Cicero and stuck out his hand. He said he was one of the vice presidents and would Cicero join him in his office. Cicero grunted and followed the man into a room behind glass walls. The man said he was sorry to intrude on Cicero's privacy but a lot of people tried to steal money from the bank's elderly customers by pulling all kinds of scams and rackets on them.

He was just curious: Why did Cicero want to withdraw so much money?

Cicero was getting mad. It was none of their business. And what had they done with his money? Maybe they didn't have it! Cicero spoke gruffly. "I'm giving it to my church. Grace Episcopal."

The banker looked even more puzzled. "I see," he said, but you could tell he didn't see at all. "Excuse me, Mr. Smoot," he said, getting up from his desk. "I'll be right back." The man was gone a long time. Cicero sat in his office. It was 9:30. Then it was 10. Finally, Cicero walked to a secretary. "If you don't get me my money," he said, "I'm getting the police." In no time at all, the check was in his hands.

Cicero could hardly wait for the week to end. He thought about taking the check straight to the rector, but he wanted to put it in the collection plate like everybody else. So he kept the check in Jackie Book no. 1. He checked every day to make sure it was still there. It was next to the picture of Jackie standing next to Lyndon Johnson when he was sworn in on Air Force One. Jackie's mouth droops open. She looks dazed. On the opposite page Jackie walked off the plane in her bloody pink suit. Cicero tried not to look at Jackie too much and get excited when he made sure the check was there. The check should be clean and pure. It was for the Lord, and for Jackie.

When the collection plate came around on Sunday, Cicero dropped the check on top of the pile of dollars. He had folded the check three times. It looked like a note passed between school kids in class. The minister said that people gave $2,000 for the organ the Sunday before. Good, there'd be more than enough money for the organ now.

Cicero stood by the front door of the church after the service. He thought maybe the rector would find the check and come out and talk to him, but he never did. The men who sat with Cicero every Sunday stood near him with their hands clasped in front of them. They had little to say. Cicero gave up and headed for the bus stop. The men walked away too.

Cicero moped around all week. Once again he didn't write to Birdy. She sent a postcard wanting to know if he was all right. She said she wished Cicero would get a telephone.

Cicero drank at home that week, not at Myrtle's. When he got back from the ABC store on Wednesday afternoon, the Saltville lady said that a dignified-looking man had come around asking for Cicero. A man, maybe the same one, came on Saturday when Cicero was passed out drunk in his room. The man left a note under Cicero's door. It said the man was on the vestry at Grace Episcopal, and he hoped Cicero would be at church on Sunday so they could all thank him for his gift. Cicero could hardly sleep that night. He'd been thinking that maybe his money wasn't good enough for them.

He got to church early the next day. As he walked from the bus stop to the front door, a cluster of men turned toward him. The rector glided his way in his black robe. "Mr. Smoot! Mr. Smoot, we're so glad to see you. We've been waiting for you."

The rector led Cicero downstairs to his office. "Mr. Smoot," he said, having Cicero sit in a leather wing chair, "we're overwhelmed by your gift." Cicero hung his head shyly. "But we're worried that maybe you shouldn't be giving us so much of your money."

Cicero squeezed the brim of the gray fedora in his lap. "Oh, yes sir," he croaked like a schoolboy accused wrongly. "I have more money than that. Now, you take that money. I want you to have it."

"But why," the rector inquired gently, "are you giving it to us? You've only been coming to church here a few weeks and you aren't even a member yet. Of course, we hope you will be."

"I done it for the Lord," Cicero said, "and for Jackie."

"Jackie?"

"You know," Cicero mumbled, staring at his hat. "Jackie Kennedy. Jackie *Onassis*."

There was a long silence. The rector stared at the top of Cicero's head. "Well, do you know Mrs. Onassis?" He spoke now as if he were talking to a child.

"Lord no," Cicero snorted deep down in his throat. "Well, not really. I know all about her . . . . . I love her." Cicero drew his shoulders up and hung his head low.

The rector gazed at Cicero's sagging cheeks and oily hair. "Oh," he said.

Presently, the rector stood up and walked softly around the Oriental rug in front of his desk and stood beside Cicero's chair. "But Mr. Smoot, won't you need that money to take care of yourself as you get older? Don't you have a wife or children who ought to have it?"

"No, sir, I'm all by myself. I just got one sister and she don't need the money. Her husband's retired from the telephone company and he gets a good pension. I don't need much money to live on. And I've got some money left over. That's a good check, if that's what's worrying you."

"No, no, no, Mr. Smoot. No, we know from your bank that your check is as good as gold. They called here to make sure your money was going to a legitimate cause. When we opened up your check and saw how much it was and how you wrote 'for the organ' on it, we could hardly believe it. We're touched by your generosity." He patted Cicero on the back.

Cicero looked up at the rector. "Then take my money and get that organ. It's what I want." Cicero stood up.

The rector put his arm around Cicero's sharp shoulders. "All right, Mr. Smoot." He gave Cicero a little hug. "That's what we'll do. You go on up to church now and I'll be along shortly."

The rector was beaming at Cicero and seemed about to cry for some reason. It was embarrassing to Cicero. "The Lord does work in mysterious ways, Mr. Smoot," the rector said, his voice full of emotion. Cicero hurried out the door.

Cicero went up into the church and headed toward the back pew where he always sat. But a man who usually sat there with him stopped him and insisted that they sit up near the front. In the middle of the service, the rector said that a Mr. Cicero Smoot ("Will you stand, Mr. Smoot?") had given $65,000 for the organ in honor of a friend. Cicero liked how he said that. Cicero rose slowly to his feet and stood there a moment. The people clapped for him. Out of the corner of his eye, he could see the people smiling at him, even the old librarian.

In the spring, the organ was shipped in from England. The rector asked Cicero to come over to the church for tea when the men were putting the huge pipes together. Sometimes on those afternoons Cicero and the rector would drink brandy. Cicero told stories about his days with the railroad. The rector asked him about Jackie. Cicero had never met anybody who didn't laugh when he talked about her. The rector didn't laugh at all.

With the brandy baking his innards, Cicero tried for the first time to tell another person why he loved Jackie.

"She's better'n most of us humans," he said. "The good Lord

made her good. He made her beautiful. Now he made me ugly. When I think about her, I pretend like I'm not a pug-ugly old good-for-nothing. In my mind she loves me back."

The rector still didn't laugh. He wanted to know something. "Have you ever been with a woman, you know what I mean?"

Cicero looked up at him with a red face and a wicked grin. "Yeah. Way back when I was young. But girls always made fun of me and I quit fooling around with them. I didn't want 'em anymore anyway when I saw Jackie."

The rector asked Cicero if he wanted to write to Jackie to let her know that this fine organ had been bought in her honor, but Cicero said no, he didn't want to bother her with it. He had never had the courage to write her. The rector wrote to Jackie anyway. He sent her a photograph of the organ and a letter saying that out of admiration for her, a very generous donor named Cicero Smoot had given the church this extraordinary instrument of praise to the Lord. Jackie wrote a brief note to the rector. Just two paragraphs. The rector had it framed for Cicero. Cicero's favorite part was where she said, "Please express my pleasure to Mr. Smoot for his magnificent gift to your church." For weeks, Cicero looked at those words several times a day. She had said that about him! Mr. Smoot! He kissed the glass where her signature was.

Birdy and Gilbert came up for the organ dedication. The rector ordered a brass plaque and had it screwed into the wood above the organ keyboard. It said: "For Jackie, with love. Cicero Smoot," and it gave the date of the dedication. Cicero almost cried when he saw it. Birdy wanted to know who Jackie was, but before Cicero could figure out what to say, the minister cut in and said, "She's an old friend of Cicero's," and winked at him. Birdy looked at Cicero kind of puzzled but she let it pass.

Cicero's been going to Grace Episcopal ever since. They keep asking him to become a member, but he says he doesn't want to.

He goes to weddings and Thanksgiving services and Christmas pageants, every occasion, almost, when they play the organ. He shows up for choir practice sometimes and sits way in the back. He wanders in on weekdays and listens as music students practice on the organ. He sits in the darkest corner of the back pew. He closes his eyes.

gloves off   slip fingers   under arm   leg cross
lay foot   on my foot   lean head   lean here   hair
smell   hair touch   fingers twist   skin slide
eyes brown   up look   heaven music   angel face
god   mama   love   me   lift me   up
up   up   up . . . .

Cicero aches for Jackie when he hears the organ, but he behaves himself when he's in church.

DON BELTON

The Dreams of Children

Lazarus, come forth.
—John 11:43

He has come home, unexpected and unrepentent. He occupies the third floor of the West Philadelphia brownstone. His father is dead, and the house is his father's memorial. Boaz realized this the moment he set his satchel upon the front steps. But now that he has unpacked in his old room among the old things, he realizes his father occupies the house in more than memory. He senses his father is present and always at the point of materializing in a corner of a room or along the stairs that form an elongated spiral through the house's core. Everyone speaks and moves in the house as though at the edge of their consciousness there is always the thought: Pompey Featherstone hears and sees everything that goes on in this house.

The neighbors pretend not to notice Beryl Featherstone's only son has returned. They pretend that the Featherstone house no longer exists. They have pretended this since Pompey's murder. It is summer. They talk about the heat, baseball, the dying city, the police, church, the president of the United States. They sit on the stoops, laughing or moaning in dark, closed faces. Even the old ones, who witnessed Boaz grow from a baby, barely acknowledge he is back when he comes to sit and smoke on the stoop late at night or walks down to the Korean market and back each morning, with that slow flowing stride that recreates his dead father.

When Boaz came home on a Monday morning, his father had been dead for three days. It was another "Blue Monday," his mother's laundry day. He found her in the kitchen sorting dirty clothes. He had let himself in with the key and walked through the downstairs. Beryl was crouched at the floor with her arms full of laundry. She saw him in the corner of her eye and dropped the clothes. She straightened her knees and declared, "Lord, look here."

She hugged him so hard his hat fell off. Then she held him back a little so she could look at him. Her boy had become a tall, grim-faced man. He had a noble, anguished mask of a face. His face was a tribute and a testament to all his people.

"I wanted to surprise you, Mother," he was muttering. He drew a long breath. "I just wanted to come home."

Beryl pushed the pile of laundry against the double-load washing machine and put the coffee on to reheat. Boaz sat down at the kitchen table and put his satchel at his feet. He rested his hat on the satchel.

"Boaz, son," his mother began over her shoulder at the stove, "you look good, boy. Your sister's here, you know. She's at the doctor's right now. She's alright. She's just having a checkup."

"When did Nina move back home? I *thought* that looked like a lot of laundry with only you living here. What happened to her job with the advertising firm in Atlanta? She was making good money."

Beryl wore a head kerchief, a tent dress, and sandals. She gave him an admonishing look. "You stay out of touch with your people too long. It's more kinds of trouble in this world besides money troubles. Seem like you children can't see that."

Boaz said nothing.

"Seems like this house drew both my children home. She came back in April and realized she's pregnant. I could tell it before she could. She and the man she was with in Atlanta didn't get along. Anyhow she had some species of breakdown over the whole thing, and your father wanted her here, where we can help her better. And she's wants the baby. I'm just telling you everything now. I don't want you bothering her with none of it unless she feels like talking about it, you hear?"

Beryl came to the table and laid out cups and saucers and spoons. "A year is a long time," she said, looking at him, "without any word. I thought we'd get a letter at least. In all this time. No matter how you and your father parted. He's always going to be your daddy. I'm your mother. This is your home."

She went to the stove and turned her back again. "Of course, I been fine, trusting in the Lord. It's nothing but God's promise to the righteous that has kept me. And, well . . . your father's dead. Murdered."

Boaz handled the salt and pepper shakers. They were fashioned to represent a black dog and a white dog.

Beryl returned to the table. She held the coffeepot. "Coffee?" She stood beside him.

Before he had time to say anything, she was pouring the steaming coffee into his cup with a terrifying smile.

"Yes, boy," she said, "your father is gone. Sold his lot in Egypt for an estate in Paradise. His body is up at Isabel Powell's funeral parlor right now. I believe he made it to God's side. The Lord had him to suffer so. I was sitting right where you sitting now when I heard all the commotion out on the front steps."

Boaz was a long time finding his words. He sat studying his hands at though they belonged to someone else. "Mother," he said at last. "I knew he was dead and that's why I came home."

His mother sat down, her eyes glazed. "Baby, what are you saying?"

"I dreamed it two nights ago in Paris, and I've been getting back here as soon as I woke. I went straight to the airport and bought my ticket. Waited five hours in the airport until the next flight.

"In the dream you and I were sitting here having coffee and you told me Daddy was dead."

"Well, you always have dreamed. Since you was a boy. That's what your grandmother said about you. The Bible says your old men will dream dreams and your young men will see visions, but you dream like the old people. I know I dream sometimes too. Not like I used to. I asked God to take the sight from me. The weight was too heavy. Seemed like I woke up every morning with my pillow wet with tears. Still I dreamed of you every night you was away. I saw the places you were. And I prayed for you every day. I prayed that you would fulfill yourself as an artist so that your dreams could grow to something good in the light, unlike mine."

Boaz leaned back in his chair and raised the front legs off the floor.

Beryl removed her head kerchief and smoothed her hair with her hand. There was not a gray hair on her head.

She said, "It was about seven o'clock. Getting near the time he usually went out every morning. I had been up since six. I was down here with his breakfast waiting on him, when I heard him up the stairs arguing on the telephone. I didn't think no more about it. He come in here. I had made coffee and biscuits and fried a piece of fish. He sit at the table a while. He didn't say nothing, didn't even look at me, just look at the food, studying. Then he got up. Didn't even touch his food.

" 'Pomp,' I said to him, 'baby, you sick? You want to go back and lie down?' He just frozen there standing over the table, studying. I looked at him. He couldn't even see me or hear me. It was like he was somewhere else with his body left in here with me. Then he come back to himself. He just snapped out of it and said, 'I was just figuring . . .' "

Beryl stopped. Her mouth was dry. She refreshed herself with coffee before she went on. Boaz sipped his coffee too.

" 'I was just trying to figure what did I do with my pistol,' he was saying. 'Them kids ain't been messing in my things, have they, Beryl? Go wake up Boaz and tell him to come down here!'

"I said to him, 'Pompey, Boaz isn't in this house. What are you talking about? Nobody messing with none of your business. What's the matter with you?'

"I thought he was fixing to have a stroke, tell you the truth. That's how people get with strokes. But then he seem to come around from where his mind had gone, and he grinned like himself and kissed me on my face.

" 'What's the matter with me?' he said. Then sorrowful: 'You poor woman, Beryl. You should have never married an old man. I knew I was too old for you when I met you, but I loved you so much, and you loved me. I'm always going to be loving you, Beryl.'

"I knew he was starting to be senile. First it was little things. You know how particular he always been about his clothes. He started to leave his clothes wherever he took them off at night—on the floor or a chair instead of hanging his things up. Seemed like he was scared to go to sleep without the radio on in his bedroom. Then when I'd go in there to shut it off after he fell asleep, he'd wake up, shouting, 'Turn it back on. I'm listening at it.' I thought it was funny really how men can be. But he kept on taking care of his business, and though I have prayed God to take him out of that hellish life since I

was saved, I didn't interfere with him. He always tried to keep his
business away from me since I met him, away from this home,
running numbers and, now I come to find out, loan-sharking too. I
never judged my husband and I didn't raise my children to judge
him neither. I know the moral shipwreck of these streets. I have
walked them every day of my life. Your father was a man. I have
God for a god, and I married your father to be my man, and he did
what it took for a man to pull out a living from these dead streets.
That was *his* business. God had to deal with him on that count.
Your father loved me, and he respected me and my children and this
house.

"'Pompey, baby, why don't you go back upstairs and lie down. I'll
be up there in a minute. You're not well today.'

"Of course, he said he was alright, said he was going to *be* alright.
He promised he would come home early, and I let him go. . . . I was
sitting where you sitting right now when I hear the gunshots
ringing from outside. He fell down the steps. They shot your daddy
seven times. They caught him leaving the house. Must have been
out there waiting on him. I didn't scream. I didn't cry. I wasn't in
shock neither. I was just clear. I was so . . . clear. I never felt so
awake in my life. I could smell his burnt flesh where the bullets had
tore up his chest and head. The Lord helped me to stand it, Boaz.
To witness it. Then I came back in the house and called the
ambulance."

Late. Soon it will be light again. Birds will start to sing at the front
and back of the house. Boaz cannot sleep. He tries to read in his
room. He draws in his sketch book. He sketches himself. His long
dredlocked hair, jungled and dangerous. The week's growth of hair
on his chin. His wide cheekbones and deepset forehead. The mouth
and eyes are comprised of petal-like shapes, like petals on a shining,
night-blooming flower. It is hot in the room, on the third floor of the
house. He removes his shirt and socks and shoes. He prowls bare
chested and barefoot through the third floor hallway. He stands at
the bannister. His mother sleeps soundlessly in her bedroom with
her door locked. Boaz hangs there, listening, imagining himself
small again.

He hears music hissing from his sister's bedroom at the back of the second floor. He comes down the stairs and taps at her door. Nina says, "Hey," and he enters.

Nina stands in the middle of the room, naked to the waist. She holds a length of purple and black patterned fabric around her, knotting the cloth at one hip. Her black-tipped breasts rest atop her extended stomach. Boaz thinks she looks as if she has swallowed the world and the world is stuck in the center of her body.

"It's burning up in this house," she says lightly.

One of her old Motown records plays on the stereo their parents bought her for her sixteenth birthday. He recognizes the Marvellettes singing "Forever."

"Come on in," she says, pulling a shawl from the bed to cover her upper body. The shawl was their grandmother's. Nina is so beautiful to Boaz. He forgot how beautiful. She has cut her hair short. Her long straightish hair was always her pride and sometimes only comfort when she was a teenager, attending Springside, a WASP private girls school in Germantown. Now she wears her hair close-cropped and wavy like rippling blue-black water running over her head. Her eyes and mouth are his eyes and mouth. She is twenty-seven years old, and he is twenty-three.

They sit on her bed.

"Are you alright?" he asks her.

"I'm fine."

"Do you need anything?"

"I could use some company."

"Me too. I'm not sleepy." He looks over at the clock on the bedstand. "It's nine-thirty in the morning in Paris."

The bed is a canopied Queen Anne that Nina bought when she was in the eleventh grade, working part-time downtown as a salesgirl. The bed, like Nina, smells of rose and sandalwood oils. Boaz lifts his sister's feet and puts them in his lap. The feet are horribly swollen.

"I'm retaining my water," Nina explains. "The hot weather makes the swelling worse. The doctor said for me to stay off my feet as much as I can, but I get tired of lying around all the time, and since Daddy's death I've been trying to do what I can around here to help Mother. After all, I'm just pregnant, not sick."

Boaz massages her feet. "Mother doesn't want you to attend the funeral."

"I know. You know colored people think it's unlucky for a pregnant woman to be at a funeral. I'll probably stay back here and help get things ready for when everyone returns from the cemetery."

"Do you think she's alright?"

"Who? Mother?" Nina laughs. She can laugh, and Boaz loves her for that. "She's alright, bless her heart. It's not just because she's strong, because she *is* strong. She's so damned resolved—always was—about the way Daddy made his living. *That* was the beauty of their relationship. They respected each other for who they were. Daddy accepted it when she became a churchwoman. She accepted it that her husband was a criminal, and he would always be a criminal. But Beryl and Pompey Featherstone loved the hell out of one another. She always knew he could die the way he died. He played at the top of his game out there for a long time, fifty years. It was only a matter of time before someone took him out. She's known her role was to love him and it would also probably be to bury him.

"I'm the oldest. I know our parents in a different way than you. I remember when I was tiny, watching her wait up for him if he was out late, taking care of his business in nightclubs and bars. How she would stand, keeping watch for him by the living room windows. How they laughed and spoke softly to each other when he came home. They used to play records in the living room and slow-dance even after she'd given her life to Christ. Daddy would rock her across the floor like he was the ocean and she was a ship. I'd hold on, hugging Daddy's legs, between them, feeling how much they meant to each other."

Boaz finishes massaging Nina's feet. She lies back on the bed, and he rests his head at her stomach.

Nina pulls a pillow beneath her head and fluffs the pillow. "Boaz, may I ask you a question?"

"Sure."

"Are you gay? Is that why you and Daddy fought? Is that why you went away the way you did?"

He waits a long time before he says, "Yes." Nina's stereo has shut itself off. The house is suddenly so quiet.

Boaz takes his sister's hand and holds it. "Your MBA had gotten you that job in Atlanta by then," he says. "I'd come home from college and didn't know what I wanted to do. I knew I wanted to be an artist. I knew I wanted to paint, but I didn't know where to start.

I got a job at a restaurant and set up a studio in the basement. Then I got the fellowship at the international colony for artists in France. Daddy didn't want me to go. He was just so disappointed with me. I could see that, but I wanted him to be proud that I was doing what *I* wanted. But he just couldn't see spending four years in college and then scrounging around even in Europe just so I could paint pictures."

He looses Nina's hand, but she does not let go. He says, "I never talked to anybody in the family about my sexuality, even you, because I didn't think it was something anybody would understand—least of all Daddy. I didn't understand. I had just as much fear and hatred of what I might be as anybody. The sad thing is that I secretly hated all of you in a way for not fully knowing me, although I couldn't risk revealing myself. Ever since I turned thirteen I knew I was attracted to boys and men. I felt wrong and dirty. I felt like I was in trouble. I was a criminal, dating girls, lying, hiding my crushes, at first, and, later, my real love affairs, afraid a gesture, a tone of voice, a look might betray my secret and bring down condemnation from all of you.

"The closer it got to the time for me to go to France, the more strained my relations got with Daddy. Finally we had a big argument, initially over nothing, but he ended up saying he thought I was wasting myself. In his eyes, I could be a lawyer or a legitimate businessman—opportunities he'd never had. He said I was running away from my responsibility. He said I wasn't a man. 'You're a spoiled little sissy,' he said. He said I should be married by now, thinking about a family. He wasn't even addressing my sex preference. I knew that. He thought I was disinterested in girls out of selfishness. But then I told him. I wanted to shock him. I told him I would never marry a woman because I love men. That I wanted a man. He got furious. He told me to leave his house, and I said that was my plan and I was never coming back. I told him to go to hell and that I hated him. For the first time in my life, he hit me. Neither of us gave the other a chance. I left the next afternoon."

They listen to the silence return. The silence casts a soft jeweled net over the room and house, and Boaz, taking cover of it, cries.

He falls asleep crying and holding his sister in her bed as the birds begin singing. He dreams he is in the living room. His mother and sister sit in the room staring into the air. It is night. Someone is trying to break into the house at the front door, battering the door. In his dream, the door is made of steel, and there is a steel bar on the door.

"Get away from here," Boaz hollers. "Leave us alone."

The pounding continues and soon the door begins to come down. A huge man erupts into the living room catching up Boaz, his mother and sister in a turbulent embrace. It is not until Boaz hears Nina's light, rainlike laughter that he realizes the man is his father.

MADISON SMARTT BELL

At Sea

(from the novel *The Stone That the Builder Refused*)

De M. Y. Chabron, ship's officer, à M. C. Agneaux, negociant au Havre:

17 juillet, 1802

Mon cher oncle,

Je vous envoie, ceci avec, un cahier, des papiers, et d'autres petites choses appartenant à Philip Brown, dit Phillipe Lebrun, un anglais qui se faisait passer pour créole, mort soudain pendant notre voyage de St. Domingue, de la fièvre jaune apparament—sa mort faisait peur, mais il n'était pas d'épidemie suivant à bord le vaisseau.

La plupart des papiers sont sans grande importance, et je ne vois rien de dangereux au cahier. Si vous êtes de mon avis, j'éspère que vous trouverez le moyen d'envoyer tout ce triste paquet à sa malhereuse famille en Angleterre. Je voudrais ça, absolument, parce que n'importe quoi il écrivait sur moi, je suis homme d'honneur, comme vous le savez bien.

Cela suffira. Pour son épitaph, je ferais, "Il n'a déçu personne que lui-même."

Hors de cela, le débarquement s'est passé sans incident. J'éspère à vous rejoindre vers le premier août. . . .

Je suis . . . . . .

Yves Chabron[1]

427

June 7, 1802, Le Cap

And now after so many frustrations and delays it appears reasonably certain that I shall succeed in quitting this country—I will not call it godless, for there are too many gods here, notwithstanding the efforts of the atheistic Jacobins. I shall be more than happy to see the whole island with all it contains receding behind me; let the ocean roll over it entire and I would not miss it one whit.

I count my berth on *L'Héros* secure, as it ought to be when I have squandered so much of the small substance which remains to me in bribes, but it remains unsure when the ship will set sail, and I have determined to remain for the moment in town, although it is unhealthy here, with so many soldiers in barracks at the onset of the fever season. General Leclerc would have done better to put more of his men in the interior, where the air is not so noisome, and fever less prevalent among our people. With the submission of so many of the brigand chiefs the fighting has sufficiently subsided that he might have done so with small danger. Though, to be sure, he is not to be bidden by me, nor is he likely to inquire after my opinion.

The climate shipboard is equally fetid and dangerous so long as the ships remain in port, therefore I have concluded to pass these days, I hope they will be few, here in Le Cap. Given my particular weakness I have no desire to board the ship any sooner than I absolutely must. In the meanwhile I will seek such opportunity as may present to furnish myself with some small provisions for the voyage.

---

[1]   July 17, 1802

My dear uncle,

　　With this I send you a notebook, some papers, and a few other small things belonging to the late Philip Brown, the so-called Phillipe Lebrun, an Englishman passing himself off as a creole, who died suddenly during our voyage from Saint Domingue, apparently of yellow fever—which caused alarm, though there was no following epidemic on ship.

　　Most of the papers are without great importance, and I see nothing dangerous in the notebook. If you share my opinion, I hope that you will find a way to send the whole of this sad packet to his unfortunate family in England. I wish absolutely for that result, for no matter what he wrote of me, I am a man of honor, as you well know.

　　That will do. For his epitaph I would write, "He deceived no one but himself."

　　Aside from that, our debarkation took place without incident. I hope to join you around the first of August. . . .

June 10, 1802, Le Cap.

I who so dearly had believed myself to have passed the peak of my misfortunes now discover it is not so. Having drained my resources almost to the very last to secure a cabin to myself I now find that I have been robbed of this costly purchase. No complaint to Captain Savary has been availing. He will say only that it has become necessary to embark a number of new passengers, and this for some obscure (and undoubtedly fabricated) reason of state. He was of course unmoved by any reference to the sum already paid, as I of course was a great fool to have proffered the whole amount in advance. I depended too much upon French venality, by which I should have known better than trust a Frenchman to stay bribed.

What hope Savary may have of obtaining still another favor by this ruse must be vain—I have no means left to tempt him, though I shall not let him know it. At the same time, I dare not protest too loudly, lest by striking some false note I should betray myself. During my weary and fruitless time in the interior I have become sufficiently familiar with the barbarous argot of this place to pass for a creole, and have thought it best to do so. Never mind the peace, at such a distance from Europe. And in this place one cannot certainly distinguish friend from foe, or know by what reason any stranger might prove to be one or the other. It was on this same account that I wished so fervently for a cabin apart, since it is a great strain on me to maintain my pretense day and night without cease.

Come what may I shall board the ship this even. It may be as well to do it, as there have been a number of small disturbances in the town. I keep clear of all French officers, but the town's mob, whether black or white or particolored, is rife with rumors of the arrest or assassination of one of the more important brigand leaders, Christopher or Toussaint or Dessalines it has been variously noised about. Given the late submission of all these three to Leclerc's authority, I find these tales to be most improbable, but that will not matter if they are believed. With so large a part of the French garrison undone by fever, the town hangs in a more delicate balance than one would willingly acknowledge, and a rising might easily throw it over.

Moreover, once aboard *L'Héros,* I may manage to improve my situation there, or at least defend it from further erosion. I carry with me 2 pounds of chocolate, 4 of coffee, and a box of lemons, these latter to relieve the monotony of the constant salt provisions. Also a bottle of French brandy, purchased at a completely ruinous price, and 2 of local rum. No wine is to be had here for any amount of money.

June 12, 1802, Aboard *L'Héros*.

It is most still in the harbor, and yet I am constantly uneasy, in the expectation of a movement which continues not to come. Whenever I look to the shoreline I expect to see it go careering away from me. . . .

There are a good many sharks in the harbor. Though all is nominally quiet and peaceful in the fleet and in the town, they are somehow being fed.

My sleep this morn broken by a clatter and banging, in the next cabin but one to my own, so it proved. Investigation discovered the ship's carpenter engaged in building what looked to be some sort of fortification there, for what purpose I could hardly say. The carpenter replied to enquiry with only a grunt, and I left him to the oppressive importance of his secrecy. The cabin is quite considerably larger than the one which I occupy.

Likewise this morn I had the pleasure if it is so to be termed of making the acquaintance of my berthmate, the ship's third officer I believe, who pressed himself upon me under the title of *le Citoyen Chabron*. I believe that not so many years ago he would likely have styled himself *Chevalier,* or something of that kind. Well then, we are both pretenders. But at whatever time, in whatever guise, I think he would remain this self-same spangled popinjay, as light of mind as he is in years.

By the time of his arrival I had to be sure already taken the wooden bunk to myself and stowed my small provender and smaller baggage beneath it. There is no question of my surrendering it under any circumstance whatever. In this wise I am able to remain *in character,* profitting by the creole's natural assumption of the absolute priority of his own wish, be it ever so trivial. Let *le Citoyen Chabron* string his hammock where best he may.

June 15, 1802, Shipboard.

Awakened in the small hours this morn by some commotion in the passage without, sound of voices, shuffling of feet &c. Arising with the dawn I found the ship already entering the channel. The secrecy of the embarkation of these final passengers, together with the sudden haste of our departure, would suggest a greater veracity in Captain Savary's claims that I had heretofore suspected. Also there is a sentinel posted outside the door of the cabin where I had previously found the carpenter at work. On deck I asked no questions, but observed a state of grim tension among the ship's officers, as though they could not be at ease before we were well away.

Which sentiment, at the least, I can most heartily share. The town of Le Cap has twice been burnt to the ground these last ten years, but even at the height of its ostentation it could not, when seen at such a distance, have seemed any more than a most precarious foothold on this savage shore. Rounding the cape, I see that city give way to rocky escarpments plunging vertically into the waves, and above these the incomprehensible blankness of the forests, or, where the trees are cut, the peaks standing out as bare and sharp as needles' points. It is such reckless timbering that brought about the terrible floods I witnessed in the Artibonite, but shall I call that undertaking more foolhardy and destructive than another? Here no enterprise has managed to achieve a good result—the hand of civilized man has done no more than make of a wilderness a desert. Perhaps before Columbus landed, it was some sort of savage Eden here. I believe it would have been better for all if he had never come.

June 16, 1802, Shipboard

Today the inevitable. It came upon me when I was at meat, sharing the table with the ship's petty officers. The vessel had been rolling heavily for most of the day with considerable swells, but somewhat to my own surprise I had so far withstood the customary effect of the movements. It came upon me of a sudden, as I watched a steward effecting a difficult advance upon the table with some dish or other, first straining against an upward slope, then lurching forward as the floor assumed a precipitous downward pitch. I was then obliged to hasten away, so as not to shame myself before the company, stumbling and staggering and clinging to the walls.

Still the nausea will not abate, though I am empty as a shell. M. Chabron has lately put his nose into the cabin. I do not take his enquiry after my health to be at all well-intentioned. With a supercilious smile he informed me that after all this sea was not an especially heavy one—as though that were a comfort. Having a bit of a lemon peel clamped in my jaws, I was unable to reply, but showed him my teeth.

June 18, 1802, Shipboard.

Difficult to credit it was four years ago when I took ship for the outward portion of this unlucky expedition. I can remember as clearly as if it were yesterday that horse I saw loaded aboard the ship at Southampton. A big bay gelding, which the sailors secured about the middle with a canvas swing, then hoisted by a wooden crane from dock to deck. Midair, the horse thrashed all his legs helplessly upon nothing, and tossed his head wildly to and fro and let out desperate windy whinnies which sounded almost like human cries. And still at any hour I can see him swinging toward me, so near I see the whites of his rolling eyes and the wet red flaring of his nostrils, and feel the touch of his panicked breath upon my face. . . .

The image is so definite and so lively I cannot always say if it is memory or dream. I pass the day in short uneasy snatches of sleep, my usual state an unsatisfactory compromise between slumber and waking. The nights the same, with twinges of delirium. I worry that I may be talking in my sleep, for if M. Chabron were to rouse himself to hear it my disguise would be undone.

June 22, 1802, Shipboard.

Better today. I was able to go on deck for the first time in many days, and could think of taking nourishment. The weather was fair, and I am given to understand that we have fallen in with the trade winds, which will speed our journey.

Several porpoises observed midday at a small distance from the ship. They jump with such vigor as to bring their bodies out of the water entire, or they may surface only partially, to disclose the top fin and a part of the back . . . very graceful, a sort of curveting.

June 24, 1802, Shipboard.

On deck today I encountered a curious party of blacks and mulattoes, four women and four men—they appeared to be passengers of some description, rather than any sort of effectives on the ship. Indeed, from their rather unsteady comportment I should surmise they are no better sailors than myself.

Finding M. Chabron draped upon a taffrail or some other such nautical fixture, I asked about the group and was given to know it is nothing else than the entourage of Toussaint Louverture! For although I had until lately been far too ill to give any thought to the matter, it is none other than Toussaint himself who has been kept so closely guarded in the cabin which, but for his presence, I might have occupied myself.

Standing at a slight remove, Chabron pointed out the members of the party one by one. The eldest (and by far the blackest) of the women is Suzanne, the wife of Toussaint. She is said to be older than he, and showed her years, appearing confused at moments, appearing not to know just where she found herself or how she came there. But for the richness of her dress (which was, however, modest) she might have easily been taken for any ordinary household servant in the colony. The three young mulatresses in her train (a niece, a daughter-in-law, and a companion as I gathered) struck me as rather more *soignée,* wrapped in that thin layer of hastily acquired sophistication with which I have often met in women of their type.

The lightest of men is Toussaint's eldest son, Placide, though as Chabron reminded me there are some doubts as to his parentage, suspicion that he may be an illegitimate child of Suzanne's prior to the marriage (though Toussaint acknowledges and indeed is said to favor him). His light color may have occasioned this speculation, though often the Aradas, from which tribe Toussaint is extracted, are similarly light, or of a reddish hue.

As for the two younger sons, Isaac and Jean, it is plain at a glance that they are full-blood negroes. The former wears a most extravagant uniform, every inch of it bedizened with gold braid and rosettes, complete with an enormous sword, the tip of it dragging the boards of the deck, whose bearer appears to have no notion of its use. The hilted weapon seems only to encumber the natural movement of his hands along his sides. With all its meaningless pomp this uniform shows marked signs of wear, hard wear at that, and Isaac seems to sulk inside it—a bedraggled peacock, caught in a rainstorm.

According to Chabron, this uniform was the personal gift of Bonaparte to Toussaint's second son. Placide was presented with another like it, on the same occasion, but no longer wears it.

The eighth and last of the party looks a miscellany of ill-assembled and badly chosen parts, being overly tall, gangly, poorly proportioned and clumsy in all respects, all thumbs and elbows. His neck is elongated, with a busy Adam's apple the size of a garden spade, and above, his head appears ridiculously small. He rolls his eyes, and stutters when he speaks, and his outsized, long-fingered hands creep about all over his person like great agitated spiders the while. This singular creature is Toussaint's valet, known by the fanciful appellation of *Mars Plaisir.* For the moment, he cannot practice his intended vocation, since Toussaint is strictly sequestered from all this retinue, not permitted to see any of his retainers or even any member of his family. A pointless severity, I should think, yet I would willingly be deprived of the attentions of a *Mars Plaisir.* In almost any European village I would expect a creature such as he to be set upon and stoned to death.

June 25, 1802, Shipboard.

Last night, in the cabin, Chabron raised his head from the sag of his hammock, to relay to me a curious remark he had heard made to Savary by Toussaint when he came aboard. A continuation of our earlier conversation he may have thought it. I was surprised by the accuracy with which he affected to remember the sentences:

En me reversant, on n'a abattu à Saint-Domingue que le tronc de l'arbre de la liberté des noirs; il poussera par les racines, parce qu'elles sont profondes et nombreuses.[2]

I could not say why Chabron chose to repeat to me this titbit. Perhaps he thought to impress me with his having been privy to conversations of the . . . notorious, if not precisely the great. I found, however, that I was moved by Toussaint's words, futile and vainglorious as they may have been. But it seemed unwise to show any admiration, considering the creole's unfailing contempt for any pretension of the blacks. I thought for a moment of the part I had to play before I spoke.

---

[2] In overthrowing me, you have done no more than cut the trunk of the tree of black liberty in Saint Domingue; it will spring back from the roots, for they are numerous and deep.

"Who taught this gilded nigger such fine phrases?"

Chabron vouchsafed no reply to this. He snorted once, a laugh perhaps, and turned his face back to the wall.

June 27, 1802, Shipboard.

A great many flying fish were seen today, running alongside the ship and in the same direction. They will launch themselves from the height of a billow, and can fly or glide a remarkable distance on their translucent wings, which seem to whir, like the wings of a dragonfly. The big blunt-nosed fish called dolphin follows them and preys upon them, and these our sailors try to catch, lancing at them with a long five-pointed spear. Several dolphin were caught in this fashion in the course of the forenoon. The living fish is rather beautiful for its color: gold, green, and blue in many shades, with a gleaming iridescence suggesting many other hues as well. But once taken from the water, these colors soon dull, and the dolphin dies. So too with any creature taken from its natural place.

The meat of the dolphin is sweet and healthful, making a welcome change from salt meat and hard biscuit.

To my son Robert, if you should read these pages in my absence, be guided by my precept rather than my example, undertake no reckless voyage or adventure, but trust to your own people, your own place.

June 28, 1802, Shipboard.

I woke this morn much earlier than my accustomed hour—could not return to sleep owing to the din of Chabron's snores—and in taking a turn upon the deck I passed a small and unremarkable negro man standing at the stern and staring intently down into the water. He was under guard of a dragoon, yet I, my mind still obscured by sleep, walked by him without immediately understanding who it was that he must be. I believe it was the incongruity of his dress that prompted me to turn to him again: he wore a loose white shirt or smock, coarsely woven and open at the neck, over tight trousers from a military uniform, and a pair of high cavalry boots. There was a kerchief bound over his head, and I remembered hearing that Toussaint affected such a covering, not only in his *déshabille,* but often even on occasions of state.

I stopped and stood at a few yards remove from him. He did not seem at all aware of my proximity. I suppose his keepers must have concluded to bring him up at an hour when he would be unlikely to encounter anyone on deck. Not knowing what to say to him, or if I ought to speak at all, I was silent for some minutes before inquiring what it might be that he was so carefully regarding.

And here the sentinel's attention abruptly returned to his charge, and he undertook to prevent our conversation, but I overrode him, repeating my question and adding to it, whether Toussaint was looking back toward the island of which he had lately been master, and whether he regretted it?

At this, Toussaint turned half toward me, and looked at me with half a smile, but without immediately speaking. I suppose he must have gone a lengthy while without much benefit of human discourse. Still there was a sort of slyness in that smile. His lips were full and heavy, his teeth long and yellow, he lacked an eyetooth on the left side. The jaw long and slung far forward, stretching and lowering the deep oval of his face. His nose was long also and typically flat, but his forehead was high, and his eyes, with their yellowing whites, were large and expressive—his best feature. All in all, a most arresting ugliness, and certainly not a face one would soon forget.

He was smaller than I somehow had expected, standing no higher than my breastbone. His disproportionately long trunk was set on little bandy legs—undoubtedly he would appear to best advantage on horseback. Some grizzled hair appeared at his shirt's neck, and the grey pigtail hanging from under the kerchief was fastened with a bit of frayed red ribbon. I would have put him in the middle fifties. He was narrow hipped and distinctly thin, though not to the point of frailty—I could guess great strength remaining in his arms and his hands.

He returned my looks, taking my measure also it may be, and then resumed staring at the water.

"*Guinée,*" he said, but so softly I scarce caught the word at all.

"Africa?" I said, with some surprise. Of course he was not looking in the right direction, but one would hardly expect him to be a master of geography, outside of the colony. He is himself a creole and I believe this must have been the first time he had ever

been to sea. I found that my gaze was drawn after his; he continued
to inspect the surfaces of the ocean for some time before he spoke.
The sun had not yet risen, and the water looked steely, with a sharp
steely glitter; I could not know whence it drew its light.

"*Guinée, on dit, se trouve en bas de l'eau.*"[3] Still Toussaint kept his
eyes fixed on the water.

"But you are a Christian," I said, for I was again surprised,
though it was not the first time I had heard of this belief. One often
finds the slavers complaining of it—how their new-bought slaves
will fling themselves off the ships in droves, believing that they may
pass beneath the ocean to regain their original homes in Africa.

Toussaint glanced up at me with that same sly smile. "*Bien sûr
que je suis chrétien,*" he said. "*Mais j'aimerais voir l'Afrique tout de
même.*"[4]

But at this juncture, M. Chabron quite suddenly appeared, fully
dressed and disconcertingly alert, and desired me to come away
with him at once. When I demurred, he gripped me by the wrist, as
if he meant to retain me there by force, while the sentinel, with
small courtesy, conducted his charge away in the opposite direction.

Unfortunate fellow, I should not suppose him likely to ever see
Africa—not, at least, in this lifetime.

July 1, 1802, Shipboard.

These past two days we have suffered through a gale. No genuine
danger, I am assured, but much rain, and tearing winds, and heavy
seas. I took some pride (and even more comfort) in the discovery
that my *mal de mer* did not return.

Toward the end of this bout of heavy weather we were hailed by a
British merchantman, outward bound. There was an attempt to
exchange letters, but the sea was too rough for the successful
lowering of a boat.

The weather is fair and warm today, but strangely I do not believe
I feel quite so well as I did during the course of the storm. I suffer
some slight pain in the joints, and a sort of ague, though not severe.
I have broached the bottle of French brandy to warm me.

---

[3] Guinea, so the story goes, is at the bottom of the water.
[4] Certainly I'm a Christian. But I would like to see Africa all the same.

July 2, 1802, Shipboard.

This even, going along the passage, I heard a voice coming from that cabin next but one, and (the sentinel having absented himself, perhaps to the jakes) I paused to listen. The occupant was reading in a loud sonorous voice, this passage from the end of Deuteronomy:

> And Moses went up from the plains of Moab under the mountains of Nebo, to the top of Pisgah, that is over against Jericho. And the Lord showed him all the land of Gilead, unto Dan.
>
> And all Naphtali, and the land of Ephraim, and Manasseh and all the land of Judah, unto the utmost sea.
>
> And the south, and the plain of the valley of Jericho, the city of palm trees, unto Zoar.
>
> And the Lord said unto him, This is the land which I sware unto Abraham, unto Isaac, and unto Jacob, saying, I will give it unto thy seed: I have caused thee to see it with thine eyes, but thou shalt not go thither.
>
> So Moses the servant of the Lord died there in the land of Moab, according to the word of the Lord.
>
> And he buried him in a valley in the land of Moab, over against Bethpeor, but no man knoweth his sepulchre unto this day.
>
> And Moses was a hundred and twenty years old when he died. His eye was not dim, nor his natural force abated.
>
> And the children of Israel wept for Moses in the plains of Moab thirty days: so the days of weeping and mourning for Moses were ended.

Here Toussaint stopped, and after a little period of silence began again but in a lower and less certain tone, a murmur unintelligible to me—perhaps it was a prayer. This was for all the world like a regular church service, though with the one man playing the roles both of priest and communicant.

Hearing a footfall on the ladder I hastened away, though after all, what had I to fear or conceal? I have looked for Toussaint on deck at all hours, but have never again met with him. If my approach has cost him his opportunity for air and exercise, I am sorry for it.

My health continuing somewhat worse this day, the ague more

frequent, and a sharpish pain in the belly. The brandy does not much relieve it.

How I shall welcome the first sight of a European shore!

July 3
Very ill today by what reason I know not. Worse pain in the stomach and in my joints. And a lack of clarity. When I dragged myself abovedecks the light was sharply painful to my eye (though the sky was clouded over) and the scene around me seemed distant, not fully real, like some poorly rendered drawing.

Returned to my bunk I suffer fever and ague in swift succession. If I cover myself I soon break into a fever sweat and must throw off the blanket, whereupon I am racked with chills and must cover myself again, so continuing.

With the ague I can scarce grasp the pen. With the fever I cannot clear my mind to write.

The pain in my head is most severe. Difficulty swallowing also.

July 4 I believe it is I am not certain of the date   Have not left the cabin but

an image of the ship's doctor, that buffoon, leaning over me, saying he had never met with a case such as mine following so many weeks at sea. As much as to declare his helplessness.

Chabron, his face hovering behind the doctor's I saw the fear in his eyes he would not so willingly force his company upon me now

Ha! I wish I had not ever met a Frenchman.

Feeling under the bunk for a lemon I could not discover the box. Is Chabron so base as to steal my food?

? Still at sea at any rate what would I not give to be on land any land now   To wake is misery but I will gladly bear it to be spared the terrors of my dreams   those horrors I know too well their source I have supped full with them

why should I dream of Chabron holding my head and guiding it
A basin at my bed's head w/black bile in it   How it came there I know not   there is a horrid stench it comes from me

? not so feverish now though the pain in my head is blinding and I feel very weak. . . . I feel my clarity come and go

I put these words together like beads on a string to guide me though I don't know where they lead

there on the island there are those who would make a string of stones or as readily of the bones of their own children I will not think of that not write it

see words are like a cloud of biting insects which from a distance appears to have form and sense but coming nearer I discern that each is separate and has no relation to any of the others

? I could not say if it has been hours or days   I believe my fever is worsening

NOTES ON CONTRIBUTORS

~~~~~~

MADISON SMARTT BELL (MA '81) is the author of two collections of short stories and six novels, including *Soldier's Joy*, which won the Lillian Smith Award in 1989, and most recently, *Doctor Sleep*. Since 1984 he has taught at Goucher College, where he is currently Writer in Residence, along with his wife, the poet Elizabeth Spires.

DON BELTON (MA '82) is the author of a novel, *Almost Midnight*. His story "My Soul Is a Witness," the basis of his novel-in-progress, appeared in *Breaking Ice: An Anthology of Afro-American Fiction*. He has been a fellow at Bread Loaf, MacDowell, and Yaddo, and he teaches literature and fiction-writing at Macalester College in Minnesota.

ROBERT BESS (MA '81) is an academic advisor, peer-tutoring program coordinator, and adjunct instructor of English at Roanoke College. He would like to thank Zebulon Vance Hooker II for contributing the title of the Oswald poem.

MARY BISHOP (MA '89), a reporter at the *Roanoke Times and World-News*, shared a Pulitzer Prize while at the Philadelphia *Inquirer* and has since won the George Polk Award and other prizes for journalism.

IRV BROUGHTON (MA '71) is a filmmaker and poet who lives and teaches in Spokane. He is the editor of *The Writer's Mind*, a three-volume collection of interviews with writers.

AMANDA B. BULLINS (MA '72) serves as Community Services Director for the League of Older Americans Agency on Aging. Her poems have appeared in the *Virginia Quarterly Review, Landscape and Distance: An Anthology of Virginia Poets, Artemis,* and other journals.

GEORGE BUTLER (MA '68), a noted photographer and film director, is the coauthor of five books and the author of *Arnold Schwarzenegger—a Portrait.* His films include *Pumping Iron, Pumping Iron II: The Women,* and *In the Blood.* He was a VISTA volunteer in Detroit in 1970 when the photographs in this book were taken.

ROSANNE COGGESHALL (BA '68, MA '70) is the author of two books of poetry, *Hymn for Drum* and *Traffic with Ghosts.* "Moving in Memory" is from her new collection, *Fire or Fire.* She has also published short stories in such magazines as the *Iowa Review, Southern Review, Epoch,* and *Carolina Quarterly.*

WYN COOPER (MA '81) is the author of a collection of poems, *The Country of Here Below.* A former editor of *Quarterly West,* he was also, while in high school, the first filmmaker to use Madonna in a film.

JOHN CURRIER (MA '70) died while still a young man, the victim of cystic fibrosis. His poems appeared in a number of journals, but his wonderful thesis, "The Big Immense Pig," has never been published.

ANNIE DILLARD (BA '67, MA '68) is the author of seven books, among them *Pilgrim at Tinker Creek,* which won the Pulitzer Prize in 1975, and most recently *The Writing Life.*

MINDA LOUISE DRAKE (BA '65, MA '68) is a teacher and tutor at The Meher School in Lafayette, California.

LINDA DUNN (MA '89) has published short fiction in the *Chattahoochee Review,* and she is currently working on a novel, tentatively titled *The Once Over Twice.* She has, to her knowledge, never hosted parasites.

GARRETT EPPS (MA '75) is the author of two novels, *The Shad Treatment,* winner of the Lillian Smith Award in 1977, and *The Floating Island.* He was a staff writer for the *Washington Post* from 1978 to 1981 and was associate editor of Algonquin Books of Chapel Hill from 1985 to 1986. He is currently a law clerk for a federal appellate judge.

E . A . G E H M A N (MA '87) was a Henry Hoyns Fellow at the University of Virginia. Her poems have appeared in magazines around the country.

M E G H A N G E H M A N (BA '85, MA '88) won the 1989 Virginia Governor's Prize for Screenplays, and her fiction has appeared in *Gargoyle* and other magazines. She was a Henry Hoyns Fellow at the University of Virginia and is currently an assistant professor of English at Randolph Macon Woman's College.

J A N E G E N T R Y (BA '63) has appeared most recently in *Harvard Magazine, New Virginia Review,* and *JAmerica.* Her work was a winner in the Frankfort (KY) Arts Foundation 1991 Chapbook Competition. She teaches creative writing and Honors Colloquia at the University of Kentucky.

D A N A G I B S O N (BA '88) was a Hoyns Fellow at the University of Virginia. She received an award from the National Society of Arts and Letters, and her fiction has appeared in *Ploughshares* and *Charleston Magazine.* She teaches English in Baton Rouge, Louisiana.

M A R G A R E T G I B S O N (BA '66) is the author of *Long Walks in the Afternoon,* the Lamont Selection for 1982, and *Memories of the Future,* which won the Melville Cane Award for 1986–87, as well as two other volumes of poetry, most recently *Out in the Open.* She is currently visiting professor in the MFA program at Virginia Commonwealth University.

D E N N I S G I O V A N E T T I (MA '90), a jazz bassist and former instructor at the Naropa Institute, is at work on a new novel.

B E N G R E E R (MA '73) has published four novels, most recently *The Loss of Heaven.* He is an associate professor of English at the University of South Carolina.

L I Z H A H N (MA '88) has taught English at Radford University, has worked as an editor, has sung in a blues band, has published travel articles, and is working on a novel.

C A T H R Y N H A N K L A (BA '80, MA '81) is the author of a novel, a collection of short fiction, and two volumes of poetry, the most recent of which is *Afterimages* (1991). She currently teaches in the writing program at Hollins College, after two years of teaching at Washington and Lee University.

SUSAN HANKLA (BA '73) is a visual artist and author of *Mistral for Daddy and Van Gogh* and *I Am Running Home*. She works as a poet-in-the-schools and is creative advisor for *Paint Pot Alley*, a children's television show.

SUSAN HARKNESS (MA '90) has published poems in such anthologies and magazines as *The Poet's Domain, Artemis, Blueline,* and the national Jesuit magazine *America.* She is a writer and production editor for *Jewelers' Circular—Keystone.*

JUDITH HAWKES (BA '70) is the author of *Julian's House,* the jacket photo of which was chosen Best Author Photo of 1990 by *Entertainment* magazine. She is working on a second novel.

JENNIFER M. HENGEN (MA '90) lives and works in New York City.

MARK HERRERA (MA '91) worked in publishing before attending Hollins. He is the great-grandson of the Dominican poet Primitivo Herrera.

BLAIR HOBBS (MA '90), an Alabama native, is pursuing an MFA in creative writing at the University of Michigan. She has published poems in *Prairie Schooner,* the *Laurel Review,* and *Southern Humanities Review.*

DAVID HUDDLE (MA '69) is the author of four books of short stories, most recently *Intimates,* three books of poems, most recently *The Nature of Yearning,* and a collection of essays, *The Writing Habit.* Professor of English at the University of Vermont, he also teaches at Bread Loaf.

JULIA JOHNSON ('93) is a junior at Hollins College. Her poems have appeared in the *Louisville Review* and *Ellipsis,* and a story in the *Nassau Literary Review.*

EDWARD KLEINSCHMIDT (MA '76) is the author of two books of poems, *Magnetism,* which received the 1988 Poetry Award of the San Francisco Bay Area Book Reviewers, and *First Language,* winner of the 1989 Juniper Prize. He teaches English and creative writing at Santa Clara University.

BRETT LAIDLAW (MA '86) is the author of a novel, *Three Nights in the Heart of the Earth*, which received the Great Lakes Colleges Association's New Writers Award in 1988.

JEANNE LARSEN (MA '72) is the author of *James Cook in Search of Terra Incognita*, winner of the AWP Poetry Prize in 1979, a literary translation of the poems of the ninth-century Chinese poet Xue Tao, and two novels, *Silk Road* and *Bronze Mirror*. She is an associate professor of English at Hollins College.

ANDREA LASLEY (BA '91) is the author of the story "Happenstance," which was chosen for the special Workshops issue of the *Mississippi Review*.

JEANNE LEBOW (MALS '82) is the author of a book of poems, *The Outlaw James Copeland and the Champion-Belted Express*. A Fulbright lecturer in West Africa in 1987–88, she has taught at Memphis State, the University of Southern Mississippi, and Northeast Missouri State.

KAREN LONG (BA '67) has been writing fiction in her closet for over twenty-five years. She has been a contributor to various newspapers and magazines throughout Vermont, an advertising copywriter, and originator of several successful housing grants. She is currently writing herself out of that closet for good with her third novel.

KATHRYN ETTERS LOVATT (MA '89) serves as fiction editor for Carolina Wren Press. Her story "The Year Alice Moved to the Attic" won second place in the 1991 North Carolina Writers Network competition, judged by the editors of *Story*.

KATIE LETCHER LYLE (BA '59) is the author of a book of poems, five young-adult novels, two books of historical nonfiction, and dozens of articles and stories. She is working on a biography of Elizebeth Smith Freidman, a government cryptanalyst from 1920 to 1956, and a collection of excerpts from nineteenth-century Virginia women's diaries.

SALLY MANN (BA '74, MA '75) is a noted photographer and author of two collections of her photographs, *Second Sight* and *At Twelve: Portraits of Young Women*. Her third collection will be published soon.

RICHARD McCANN (MA '72) is the author of a book of poems, *Dream of the Traveler,* and editor (with Margaret Gibson) of a poetry anthology, *Landscape and Distance.* He teaches English and creative writing at the American University.

JILL McCORKLE (MA '81) is the author of four novels, most recently *Ferris Beach,* and a collection of short stories to be published in 1992. She has taught at Tufts University and currently teaches creative writing at the University of North Carolina in Chapel Hill.

THOMAS McGONIGLE (MA '70) is the author of *The Corpse Dream of N. Petkov, Going to Patchogue,* and *In Patchogue.* He writes with some regularity for the *Manchester Guardian,* the *Washington Post,* and New York *Newsday.* A Bulgarian translation of *The Corpse Dream of N. Petkov* was published in 1991.

CHARLES MOLESWORTH (MA '64) is the author of *Marianne Moore: A Literary Life,* and five other books of poetry and criticism. He is chairperson of the English Department at Queens College in New York City.

ELIZABETH S. MORGAN (BA '60) has published a book of poems, *Parties,* with a second, *The Governor of Desire,* forthcoming. Her fiction and poetry has appeared most recently in *Virginia Quarterly Review, Southern Review,* and *Shenandoah.*

DANIEL MUELLER (MA '89) was a Henry Hoyns Fellow at the University of Virginia. His story "The Night My Brother Worked the Header" won the 1990 *Playboy* Fiction Contest. His stories have also appeared in the *Crescent Review, Timbuktu,* and *Henfield Foundation Prize-Winning Stories: 1981–1990.*

HOWARD NELSON (MA '70) has published two books of criticism on the poetry of Robert Bly and Galway Kinnell, and two books of poems, *Creatures* and *Singing into the Belly.*

KAREN OSBORN (BA '79) is the author of *Patchwork,* a novel. Her poems have appeared in the *Southern Review, Kansas Quarterly,* the *Wisconsin Review,* and other magazines and journals.

STEPHEN PETT (MA '74) is the author of a book of poems, *Pulpit of Bones,* and the novel *Sirens.* He is the coordinator of creative writing at Iowa State University.

MICHAEL PETTIT (MA '75) is the author of two books of poems, *American Light* and *Cardinal Points,* winner of the 1987 Iowa Poetry Prize. He teaches at Mount Holyoke College.

DALE PHILLIPS (MA '85) has published fiction in the *Atlantic, Esquire,* and *The Best American Short Stories of 1989.* He teaches at Elon College and is finishing a book of stories, *What It Costs Travelers.*

STEVE POLANSKY (MA '72) has published short fiction in various journals and magazines. He is associate professor of English and creative writing at St. Olaf College.

CAROL POSTER (BA '77) is the author most recently of *Selected Poems of Jacques Prevert.* She is an authority on, among other things, canoeing, shredding, and prosody.

CONSTANCE J. POTEN (BA '71) produced and directed *Contrary Warriors: A Story of the Crow Tribe,* which received ten awards including Best First Time Director at the American Film and Video Festival. She has published fiction in the *Missouri Review,* and her article on the illegal trade of wildlife in America appeared in *National Geographic.*

MARNIE PRANGE (MA '77) has published her poems in *Black Warrior Review,* the *Missouri Review,* and *Poetry Northwest,* among others. In 1988 a group of her poems won first prize in the National Poetry Competition of the Hackney Literary Awards. A member of the Rattlesnake Ladies' Salon, she teaches community-based workshops for Hellgate Writers, Inc., in Missoula, Montana.

JULIE REED (MA '91) has taught at Colorado Mountain College in Aspen. She is working on a novel.

KATHERINE REED (MA '91) is a former victim's advocate and police reporter. She is at work on her first novel, which won Hollins's Melanie Hook Rice Award (1991) for a novel in progress.

LISA RESS (MA '80) is the author of a book of poems, *Flight Patterns,* which won the AWP Poetry Prize in 1983, and her poems have appeared widely in journals. Winner of the Word Works' Washington Prize in 1987, she teaches at Knox College.

CYNTHIA ROSE (BA '72) is a journalist and broadcaster who has lived in London since graduate school at Newnham College, Cambridge. She is the author of *Living in America: The Soul Saga of James Brown* and *Design after Dark: The Story of Dancefloor Style*. A former editor of *City Limits* and *Wire*, she has been a TV presenter for BBC2's *The Late Show* and appears regularly on BBC Radio 4's *Start the Week*.

MARY RUEFLE (MA '76) is the author of three books of poems, *Memling's Veil*, *Life without Speaking*, and *The Adamant*, which won the 1988 Iowa Poetry Prize. She has also received an NEA Fellowship and lives in Shaftsbury, Vermont.

MARK SABA (MA '83) has published poetry and fiction in such magazines as the *Panhandler, Kentucky Poetry Review, Artemis, Confrontation*, and *South Dakota Review*.

MARY SANSOM (MA '89) lives in West Virginia and has begun to publish her poems in journals.

KERRY SHERIN (MA '90) was New York production assistant on Jim Jarmusch's film *Mystery Train*. She has a poem forthcoming in *New England Review*, and this is her first published story.

MELISSA SITES (BA '90), a native West Virginian, studied English and music at Hollins and wrote an honors thesis on West Virginia poetry. She is currently a fellow in the MFA program at the University of Maryland.

LEE SMITH (BA '67) is the author of seven novels, most recently *Fair and Tender Ladies*, and two collections of short stories. She teaches at North Carolina State University and currently serves as a fellow at the Center for Documentary Studies at Duke University.

MATTIE QUESENBERRY SMITH (BA '85, MA '86) has published poems in *Appalachian Heritage, Wind, Virginia Country*, and *New Virginia Review*.

MATTHEW J. SPIRENG (MA '71) has published poems in such journals as *Tar River Poetry, Wilderness*, the *Cape Rock*, and the *Hollins Critic*. An award-winning journalist, he is the assistant city editor for the Kingston (N.Y.) *Daily Freeman*.

HAINES SPRUNT (MA '91) has published poems recently in *Carolina Quarterly* and *Shenandoah*.

STEPHEN STARK (MA '84) is the author of two novels, *The Outskirts* and, in the spring of 1992, *Second Son.* His short fiction has appeared in the *New Yorker,* and he is the coauthor with Robert Altman of a feature-length screen treatment, *The Chicken and the Hawk.*

DEBORAH HILARY SUSSMAN (MA '91) is currently a Hoyns Fellow at the University of Virginia. The former editor of Scholastic *Scope,* a national language-arts magazine for teenagers, she is working on a novel based upon her father's childhood in German-occupied Amsterdam.

HENRY TAYLOR (MA '66) is professor of literature and codirector of the graduate creative writing program at the American University. His books of poems include *The Horse Show at Midnight* (1966), *An Afternoon of Pocket Billiards* (1975), and *The Flying Change* (1985), which received the Pulitzer Prize in Poetry.

SONYA L. TAYLOR (BA '87), while waiting to be discovered, works in the advertising department of Richmond Newspapers, Inc. She is working on a collection of short stories.

ANITA THOMPSON ('92) is a senior at Hollins College, working on an honors thesis in short fiction. Her stories have appeared in the *Texas Review* and the anthology, *That's What I Like (about the South): Southern Stories for the Nineties.*

BURN THOMPSON (BA '78, MA '81) is a physicist as well as a poet, who lives in Roanoke, Virginia.

NATASHA TRETHEWAY (MA '91) is currently a student in the MFA program at the University of Massachusetts. Her poems have appeared in *First Things.*

PHILLIP WELCH (MA '90) has published poems in *Black Warrior Review, Chelsea, Kentucky Poetry Review,* and *Shenandoah.* He is currently working on a novel.

EDWARD WESTON (MA '86), former saxophonist for the legendary punk-rock band Boy's Life, is a poet and writer of short fiction.

TOM WHALEN (MA '71) has published fiction, poetry, and criticism in over two hundred journals and anthologies. His collaborative translations of Robert Walser appear in *Selected Stories* and *Masquerade and Other Stories*. He teaches creative writing at Loyola University and directs the creative writing program at the New Orleans Center for the Creative Arts.

S. LAUDERDALE WHITE (BA '83) is currently completing a master's program in special education at James Madison University.

SYLVIA WILKINSON (MA '63) is the author of six novels (most recently *Bone of My Bones*), three nonfiction works, and sixteen juveniles.

JAMIE YATES (MA '76) is writing and publishing poetry and new work in fiction and nonfiction. He teaches for the Arts Commission in Columbia, S.C.

LEE ZACHARIAS (MA '73) is the author of a collection of stories, *Helping Muriel Make It through the Night,* and the novel *Lessons*. She teaches at the University of North Carolina at Greensboro.

HEIDI A. ZINSMEISTER (MA '89) has published stories in several literary magazines. She lives in the San Francisco Bay Area.